I Am Here and Not Not-There:

An Autobiography

Margaret at an Evangel Hall window, 1972.
(Credit: John Reeves)

Margaret Avison

I AM HERE AND NOT NOT-THERE

An Autobiography

The Porcupine's Quill

Library and Archives Canada Cataloguing in Publication

Avison, Margaret, 1918–.
I am here and not not-there / Margaret Avison.

Memoirs and letters by Margaret Avison and interviews with the author.
Includes biographical references.
ISBN 978-0-88984-315-8

1. Avison, Margaret, 1918–.
2. Poets, Canadian (English) – 20th century – Biography. I. Title.

PS8501.V5Z464 2009 C811'.54 C2008-906899-8

1 2 3 • 11 10 09

Published by The Porcupine's Quill
P.O. Box 160, 68 Main Street, Erin, Ontario NOB 1T0
http://www.porcupinesquill.ca

Edited for the Press by Stan Dragland.

The cover is after a painting by William Gill entitled 'Winter Twister' (acrylic on wood panel, 2006). Courtesy of / from the collection of Susan Sherk.

Represented in Canada by the Literary Press Group.
Trade orders are available from University of Toronto Press.

We acknowledge the support of the Ontario Arts Council and the Canada Council for the Arts for our publishing programme. The financial support of the Government of Canada through the Book Publishing Industry Development Programme is also gratefully acknowledged. Thanks, also, to the Government of Ontario through the Ontario Media Development Corporation's OMDC Book Fund.

Canada

ONTARIO ARTS COUNCIL
CONSEIL DES ARTS DE L'ONTARIO

Canada Council for the Arts
Conseil des Arts du Canada

TABLE OF CONTENTS

FOREWORD

Before Margaret Avison died, on July 31, 2007, she had almost completed a draft of her autobiography, had revised it, and then revised roughly half of it again. She left notes toward further revising a couple of the later chapters, and a file of materials that she had intended to work in, or to include in one way or another. Some of the primary composition was yet to come. Throughout the process, which slowed as she became more frail, she worked closely with her long-time friend and editorial assistant, Joan Eichner. Margaret sent the first rough draft to me, asking whether I thought the project was worth continuing. Of course it was. She pressed on, with me now involved as editor. She would revise a chapter and I would read it and send my suggestions for further revision, most of which she accepted, no doubt in consultation with Joan, who then incorporated the changes and returned them to me.

With the project left incomplete after Margaret's death, Joan and I felt lucky to have gained a good sense of the sort of editorial suggestions, for clarity and directness, that Margaret welcomed. Otherwise, we would have felt even more trepidation than we did in preparing the work for publication. To Margaret's 'automatic writing' poem, 'September, 1939', we added punctuation missing from her typed version. We have made some changes for the sake of consistency in the text. In a very few places, we have silently corrected or omitted what we found to be an error of fact. Joan's long-term close relationship with Margaret was an invaluable source of accuracy in matters like chronology. We have tried to keep our own presence minimal, but have on occasion contributed bracketed insertions and footnotes which are intended to inform or clarify or expand on some point or other.

We could not on our own integrate some of the materials that Margaret marked for inclusion, so we have prepared a 'Documents' appendix to the autobiography proper. To the material in this section, now and then risking some repetition (but with a gain of variation), we have added a few other texts – essays, letters and interviews – which flesh out the sense of Margaret Avison as person and poet. She was considering some of this material for inclusion; she thought all of it relevant. 'Poets Learn from Poetry' might have been part of this appendix, but Margaret always intended it to be her last chapter, whatever concluding remarks she might eventually have felt moved to make.

The letters to Eleanor Graham are fascinating to compare with briefer accounts in the autobiography proper of her Indiana summer school session. In most of the included letters, like the two essays on Tolstoy and the Doukhobors, especially the latter, Margaret is in full flight on artistic matters. She retrospectively devoted much less attention to these than to her history of employment and the importance of her faith. The glimpse of her epistolary skill recalls her friend Miriam Waddington, speaking of *Contemporary Verse*'s Alan Crawley. 'His letters to me,' she says, 'as well as those from Livesay, Avison, and Marriott, are still so alive, so full of vitality, that I believe the correspondence between writers and editors of the forties – if it is ever collected and collated – will be every bit as exciting and intellectually varied as the letters of the Bloomsbury Group – always, of course, allowing for the different Canadian context' (*Apartment Seven: Essays Selected and New*, 24). We have made some cuts in the letters, always of innocuous material extraneous to this book. In a sense, of course, nothing is irrelevant. Margaret's letters should some day be collected and published whole, at which time every iota they have to contribute to her story will be in print.

Discussion about the inclusion of appendix material – essays and interviews especially – began while the text proper was still under preparation, but was necessarily left inconclusive. Austerity and self-effacement were characteristic of Margaret's life and her attitude to her reputation, so we cannot be sure she would herself have included some 'documents'. Now and then, though, it was two against one: Joan and I ever so gently applying pressure and Margaret yielding. At other times, she resisted pleas for a little more story. With Margaret's example of the keenest integrity burning in us, we have done our best not to take undue advantage of having the final say.

Margaret had in mind *Not Not-There,* a shorter version of the title of this book, for what became *Momentary Dark* (McClelland and Stewart, 2006). It was rejected at the time as unintelligible without context, leaving a longer version available for this book, where some of the context for it appears. The epigraph is the bones of it, now intelligible though fascinatingly enigmatic.*

'Too much autobiography,' Margaret says in one of her letters to Miriam Waddington. The remark resonates with the injunction of Gladys Story, her grade nine teacher, to avoid for ten years the use of the first person pronoun in poetry. The poet e.e. cummings has pointed out the impossibility of discovering 'a single peripherally situated ego,' meaning that everyone is, in a technical sense, egocentric. But he also said something else that Margaret would probably endorse, that 'who I am is what I write.' Margaret lived for poetry, putting it second only to her Lord. The role of poet was of no interest to her. She even had trouble with public honours. Nobody who knew her would expect a confessional.

You hold in your hands a self-portrait by one of the country's best and most revered poets, a woman of almost unparalleled humanity and humility. Because she could not finish it herself, it is not the book she envisioned. She would have wanted it all of a piece, not trailing an ellipsis of documents. Still, the book is almost all Margaret Avison, and *that* is always really something.

STAN DRAGLAND

---

* Margaret's fullest annotation of the title appears in 'Understanding Is Costly', lecture two of *A Kind of Perseverance*, but the reader who seeks it out should be cautioned that there appears to have been a slip of the pen in the last 'proposition', which reads: 'The true believer's problem: how to say "I am here," and not be saying "I am not not-there".' Too many negatives; consistency would require that 'not be saying' be removed.

AUTOBIOGRAPHY

This question was put by a registrant: 'What makes a poet's language distinctive?' We all fell silent, trying to pin it down, then tried to answer. Not just affection for words, which is common to all good writers; not necessarily a matter of cadence, formal structures, rhythm. The answer that came to me, forced out of minutes of dismissing options, was new to me too: 'It is saying "I am here and not not-there."'

Margaret Avison, Vancouver 1963

Mary, Ted and Margaret with their Kirkland grandparents.
(Credit: University of Manitoba Archives
and Special Collections,
Margaret Avison fonds, Box 1, PC151)

BEGINNING?

Tennyson said, in 'Ulysses', 'I am a part of all that I have met.' If I may take on his 'I' as meaning 'me, Margaret', it might explain this book. It certainly does apply to this poem which occurred to me during the hours of sleep at age eighty-eight. (I had to get up and write it out or I knew I'd keep myself awake for hours trying to hang on to a 'lead' without squashing its life out.)

What I had been dreaming I could not remember, and the aunts of the poem are none of mine but drawn from 'all that I have met' over nine decades. Why not? The poem, then, and my story.

A Novel in Miniature

My aunts are robust. I
still have all
four. Do
yours come vividly
to mind at mention of
a comment at first
glimpse of the
no longer new baby?

'Look at the X nose
on the wee face!' (Or
any kinship-logo-feature they
spot, or think they do).

That may be why
the X family keeps
a keepsake portrait of great-
grandfather Jock in the
dark or a
wall near
the front stairs landing but
not near enough for you
to stand and view it.

April 2006

Margaret sitting on the steps
with her older sister, Mary, in Regina.
(Credit: University of Manitoba Archives
and Special Collections, Margaret Avison fonds, Box 1, PC151)

EARLY CHILDHOOD

The family's move from Welland, Ontario, to Regina, Saskatchewan, occurred in 1920 when I was about two. My earliest memory is in Metropolitan Methodist Church there. What recurs to me, very clearly, is spitting up into Mother's dainty, lavender-scented church handkerchief during the service, and its soft damp silky touch on my chin.

Some other Regina memories are equally insignificant, for instance a tin bathtub by the stove in the kitchen for Saturday night baths, before we were put into sleepers with feet in them. (Children's nightwear in the early 1920s was better than outdoor wear. We had no 'snow suits' then, just thick scratchy woollen stockings with a bump at the ankle from stretching, and wool socks pulled up over them. Winters were bitter.)

Daddy's study was somewhere across the hall from the kitchen. It was out of bounds. The parsonage layout is no longer clear to me, but I do remember a narrow wooden ledge which ran around the outside of that house, painted pale yellow, within stepping distance of the small back porch. I think one of my two Regina concussions came from walking that ledge, unsuccessfully.

My life's first remembered winter is defined by the Regina morning when, as always, I had been bundled up and put out to play, alone. Mary and Ted were, respectively, in 'infant school', mornings, and public school, all day. Things did not look right to me. A dusting of fine snow was everywhere, and a great hardness underfoot. Where was the earth? I fetched my sand pail and tin shovel, and tried to dig down to the beautiful ground, but a glaze of black ice everywhere was all I found. Despairing, standing there alone, I felt the wind as an assault 'from dark Arcturus down' ('New Year's Poem', *Winter Sun*) and stood paralyzed with a deep sense of desolation. Children feel all human emotions but they lack words, alone in whatever washes over them. Over the long years I have tried to remember that when children are staring, transfixed, some impression is going down into memory for them.

Next came the Christmas in Regina which established my father as the Christmas celebrant he remained throughout his life. He had

had no family, no festive times, in his childhood, so enjoyed the ones he devised for us now: the tree, parcels, excitement in the air. He was up and dressed when I ran down to join him that Christmas morning, the other early bird in the family. He watched as I stopped in the doorway, dazzled by ornaments all over the tree. On the floor were flakes of white, with big footsteps imprinted in them. I remember knowing instantly that he wanted me *not* to notice that the flakes weren't melting. With a surge of love and a flirt's duplicity, I played up to him there.

Does spring come with particular grace after a harsh winter? How keenly I sense again the prairie grass, a clear bright sky, and the ground brushed with a lilac bloom clear across to the far horizon: crocuses! Not the frail party-dress garden kind called by that name in the east, but true crocuses, soft to the touch, both stem and flowers, with invisible fur, purplish blue, everywhere, everywhere. Whoever brought me there gave me some newspaper to hold the ones I picked. They lay there, fading now in the sun, small ants running from them along the folds.

There are photos of Regina days: for example, one where my sister Mary and I sit on the steps in front of the church wearing straw hats, reefer coats, white stockings, black patent leather shoes with straps and buckles; or one where I am all dressed up as someone's flower girl, after a wedding. The church building became familiar in all its corners. But once, when some group was putting on a play, Mary was roaming on her own (perhaps Mother was involved in directing) when she suddenly trotted out of the hall onto the stage. The actors came to a sudden standstill, the audience laughed at their frozen panic, and Mary fled away in flushed misery.

One afternoon, reportedly, I had the attention of a small group of parishioners who were 'minding' me until Mother was free to come home. Trying to sustain this attention I apparently told them, punctuating the outburst with a fist on a palm: 'My father said "There was no spirit in that meeting...."' Preachers' children learn, painfully, to avoid the spotlight.

All three of us had scarlet fever in Regina. I was placed with next-door neighbours when Ted and Mary were both down with it, to protect me from infection. The neighbours were kindly, sensible people in a sunny house with mirrory hardwood floors. When Mrs Musselman ran her electric polisher with its terrifying roar, I remember bawling inconsolably, but not loud enough: its voice drowned mine. I remember, too, my astonishment, running from bed early through the upper hall and seeing someone, not my daddy, in undershirt and braces, standing at the bathroom mirror, shaving. He leaned down to dab some foam on my cheek, just the way Daddy did.

When my turn came to catch scarlet fever, Mother had already served two terms in quarantine, nursing Ted and Mary. What strikes me now are just two memories. One is of Mother, standing at the tall bedroom window, her forehead leaning against the cool glass, gazing at the outside world.

The other memory is my grief over a cherished book. Nobody remembers the feeling of pain or acute discomfort. What the fever meant to me was lying in a grown-up's bed, in the 'sickroom', with a magical book, illustrated in glowing primary colours, telling the story of a child with a ball he could toss up and order to stay up, or move sideways, and it would come back down whenever he allowed it to fall. But everything in the sickroom had to be burned after the quarantine was lifted. When later I needed to reread that favourite book, I found it had vanished forever.

The grown-ups who visited our house in Regina often talked about how they had escaped during the 1912 cyclone. A tornado had ripped through Regina in the summer of that year. Two odd stories I remember. The first rings true, given a child's trusting ear, and a man's awkward way of putting things on a child's level. Had I been staring at the man's face, or had I even innocently asked him about it? What he told me was that the marks on his face were scars from the cyclone, which had blown scores of tiny nails out of a smashed piano into his cheeks!

The second tale has the sound of a real news report. Its hero was canoeing on a small lake at a holiday resort some miles north of the city when the storm swept in. He was lifted high, high, and came to himself when he was set down again, gently, in the Regina city hall square, with his legs still comfortably under the thwarts. What a storybook city Regina must be!

The terms of Methodist pastorates in those days were limited. Since 'the Western Conference' was to be the locale of our next move, inevitably further west, my parents availed themselves of a special bargain railway rate from Regina through to Quebec City. They needed a vacation, and for Mother travelling was the ideal kind. We all set out together for the head of the Great Lakes; from there we would travel by boat to Sarnia.

But one dark horror marred that boat trip. In the retelling I realize why Mary and I were free to run about on deck in the sun and on a big curving carpeted staircase, and were given balloons by strangers who also played games with us. Ted, six years older than me, was sick. The doctor on board was not sure what it was, but he knew it was serious and for a while feared it might be contagious. I overheard one worried passenger tell her husband 'The child's vomit is black!' They threw the sheets overboard when they changed Ted's bed. The apprehension meant that everyone on board knew that he 'might die' and therefore my parents had little time for Mary and me. So we basked in others' attention and evaded worry, as small children do. Later I learned that Ted had had ptomaine poisoning.

By the time we docked in Sarnia, Ted was strong enough to sit on a potty in the hotel, or dockside shelter, where Uncle Orville and Aunt Elva stayed to meet us and take us children on to the farm. Nothing remains in my memory of that first visit there. I have been told that when my parents returned to pick us up for the journey home, they were informed that 'Margaret didn't make a single misstep.' I was a well-behaved child, on guard with anyone but the family, where the youngest fared well, and where we were trained to be aware of people's expectations of a minister's child. I was happy to conform, until, much later, we left the West and the long homesickness began.

On an earlier visit east during one of my father's summer holidays while I was still small, I had met my maternal grandmother for the first and only time. As soon as I saw her, I trusted her completely, following her everywhere, settling down wherever she did. What I remember is a glorious game she invented, doing dishes. She lifted me onto a high stool drawn up at her left side, and gave me a little paddle-shaped piece of silver to slosh about in the hot water as she added some soap powder. What foam we made! Then she scalded the kitchen knives, setting them aside on the tray to her right. Finally, two at a time, she handed me spoons and forks to dry. Each piece had a personality as she introduced them to me, and to this day I sometimes have a word to say to a spoon or a ladle as I take it off the draining board to put away, briefly aware of Grandma's eyes twinkling, long ago.

Grandma Kirkland is cherished in many stories told me later, but I am thankful for that three-year-old's visit to the old home in Galt. Without that, Grandma would exist only in the stories, authenticated by the exciting pudgy parcels that came at Christmas, and the downy feeling of flannelette nighties with pink hemstitching at the neck, or sleepers with feet in them.

Her memories of her parents in England made stories Mother sometimes relayed to us, along with old songs. Those songs we heard at night when we were ill, or on days when we were in bed, feverish. My sister later sang them to her children, and they likely did to theirs. Once, years later in a lecture on Chaucer at St. Michael's College, a professor reviewed rhythms and types of medieval folk songs which included a rhythm called 'hocketing'. It fitted Grandma's narrative song: 'On a calm still night/when the moon was bright/two foxes set out for their prey....' After class, the professor confirmed what my ear had suggested, namely an unbroken link of chanted stories, over English centuries, from mothers to children.

Grandma was a comfortable person to be with, staunchly Methodist but never talking it. It is said that when gossiping started in a ladies' group, she would suddenly stand up and say 'God save the Queen!' Her sagacity still impresses me. For example, 'You can learn something from everybody,' she would say, 'something to do, or something not to do.' [See 'Listening (for Grandma)' in *Listening: Last Poems.*] Mother was far away in Calgary when Grandma died, of diabetes *just* before insulin was discovered. Her mourning was a quietness in my mother, over days. Grandpa Kirkland came to live with us some months after. They helped each other, I suspect. It was for me very special, in Calgary, to get to know and love Grandpa.

He took the upstairs west bedroom, with its windows on spacious sky and, on clear days, the mountains, their snows catching first and last light. My bond with him developed through shopping trips to the meat store, to the fruit and vegetable market, to the grocer's. He had to walk slowly because of a heart condition, and I kept his pace more naturally than the two older children. I took to settling down in his room often, made welcome there, given satisfying answers when I plied him with questions. 'Tell me about when you were little.' 'Well, my girl, we were lace makers in the Old Country, in our family. They brought me out to Canada, to grow up on Peach Grove Farm ...' I interrupted:

'Oh, I remember how Mother told me she used to play there in a corn crib when she was little.' The corn crib (see 'Harvest', in *Momentary Dark*) was set up on stilts the way they were in wet, old England to keep the grain dry. She'd play with her doll there. A large old dog called Prince looked after her. 'That's right. By that time we had the drugstore in Galt, with our living quarters behind the store where I brought my wife. That was our first home. I had been away from home before because pharmacy was taught only at Rockwood Academy, in our area anyway. So I'd had to go away to qualify for a licence. Sarah, my wife, left her first home only when she made a second home, our family's home.

'She was a great hand with the accounts, too. Once when I felt able to make an investment in a new mining company, she advised against it, but I talked her around: "It stands to reason: the ore is down in the rock, you need costly equipment to break through and bring it up and for that you'd have wages to pay! All those expenses before one cent of profit. Investing makes it possible. Then, when it pays, the profits bring your money back again." She gave in. We lost that money. She'd been right to be careful.'

The portrait of Grandma, Sarah Maria Bainard Saunders, had been built up by my mother's stories, and our early visit. She fitted in comfortably with Grandpa's account. He and I often sat together after supper. The glowing western sky quieted us: in that latitude dark came slowly, and sunsets seemed to linger. Grandpa would speak into the silence at times, with different stories that held me in the same absorbed musing stillness as his own. Some of his stories were not new to me, but Grandpa's concentration lifted them off the pastel-tinted shiny Sunday school papers, from which I had heard them before, into the very reality of that room, that dying sunset. One, about Abraham, became my recourse down the years, not the Joseph stories, though the tangle of brothers and grain sacks mattered, the building of suspense, the level place it all came out. Grandpa filled my imagination with one picture about Moses, the river-sedge scene, the basket afloat, the baby secretly watched by little Miriam. When Pharaoh's daughter came, he made ancient Egypt permanently a vivid part of geography for me. That's all I remember of what he told about Moses.

Best of all he liked to get to Abraham. 'Ur of the Chaldees' was a locale he made more remote, stranger, than any fabulous land in our children's books. Abraham was already on in years, 'about my age, maybe'. Grandpa got up and walked, solemnly, down the room, his face rugged, set: 'Abraham was told to go, and he faced away from all he had known, under orders that were only "depart from...." Where he was headed, time would unfold.'

Grandpa's stories were of people and places. Why they mattered to us was the unspoken wonder of those evenings. The closest I came, as a child, to sensing God's pressure, presence, was when Grandpa finished the Abraham stories with the father and son, Isaac, off early one morning for some special ritual, the boy alert and confident, the old father concentrated, steady, with few comments as they travelled. How did he manage to make the 'sacrifice of Isaac' so real, so awesome, to a listening child? Was he depending on the tradition of most children's stories where the prince finds the princess in time, or a chance uttering breaks the spell and makes the evil ogre wisp away into nothing? I do know that in Grandpa's room I first sensed the near presence of God. The unbidden awareness would recur over the years, the quiet of an evening service, or a family walk after supper in the late fading daylight when everyone comfortably kept still, exchanging with one another in ways better than talk. All moments of that kind recalled to my awareness some central significance of that timeless story of Abraham.

Your mild eyes mirrored an
Ontario room with Grandma,
turned into marble, long in her best dress.
Moving in the Alberta house,
preoccupied but kind,
you soon made friends with me.
I'd confidently seek you out
in what had been my brother's
upstairs room; the windows
gave on miles and miles of clear
air, and foothills, then
the mountains. Usually in light aslant
late in the day, I'd visit.
You had a rocker, at the window,

and, your eyes far away, your voice
a little sad at first, would tell me stories:
Joseph's, Gideon's, David's.
I knew, over those months,
you cherished most the
stories about Abraham.
All the stories absorbed
the child on your knee. My eyes
must have been on your face
but I remember no sign that that disturbed you.*

The farm, Uncle Orville's near Union, Ontario, was a fixed point in a vast world for many years during our time out west, and even later. As children, my mother, Mabel, and her younger sister Elva had been satellites around the youngest sister, Laura, the most gifted (music) and the most fun (athletic and serious and funny and witty, from moment to moment intensely alive). After Laura died at eighteen, of a burst appendix for which there was no surgery as yet, Mother moved into Laura's piano playing, and Elva developed aptitudes of her own – mathematics, singing and drama, directing pageants in Sunday school. Their father mourned Laura for years. Their mother had to summon all her will-power and practical Methodist faith in order to help keep the family on as even a keel as possible.

Sisters! I sense that Mother regretted choosing to stay at home much of the time, even quitting high school halfway through grade ten in Galt Collegiate Institute, because the mathematics master despised women who wanted an education, mocked their efforts, eliminated most of them. At home she played and practised more and

---

* Margaret's draft of this poem, titled 'For my Grandpa Kirkland who Died 72 Years Ago', has a fascinating first stanza completely unrelated to the rest. She might have found some way of making the leap work, but it seems more likely that stanza one would have led to something else entirely. Since Margaret's grandfather died in 1924, seventy-two years later is 1996. The poem was among the candidates for inclusion in Margaret's last book of poems, but, with the two parts ill-connected, it had clearly not reached final form. The decision of the editors was to place the second part here.

more on Laura's piano. She accepted Elva's wider-ranging young life, not envying though sometimes wistful, and remembered years later, contentedly, how their mother worried about all the perils Elva might be, and never was, 'ruined' by. (The worst that happened was an early unwise engagement that evaporated later the same summer). Uncle Orville, the young man who moved into her life and became her husband, was as sound as a good apple tree.

Mother graduated in piano and taught, at home still. She became engaged, in time, to a young baritone whom she'd been asked to accompany at somebody's house on one of those 'evenings' that constituted the entertainment in those days. But her engagement ring was alone on her finger a long time until his arts and theology degrees were completed, and then his student postings.

When they finally married they came to Toronto to the Walker House for the first night of their honeymoon, then on to Muskoka, returning two weeks later to begin a ministry at Paisley Memorial Methodist Church, Guelph. All this was a travelled and different world, viewed from home base. Perhaps Aunt Elva's slight edge,

The whole family at Lumsden Beach, Regina.
(Family photo: courtesy of Karen McKim)

obvious manager's skills and competence betrayed a bit of bridling, and perhaps Mother's uncharacteristic self-deprecation was a defence, but I was aware of their sisterly uneasiness when we stayed at Uncle Orville's farm.

The farm, and one memory of the time when Aunt Elva's reaction to me came as a shock, generated all this speculation about the sisters. I was about ten. Their five children, we three Avison children, the four parents and Uncle Orville's mother, who lived in a private set-up off the farm kitchen, made for a strenuous household. When the boys woke at daybreak and tiptoed off the sleeping porch where all our cots were wedged side by side at night, I wakened too. The other girls seemed barely interrupted in their slumberous breathing. For what seemed like hours I stuck it out, though eager to see the quiet morning countryside, but at last I crept free, found my stuff inside where we girls had undressed, and went out a side door. I could hear sounds of my aunt in the kitchen preparing breakfast for the men who would come in from chores through the back kitchen where boots and overalls were kept.

The early roaming in the lane and around the edges of the farmyard, I can't remember. Due caution was always taken at the fence nearest an old sow who seemed to me huge and menacing, given to snorts and little rushes at the fence. But perhaps not that day. I do remember a sense of wholeness, the newness of the dew-drenched grass, and long shadows in the slant early sunlight. Somewhere I must have settled on a log or fence-post and set down my string-bag. Wherever it was, outdoors, I wrote a poem, and brimmed with the excitement of catching the lovely contrast of all this country quiet with the clatter of the day now audible from the farmhouse.

Therefore I couldn't wait to bound into the house and show Mother, but since she wasn't yet down for breakfast, I scrambled into my own place to eat and thrust the poem on Aunt Elva. The only line I remember of it she made indelible in my mind by her response: 'Those whose *sole* (I can still hear the emphasis) concern is toast and porridge....' I had meant only to define the indoor busyness that way. But as Aunt Elva read, repeating my words aloud, she added, 'You think we live to work and eat here, so the rest of the world can do all the other things,' as though we did not all know about her contralto solos, and her involvement in London's Little Theatre.

Sisters, the next generation, at the farm: two sets were paired off. My sister Mary and our cousin Betty were the same age, and Jean and I were at about the same stage and, fortunately, congenial. Mary and Betty were continually in trouble and lovable. After they cut the blooms off all of Aunt Elva's garden flowers to make a bouquet, scolding resounded from both mothers. Their punishment was to have their hands tied behind them, for a time. But instantly they ran about backing up to things, testing what they might do with their invisible hands. Soon all of us, boys first of all, were in the house asking to have *our* hands tied too.

What did Jean and I play together? I remember sitting at a table on the side porch, mornings, with crayons and a small pile of cardboard picture outlines for children to colour that came with Shredded Wheat. The cardboard was a dirty grey colour, and our wax crayons went on speckly.

Jean took me out to the hayloft one day, I remember. Nobody else was around. She was up the ladder in a flash then jumping down from a beam onto the hay piled below. I was terrified. She dared me. Halfway up the ladder my fingers and knees were trembling so that I had trouble hanging on, but the thought of trying to feel the rungs below and go back down was worse, so I finally made it to the top. How was I to get down again? 'Jump,' said Jean. *These city kids don't know what fun is,* she was probably thinking. 'I'm scared,' I said. 'O come on, jump. It can't more than kill you!' she replied. True. 'Die, then!' I dramatized to myself and jumped, bouncing on the hay pile, just as Jean had done. We went happily on to the next thing, whatever it was that day.

That particular summer Jean was lofty towards her younger sister Patricia: sisters too close in age are usually scornful of the stages they have just moved on from. I had no younger sister, so Trish delighted me – dancing about naked in the morning, or down at the pond: 'Betty, Betty, where's my shite?' (her way of saying 'shirt').

On the hottest days Jean and I were sent up to Aunt Elva's bed to have a rest. One afternoon was pure pleasure for me: I dug out my scribbler and two pencils and we wrote stories. O bliss! Such days with Jean were like days with Margy Hayden later on in Calgary. (Our stories on those hot afternoons would fizzle out when we grew impatient to be allowed up to resume real life.)

Mabel Kirkland Avison
as a young lady.
(Family photo:
courtesy of Karen McKim)

H. Wilson Avison's
graduation picture.
(Family photo:
courtesy of Karen McKim)

Mary and Margaret in Regina.
(Credit: University of Manitoba Archives and Special Collections, Margaret Avison fonds, Box 1, PC151)

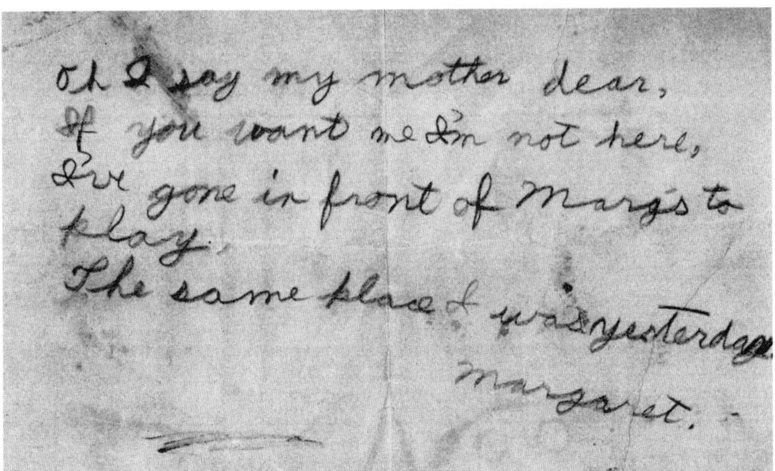

Oh I say my mother dear,
If you want me I'm not here,
I've gone in front of Marg's to
play.
The same place I was yesterday.
Margaret.

c1926

Margaret's note to her mother (see page 28). (Credit: Joan Eichner)

CALGARY

Oh I say my mother dear,
If you want me I'm not here,
I've gone in front of Marg's to play,
The same place I was yesterday.

My mother saved this note-in-verse over the many years after our time in Calgary (1924–29). 'Marg' was Margy Hayden who lived on the lot behind our 6th Avenue West house, in young Calgary. She often came over, or I went to her place, climbing the back fence on the old barn corner. I remember well the surroundings of our house – the front yard in grass, the back yard a garden for Daddy, with a disused barn in the back corner. Up by the house stood Mother's piano box (her piano had been specially crated for railway baggage car handling), the site of our club, though we played in the tool shed by the driveway as well. Alongside the driveway were two hedges, caragana, with little yellow flowers, and an all-green leafy one with soft-spiked squashy round green fruit that we could throw at each other, unhurt. (In the 1960s, I looked up the old 246–6th Avenue West house. It had been replaced by a huge downtown medical arts building!)

Daylight prevailed. The latitude, being further north, permitted us children to play 'Run Sheep Run' well on into the evening. It was called 'Hoist Your Sails' in Ontario, I learned later. Some war veterans, who had endured mustard gas attacks and moved west because they found breathing easier in the high, dry climate, were family friends who made World War I very immediate to us: we ended our ball-bouncing games with 'turn-your-back-on-the-KAI-ser!' Time outdoors in our clubhouse, or, in winter, building snow forts that would vanish in the morning when a chinook wafted in with warm Pacific air: these are treble clef. The groundbass was my Grandfather Kirkland.

All my stories nourish me now as I write them down because I had, in the west, a happy childhood. Oh, there were bad moments too. As well as the piano box (south) and barn (north), our back yard had a small shed for garden tools behind the hedge line (east-northeast). The shed became a clubhouse where members met, but in the piano box special members held 'cabinet meetings'. We considered membership to be a great privilege. The process of inviting someone to join was easygoing and yet it worked out all right. We designed our own money – bills, not coinage, and kept the treasury in a box under one loose board in the tool shed floor. There were ways of making and spending the money, but I cannot remember what they were.

I do remember the time when Billy Grogan and I were out of 'bills', so we used some India ink and crayons to make our own. Though it seemed a good idea at the time, it left me mopey at suppertime. My mother asked what was the matter and I told her what we had done. 'That is committing forgery,' she said. 'You and Billy are going to have to confess and let the other members deal with you!'

Thanks to the lingering daylight we got the confession over with the same evening. A cabinet meeting was held in the piano box next day. It was decided that a court would be set up to try us and mete out punishment. All I remember is the relief I felt! The penalty must have been quite endurable, for occasions were contrived later to hold other trials, it had been so much fun!

An almost unclouded world it seemed. Only on chinook days did we see a heavy cloud-mass above the clear band of greenblue sky at the horizon. Storms 'broke' to the west on the mountains in the west-east climate flow. Normally life was sunny like the Calgary climate. ('Sunshine every day,' we sang in Central Public School.) In hindsight I marvel at the prevailing sunniness. It didn't seem to matter, for me, that none of my friends turned up at church events, though these were central in our family's life. The wide open space that accommodated us all was free time, to play together, outdoors.

When we moved to Calgary, Ted and Mary were already accustomed to school. For me it was a great adventure ahead, after summer holidays. Ted and Mary probably walked with me the morning I began grade one in Central School, within a block and a bit of our house on 6th Avenue. Even then, my sense of direction was unreliable. At lunch time a stranger found me wandering near the school, in silent tears. When he heard my address, he kindly steered me home.

Once a school friend, setting out past our yard, on her way somewhere with her grandfather, invited me to come too. I addressed him: 'Are you a strange man?' He twigged to an odd question, and kindly knocked at our door for Mother's permission for me to be included.

Lining up to march into school, sitting in rows, hands behind our backs, forming words with sharpened pencils on clean notebook paper, listening to stories: school was orderly and fast-paced enough in the early grades. Once, only once, we had a 'media presentation', a jerky, greyish film, projected onto a sheet, about modern-day Egypt. That fizzled. The big maps on the wall had good shapes, and the ocean parts looked nice, but the land parts were in washed-out colours, unrelated in my mind to land as I knew it, mystifying, not deciphered for us. Perhaps the maps were only decorative, before there was any geography on the curriculum.

Lunch on school days was a glorious time when there were no meetings at the church. The food was simple, ready. We sat at the table, Mary and I, with Mother and Daddy (Ted must have been some distance off at high school by then). Was the sunlight always flooding the front room, and did Mother always play lively pieces we could jump around to? Best of all was when Daddy reverted to the days of their courtship and became a baritone soloist well pleased with his accompanist: 'I am a band-e-ley-ree-o, a King with a sward for a pee-e-lo' [pillow] was my favourite song. Brimful of my parents' unaccustomed frivolity Mary and I rushed back for classes. For some months I set my heart on a grass pillow. The 'sward' I kept as a new word, only.

In that period, elocutionists could fill a concert hall as musicians now do. One woman who gave public performances was a member of our congregation. When she was a guest at home after church, she would sometimes consent to give a recitation. I suspect I begged her to do so. The cadences and shapes of word-sounds entranced me.

In the autumn of 1927, our busy lives were disrupted. The polio epidemic was so severe that all schools were closed, and children were to be kept out of contact with one another throughout the city. Teachers prepared daily lessons which were printed in the *Calgary Herald,* and we were to work the sums and do the daily problems and assignments, writing carefully in our notebooks, for marking when school re-opened.

It was torment to stay indoors, wasting the end-of-summer days. I was allowed a small table and chair in the back yard, and, as I had hoped, my friend Margy Hayden saw me from her back door and was over the fence in a flash. Bit by bit, clandestine visitors found secret passages (there were those hedges between buildings and lanes). We had to be very quiet: the clubhouse was ideal. Once the lessons had been handed in at home, nobody was checking up. Undeservedly, but happily, not one of us caught polio, although when school re-opened after the cold weather settled in, we found out how many others had been infected and how lucky we were.

We went to church Sundays, morning and evening and, in between, to Sunday school. Most people did, in the twenties. It was like everybody's going to school on weekdays, or to their work. It was just the shape the weeks took. People found plumbers when they needed them, or piano tuners, or dentists, in their home congregation. To achieve standing in local politics would require regular church attendance Sunday mornings. The reason I always preferred the evening service as a child was the small group in the big, shadowy sanctuary, there because they wanted to be there, singing the hymns with their hearts in it. The words of the Psalms, often sung as well as read, gradually recorded themselves in my mind without 'memory work', although the unexplored sense of the words occurred to me only after years of happy misreading.

No sense of a subculture rose out of our routines, in Calgary or, later, Toronto school days. It was not upsetting that among school friends there was an Anglican, a Roman Catholic and a Baptist. Children went where their parents went. It was simple. My grade four teacher was Jewish, as was Mary's best friend in high school. My 6th Ave. Calgary friend, Betty Purchase, was Burmese. Ted, in high school, had a Chinese friend who played on the same baseball team, and through jobs in car-repairs and bus-driving, and through sports, he met a wide range of people. Thankfully, I see how open my parents were to differentness, uncritical of anybody we brought home, but no doubt with their antennae out, at need.

Every place has some insider term. In Calgary, to my ears, it was the word 'Stampede', new even as a noun. A child is brought into the picture faster than an adult: at recess schoolmates gave me early tips. I was to wear khaki all week. I would be safe on the streets that week, but it would be a little scary, though fun. Tickets to the bleachers would cost too much, but newspapers would have pictures almost as good as seeing with your own eyes. (This was long before TV, and before our first radios.) Mother discovered that children's khaki suits were everywhere, and inexpensive, in soft cotton material that buckled under the knee and flopped above it.

Though the excitement mounted daily, the actual day the Stampede began was astonishing. Our house was a block or so from the Hudson's Bay Company. I headed that way, early, following anybody and nobody, in the buttery-echoey sound of hoofs down canyons of tall buildings (so they seemed, in the early 1920s). Whoof! Something caught me up from behind, a rope that closed my arms around my chest: I had been lassooed! The friendly cowboy who had roped me in worked fast to undo his slip knot, to set me free. 'Go just around the corner for a free breakfast,' he said. 'They are making good flapjacks on the end of a chuckwagon.' Timidly, I explained that I had already had breakfast.

Other stragglers still headed towards the Bay department store, where, for the first and only time, I walked in alone, with nothing in the pockets of that khaki suit but my fists. Shopping was a child's ordeal. But, behold, *this* time there was none of the usual reverent bustle. Some counters had throws over them in materials as bright as the big kerchief around my neck, prescribed for the khaki suit. And then, cloppity-clop, a cowboy rode his horse right down an aisle! In the first hour of the first day of the Stampede I too was a Calgary insider.

One other memory of the Bay store I record here in the hope of sparing future staff the embarrassment of being used as interim babysitters, for a set period when mothers freely shop and hide secrets in Bay bags. That December the locale was a dining room, set up for us with children's tables and chairs. We were kept quiet a while with ice cream and wafers. The situation was uneasy, not one where we felt free to stir out of our chairs or make much noise. When ice cream palled, entertainment followed, big girls in pink tights with lacy tutus and small, glittery crowns and wands – our fairy princesses, they said. They were trying hard but they did not believe it, nor did we. With children, only a good storyteller is a substitute for absent mothers (promising to be back soon, of course).

If the Bay store's children's Christmas entertainment flopped somewhat, the city-wide 'Sunday school rally' at New Year's was worse, though different. The large, galleried auditorium filled up too slowly, with wan teachers filing in behind higgledy-piggledy lines of corralled children. Delay inevitably meant restless sections, 'settled' but soon stamping, whistling, calling out to newcomers sighted in doorways. The din swelled and got altogether out of control.

My father's best friend in Calgary, Paul Brecken, an elder whose wife had already shepherded her class in, me included, appeared at last on stage in a sudden spotlight. He taught high school science, knew how to project his big voice, tried, but encountered cheers and clapping added now to the earlier din. When a political leader takes the podium at his party's convention, he expects this uproar. Our friend Mr Brecken, as rally chairman that day, did not. How it ended I can not remember, only the headaching discomfort, the knowledge that this rally was really not for us but, rather, was some brain-storming parents' device for a little sleep-in on New Year's Day. We sang Sunday school songs, no doubt, and we all got through it that once, but I remember no recurrence.

The Sunday school teacher, Jessie Brecken, whose husband had to control us at New Year's, was, to me, the first sensible, beautiful teacher I'd ever had. I wanted to express my appreciation to her. Plunging headlong into moral hot water, I filched one of mother's 'good' handkerchiefs out of her drawer, preparing an alibi: by sneaking it out and laying it down on 6th Ave., I could say I had found it on the sidewalk. Satisfied with my well-devised plan, I gave my present to Mrs Brecken with glowing thanks the next Sunday.

Now it happened that Mrs Brecken was a violinist and my mother was her accompanist. This I had overlooked. At their next session together, my teacher, as might have been expected, conveyed her thanks to Mother for my gift. Mother confronted me when I came home from school. Now I trotted out my alibi, not fully confident that it would 'do'. Her response was direct. Her words 'stealing' and 'lying' had already been whispering in my conscience. I was told to think about what I had done, left alone in my room while the family ate supper. Mother would bring me a glass of milk when the dishes were done. My disgrace was now public. Some lessons are hard to learn, but what if I had never been caught?

Even apart from parents, in a child's unsupervised jungle conscience acted as a control. It may have been family Sabbath observance that gave me a furtive feeling one Sunday towards suppertime. My new friend up the street, Betty Purchase, who said she was a Buddhist, was free to play on Sundays. When wandering along the street that day I couldn't resist joining her, unhappy at the happy, dusty, overwarm sensations of an ordinary playtime on the Lord's Day. But when I went home, nobody seemed to mind beyond making me wash my hands.

Another new girl our peer group rejected. She lived further south, closer to Mount Royal College where we were sent for piano lessons. She came from Ontario, dressed in navy serge, had tie shoes with Cuban heels, wore a hat, and, worst of all, carried a black briefcase. We would run and hide when we saw her coming. It's horrible now to realize how her stiff, solitary progress towards school megaphoned, in 'body language', her loneliness, and probably as well the awareness of unfriendly eyes.

Another child, still pre-school, lived briefly in our neighbourhood. Her mother dolled her up in starched dresses, white socks, pretty sandals. As soon as she came out to play we would pounce, smudge her dress, then run away when she cried. She didn't explain, so her mother washed her face and arms, put a clean dress on her, with short puffed sleeves this time, and sent her back out to play. I remember the shame, once – may it really have been only once, never again – when we took her out of sight of her house, made her keep quiet with terrifying threats, and smudged all her clothes. Suddenly it was not fun any more. I cringe still at our spontaneous cruelty.

Even the backdrop of our days was not all benign. The First World War had generated a widespread climate, dispirited, directionless, which children accepted as they accept the weather. In hindsight I recognize the poverty: Ruby's house was best for playing jacks because there were bare floors and little furniture in our way. Thefts were common too, but of a friendly sort. Once, mother's 'kitchen purse' was rifled, but when we tested the mission's 'mite-box' it still rattled satisfactorily and we found a note that said: 'Sorry about your purse. I put two dimes in here.' One Sunday Mother went out to the back kitchen which was just cold enough to serve as a refrigerator, and came back with no dessert, just two empty plates and a note: 'The pies were good!'

My writing did not tap into day-to-day impressions and events – far from it, judging from scraps of juvenilia Mother saved. Early poems picked up rhythms and rhymes from familiar books such as R.L. Stevenson's *A Child's Garden of Verses,* and from chants for rope-skipping or ball-bouncing. And then there was my poem about an imagined Ontario orchard displaying apple blossoms 'blue and pink and white'.

I declare, though no evidence remains, that I composed a few rhymed quatrains about the beheading of Charles I (an event salvaged from boring history books about faraway British Empire matters – all that the curriculum ever offered) and submitted the poem to my teacher, a wiry, black-haired, square-faced older woman, who rebuked me for passing off someone else's work as my own. She must have been the grade five teacher. I was upset, so tore up the piece. I would suspect this memory, if it had not been quickened by a much later reading of L.M. Montgomery's parallel experience, recorded in fictional form in *Emily of New Moon.*

The early years in Calgary were the last when Ted, Mary and I were children together, at home, upstairs in our quarters, late afternoons and after supper. The focal memory of that time is when we all three had chicken pox. Ted, being older, had more fever, so we played mostly in his room. The family doctor, central to our 6th Avenue days, is the hero of this memory. Dr Gibson's 'surgery' was right next door. When I had a swollen wrist once, Mother noticed it and told me to run in and ask Dr Gibson to look at it. What I remember is being sent in alone, and coming back with a new word, announcing buoyantly: 'I've broken my *epipheseme* bone!'

Mary and I were the same ages as Dr Gibson's daughters, Patricia and Marian – 'Pat' and 'Mike'. We four sometimes played at their house, out in residential Calgary, but we did not all play together. Pat and Mary, who considered themselves grown up, *almost* teenagers, despised 'little kids', and they would stroll along the sides of the garden in serious talk while 'Mike' and I devised ways of plaguing them, rewarded when they'd turn and scold us. Did Dr Gibson arrange these visits or was it our plan? A little sting of having been 'sent' there on our part, and having to accept us on theirs, may have overheated those Saturday afternoons.

During the chicken pox days, right after he had diagnosed our spots and told Mother what we had and what to do, Dr Gibson ran back in with an armful of things, to 'keep the kids quiet'. There was a big scrapbook for each of us, some safe little scissors for me and proper ones for the other two, and piles of magazines, already thumbed ragged in the office waiting-room. We were organized by Ted with a 'clutch' of magazines apiece, and passing-on rules. Only the completed scrapbooks stay in memory: Mary's had scenery, sunsets, country farmyards; Ted's had all different makes of cars; mine had faces, most of them babies'. (I used to collect all my dolls and put them on the hall seat in attentive positions. There I would tell them stories, pretending they were my family.)

Cars were still a novelty, before driving tests. Every owner was ready to fix the motor if somebody aboard had hairpins and chewing gum. My father's rather high-spirited approach to driving goaded Ted to demand a turn at the wheel. (He had long been fascinated by motors: as a boy he had been allowed to drive a tractor up and down the lane at the farm; before we left Calgary he worked as a mechanic and later came back summers to drive buses in the mountains for student earnings.) When Ted learned that we would be moving to Ontario, he astonished Mary and me by saying: 'The roads there are fine, so wide that two lines of cars can go along one way and two lines the other way, almost all the time.'

Our 'drives' were at first tentative, after supper, around town. 'What do you do when you come to a hill?' my father asked Ted early on. But driving gradually became a form of relaxation for my father after the tension of two Sunday services, or a funeral. (He told me years later that the hardest time he ever had as a minister was during World War I days, when overseas chaplains would telegraph lists of casualties to local ministers who then were to break the news to families. Funerals followed, too many, too often. Officers' letters of sympathy would follow later.)

In Calgary, school day or not, it didn't matter, some mornings he'd wake up and shout 'Let's go to Banff!' There was a family routine: wash, dress and line up in the kitchen, each with a slab of bread, where Mother had a panful of bacon waiting. We'd have our open-face sandwiches in hand, all round, as we climbed into the car. (Breakfast oranges were offered only once a year, in the toe of a Christmas stocking. The orange-rind smell evokes pine-needle scent to this day.)

Mary had reached the dreamy age, happy to stare out the window. I sat in the middle, trying not to see motion too much, and Mother kept the window open for my sake. Ted sat in front, waiting for 'his turn'. Once it came when a white horse was cropping behind a fence, near Midnapore. The horse began running from the unfamiliar noise and dust of traffic, thus inspiring my father to a race. The horse won, Daddy accepted reproof and Ted took the wheel.

The roads were skiddy gravel. On hairpin turns in the mountains there were no guard-rails at the sheer drops. Roads were one-way, with occasional 'Pass Here' places dynamited out of the rocks, so the inside driver might have to back up a fair distance. Heights used to make Daddy dizzy but he was resolved to master his queasiness in the interest of family safety. There were times, though, when he'd pull into a 'Pass Here' place and let Ted take over.

Family trips to and through the Rockies blur in my memory. The very first one I anticipated with keen excitement. What it would be like to 'go into the mountains' had disastrously been left to my private imagining. Setting out was exciting, tension mounted through the obvious changes outside the car window, but at the final turn, when the mountains surrounded the car, my parents announced 'Now we are *in* the mountains!' Oh no! It was a great let-down. I had expected a long dark cave opening into a huge under-earth world, with its own weird cities, vegetation, and some kind of illumination deep down out of sunlight. Recovery was quick, though. What we actually saw soon proved to be no disappointment.

I also remember Storm Mountain. Was it on the Calgary–Banff, or the Banff-westward road? I'm not sure. What was memorable was the wonder of coming out of fair weather up into clouds and rain, seeing, always, 'the house on Storm Mountain'. Somebody *lived* there. *On purpose!* I could hardly believe that.

Summer holidays in Calgary always meant going further west. My first memory of Vancouver must have been from our first western holiday when I was seven. From a heretofore unknown uncle, a red-headed Catholic wheat farmer who hunted us up one Sunday because he had seen my father's name, we had learned about the existence of a great-aunt in Vancouver. This trip, then, was proposed by Mother in order to find this relative of Daddy's. I can barely picture her now. What I do remember is a white-painted little house, with a yard where a few chickens pecked in the sunshine. The new great-aunt had only fumbling recollections of my father's father, John Avison. He had been much younger, a fading memory for her.

I knew Daddy had been an infant when twenty-nine-year-old John Avison died. A special Calgary memory is kept in a jewel-box on black velvet. One night on the North Hill, I had been sitting in the car while my father made a pastoral call. When he returned, he opened the car door and suggested a little walk. It was a sparkling clear night, very deep, steep sky and stars as city people seldom see them. We stood and saw the city far below, and that sky above. In the hush of the moment my father said: 'Whenever I look into a sky like that, I wonder which light is the one where my father is.'

My father's tension, his up and down extremes, still reflected his foster-childhood with no fixed home between age five, when his beloved foster-father 'Mr Wilson' died, and age fourteen, when his mother and stepfather caught up with him and took charge. His violent outbursts and days of withdrawn melancholy made childhood exciting for us. As punishment for infractions, few of which I can recall, we would be strapped until bawling. We would next hear 'Stop that crying or I'll give you something to cry about!' Finally the sun would break through the clouds and my father would be trailing us up to the corner for ice-cream cones. Ted used to ask for, and get, money instead.

We would usually be in trouble together. What had we done? Gone to the far-off skating rink through dangerous traffic? Come home late for supper? Once I was *not* strapped and hated sitting apart in my virtue, left out. The odd thing is, once when I was strapped at school, and dutifully reported the fact at home, sniffling a little because of my stinging palms, my father saw that both hands were badly swollen. Instead of sticking to the parental rule of 'punished at school, punished again at home', Daddy marched me right back to the teacher: 'Look at the state of this child's hands!' His eyes must have blazed for she began to cry as he persisted 'What did you do it for? Why?' We girls had gone to the boys' baseball game, against instruction. Baseball *he* loved, too, so the poor woman had no defence. Was she the teacher who had scoffed at my history poem? I can't be sure.

A quarantine we felt keenly happened during one of our holidays in Banff. The town was quiet, before paved roads, before touring became popular. But that summer, when our family had rented a cottage on a hill just east of town, we felt victimized by the tourist officials when Ted came down with mumps. Mother used to say that the Banff officials quarantined us more rigorously than Regina ones had for scarlet fever, lest a visitor to Banff should be infected: word would spread and the infant tourist industry would be in peril.

From that cottage time I remember two events. A school friend of

Ted's with a summer job in Banff put a stepladder outside Ted's window and perched on top. They had daily visits that way. And from that cottage we would walk on the long empty hillside after supper, four of the five of us, in procession. My father felt responsible. Twilight, he believed, brought the animals out of the wilderness. Sure enough, one evening we were far out of reach of shelter when one wolf howled and others from another height answered, a wild echoing chorus rising and falling. Poor Daddy! 'Don't run,' he ordered, grimly taking somebody's hand, and two by two we were marched back to our safe doorway.

Over the years people told us what to do if we met a bear. Once, in the Valley of the Ten Peaks, I was alone on a grassy knoll, not very near a road or people, when a brown bear broke slowly through some shrubs where he had likely been feeding. He shambled toward me: curious? I knew not to turn but to stand my ground, and to use my voice to dominate him. My first try was soundless and he still came on, those forepaws looking huge. Finally, I swallowed then resolutely shouted 'Shoo! Go away!' To me it sounded more like a soprano squeak then a shout, but he paused, looked at me for a few seconds, his head swinging back and forth, and then turned his backside to me and ambled off into the bush again. I remember my knees suddenly feeling so weak that I sat down on a big stone until I was able to scramble back to the road. Probably bears in those days were more tolerant, rarely disturbed by people turning up in their territory.

When I found the family again, preparing our picnic lunch, I was glad to see our friends the Breckens had turned up too. A few other newcomers were wandering nearby when someone keeled over. 'It's the altitude,' one of them pronounced. Mr Brecken, a veteran, remarked thoughtfully, 'She'll be all right. When they die, they fall backwards.' Why is one such statement indelibly clear, more than seventy years later?

We have, or used to have, snapshots of another bear encounter, this time a family one. Our picnic was set out on tables in a small park at the Alberta-British Columbia border – the Great Divide. When two bears with a cub approached, drawn by the smell of our food, we withdrew to our parked car. The intruders found the food to their liking. In the snapshot one (was it the cub?) was sitting happily on a picnic bench, his legs apparently wagging.

For a minister's child holidays stand out, bright with variety and radiant with the unaccustomed family time all day every day for anyone who chose another's company. The variety, for us, may have been Mother's joy in discovery of new places. Moreover, when we spent our month at a distance, Daddy was less likely to be called back for a church member's crisis. The radiance was my father, free – no meetings, no scheduled congregational visiting, no hospital visits, no weddings, no preoccupation when a family suffered illness or disputes or loss. He would swim enthusiastically, out, out, out into a lake, floating face-up into the sunshine at will. Mary and I relished beaches with him. Mother did not like 'going in', and Ted, after a bad initial experience without Daddy present, went into the water only to soap, rinse, and wade shoreward, blue to the lips.

The Kootenay summer, at Balfour, began a tradition of holidays with the Breckens. The water was icy there. Mr Brecken and Daddy would yelp and hop about on the edge, while we shouted from further out that the water was *fine!* Ted's first plane ride occurred there. In those days even adults stood staring at the sky if a plane droned overhead. And Ted's ride was with royalty, though he was just twelve years old and we were nobodies.

He had rowed across Lake Kootenay to the town, then a cluster of buildings where, that day, flags were flying and people were gathering to greet Edward, Prince of Wales. He was doing a royal tour to outlying places from his ranch in Alberta. We, too, watched as his seaplane plumed in and settled down at the far wharf.

We heard at home later: the Prince emerged, shook hands all round, and (noticing one boy's eyes on the plane?) asked Ted if he'd like a ride. And how the plane roared and shook, up in the sky, and how different the world looked from away up there! I wonder if his arms were still trembling when he took the oars and headed home, after the Prince had left in a final display of foam-dazzling speed.

Another summer, we went to Brentwood on Vancouver Island. The swimming was full of wonder, those first days: jellyfish, in 'schools' (they left a red streak on your arm if you accidentally swam through them); starfish on the rocks, gritty to the touch but good to stare back at. But, alas, a few days had barely whetted our curiosity when a tanker leaked oil into the bay. This meant no more swimming. Instead, we learned first-hand how oil settles troubled water: the rowboat glided so easily it almost skidded along that surface, and the oil made an awful mess of the wooden boat.

One day we rowed around the bay to a wonderful place. Nobody challenged our beaching there: it was the valley part of the Butchart Gardens we had come upon! The shoreline led, in the other direction, to a place where bracken ferns grew so tall that we could weave little houses, and sit in them (see 'Spaces, Verticals' in *Momentary Dark*). The sap smell is still on my fingers as I write.

Once, somewhere in British Columbia, we drove along one of the twisty roads which had a steep drop on the left. Happily, we were on the side of the rock wall, opposite. Coming towards us in the left lane there appeared a lumber truck piled high with fresh-cut logs, roped on, side to side. Whether our approach distracted the driver, or the road-edge was crumbling, the tall load leaned. We slowed, then stopped in horrified witness as the truck toppled to one side and *all* the logs rolled off down into the valley below.

The driver? He was not only unhurt; he and his workmate scrambled out of the cab, their Sikh turbans undisturbed, peered over the edge of the valley and broke into laughter, whacking their knees as they put their whole bodies into that laughter. Finally one of them guided us over the hill ahead – no cars approaching – and then probably joined the other who had gone off down the hill to assess the situation.

Summers provided a necessary relief from Calgary winters. There on the coldest days we hated how our teeth ached with cold, biting into an apple, and how wisps of wool from our mitts strayed onto our tongues. Once the three of us were caught in a blizzard, sudden fine-driven snow blinding and choking us, and sweeping winds away below zero. We had to be treated for frostbite when we got home, though if Ted had not been stronger and surer of our direction, Mary and I might have fared far worse.

These blizzards broke suddenly. At school there was regular yard-drill, in case one happened at recess. The strongest people stood on the outer end of a 'rescue line', the inner end hanging on to the school door so that the whole line could fan through the schoolyard, handing back, person to person, any little ones who lay face-down in the snow for protection. If the storm broke when classes were in session, we had magical, night-light informal times right at school, till one by one each child was called for by a rescuing parent. Dramatic, those dark windows, that scream of wind outside, and the party atmosphere inside, with teachers playing games and sometimes even producing food and drinks!

It was, as I said, a happy childhood. Yes, there were the usual squabbles. Mary and I would be victimized by Ted and his high school friend, Art, teasing us, talking French to hide something from us. We would escape up the back stairs. We sometimes pouted about hand-me-down clothes, too. But such moments only provided a foil to the happy times.

People often attribute their problems to a troubled childhood. It struck me that, in contrast, my father resolutely set out to generate a climate for his family that would compensate for the lonely, unsettled years he had experienced between the ages of five and fourteen which might have made him inward and difficult. Indeed, an early photograph taken at college shows him with a dark, brooding look.

His life in our home said more about the faith that restored and sustained him than any exposition from the pulpit could. He wrestled with doubts, read with an open mind both devout and skeptical theological books, and was most at home with Charles Dickens's *Old Curiosity Shop.* Music helped heal him: he spoke of a student assignment in Meadowvale where a string quartet had delighted him with Mozart and Haydn. Singing had also been part of his student years.

Mother brought a stabilizing 'chapel' background into her marriage. Her inheritance was Wesleyan. As a child of seven she was included in a small believers' group with a few older men and women, the Methodist 'class' of the early 1900s, where Bible study, encouragement, rebuke, confession, reconciliation, all built moral discipline. Her faith was secure enough to work through jagged disparities between her early but sure convictions, and Daddy's struggles to plot a course through the angers and doubts of Depression-racked parishioners. He felt with them. He wrestled with his sermons until late evening on Saturdays, sometimes, and would summon Mother once, or even twice, to hear him through his outline. If we were in the hall, we'd tiptoe past.

Every phase of his mellowing over the years was supported by Mother's passing on the encouragement and honest speaking of her childhood 'class'. His wide reading she respected. They both enjoyed the same music. They built wholesomeness into the family's life, conferring and coming to agreement before dealing with us, not in our hearing. Consistency was Mother's contribution; warmth and occasional thunderstorms, Daddy's.

Mother's mind could turn to practical, applied mathematics. On somebody's authority I was assured that when our 6th Avenue and 4th Street area was burgeoning with new shops and office buildings, and a new parsonage had to be built, Mother drew up the plans. They proved workable when submitted to the relevant permit office. I asked her about that house once, when she was in her late eighties. She said, with a dreamy smile, 'It was good to design a laundry chute from the bedroom level upstairs to the basement tubs.' Before there were automatic machines, the old washing machines, although an improvement over hand-scrubbing, still involved hard labour – carrying baskets of clothes down to the basement, squeezing them through a wringer after they were washed and rinsed, then carrying them again, wet still, up the back steps to an outdoor clothesline and hanging them up with clothespins. A chute would have saved one step.

We left our 6th Avenue house for an apartment. The sense of how other people lived, the smells of unfamiliar cooking, made that interesting. Besides, there was a courtyard where balls could be bounced or batted against walls. It was not far to the public library park, long a favourite place of mine. Once I asked permission to invite a friend home for lunch. 'Who is it?' 'An old man I met in the public library park.' 'Yes,' said Mother resolutely, 'do invite him.' 'Daddy Lowe' was my name for him, an Englishman who often sat in the park because after his wife's death he had finally sold their home and rented a room. He became a regular visitor, a friend of the whole family, and when we left Calgary he gave me a beautiful ring, a ruby set with tiny diamonds, his mother's ring. I wore it until the stone dropped out somewhere in Toronto seventy-odd years later.

Leaving the old house was not painful. Our last months there were not easy. Mary had diphtheria, Mother was quarantined with her, Daddy and Ted moved out to a boarding-house, and a Scottish newcomer to Calgary was hired as housekeeper (see the second part of section 6, 'Other Oceans', in *Concrete and Wild Carrot*) and to look after me, doing whatever Mother instructed through the sick quarters door. Mary told me later how the worst thing about the illness was looking in a hand-mirror at her sore throat and seeing white strings all across it.

Dr Gibson had read about a newly tested serum and sent for it. He injected what he thought would be a maximum dose. It could have been much stronger, but the dose he gave certainly moderated the later part of the fever. (The early tests had not yet been completed on the much larger doses which they did not yet know could be used safely.) Mary's convalescence was slow. After-effects were recognized and treated only after we had lived some years in Toronto.

Margaret dressed up in a Calgary Stampede outfit.
(Credit: University of Manitoba Archives and Special Collections, Margaret Avison fonds, Box 1, PC151)

TORONTO

When we left for Toronto in the summer of 1929, I had mixed feelings. For me the unthinkable, leaving my friends, was transmuted into a dark story with a perhaps happy ending ahead. Then reality hit. A dim sense remains of the departure and the trip: a muddle of Calgary people, luggage, coats, the exciting steps up into our railway car, travelling across prairie and bush country, trying to keep my balance in a clattery washroom among strangers in the morning, nervous attempts to walk up and down station platforms along the way before the 'All Aboard'. These experiences did not overide a dominant apprehension.

Finally we arrived at West Toronto Station, Keele and Dundas, bag and baggage. Someone drove us along Annette Street to our new parsonage next to the big brick church on High Park Avenue. We had arrived in a heat wave. No holiday this year. For the month of July we would all settle in. The first pay cheque was due August 1st.

Ted, Mary and I were assigned the two bedrooms on the third floor, though on the hottest nights we slept out on the grass. Our room was larger than his, with two beds, a desk with a kneehole to accommodate us face to face, and a dresser with a tilty mirror where, when she sleepwalked at night, Mary would terrify herself awake, looking into that mirror in the faint glimmer of street lights far below. The gables meant a sloping wall by one bed, the opposite slope in Ted's room, and two windows on our side. The second floor had my parents' room, a guest room used as a sick room for times of flu or fevers, Nanny's room, and two bathrooms, one for the toilet, the other for tub and basin. Showers were unknown to us.

Nanny was Daddy's mother who had just sold the house where her second husband had died. Her daughter lived in Toronto but was too far from a church for Nanny to walk. From her second marriage she had three sons who lived in other cities. The High Park parsonage had a room she could furnish with her own things, and it suited her, although climbing to the second floor became painful over our time in Toronto. That discouraged her from staying on at my father's next charge, eight years later. The stairs in 270 McLaren Street, Ottawa, were so forbidding that Nanny returned to Toronto and moved into Belmont House for the rest of her life.

July was a discouraging start. It took us more than one summer to adjust to the humid heat, interspersed with thunderstorms. No mountains broke the bad weather here. We did have an icebox in the new kitchen, with a drip pan. Emptying it was one of our chores, rotated weekly with meal duties, bed-making, dusting and carrying out the garbage cans. There was a side door in the kitchen, and space enough for a work area opposite the sink and stove. Until my father got at it the next year, the garden was all vegetables: hills of potatoes, rows of beans and beets. We fed on beans and beets and boiled potatoes all that first July! The one concession to beauty was a grape-arbour.

It took some painful months before I stopped expecting children in West Toronto ('the Junction') to be somehow like those in downtown Calgary. My first playmate came to visit at her mother's bidding. I took Norah out to the grape arbour, guilefully, for I knew that the vines were infested with furry caterpillars that could be counted on to drop on us. I flipped mine off my arm or neck nonchalantly, and hoped Norah was squirming. All this venom had been generated when my hope for a congenial playmate died the instant she arrived: her mother had dressed her up as if for a party. Pretty and petite, she came leading a little Pekinese on a ribbon, not a leash. Is that memory edited to justify my boorishness? Probably.

If Norah came to visit reluctantly, under orders to be nice to the new girl, she probably couldn't get away fast enough, that day. At high school we did become friends, and long years afterwards our paths crossed again. Her name had become well-known and was still associated with caterpillars! She had married Dr Frederick Urquhart, the biologist who, with her, first tracked the monarch butterfly's long migration south. The Urquharts were a distinguished couple in the University of Toronto community by the time Norah and I met again.

Children in Toronto were no substitute for the cherished ones left behind in Calgary – forever, I began to feel. No letters back and forth, and on one return visit, far into adult years, only two could be located, though both reunions were friendly. Such was the lot of a Methodist minister's child. Until the United Church absorbed Methodists in 1925, they moved their clergy every three years. I should have been used to arriving in new places as a stranger but this move was cataclysmic. In Calgary lots of children would be playing outdoors; here the nearest neighbour my age was a Dorothy who seemed to sit all day on her veranda doing nothing, *nothing*. We became friendly in time, but with distance.

On into August, more children surfaced, home from summers away, but preoccupied with silly little cardboard trays they showed one another and me – samples they had collected at the Exhibition, to trade or gloat over. 'What is the Exhibition?' I asked. 'We'll go next year,' someone promised, unwisely adding 'It's like the Stampede.' Nonsense! Fiddly little things on trays!

On the first day of school my isolation was completed. Mary and Ted were going to be in other schools, but I had to take grades seven and eight in Annette Street Public School. Somebody took me there, registered me in the principal's office, then left. I trailed along a hallway to the door indicated on my new admission paper, and opened it just as the teacher up at the far end of the room was asking 'What is your name?' I told him. And all the heads at the rows of desks pivoted round, bursting out laughing while I stood frozen in misery. 'No, the person who had not received a pencil – *your* name?' he said, quieting the new class and coming towards me to take my paper and assign a desk. I remember thinking, savagely, 'Just wait until they hear me read!'

The man who taught us was likeable, well-organized, irascible. Students who had failed one or more years but by law had to remain at school until age sixteen washed up on his shore. He seemed to accept the sprawling, older few. One had a desk just behind mine, and during a North American geography lesson one morning he told me, 'My dad and I have been all those places, hoboing and riding the freights.'

One morning, that teacher came in looking very flushed. After roll-call he paused, started to shuffle papers, put them down, seized a pencil, began whittling it fiercely into the wastebasket, then said: 'Sally is not here. She was fine yesterday, but during the night she began coughing, then she coughed blood, and then she died.' The day went on as usual, but for weeks anytime Mary or I coughed, I would expect death by morning.

One friend eventually emerged out of that grade seven class – Maisie Cameron, another young writer, whose reading of her own poetry was featured on a Friday afternoon towards the school year's close. She lived nearby, liked walking, showed me around the district or included me when she took her little brother Duncan for walks.

Supper hours were very strict in her home. Her mother devoted herself exclusively to domestic duties, doing all the cleaning, washing, ironing, preparing and serving meals, for her husband and three children. No children's chores in that household! Her husband, a Scot with Boy Scout credentials, focused on the children, co-opting the dining room table for games and puzzles until his wife had to clear it to serve a meal. It bothered me that in this family nobody seemed to help her. I realize now that Mother assigned us household chores so that we'd be used to routines.

Maisie I considered my special friend. But another girl at school called Helen, frail-looking, golden-haired, liked her company too. Helen was erratic. When she wanted someone's company, she wanted it, and when she didn't, she withdrew totally. Maisie seemed to suffer in this on-and-off relationship, and when it was 'on', she ignored me. I remember being comforted by my mother, once, as I cried in the bathroom, ashamed of feeling so abandoned.

That first year, Ontario stifled us. The bulk of the city's buildings oppressed, and its elms and maples, and even the gorgeous oaks in High Park, were so much clutter to us. Ted was happiest in the car. When we could, the three of us drove to the shore of Lake Ontario, stood at the edge, and stared greedily at wide-open spaces. This brought relief, if only briefly. Ted's homesickness grew until, by spring, our new family doctor was 'watching' him for possible typhus. The feverish malaise dragged on. When it neither abated nor developed full-fledged symptoms, the doctor recommended that Ted should apply for a summer job driving Brewster buses out west in the mountains. He did, and was hired. When he returned to Toronto that autumn he looked sturdy and at peace, ready for his sophomore year in commerce and finance at the University of Toronto.

That Christmas – I *think* it was that first year – was one oasis of good feeling, all round. We had been invited to the farm for Christmas Day, and Christmas week had brought beautiful quiet deep snow. Our stress over the Christmas Sunday evening service was behind us. For this service, a crowded family affair, Daddy had announced a Charles Dickens recitation. Over the years he had enjoyed *A Christmas Carol* so often that he knew it by heart. But to recite it in public? Without a prompter? To this day I remember the tension at home and, later, Mother in our pew, spasmodically kneading the handkerchief in her lap, intent on supporting him through every word, every inflection. It went without a hitch. And two days from now would be Christmas.

On Christmas Eve we set out merrily for St Thomas and the farm. It snowed more on the way but by then Daddy was irrepressibly his holiday self, reciting passages of his favourite Dickens novels, off and on, to while away the time, and so well adapting his driving to roads and weather that I think Ted did not once ask to drive. At the farm, in Union, past St Thomas, the white frame gabled house was aglow with lights as we drove up the long lane between the pines. Those old trees made a wonderful surf sound when you stood under them in the windy darkness.

Morning, with their family of eight and ours of five, was a tumultuous reunion. Every window looked out on a Christmas-card picture. Inside was a tree, decorated with their family's traditional pieces in among the tinsel and colourful paper chains. After dinner some of us walked with Uncle Orville out in the snow, in the lee of a fence, to a place where a brook broke through the drifts and danced along in the sunshine. Calgary winters had been blizzards, drifts in an hour or two, alternating with chinooks that withered away, rather than melting, the snow. Now on the farm I at last understood why my parents, out west, had been homesick for the puffy snow and irrepressible little brooks 'back East' [see 'Two Whoms ...' in *Listening: Last Poems*].

In the city, that same snow was not licked up at intervals by warm winds from over mountains. It grimed. It slushed. We three had skates, and the rink on Keele Street was a welcome resort after school, until the thaw. The grey days brought sickness to many of the aging church members, and magnified recurrent family crises in those days of the Great Depression.

At mealtimes we felt the weight of our parents' burdens. They didn't mention it but we knew by the grapevine about one businessman's failure and suicide in our neighbourhood. His family home, bought during twenties boom times, was a splendid three-storey brick house where the widow and two daughters were alone now. Nobody bought such houses after the Crash, so his widow and daughters stayed on, though I used to wonder whether they had enough food. In the manse we were perennially putting together quick box-lunches for some hungry man at our door. For families, the church bought meal tickets from a nearby restaurant, which Daddy gave out at need.

In spite of friends I'd made in public school, and new contacts when high school days began, an undercurrent of sadness ran steadily under the security of day-to-day events. My first high school poem was an ode, 'To an Apple-Core', the death-image mirroring the gloom that only a vigorous young person can safely indulge. Ted liked another poem I showed only to him: a street-vendor with a bony horse drawing his cart, in a misty rain. He put it in his wallet.

To an Apple-Core

Poor ugly, shrivelled, useless, withered thing,
The warped, dark stem, that once so joyously
Clung to the mother branch and bore its child,
Is robbed of all but these frail, worthless wisps.

Do you remember those far distant days
When mists of beauty above o'erswept your souls
And you were urged to share your loveliness
In dainty blossoms and in fragrance fair?
And then there came the soft, sweet breaths of rain
To spread white petals on the naked earth.
In pure, rapt sweeps of utter ecstasy,
Through all the cool, fresh days of later spring
You throbbed with wonder, and the perfect joy
Of being in Creation's moulding shop;
And in the autumn, dusky-cheeked and fair
And mellow with the sunshine you had stored,
The beauty of the harvest days of fall,
The strange, sweet, sad aromas, drifting by
Of smoky mystery upon the wind –

The picking, and the sudden jarring jolt
Of commerce after days of perfect peace;
The robbing of the ruddy cheeriness,
The fruit ingrained with sun, and rain, and wind;
And now swept off into oblivion

Alone, forgotten, empty, useless, old,
You sink into a lost thing of the past.

And can it be that we, as you, must end,
By death robbed of all beauty, of all worth,
Cast in a sorrowing, forgotten tomb, –
Dust 'neath the feet of onward marching men
Who soon must join those soulless drifts of dust?

Oh that my eyes were opened! I *must* see
A future glad as yours is void of hope.*

In grade seven I had been a solid, pudgy child, good-humoured in spite of missing Calgary. At puberty I hated the changes in my body. Was I to become like Pat Gibson and my sister who had put on lipstick and carried little purses as they strolled about at the Gibsons'? This physical change was the last straw. I resisted it. I wanted to remain a child. In order that my body should lose its new swellings I resolved to stop eating and to walk off my fat. I took long walks out Annette Street to the heights over the Humber River, then up and down beside the river, which was a country walk in the 1930s. There were market gardeners stooping and rising on the steep east side of the river, and gravel and scrub on the west side.

The range of the walks kept widening. In and out of unfamiliar streets beyond the West Toronto Station, past the railway underpass, into abandoned factory stretches, or northward past the Heintzman piano factory into an area of small frame houses I walked, through grey streets where grey, solitary old men rambled aimlessly. I coveted the bony wrists poking out of their worn coat cuffs. In skating days I had liked walking past cheerful houses very different from ours, different perhaps because of a copper coffee-kettle in a window or the Scandinavian smell of the cooking.

Compulsive walking works best in small side streets, where the pace's hypnotic rhythm is seldom broken. Such walking allowed me to shed, temporarily, the self defined by family, school, home

---

* The poem appeared in Humberside Collegiate's magazine, *The Hermes*, 1932.

neighbourhood, and so on. Freed from such frames, I could appropriate a new identity as though I'd become some unknown person as suggested by new views: lonely scenes glimpsed through front windows. A heavily overcast day, or twilight, would be most conducive, with perhaps a lamp lit inside those windows. Exploring other people's places made life spread out, away out, dotted with potential new discoveries.

A librarian in the Annette Street Public Library also challenged me to explore, through reading. For me, the library had always meant the children's collection. There were adult bookshelves in plain view, as there were at home, but somehow they seemed out of bounds for me. This librarian broke the jinx. She noticed me re-borrowing books I had read already, and firmly led me upstairs to show me the sections for history and geography project materials, the fiction shelves, and the big dictionary to use if I needed to learn a new word. I went home that day with my first adult loan, Caroline Dale Snedecker's *The Perilous Seat,* a story about ancient Sparta, chosen for me by that librarian. She freed me into a new kingdom that supplemented my first-hand experience with that of other persons in other places and times. In those days I kept a list of books I read and today I wish I had continued that practice.

Choosing a book must have been part of the sense of discovery. Other places and times were always turning up in our set of *The Book of Knowledge* at home. Nobody guided our explorings when we filled in time downstairs before some outing with any volume, at random. One chance landing I remember, and have had revivified. The word 'tsunami' did not enter my vocabulary then, but the fact of a tidal wave became very real. The disaster, the wave advancing like a wall of water, swallowing up little boats and seaside villagers, the appalling devastation: every detail burned itself indelibly into my memory. My nightmares were full of tsunami associations.

In our new back yard was a climbable cherry tree. Contriving exalted pictures of myself one summer day, I marched out to that tree with a cushion and one of Mother's books, Palgrave's *Golden Treasury of Songs and Lyrics.* The cushion kept sliding between branches; sitting up there meant controlling it, myself, and my place in the book. I read the words without difficulty but found nothing I liked, even a bit. A humbling afternoon that was. I was outside the magic circle.

When I began high school in September of 1931, I approached the poetry club timidly. Should I bring a poem, as the club notice encouraged newcomers to do? Students from all grades were invited. The classroom where we met was full of windows looking onto the beautiful fall landscape we three young Albertans had scorned just two years ago! Was dimming daylight the only light in that room from four o'clock to almost the end? I think so. Big fellows, seniors, two older girls in suits with blouses, and many others were there, but few newcomers. Those older girls, I learned, were now university students.

The teacher who presided collected poems from several of us. She opened the meeting herself by reciting a lovely quatrain, not like a performer, but as though realizing someone else's thoughts out loud. She read us things she liked and let us comment. She was open to readings by club members and some, prepared by last year's meetings, had brought poems or paragraphs from longer books they wanted everyone to enjoy. Miss Gladys Story was a teacher looked upon as a friend by students and staff alike. Even in the informal times, like the Poetry Club, she never spoke of herself and yet became, in our eyes, part of everyone's trusted inner community – so much so that, when she was away, ill, it seemed natural that a couple of her grade thirteen girls would go over to her apartment near the school to do things and make tea for her.

One glimpse into her private experiences emerged from her readings: any reference to the 1914–18 war seemed to touch on acreages of sorrow. The stories of Katherine Mansfield (1888–1923) from this period moved her, and us as well from her reading. Since trying to like those *Golden Treasury* poems, I'd dimly felt that the Old Country was foreign, alienating to a young Canadian of my time. These barriers were dissolved in that after-school hour by Miss Story's hypnotic reading of Scottish ballads and flashes of song from lyricists of Shakespeare's day and any later century.

When discussion died out, that first meeting, Miss Story gave us her form room number and offered times when contributors would be able to pick up their work. Then she asked the person who had contributed 'the ode' to stay behind a minute. I did, and she asked me whether I had other work, and if so, would I mind letting her see it. The extent and range of her influence, in those short months, make it hard for me to be sure whether I saw her for a one-on-one session just once, or went over my poems with her in several four o'clock sessions.

Before the end of that school year, after more intervals of absence, Miss Story was dead. The news devastated the school. We all gathered for a memorial in the auditorium. The room must have been hot and crowded. Former students had swelled our numbers. The grade thirteen boys stood at the back. At intervals, one of them would fall over and be carried off like a log; three or four fell in a marbled silence – no whispers, no head-turning. The fainting spells seemed just part of the unbearableness, the inevitable sad ending, a rare light in our midst having gone out. I remember trying to reassemble my tear-swollen face in a washroom afterwards, and how Maisie, my more self-contained friend from public school, waited out in the hall so we could walk partway home together.

The fine red-ink comments in my notebook went on instructing me: 'Too much here. Save it till it builds, and justifies such a term.' Or, '*You* underline, Margaret, the two places in this one that are insincere.' Across one margin she had written: 'For ten years, do not write any poem with any first person singular pronoun in it.' Within the ten years it was necessary, in some poems, to use an *I* or *me,* but I had radar out against using them for any self-indulgent reason.

Though the high school years were sombre, there were redeeming factors. It proved possible to keep on keeping on, even at the worst. For one thing, home was secure. My parents' confrontations were wholehearted on both sides, and blew over, faster for my father; my mother needed time to venture again into safe weather. Our regular chores kept us sane and kept us from moping for long. One Monday morning I was sitting on the top step of the cellar stairs when Mother came up, panting, with the first basket of wet clothes to hang out on the line. She thumped the basket down where I'd made room and asked what was wrong. I moaned that I still had homework to finish and beds to make and school was in an hour and it was all impossible. 'Well,' said Mother, picking up her laundry, 'it certainly won't get done with you sitting here,' and she proceeded, unsympathetically, to the outdoors.

From this distance I see that my classmates' implicit friendliness meant ease with this one and that one. I fished for crayfish with someone, or walked in company, sometimes, in High Park, even joined somebody from Sunday school to walk in the Easter Parade on Sunnyside's boardwalk, though only once: my shoes hurt.

Nonetheless, gloom kept deepening in my personal climate. The Great Depression was part of it. But poverty? We were secure, and had status. Down the years I have seen three kinds of poverty. How to encapsulate them? *First,* the pioneer poverty, expected, borne in courageous resolve to succeed, soon: that furniture-less house in Calgary that we liked for its bare floor where we could play jacks. I happily remember the oil boom in Alberta with its promise of fulfilling those pioneer dreams.

Second, the almost-universal, shared poverty of the thirties. The financial crash of 1929 had dumped one after the other into financial limbo. Before long, jobless men were trying any kind of work. But who could pay them? Hunger and helplessness undermined their stubborn hopes. Government relief was a deferred response. 'Billy', as people called a colleague of Daddy's, set up his private soup cauldron downtown, where the cheapest rooms were and the most places to try for work. He wore gauntlets so he could handle the ladle which he kept hot on coals. His clerical vest was usually daubed, his cheeks streaked with smut from the fire irons, his welcoming smile all the better for it. That scene registered – a good man doing something about the thin-wristed starvelings I had seen wandering the streets north of Keele and Dundas.

Third, the poverty which settles in among families on public assistance, somewhat sheltered but still insecure. Even after relief was organized, the cheques did not cover dependants aged sixteen and over. One, at age sixteen, resolved to get work at a nearby car wash. He walked up and down the opposite side of the street, trying to get up courage enough to cross over and apply. He never got up that courage. When another reached sixteen, his mother had to cut him off, as his healthy raiding of the fridge and gulping a quart of milk after school meant they'd run out for the younger children. He ended up on a bench in a small park disconsolately eating stolen buns.

Poverty, for some, is a temporary hindrance. They may start small, with plans promising enough to justify financial backing, in prospect of much more when business picks up again. The poor in low-income neighbourhoods all, alike, make do, going without that new coat again this fall, preparing plainer meals, walking rather than spending money on public transportation, and so on. All this soon becomes second nature, not a hardship. Finally, there are the chronically poor who are undernourished, listless, usually undereducated.

The encompassing Depression weighed on us. My sister was not well. For some four years her symptoms, which included excessive weight gain, were not recognized as glandular deficiencies, perhaps the after-effects of diphtheria. Was there no metabolism test as yet? In any case, she suffered unduly from any negative comment she overheard, even from Daddy's half-brother who hadn't seen us in years and was taken by surprise when Mary came down for dinner. She fled to the third floor, refusing to come back down that evening, or ever thereafter when there was company – not even the amazing time when the guest had no arms, and washed his feet before the meal so that he could rest a heel on the table to hold a fork or spoon with his toes. He managed even dessert, a dish of maple syrup, without making a single spot.

Eating with the family was beginning to be a dread occasion for me. The physicality of chewing and swallowing suddenly seemed repulsive. Incipient anorexia nervosa would be identified sooner nowadays. At that time it must have struck our doctor as inconceivable that somebody provided with basic nourishment should deliberately refuse to take it, when so many were out of work and semi-starved in the city around us. He treated me for digestive disorders, even once overnight in hospital to absorb through a suppository the medication he assumed I would be unable to keep down. In fact, my digestive system was fine, in spite of shrinking capacity as I ate less and less. I continued to be hungry: on one of my two-hour walks around West Toronto, I remember stopping to stare longingly at a bakeshop's rolls and cakes, torn between appetite and steeling myself against it. Willpower can turn resolution into a compulsion, and therefore become addictive.

When a person keeps growing while starving herself, failing weight becomes more obvious. That summer a family holiday was planned; the Breckens from Calgary would come too, to Prince Edward Island. I loved the walks on the sand, climbing around the cliffs. Once I crawled through a hole in a craggy place, feet first, and when my head was through far enough I saw that the other side was a sheer wall of rock. With the rocky shore below, the ocean looked a long way down. I remember clinging in the hole while my fingers slipped, bit by bit. I fell – into water deep enough, at high tide, for me to *swim*, among the rocks, to shore. My wet shorts and top, shoes and socks, had dried a little by the time I reached our cabin but still betrayed how thin I was. Mrs Brecken told Mother later she thought I needed better medical help, and soon.

A specialist was recommended when we were home again. He was pleasant-faced, imperturbable, careful in writing out the history and listening to my account. He did not treat my psyche. He admitted me into a thirty-bed ground floor ward of the old Toronto General Hospital. The first test, hard to take, established that my digestive system was healthy. It rewarded me when the doctor encouraged a patient nearby to swallow the gastric tube he had to push down her throat: 'That young girl next to you swallowed it at first try, gagging only at the start, and lay quiet till the test was over and it could be pulled out.'

Thereafter the treatment was painful force-feeding of huge meals. (If the quantity was painful for me, it must have been more so for the other patients because *their* Depression-era trays were meagre: one slab of hard, cold, precooked fish for supper, once, I remember, with some bread.) To prevent my sending back food they brought, the doctor resorted to insulin-shock therapy. He explained that after each injection I would *have* to eat to allay the discomfort, which turned out to be a dry mouth and eyeballs almost crackling with dryness. I ate. And my trays were high-calorie ones. Soon I looked forward to mealtimes, but it took weeks before the doctor was sure I was on my way to normal eating and would not revert to old habits.

The three months taught me a lot. They awakened in me 'populist' sympathies, a term I did not know until the 1950s when a Hungarian refugee introduced me to it. One small white-haired lady, who had liquid liver injections for pernicious anaemia, and hated how she tasted the liver all the time, taught me how to knit. Another patient lay dying in the bed next to me one night. A curtain shielded her from passersby but not from me: either it was too skimpy at my side, or her sister, sitting in her coat at bedside on a wooden chair, had disarranged the curtain. In any case, what I remember is the sister plodding into the bathroom at intervals, the scrunch of her steps, still wearing overshoes.

Then there was a bony, short man who came through the ward twice a week. He would seize the railing at the foot of the bed, fix a slightly cross-eyed glare upon each of us in turn and demand, 'Are you saved?' When I answered that I didn't know, he declared my illness a judgement. Finally, when he came into sight again one day, I changed my answer: 'Saved?' 'Yes.' He simply said, 'Praise the Lord,' and never stopped at my bed again. Now I honour his motive. Who knows, his way may have been the right way for somebody else.

One morning when I went into the bathroom, where the toilet stalls were beyond the big bathtub, I surprised a gaunt woman trying to lift the big can of disinfectant from its place beside the end of the tub. She froze, then said fiercely: 'If you tell a nurse I'm drinking this, I'll kill you!' Of course I told, they restrained her, and she was moved to another area of the hospital.

It chills my blood, as I try to speak truthfully about those years, how my *feelings* seemed cut off from all that I was carefully *observing.* Where, in me, was any clue to what I was putting my parents through, emotionally and financially? And now a final extravagance was demanded: the doctor wanted to widen the distance between my days of illness and my ultimate resumption of normal routines. For this final step, he counselled that I complete my fourth year of high school in a private school. It would be a late start, on in November. Since Mother had done her graduating year in piano at Alma College, St Thomas, she and Daddy concluded that my boarding there would be the solution.

Through those months, and throughout their lives, neither of them ever referred to that bad time. Only now, looking down the decades, do I glimpse what generosity they showed then and thereafter. A typical teenager fighting free of home? Why the daily misery, then, at Alma College, after classes, lying on my bed in a cold room with homesick tears trickling across my face? (At least I could count on a hot bath before dressing for dinner.)

Ladies' comportment was a new training here. Weekly teas were served in the dean of women's drawing-room followed by gentle, private comments on what had been correct, and where we might have slipped, this time. Classes, on the other hand, were buoyant compared to a city collegiate's. Smelly chemistry experiments were done out under the trees. Literature, too, might be taught in a quiet corner of the ravine, or out in the spring sun.

At first there was constraint at mealtimes: I was not only new; I had arrived halfway through the first term. But in time I looked forward to my tablemates. So far my skinny appearance persisted but my appetite flourished. A local farmer had apples, more than he could market. He would bring big hampers of rain-cool apples to the side door of the wing where our bedrooms were, and we were to help ourselves. The hamper was replenished regularly.

The year circled towards May Day (not the Workers of the World's Day) at a rhythmic pace. We rehearsed our maypole dance until it was perfect, then flowers and ribbons and lovely weather were added, and the park and ravine full of visitors. A truly happy-ever-after ending of a year that had boded no good. Mother and Daddy must have been glad of their extravagant plan when they brought me home energetic and healthy. In the fall, familiar routines ought to have taken over for me in Humberside Collegiate. Then why the struggle to adapt? At first my normal circle of school friends seemed distanced for me by all that had happened since grade eleven, in their lives as well as in mine.

By then I had taken the communicants' classes at church, sincerely enough, and had been admitted to church membership. Now I willingly accepted a Sunday school class of much younger children. Whenever the printed lesson plan felt artificial to me, I hit the topics my own way, based on the assigned readings. It came as a shock when the youth pastor asked me to withdraw because my teaching was disturbing someone. He had no need to tell Daddy's daughter that it's politically wise to avoid upsetting long-established church families.

Those were uneasy days still, in our denomination. Church union, which had been embraced in the west, was resented in Toronto by the old guard. The group from the local Presbyterian congregation who had opted for the United Church did join the former Methodist group in our building, but they met at first in separate areas, Presbyterians in the basement, Methodists in the sanctuary. Daddy's indignation burned hotly when he saw the situation. He insisted on one common service in one common sanctuary, and he persevered in working, as fellow pastor, with the retired Presbyterian clergyman who, with his flock, at last joined the upstairs congregation.

If to me this was confusing at the time, I can imagine how ludicrous it may sound to anyone hearing about it in the twenty-first century. Many who have drifted away from a churched upbringing, and more who have no roots at all in Christian faith, tend to form theories about the basis of such pigheadedness and opposing passions. Wars, they say, Christian bastions, divisions, that's all you see; and where is their Prince of Peace? True, it is sad when a church gets into disputes among members. But such disputes are not unknown in political parties and other institutions. In High Park United Church, divisions never grew into schism. Learning to acknowledge differences led to accepting them, with good will. Learning to know what underlies animus usually changes it into friendly debate, I suspect, as the two factions at our church soon demonstrated. For example, the hymns of each tradition became part of a new tradition, enriching both groups. The quiet evening service continued to soothe my spirit.

One friend, whom I met at church, appeared first as piano soloist on some festive occasion. She was non-conformist in every sense: slangy, wild, with rather dry blond hair. Tallish and thin, witty, unpredictable, she made flip references to topics I had barely heard about, and then only in counsels to be cautious. And she taught me how to roll my own cigarettes. Her name was Kay. She questioned my father sharply about things he said from the pulpit. She was clearly full of hunger to read more books, and think more thoughts, all from a standing point in a fast relay race, as she perceived it, and as I came to understand.

Mother and Daddy invited her home, once, after some meeting. And a while later, Kay invited me to her home. It was out northwest of Toronto, at that time a scatter of low-built houses and small shops. Was there a tramline out of the city? I'm not sure now. To me, the whole area was still soaked in misery, from memories of Aunt Lena's funeral out there. I had not taken it in that Nanny *had* a sister, until I was asked to accompany her to the funeral. That was Weston, then, for me.

Kay's home was one of the small frame houses, about the size of a trailer-and-a-half. The door was unlocked. She marched in and ahead to a far corner where her piano and cot were, behind a divider-curtain. Her father was home, tall and thin too, with patches of black hair in odd spots of his bald skull. He was drunk. Kay said it, and his behaviour increasingly bore it out. 'We don't have to bother with him,' Kay said.

She showed me her books: a library-book history of modern France I think was her current reading. I told her about Maeterlinck, and Hardy's *The Dynasts,* which absorbed me around that time. At some stage I remember telling Kay that I had tried to read Mother's copy of Robert Bridges' *Testament of Beauty,* but that to me it fell flat. Kay made us a sandwich, and brought back mugs of tea on a tray. It was becoming a wintry twilight by then. Somebody else had come crashing home, taken in a situation he grasped in a moment, and crashed out again. The trip home I do not remember. But I understood why Kay turned up in church those peaceful Sunday evenings. Years later, married and more prosperous, she still came sometimes. 'It's a place to sit and be quiet,' she said once.

Our different neighbourhoods kept our friendship intermittent at first. But when Doug and Kay introduced themselves as engaged, and asked my father to marry them, the relationship stabilized. Their new home was not far from ours. I remember hearing, from Kay when *her* son married, 'I've lost a son but gained a garage!' In adulthood she and her daughter met a drunk driver on a hilltop, on the wrong side of the road. Their injuries were awful. She developed a new edge to her humour through the years of surgery, plastic surgery, re-learning to walk.

Another atmosphere somehow alien to my childhood upbringing was the Toronto Conservatory of Music. It stood on the southwest corner of University Avenue and College Street then, a rosy brick building, three storeys high. Sounds of tenors singing scales or instrumentalists practising toots and twiddles floated out the windows. My teacher there was to be Miss Alma Cockburn. Mother had asked around, and had been given her name.

But there was competition for piano time at home. Mother kept up her technique and much of her repertoire, even into old age, by playing whenever time permitted. Nanny had been a soprano soloist; before dinner she sometimes chorded with arthritic hands, and sang hymns. Mary had volumes of songs and *Étude* music books, was a good sight-reader, and kept up her piano enough to handle her kindergarten teaching job years later. Ted was the best pianist of us three, and applied his technique now to jazz.

In his freshman year, he brought a classmate home from university: Northrop Frye had a small, piquant face, a big cloud of fair hair around his head. He was very shy. Before dinner he sat on the piano bench with his back to any threat of social interaction, thumbed through several music books, found some of Mother's Bach preludes and fugues and proceeded to play through them from the first to whichever one he'd reached when Mother summoned us all to dinner.

Piano practising time for me was from seven to eight in the morning. Daddy and I were early risers, and often had breakfast together before then. Beginners' lessons in Calgary had made it possible for me to play a little – MacDowell's 'To a Wild Rose', pieces from Mary's *Étude* books and, in exasperation with my clumsy fingers, 'Chopsticks', with somebody else thumping out the bass. Alas, I was a late starter. The Conservatory lessons meant scales and arpeggios, finger-exercises, studies that were more tuneful than the exercises, but, at that level, not much more. Slowly, very slowly, strength increased a little. I worked doggedly every morning, did all that was bidden in my lesson book, but trailed home, discouraged, after every lesson. Miss Cockburn was not unkind; she found encouraging things to say. But on her studio piano my fingers felt like cold spaghetti. The action on our keyboard was very loose, and on hers, resistant. Even more discouraging was auditing Miss Cockburn's class recitals, with gifted and experienced students, some much younger than I, who performed dazzling, thunderous pieces.

Yet I was to play my Mozart at a public recital. This involved rehearsing on a stage, then an evening performance, sitting huddled in side-stage places until Miss Cockburn signalled one's turn, held back the curtain you entered by, and afterwards smiled you back inside. My fingers shook so much that I don't know how I got through the piece. Mine was the only knee-length dress. My brother Ted was the only family member present because Mother was in hospital.

The entrance hall of that old Conservatory was often buzzing with people who seemed exotic and sophisticated. Among them would appear celebrities, in easy conversation: Lois Marshall, the widely acclaimed soprano, bearded older men who evoked my picture of Brahms. The whole area was literally perfumed, a distinctive fragrance, furs and scent, always evident at the late afternoon hour when my lessons ended.

Just as the church's problem situations ate away at my catechist's sureness, so the glimpses of different and wider-ranging ways of living confused and, increasingly, pleased me. These factors undermined the careful structures we had inherited, which home and church had reinforced for me. I did not realize, at adolescence, how much I owed to that godly home base: fragments of pure gold which nothing could corrode or devalue.

Through our upbringing we knew the Bible as a readable book, understood by people of all kinds, easy to find our way around in. Its sections were recognizable; even the sequence of its books had been well taught. Daddy had a kind of football-game cheer (for him it would have been lacrosse) for the Minor Prophets: 'Ho-jo-AM, ob-jo-MI-na, HA-ze, HA-ze, MA'. Easy. Reading aloud at home made even the most unpronounceable names manageable, although I never felt Euodia was a fair name to give a girl, or Hephzibah, so called because she was her father's delight.

The assumptions from this background teetered now in a new balance. For example, one of the really good pianists had dazzled me at the pre-recital rehearsal. Our teacher, however, had broken in on her second number, 'Jesu, Joy of Man's Desiring': 'Stop, Marguerite! That's obscene. You're making love to the Lord!'

Marguerite was still in the Conservatory entrance hall when I came down from my lesson one day. She knew I lived in the west end too, so she walked with me. We often walked distances in those years, as from University Avenue the many blocks to Lansdowne Avenue. Marguerite Conforzi talked easily all the way to her place, a home behind and above a greengrocer's store, manned by one or another of that large family. 'Call your house and stay for supper,' Marguerite said, 'and I'll walk you partway home after.' It was a wonderful meal: a huge bowl of salad, made with everything that might not be fresh enough for tomorrow, tossed together, with a taste I found out was Italian dressing. (At home we used *boiled* dressing with salad.) And we all had a little of Mr Conforzi's home-made wine. With Kay I had learned to smoke roll-your-own cigarettes. Now my rebellion was complete. Uncle Orville, on the farm, used to say: 'If a woman will smoke, she'll drink, and if she'll drink, she'll do anything.'

Actually, Daddy's unusual boyhood and his wide acquaintance with the ways of human beings had softened the edges of Mother's Methodism. Mary and I soon began to smoke cigarettes at home and by that time Ted was smoking a pipe. The third floor, already flavoured by his rum-and-maple mix, was now designated the only part of the house where smoking was permitted. Any purchase had to come out of our allowances, which had been graduated through stages of growing responsibility, until we were to cover *all* our clothing and store expenses, everything but room and board. In those days we bought packets of papers and tobacco, or elegant boxes containing five cigarettes.

One of my new friends at school was Doris Mosdell, who also became a close friend of Maisie. In boring classes Doris and I began exchanging notes. I wish I had kept some of them. They were portraits-by-association, in words – a genre we may unwittingly have invented. For example, we'd pick a classmate and assemble our associations: Roger was 'a cliff on a sunny day, dried parsley, the colour of burnt orange, a bird – perhaps a grounded nighthawk', and so on. I always recognized Doris's portraits and she would agree about mine.

When Doris invited me for supper, I found her room wonderful, private, for herself. She was an only child, and had various touches in the décor which reflected her preferences. Her father had the complete set of Everyman's Library, a full wall of bookcases. Doris had read or was reading these volumes right along behind her father, originally a Newfoundlander, who worked for the Eaton's catalogue (printing? layout? text?). Her mother spoiled us with good food, and hovered. We did not have to stay to do dishes.

Some weeks later, Doris asked me to come to her church. We had to set out early: it was a long way to Jarvis Street Baptist Church, where in those days T.T. Shields was drawing big crowds. Her parents, I think, had gone to a Bible class before the service. We found two places at the front of the gallery. The whole service was abrasive by contrast to the Sunday mornings I knew. At the end there was an altar-call, everybody droning away, over and over, the same hymn, while many gathered at the front. I knew that Doris had been converted at her church, and I felt uneasily that she expected me to be recruited now too. We stood and stood. Finally, after the benediction came at last, we left without much to say to each other. She was resigned, and went on being my friend.

In old age I am where she was, and she has gone through, rather later than I did, the assertion of an adventurous mind and imagination. But though she flinches at some of the strictures needlessly imposed by legalistic belief, she still sings hymns, all the verses, from memory.

Once when her mother was in a nursing home at the end of her life, Doris sang hymns to her. When voices rose from other beds, Doris was encouraged to look up the whole repertoire and come prepared to sing, on request, at every visit.

The last year of high school was socially lively, but academically dull compared to our own reading, exploring, conversing. Boredom paralyzed some who would rather have been out of school, but there were no jobs and you had to be sixteen to leave anyway. Others were bored because the hours dragged, the lessons were too thin: a least-common-denominator level was inevitable, before 'streaming', except in voluntary learning like the poetry club, or when, for instance, after class one afternoon, a parting question roused our science teacher to a lucid and lively account of the structure of matter.

School clothes were not an issue in the Depression. That was before the days of blue jeans. The boys' trousers were shiny behind, ragged at the cuff. Girls wore a middy and skirt, mostly, though there were two girls in the school who had cashmere sweaters. They were both called Audrey! We cherished any glimpse of either of them. They both seemed unaware of their distinction.

Mixing poor and good scholars did have its point. No one liked to stand out for having high marks, valuing social acceptability over the principal's recognition on public occasions. In fact, I aspired to be classed with the athletes one semester, padding around the track in autumn twilight when there was a sting of cold in the air, and pretentiously carrying around 'my' Absorbine Junior (for sore muscles) when the real athletes rubbed theirs on in the dressing-room. I did not make the track team. We did attend football games, from which the plays, the rules, the rising tension of successive yards gained, built into a spectator's pleasure I feel to this day, but more in the Canadian than in the American game.

And we tried socializing. One mother collected her daughter's girl friends and, through a boy she knew, enough boys for a two-table bridge night. We all made an effort to like it. She was kind in helping us beginners learn the game – how to hold a handful of cards, play one, and remember not to let your opponents guess the strength of your hand. She also served good refreshments at the end of the evening. But I suspect we all felt manipulated. I can still see the posture of the boys, upright in those parlour chairs, creaking with unaccustomed collars and ties, their hair slicked down. I wonder if any of us grew up into bridge players.

I had friends, too, in another context. I loved to play tennis. There were courts between the church and our house. Ted taught us, with *Lacoste on Tennis* in hand, working with me until I placed my feet the way the book sketched they should be placed for forehand, for backhand, etc. We had a brick wall to practise on, out of the way of players on the court. By the time we got formal and kept score, we were ready for *some* competitors. Mary stayed with tennis and played well for many years.

In my case, an appendix operation sidelined me so long that I lost my natural flow and energy for the game. The operation was done in the original Wellesley Hospital, an old brick house. In those days incisions were longer, and convalescents were not allowed up for about two weeks, maybe three, with days of learning to walk again. It seemed a big deal, then. My attempts to do labs and cram mathematics, in the hope of following my plan of taking mathematics and physics at university, were frustrated by this interruption. That was worse than losing ground in tennis. Catching up, I now discovered, would involve staying a year longer in high school, but I could graduate with my own class if I simply completed the prerequisites for the Faculty of Arts.

Did I take the easy way out at that fork in the road? Or did I follow a natural inclination? A possible answer came through a podiatrist seven decades later. 'Yes, I completed my Ph.D. in microbiology,' he said, 'but lab work was too isolating, so I switched occupations in order to work with people coming in and out all day.' I too have liked working where people are, to balance against the solitude of writing time.

High school began to feel stifling toward the end. Classroom English I remember chiefly for essay topics, the dreaded 'oral composition' once a year, and notes to reproduce on exams. Of course, there was fun too. At some point our English teacher was the likeable man who coached the school's renowned football team. The required Shakespeare play that year was *The Tempest*. From his classes I remember only this: the seamen's line, just before King Antonio's shipwreck. For some reason it stuck, and we'd reel homeward, laughing ourselves sick, declaiming, in turns: 'Yarely, men, yarely. We split!

We split!' That was the giggling age, I guess. This kind of detail counteracts the gloomy self behind the poems of those years. We did survive school by swapping books from home, or finding new writers in the Toronto Public Library's Annette Street or Runnymede branches.

The family planned a move to Ottawa in the fall of 1937. By then I would be entering my second year of university, if I stayed on in Toronto (and I meant to stay, even though I knew that the piano would go with them, and those free tennis courts would be unavailable). Meantime, first year university was just ahead and would have to be paid for. I had the advantage that my father was known and respected by the local bank manager. That man believed I would honour his terms and, in time, repay a loan for fees. Thus the way opened to a new world of learning.

A photo of the Poetry Club in 1931. Miss Story is second row, fifth from the left; Margaret is second row, second from the right. (Credit: Humberside C. I., *The Hermes*, Humberside Collegiate)

STUDENT YEARS

My first year at university, 1936, was the family's final year in High Park Church and parsonage. Travelling to music lessons had made the route familiar: walk south to Bloor, about twelve minutes, catch a cramful streetcar on the High Park corner, and count on forty minutes, if there were no delays, to reach Avenue Road. It was in such a streetcar, home-bound and strap-hanging again, that somebody with a small portable radio turned up the sound to let us all hear, in the news, King Edward the Eighth's abdication speech.

My friend Doris was in Honours English at Victoria College too. Another early acquaintance, from Ottawa where my family would live next year, was Miriam Dworkin. We became friends on campus, though Miriam had different professors at University College. Canada came to know her as Miriam Waddington. It was Miriam who would later introduce me to the Montreal poets, and to Earle and Esther Birney.

With another friend, Rosemary Schawlow, I was struggling along Harbord Street one cluttered winter morning when she slipped and fell. A fine blowing snow was driving from the west, so, though she was hurt, she refused to stay there and freeze until help came. Gingerly sitting, then standing, she cradled one elbow. All I could do was gather up her books, with mine, and steer a little until we reached the student health centre on campus. When the nurse there eased Rosemary's heavy jacket and sleeve over her hand, we could *see* that it hurt: a bone was coming through the skin on her arm. She endured being bundled back into her jacket to go for X-rays at the hospital (I think someone drove us), and by the time the wait in emergency was over, I had a friend for life.

As a guest in her home I met her brother Bud (Arthur). One day I would attend a public lecture on laser beams by this Nobel Prize winning younger brother! But in the thirties he was the person who introduced me to jazz. He had an astonishing record collection, and helped me hear riffs and sequences, highlighting the musicians' names. My own brother Ted, who loved to play jazz on the piano, would one day build on this introduction. He liked the rolling jazz bass with treble melody line.

Roy Daniells was our professor (at Victoria College) for Renaissance literature that freshman year. His lectures were spellbinders. Flaring gown and all, he would sweep in, tall, fair-haired and bony, place one elbow on the table which stood on the raised platform and lean while he lectured. (Most professors stepped up onto the platform and used this table for notes). Sometimes he'd bring extra books to put up there, but mostly he just spoke, in a quiet English voice, directing his words towards one student or another. At the hour's end he would sweep out again, gown billowing behind him.

One morning three of the boys shifted the table so that its front legs were right at the platform's edge. We watched. They'd barely seated themselves again when Dr Daniells made his entrance and leaned that elbow on the table. It crashed down and turned over, not quite on top of him. We all sat frozen. No one moved as he hefted the table right side up, and up, up, up to the usual level. A vein stood out on his temple. But he resumed his stance and lectured, eyes out the window, sometimes fleetingly on us but not seeing us. We took notes, heads down.

This class was divided into seminar groups. My group had the good fortune to be led by the same Dr Daniells, but in discussions much engaged, enjoying the give-and-take. He still made an entrance. Our seminar was in his office, one of the academic offices then made available by Emmanuel College. Since his previous class was at Vic, he had to rush to our seminar across the grass to the casement window, which he stepped through lithely, gown flying. Doris was in this group. Adapting our portrait-notes from high school days, we 'did' Daniells. Mine I still remember:

> 'Gregory' is handsome in a tweed sort of way,
> his blazers are Oxford
> and his accent
>   his accent
> you don't hear an accent like that every day!
>
> He likes the theatre
> and tea at four o'clock.
> He likes to lean his head back
> and listen to Bach.

He likes Victor Hugo
and rain in the night,
and all of his handkerchiefs
are scrupulously white.

Nothing ever happened.
This isn't a story.
In stories things happen,
in real life never.
He just gradually stopped
being handsome and clever.

In that seminar room, Mary Gibson (later married to Harley Parker, the landscape painter) stood out from the other unfamiliar students. She was a little older, but fresh-faced and enthusiastic. Her enthusiasm centred, at that time, on Gurdjieff's mysticism. Hence she lit up when, to fill in the context for seventeenth-century verse, Daniells told us about the Neo-Platonists. 'What did they believe about heavenly love?' she interrupted, gazing dreamily at him. He fumbled an answer and got back on track, but from that moment Mary became another friend in our 'inner circle', as each circle in a small first year probably considered itself.

We were indeed few. In the Depression not many families and bankers were as far-sighted as ours had been. And there was a general view in those days that college was only for an elite. So classes stayed enviably small. My only experience of distance and anonymity was in first year Honours History. Students from all ends of the campus gathered in University College, where we entered a landing three-quarters of the way up an amphitheatre, often already filled up when our group arrived from an earlier lecture ten minutes away. Somehow, from textbooks and desperately scribbled notes, I crammed enough to pass the course. But all that remains in memory now is the huge class, the dear old wood-carved warmth of that lecture hall, and a tiny English gentleman in a gown at a dais far down on the platform below, articulating rapidly and effortlessly, it seemed, meeting no one's eyes, using no notes, just giving an occasional glance at the books and papers he piled on the dais and swept off into one hand when he left. I do remember one fragment and can almost hear his precise repeating of it: 'Pepin bushing up through the snow.' The historical relevance has melted away from my mind, but the phrase remains as a dictional delight.

In that history class we first noticed a student whom we would later know in English classes as Eva-lis Wuorio. In time she explained her comings and goings among us. She had no money, paid no fees, was not registered, but had made contact with each professor of her chosen classes to explain that she would like to be allowed to learn, would do the work and write the essays, but would ask for none of the staff's time and expect no degree after fourth year. Her tact in this role was consistent. At a time when professors salted away what they could for emergency loans to many students, this novel solution was respected. Eva-lis later became a journalist with a byline in the *Telegram*, and published several children's books.

That first year I was a day student, as distinct from those who rented rooms or lived in residence. Mary Gibson and I 'ate out' at noon for ten cents each – wide, flat muffins we called hockey pucks, and coffee, at a small place on Bay Street. Once a week or so we had the full-course meal for twenty-five cents: meat, potatoes and all the bread you could eat. Doris brought sandwiches and found corners where she could read while she ate.

Social life, especially in first year when long trips home by streetcar shortened the days, depended on friends, not on extracurricular activities on campus. It didn't occur to me to look for clubs to join, though I did enjoy volunteering with the college paper. That was identity enough to make for an attempt to draw me into the Student Christian Movement. One member approached, asking me to lead a discussion for her group on the topic 'Is it all right for an artist to be immoral?' Still defining myself by my family, I somewhat indignantly declined. In retrospect, the topic does convey how far away the thirties seem. No group would discuss such a question now because the issue would not occur to students today.

Exasperation with unemployment and the general air of discouragement next led me away from the Honours English group into another new world. 'The State and Revolution' would be the subject, at four in the afternoon, one October day. The audience was very small. The topic, I learned, was the title of a book by Lenin. Mimeographed paragraphs were distributed, giving what the convenor told us was the gist of his argument. Certain other safe tracts and news stories, also smeary with mimeograph ink, were added to our clutch. In silence we rustled papers, reading. Two people left.

Josephine Siggins (later Grimshaw), another first-year student ('The Jo Poems', *No Time*) and I stayed. This was our introduction into one cell of the Young Communist League. We studied. We obediently turned up mornings at seven-thirty to help union members hand out leaflets at whatever factory gates were not locked forever. I remember Sid, a small history and philosophy student whom we had met on some YCL assignment. He would sit tailor-fashion on his cot and beam at everyone: 'Come the revolution, we'll all have strawberries and cream!' The cell meetings were less colourful. In fact, they consisted of disciplined, dry teaching in the get-it-by-rote mode.

Eventually, Josephine and I both noticed a lag between meetings. Sid told us why. We had wanted to be free to discuss some idea from Lenin's book, so were dismissed as Trotskyites. We had been blackballed and the cell dispersed into other safe units, leaving us to our political wilderness. In fact we both *had* been drawn away from class-struggle dogma, Josephine by what she was learning in her course (Social and Philosophical Studies), and I by brilliant public presentations on the socialism of the Fabian Society by the historian 'Mr' Underhill, as the Oxford academic preferred to be called. It surprises me now that essays assigned and finals required to pass in my English course seemed inconsequential against such a background of new experiences opening new perspectives in dizzying succession.

The stone building across the grass from Knox College (now, I think, a University College library and before that for a time the medical library), was the main university library before the building of 'Fort Book' (as the Robarts Library is called) further west. The library became a retreat for quiet hours, to some extent in all four years, but most meaningfully in first year. There I went, alone, in early October, as soon as I had my student card. Card catalogues were open-sesames. Any drawer not in use would meet my need. I flipped the cards past entries like 'Institute of....' or 'International Survey....' What was I after? Anything published in 1660 (arbitrarily chosen) or earlier. The minute I found something in some language accessible to me, whether history or botany or medicine or literature, I requested it for use in the library. One find was a medical treatise on the self-assertive personae of body parts continually struggling to maintain community. This was *education* at last.

Once my first year had passed, the High Park house was in somebody else's hands. Our parents sent their furniture ahead to the new Ottawa manse. Then they sailed to Sweden, Denmark and England on their one trip 'abroad'. Mary and I house-sat on Beresford Road for Aunt Louise (a half-sister of my father's). She and Uncle Dick and their two daughters were away for the summer in Bala. It was a trim house, easy to keep clean. What our summer work was I no longer remember, but I do remember the quiet street in the cool of early morning, our turns making meals in the evening, and busy letter-writing to those afar. (Ted was by that time a commerce and finance graduate, in a job somewhere, perhaps already in Montreal.)

Mary had two suitors that summer, favouring the one with whom she had *not* gone to the Grad Ball. One evening I found her in tears. When pressed, she said, 'Bill kissed me yesterday and I'm afraid now I'll have a baby.' Years ago Kay's easy talk had clarified for me the points I had overheard Mother explaining once to Mary. Mary needed a touch of Kay to be reassured that night.

At summer's end, Ted planned to meet Mother and Daddy in Montreal and bring them to Ottawa. Mary and I were to arrive there early that day, take off the movers' dust-covers, put in basic groceries, and prepare dinner. We did. Then, having travelled by night coach and slept little, we readied key rooms for occupancy, and took time for a bath and a nap. The nap went on too long! That attempted first dinner (braised round steak) was burnt to a crisp. However, Mary's resourcefulness brought on a good dinner by the time the three travellers arrived.

Where would I now live for the rest of my university years? 'Rooms', I decided. Daddy, on the other hand, wanted to put me into a good boarding-house. He chose a solid brick house on Lowther Avenue which offered 'Room and Board'. I was 'put', but I didn't stay long. Even at the outset I foresaw an early move. 'Board' turned out to mean breakfast and dinner, both included in the first month's rent. In a month the 'and' had turned into an 'or', especially since dinners often conflicted with campus library hours or events. I chose to save the expense.

Even breakfast was a problem: it had to be eaten at table with the landlady's 'young gentlemen in business', stiffly dressed to conform to office standards of the thirties. All of us were uneasy at her communal table, polite, evasive, quick to escape. The young men in the morning impatiently took turns at the toaster, anxious to be on time for work. They ate in their shirt-sleeves, carefully slipping into their jackets at the last minute.

A woman tenant worked at home as a telemarketer. She was also struggling to give herself a business course with an old Underwood typewriter and a secretarial instruction book bought second hand. Her once-wealthy family had lost their good house and garden in the crash of 1929. She never elaborated, nor were there any signs of family contact while we were living there. Meantime, she taught me courtesy to telemarketers. Her efforts to throw off a day's abusive responses help me to be polite, even to this day, if a spiel runs on a bit.

Already oppressed by the place, I was incensed to be chided one day for keeping clean hand towels in my bureau drawer. 'Why were you checking my bureau at all?' The landlady seemed baffled by my anger. So after two months there I moved out, first to a room in the top floor gable of a big brick mansion on Avenue Road, where the Park Plaza Hotel stands now. A German gentleman was the landlord. The rent was low. He and his wife kept to themselves and let me receive visitors whenever I wanted, and when I caught cold and was coughing, the landlord laboured up to my room with a wonderful mug of special onion soup 'to make you better'. When George VI and Queen Elizabeth visited Toronto, a wooden bleacher was erected in front of the house. For a time, we had to scurry in and out through the understructure.

Leaving there was precipitated by a visit from the RCMP in *mufti* but with credentials. They had suspicions about my landlord, and wanted me to 'watch' and 'report'. I protested that it was unthinkable for me to spy on people from whom I had known nothing but kindness. They gave me a grim-sounding 'ten days of grace' to think it through. Fortunately, the dean of women, to whom I resorted, came to my defence. She urged the authorities not to demand espionage from a student facing important examinations. I moved out.

My landlord was interned in a Northern Ontario camp for the duration of the war. It seems the Nazi *Bund* had stored their literature in his downstairs cupboard, likely with him being 'glad to help' as he was *always* glad to help. I do not think he harboured designs against Canada. He just craved the comfort, in a new country, of speaking his own language and maintaining contact with his countrymen here.

The dean urged me to go into residence at the College. That would have meant Annesley Hall, by that season, not one of the Bloor Street houses, and it would have cost more than my budget allowed. Instead, I found a room facing the south side of St Mary Street, a quiet place overlooking the St Michael's College athletic field and the gardens around St Basil's. It felt like home faster than most new places. Grocery stores were a bit distant but I enjoyed escaping the desk, as any twenty-year-old would. For these and many following years, my stove was a two-plate grill; I stored supplies and dishes in a wooden crate on its side, with a little curtain for its door.

Sunday mornings, some of us ate with Helen Saari, a friend who lived in one of the five old family homes on Bloor Street, running west from St Thomas Street, that were used to house students. On Sunday mornings, the residence dining room was closed. Instead, portable breakfast foods and huge metal coffee pitchers were brought to the houses. Our friend declared there was always so much left over that we should, two or three of us at a time, come and visit and eat. Helen came from Creighton Mines, where she and her father lived in an Inco boarding house. She had a beautiful contralto voice and, when we pleaded, often sang Finnish folksongs for us. On unhappy occasions, in the same gorgeous voice, she bewailed motherlessness or a letter reporting that a miner friend had lost a finger. For Helen, Toronto was a wilderness. Homesickness persisted through all four years and she returned north as soon as she graduated. Yet she was a solid part of our inner circle, and her Sunday breakfasts still stand out.

How strange my Honours English course would seem to today's students. Over four years it included, theoretically, everything from Beowulf to Hardy. Later works, and Canadian and American books of any period, were off the curriculum. The map for the present twenty-first-century generation includes the far reaches of Asia, the Antipodes, the Arabic lands, Africa, our own hemisphere in all its variety. In the mid-sixties I met students at Scarborough College who were world travellers at age nineteen or so. Few were affluent. They had worked their way across oceans, backpacked, lived in youth hostels. For me, in 1936, planes meant bush pilots, not commercial flights. So novel was the idea of a plane trip that the gift I requested as a graduation present in 1940 was a flight to Ottawa for a family holiday there.

When most borders were closed to travel because of the impending war in Europe, our exploring was by means of times past. History papers we wrote, yes. But the past really opened out when it provided a context for the poems and novels we were learning to read and, gradually, to enjoy. The rich depths behind and beyond our own day insensibly steadied us through the era of broken spirits that had been left by the First World War. Maps were dead. But the past grew lively, more and more inviting over the four-year course.

Some students in our group began to shine. In seminars Doris astonished professors and fellow-students alike with her ready quotations gleaned from years of reading her father's Everyman's Library books. My father did not have this series. He did have, and prized, a book he had picked up in his years as a hired hand and store clerk. The title was *What a Young Man Should Know.* This was not about deportment or relationships; it was about what to read in order to build the mind and prepare for a useful life and a habit of ongoing reading.

Mary Gibson brought in associations from her faraway father's Gurdjieff and her own wondering glimpses of non-Judeo-Christian cultures. A few in the group were faithfully plodding along toward the professional training they planned on when an arts degree qualified them. Then there were two hard-working, reliable students, one determined on a First to continue as a scholarship student; she came from Saskatchewan, bringing nothing but her fine mind. (She did keep the scholarship.) The other was a true scholar in the making who would one day be editor of the University of Toronto Press.

If the others in that group have any memory of me, I wonder how they would evaluate my work? I recall the tendencies that have become more marked over the years: a tendency to evade strict prescriptions; true curiosity, but like a jackdaw's filling the nest with shiny bits from anywhere out there; a damaging facility on exam papers that often covered a scantness of information; a mind taken up with longing for greener fields just over the fence, where I'd be free in the wide, wide world.

Sometimes when course work was heavy I would evade, reading

anything not assigned. At such a time, in third year perhaps, I first read Alain-Fournier's *The Wanderer* (*Le Grand Meaulnes*, 1913) in an early quirky translation. Or did I first try it in French? Certainly I did sometimes launch into celebrated French writers' works with only high school French to steer me. When I later resorted to an English translation to savour favourite passages, I often found them diminished because my inaccurate reading had introduced intriguing odd and delusional sidelights.

How did I find my way to Alain-Fournier, one of the gifted young writers killed in a 1914 battle? Probably through Cyril Connolly whose periodical writings showed him to be enriched by wide reading. His prose style itself was alive with mental energy which inspired a following of readers, one by one. He led me to read *The Wanderer*, and *The Wanderer* led me to fantasy landscapes and elusive poetic truth.

Also in third year, I think it was, I stumbled on Goncharov's *Oblomov*. When I reread it in old age, it still stood as a universal portrait. Its impact sent me to Russian novelists in general. I was on a Dostoevsky jag during third-year examinations, and I remember wandering across the grass to Convocation Hall where an Honours English exam was to be written, reading as I walked, and reluctantly leaving *The Idiot* in a pile of texts and notebooks outside the examination hall. I wrote the paper with ease because I was still so absorbed in the story.

There were unforgettable classroom hours during those undergraduate years. Some professors are still vivid in memory – Dr Robbins, for example, who made Old English and Middle English emerge out of his own art of communicating oral tradition, such as the stories of Paul Bunyan and his ox in lumber camp frontier country, and of Br'er Rabbit (in a style, without a phony Southern accent, that gave us the subtle, sane subculture of plantation workers in an earlier age). These were only quick references in class; the true storytelling would occur at late afternoon tea parties in his top-floor office, with students sitting on an old couch or on the floor, Dr Robbins ministering tea and cookies, and, when we all settled, enjoying his third role, not as scholar, not as host, but as what aboriginals call a 'keeper of the wisdom'. From this teacher/storyteller, the text of *Beowulf* became humanity deeply rediscovered as warm and dangerous and absurd and noble.

E.J. Pratt taught Shakespeare. He delighted in the text, but only by library research did we learn much about sources, characterization, or the reshaping of a story to English political sensitivities – all the exam-writing themes. Professor Pratt had typed out his lectures, and used them sometimes, but they were stale to him and consequently to us as well. Mostly we enjoyed his side-references to productions that had impressed him, and his appreciation of characters like Falstaff.

He, too, is remembered as a party-giver. The first time, we all found our way many streetcar stops up past Eglinton Avenue; the Yonge streetcar was slow, so distances seemed greater then. We flocked in to a gala atmosphere, all on the ground floor, coats bulging on the hooks in the entrance hall, and we were very quickly enjoying a good meal. Dr and Mrs Pratt had the gift of abounding hospitality. To establish our status as guests, not students, did he offer both fruit-punch and beer before dinner? Perhaps not that first time.

After dinner, Dr Pratt turned the conversation to such topics as: soldiers with superstitions about having some article always in the vest pocket or backpack, and the wounds incurred the day they forgot the token and became vulnerable; or Newfoundland seamen's yarns of uncanny events and premonitions that came true, and sightings of spectral walkers out on the waves. The climax was his lecturing-voice-summation to the effect that some factual or scientific explanation could always be found for spooky-seeming events. As a matter of fact, he told us, a grown man could be lifted by two young people, their forefingers under his armpits, if the heavier man first breathed deeply, twice, becoming buoyant for that moment. Of course there were students who contested this notion and, of course, two of them, selected for their requisite height and slightness, were challenged to try it. Dr Pratt put the two in position, drew two deep breaths, and – we were clustered in a circle and saw it – their forefingers under his armpits lifted him nearly to the ceiling of that big drawing-room!

Soon after, having grudgingly accepted what our eyes had seen but feeling somehow manipulated, we turned like a flock of fall birds ready to migrate, said our thank-yous and left. The trip home I remember well. It was a crisp late-October night. We were too disturbed to sit in a streetcar. We chattered in twos and threes and ended up walking, and walking, south. None of us mentioned why we were hurrying. But finally there was a coffee-shop open and we all bundled in. Having been too shy at Pratt's to ask where the washroom was, we quickly formed lines to the two here.

Years later when Northrop Frye had become an international attraction, he lectured in the amphitheatre where maximum numbers could be accommodated. But when he taught us 'Nineteenth-Century Thought', he had just returned from studying at Oxford. Our seminar with him took place around a table in a small pleasant room that faced south. We tried to take notes as Mr Frye (the 'Dr' came after his major manuscript on Blake was written) walked to and fro, almost thinking out loud. It was good to listen, but few of us raised a question, or dared to respond when he asked one, braced as we had to be to catch and hang onto the tumbling-over-each-other new concepts he was developing. He told me later that, curious about the kind of note-taking that seemed to be going on so busily, he took to walking around that table and he remembered seeing a lot of interesting doodling [Margaret's characteristic way of recording a lecture or talk]. It helped us with the kind of concentrated listening his teaching demanded.

Frye remained modest despite increasingly wide acclaim. For years he was a member of the *Canadian Forum* board, deferring there to those with first-hand political experience. (I now realize that it was to Frye that I owed my 1956 Guggenheim Fellowship. At his unsought urging, they sent me a formal application, unsought because I had always hoped to avoid grants, preferring the experience of a nine-to-five job to a literary environment.)

How I wish my grudging memory would do justice to all the other professors we learned from and made undergraduate fictions about after classes. One religious knowledge pass-course requirement had options. I chose Near Eastern studies. Just as medieval history remains in my mind only as odd fragments, so does this subject. A very likeable small scholar taught us. We were a class of three in a large, chilly classroom. Not daring to skip, as we could some relatively more populous morning lectures, we would be sitting, waiting, with notebooks open.

Right on the dot, the professor would arrive, gown floating, notes and books in one arm. He lectured quietly for the stipulated hour and we wrote down what we could spell out. There was much about bulls and blood-touched stones; where it all fitted was unclear, so, lacking a textbook, we had to rely on our notes. One by one we would stop the professor privately after class with some questions, hoping to clarify obscure words in our notes. My questions would be courteously heard, and the answer elaborated, too often on the assumption that the context of these ideas was familiar to me. But these one-on-one words were easier to reproduce in notebooks and, in time, on the examination. Somehow, still mystified, we all passed.

When I arrived on campus, Jerry Riddell was lecturing in history and living on Charles St West near Burwash Hall, where he was also the dean of residence. His wife turned out to be Kay Dobson who had taught me English at Alma College. Their place became a second home for me over the early months at university. Then they left for New York, where Jerry had been appointed as Canadian Ambassador to the United Nations, and where, later, with awful abruptness, he died of a heart attack in 1951.

There were organizations that made meeting people easier, especially for students without the advantage of such a congenial group as ours in Honours English. Through the Young Communist League I met Margaret Fairley, and, through her, Professor Barker Fairley, prominent in German studies but also an artist. Through him I met his many lively protégés. I was included in visits to The Studio Building in the Rosedale Valley. Painters there, and the young sculptor Elford ('E.B.') Cox, who became a good friend, were impoverished but irrepressibly enthusiastic.

One weekend a few of us went to a cabin near town where the host and instigator of activities was a disabled man with flaming red hair whose health was endangered by the least bruise. Like the fabled Tsarist family, he was a hemophiliac. When we found him risking injury by poling himself along a muddy little stream on the property, chair and canes abandoned ashore, one of the other artists, half in rage, called him 'Robinson bloody Caruso'. A good thing the angry friend had not seen him embark!

Somehow cash was found to provide food for such outings; travel was a combination of hitchhiking and walking between 'lifts'. Ways of earning cash were elusive. Doris pasted card-pockets into new public library books, I remember. One summer I risked reading, June through August, for an essay ('Coming to Terms with Tolstoy' [see

'Documents' section]) which I thought might win me the $300 award offered. I hope my success did not frustrate any other candidates who made the same gamble, then lost out on earnings they might have had from the more usual holiday waitressing or golf course jobs, which were scarce enough, depending as they chiefly did, in those days, on tourist money.

An ominous undercurrent of war was half acknowledged among a few of us, month by month, as if all the ugliness from World War I and the Depression were precipitating out. We hung around the edges of conversations. We read newspapers and journals in the library instead of going to the reading room to focus on course work. At this point I still had the room on St Mary Street. A chilling experience defines the time there.

I had come in from a morning class where an essay was due. Mine had been finished just about breakfast time, after a whole night of false starts and feverish unravelling of notes which still lay crumpled on the floor. Fortunately it was my day for the bathtub: the bath had helped me get through the morning, along with whatever I stowed away at breakfast. But at noon I stumbled home, tossed my coat onto a hook, kicked off my shoes and fell onto the bed for the kind of immobile, deep sleep that rewards a long job finished at last.

It was twilight when I awoke. The crumpled papers still lay on the floor around my desk, but the top of the desk was strangely clear of clutter, and on the green desk blotter (we still used ink bottles and fountain pens) lay a neat manuscript, three pages of it. The writing was my writing. It was an untitled poem (later I named it 'September, 1939'), rhythmic, with alternate lines rhymed, and not a forced rhyme anywhere. Neither style nor subject matter seemed like mine at all. Such skill at speeding up some lines and slowing down others: one line even forced a lingering reading ('and the first stars bloomed slow'). Intrigued, I read the whole text. It was a premonition of war, that third-year spring term in 1939. I had no memory of getting up to the desk. The poem was wholly unfamiliar as I read it. The style was more polished than what I was writing at the time. It gave me the horrors. Automatic writing is a phenomenon that does happen, apparently, but it is not to be desired. That poem has never before been published because I did not feel it was mine. It was automatic writing, by whom?

September, 1939

A plane drones high in the stillness
And a haze of distant cries
Dissolves in the lucid emptiness
Of the afternoon – my eyes
Weigh with the long remembrance
(For it is all past and gone).

And I see the broad bay glittering blue
In the endless July sun
Laced by the circling speedboats
And the seagulls rise and float
In the languid breeze, and the awnings
Of the terrace –
                        (so remote) –

        And lazily we smoked, and stirred
        The mint leaves with the ice
        Or strolled along the leafy walks –
        An empty paradise
        Of silk and sultry perfume
        And violet-gloaming dark
        And figures drifting through the trees.
(But never the ships came back.)

They used to say the ships will come,
Their lower eyelids taut,
And sigh and stir the floating mint
And watch the shadows blot
The last pale luminous lines of sky
And the first stars bloom slow.
We didn't haunt the lookout towers –
We knew that we should know
When at last the ships spired into view –
Nor knew we what they were.
It was scarcely a presentiment,
The knowledge that would stir

Sweetly uneasy now and then
Among the shadowy blur
Of underconsciousness where sorrows
Murmured in their sleep
        And we would merely sigh and lapse
And watch the night grow deep
And rise at last and languidly
    Go up the curving stair
And lie on the small balcony
        Breathing the gentle air –

I met him on the landing.
The wind was rising strange.
We heard it as a long way off.
He saw me stop and cringe
Against the savage undersound.
He stood before me firm
Staring in my dilated eyes
One hand on either arm.
'You will stay on alone,' he said,
    'Here and only here.'
I saw his hair stream out and heard
    The outer gate go slam.
The frail French doors blew inward,
The wind shrieked, and the light
Flapped into chill unfeeling grey
And we saw the seaspume white
Dashing against the rocks below
And we stood alone and slow.
As he spoke there was nothing around us
But an infinity of snow.

'Leaves fall through all November,'
    He said, 'and rot away
And some spring come hepaticas
    Out of their dank decay
And you must wait and watch for them
Long, long,' I heard him say.

'By night forget despair,' he said,
'And empty fear by day.'

The stillness broke like windsnatched smoke
And there I stood alone.
The sky was turned a yelling fiend,
The earth a thing of stone
And from the watchtower on the bay
They shouted through the night
Against the searoar and the wind:
'The ships – they are in sight!'

We waited then and now we wait
And as the late planes drone
I see again that glittering bay
Under that summer sun
And O my eyes are heavy
For another day is done.

In the following September when war was declared, the 'real world' I had been anticipating, and where in a year repayment of my loan would begin, now appeared a grim and unpredictable prospect. While still on holiday in Ottawa, I was seeing more and more men in uniform on the streets and in the stores. (Women recruits came later.) My revulsion was physical; I felt like spitting. Unemployment solved by herding people into phalanxes and marching them off to who knew what horrors: a new Vimy Ridge, maybe, as though the 'never again' of the early twenties had never been meant.

Social upheaval was also evident back in Toronto as I began my final year. The campus was perceptibly different: students took time out for officer training, exempted from full-time service only in order to complete education that would make them more useful to the war effort. Two of our favourite professors and several of our off-campus friends volunteered. One of those professors later lost his life in the Battle of Britain, as did three of my friends.

Lectures, library hours, coffee breaks, essays, exams, all helped blot out some of this turmoil throughout the following months. I was actually dreaming that high grades and scholarship money for graduate school might justify deferring repayment of my loan in hope of better income later. Instead, I simply received a gold medal.

Between the last exam and graduation day many of us out-of-town students went home. Just as my father was preparing the car for our drive back to Toronto for the graduation event, Elford Cox, my sculptor friend, phoned. Yes, we were coming. Yes, of course he could find me: I had kept my room for the time being, resolved to stay near the people and places I knew before it all evaporated, and to find work in order to start paying off that debt.

Only on graduation day did Elford learn that the grand windup was a graduation ball at Hart House. We had to go, he said! He arranged what he needed, and my sister invented what I needed. I had one fine cotton nightie: that would make a good slip, said Mary. I protested that I had nothing floor-length to wear over it. She found somebody's old Hallowe'en costume made of cheesecloth with paper leaves and bats stitched on to it. Off these came. On went tiny roses. When the sewing was complete and I tried the dress on, only a few adjustments and a borrowed scarf were needed to finish the job.

The dance was in the outer courtyard of Hart House as well as in the adjoining ground floor rooms. It was fun for a while. When we had both had enough, Elford conceived a new plan involving a bus ride up Bathurst Street and a walk up the hill to Casa Loma. One security guard and partial fences were its only protection. 'Let's go in,' said Elford. He tiptoed ahead: 'The old man's sleeping by the fire in the hall there. We can get past him! Shall we explore?'

There was no light, of course. If any existed it was too black dark to find switches, and anyway a light would betray us. We groped up steps, around, along, up, and as the city clocks struck midnight, we stood in a topmost turret, with Elford declaring the moonlight was for me, 'an emerald shaft in a silver quiver' or some such lyricism. Creeping down again was trembly-kneed work. In daylight later I saw places where we might have broken our necks in that caper. But we escaped even the night watchman again.

Did nothing come of that night? Elford did visit me at home, and met my family. After he left I remember my father saying 'It's all right, dear, if this is what you want. Just remember, it's every morning for the rest of your life.' Our letters began to falter when Elford was on the Italian front during the war. After demobilization he was given a contract to create a fish fountain in the Park Plaza Hotel courtyard, and he married a Bowmanville friend of high school days.

According to a full page obituary tribute at the time of his death in 2003 at age 89, Elford Cox had become famous as a sculptor. His eleven-foot-high statue of Hercules, for instance, carved from a six-tonne piece of Indiana limestone, stands in his 'Garden of the Greek Gods' located near the Dufferin Gates of the Canadian National Exhibition grounds in Toronto. His friends' comments in the obituary portrayed Elford's quirky and happy personality to have been just the same throughout his life as it was when he was twenty-four.

Josephine Grimshaw, née Siggins, of 'The Jo Poems'.
(Credit: University of Manitoba Archives and Special Collections, Margaret Avison fonds, Box 1, PC151)

Margaret on graduation day, 1940.
(Source unknown: courtesy of Marion D. Cameron)

Margaret with her parents.
(Family photo: courtesy of Karen McKim)

Margaret with friends. From left to right: Marvin Gelber, Eleanor Graham, Bill Graham, Marion Johnson, Jack Johnson, Margaret. (Credit: University of Manitoba Archives and Special Collections, Margaret Avison fonds, Box 1, PC151)

Mary and Margaret in their twenties. (Family photo: courtesy of Karen McKim)

SHORT-TERM JOBS

After the flurry of celebration and a final long summer holiday in Ottawa, I returned to Toronto to find a new room and a job in order to begin repaying my education loan. An older friend, whom I had met through my brother, offered me her comfortable Elm Avenue room rent-free for the three weeks she was going to be away on vacation. Since my remaining funds would shrink fast, it was necessary to find work, and accommodation, within those three weeks.

The declaration of war the previous September had not yet stimulated the economy; at least, there seemed to be no change in disheartening want ads or employment postings. Nowadays people talk of 'resumés'. I had none. When I answered questions under 'education' on an application form, the person who received it usually said, 'You're over-qualified for our job.'

Towards the end of the third week, I had just seven dollars left. To save money, I had been walking each day from the Bloor-Sherbourne area to business and industrial districts all over town. Determination kept tightening. The morning came for getting that job, by any means. I walked down by all the back ways very early, letting the elation of Toronto trees and morning sky fill my sails. Whether it was the third or the fifth or the umpteenth building I entered I do not remember, but at the threshold of a big insurance company on King Street, near Spadina, I decided: I will *see* the personnel manager here, and, if necessary, I will find a way to *make* him take me on.

Seeing him was easy enough. But he began the familiar drone about having enough employees at the moment, and how the work would be unfit for me with my academic background and no work experience. 'And no money left,' I said, and managed to produce two or three tears. I can still see him anxiously walk out to the water cooler to give me a chance to collect myself. He brought me back a paper cup of water, and gave me a job as filing clerk, to start the next day. I could now get by on my seven dollars.

To reach stacks of lower-drawer files, filing clerks sat on little stools with wheels, alternating this with standing for the upper-drawer stacks of files. In time, I was promoted to writing up one type of easy insurance policy. There were not enough of these coming to my desk to keep me going, even if I wrote very slowly. In between policies one was to sit and wait; reading was forbidden. The second hand on the wall clock lurched through my innards every time it moved. When the minute hand hit twelve noon, an instant stampede began. Lunchtime was half an hour. This was still the era of 'Brother, can you spare a dime?' Coffee at a counter across the street was ten cents, and cheese and crackers made a prepared lunch easy to carry and consume somewhere, with an apple.

Dining within my budget involved the adventure of finding an affordable room within walking distance, wherever I worked. In recent years, Greg Gatenby compiled a book of Toronto writers' residences. At his request I provided a longish list of mine. Almost at the end came an unlikely address, the sub-basement apartment in the group of high-rise buildings on Lascelles Boulevard south of Chaplin Crescent, chosen by my sister-in-law a few years after I had brought my mother to live with me in Toronto. Only this late entry met with Greg Gatenby's approval, but even then his photographed locale for me was an elegant house further north on Lascelles. Embarrassed, I visited the resident of this house to caution her about Greg's mistake. She listened with bemused disinterest.*

My earlier addresses had changed often. It was a way of life. A campus friend, Alice Eady (later Alice Boissonneau, the novelist) and I helped each other find new places. We often moved things on foot. We worked together on the books belonging to whoever was moving – stacking piles, and roping them both ways with a rope-handle on top, in manageable lots. Shelving might or might not be carried on the first trip; sometimes it seemed easier to buy new planks and bricks. Someone's discarded door, knob side down, could be balanced on two orange-crates to provide a desk. Unhappily, most cheap rooms were already

---

* *Toronto, A Literary Guide.* Toronto: McArthur & Company, 1999. The Lascelles address was misnumbered (117 instead of 17), but Gatenby does mention Margaret's various earlier rooms and there is no photograph in his book of the 'elegant house'. A local newspaper later picked up on some of Gatenby's addresses, and that may be where the photograph of the wrong house appeared. Margaret resented being associated with an elegant house. Perhaps that is what distorted the facts about Gatenby's book in her memory.

furnished, and proved temporary for one reason or another. Other writers I knew reported the same temporary living quarters then.

It was the after-hours social life at the insurance company that eventually drove me to hunt for another job. First there were the bridal showers, which were inevitably expensive. And as an outsider, even when I'd been around long enough to know the person concerned, and was quite willing to buy her one of the presents suggested, I still found such occasions awkward. But further conformity had a price I had not foreseen: now I was expected to join the bowling league. There was no use explaining that I had other designs on my free time. My only recourse was to find a new job elsewhere.

On my walks home, I had noticed the Gage building, where paper and envelopes were produced. (My room, by then, was just west of Spadina Avenue above College Street.) I now had work experience, not just that university record, to define me to the personnel office. And perhaps the war was beginning to create vacancies, for I did get taken on in the paper factory.

The human climate here was another new experience. Physical work was new to me too – keeping stationery and envelopes 'jogged' for clean-edged stacking and packaging. There was a good lunch room, spacious with wooden chairs and a long table made of boards supported on wooden 'horses'. I think there was a hot plate and a kettle; certainly there was no need to fight the crowds at a counter outside. I could eat and read, and nobody bothered with me there.

Above the paper division was Gage Publishing. One day Mrs McCool, an editor, came into this room to have a quick lunch. She looked in again the next day, saw me reading while I ate, and approached me: 'We need to train a new proofreader/secretary upstairs. Would you be interested in trying out for that job?' My factory experience had ended!

As is often the case, promotion involved a literal move-up: heavy equipment was on the ground floor, typists and bosses on higher floors. The chief editor was in a section fronting Spadina Avenue. Mrs McCool, his second-in-command, worked in the quieter west side. Had I told her how slow my typing speed was? What I learned before graduating, in a clattering stenographic school, had been aborted when money for more fees wouldn't fit my budget. So in my next rooming house, on Kendal Avenue, I practised every evening, imposing on myself the school's requirement to repeat an exercise from the textbook until I'd typed a full page, error free, before going on to the next. There was a little girl of about six in rooms down the hall. She was intrigued by the click, click, and usually danced in and out of my room in her after-supper free time. That helped me not to smash something in a fit of exasperation. Renting the typewriter was a risk. The investment had to produce returns. In the quiet of the later evening, I would turn on the radio to any talk programme and practise my Pitman. Shorthand I enjoyed, almost – making marks with my hand on a clean page, even if it were with the required sharpened pencil instead of my blunt-nib fountain pen dipped in a bottle of black ink.

When I told Mrs McCool that I could type, I had not allowed for the silence in the office when nobody else was at a machine. I could hear in my imagination the painfully slow but correctly fingered plunk, plunk in my corner, with that little bell tinkling when the carriage was slowed for a new line. Fortunately I had been assigned a variety of tasks. When things were too quiet, I worked on editing for Canadian schools a text first published in the U.S., inching my way into it, Canadianizing the American spelling, finding equivalents to U.S. references. 'The size of Texas' had to become 'the size of Ontario', for instance. Parallel events in history, theirs and ours, took more inventiveness.

I would drop this worthy work the instant some typewriter launched on whatever sounded as if it would go on for pages. What I would finally roll out of my machine would at least be accurate. When Mrs McCool dictated letters, my Pitman and my memory made them squeak by as acceptable. Practice was helping too. Probably she had sized up my rather poor qualifications all the time I thought I was covering them! She was considerate but, I thought, aloof. Gradually I learned, from her, that her husband was already a major, in England. When he led his men at Dunkirk and was captured, the intervals between communications must have tormented her. He spent those years as a prisoner of war. She carried on with her responsibilities at work throughout, and sensibly spent much free time volunteering.

The walks home, through the Jewish community and via Kensington Market to the west, which was predominantly Jewish then too, made me feel happy, as I did not feel on Kendal Avenue. Soon I moved. My new room was back in the campus area, the first of three rooms, over the years, on Washington Avenue. There were four tenants in the small house, all sharing a second-floor three-piece bathroom. We learned each other's hours and found it workable.

The old gentleman in the third-floor apartment invited me to tea soon after I moved in. He was English, long retired. He courteously explained how our Washington Avenue community worked, with all tenancies on both sides of the street rented on the same terms. (The landlord owned all the houses on that one-block street.) My new friend was wistful about not having come when a south-side attic was available, because the backs of all the houses looked out on one block-long, beautifully kept garden. The landlord had made it for his mother; she had lived with him a long time, had designed it and loved to work in it. (I myself never had a glimpse of that garden.)

My pay allowed me to buy my own Underwood typewriter. So when Gage's editor suggested that I either revise or rewrite an earlier, out-of-date history of Ontario, I insisted that it sorely needed to be rewritten. Would I be permitted to do it on salary, but freelancing to make research and writing easier? He agreed, giving me a deadline. The new arrangement felt good. The hours of work could not hold clocks over me: that second hand on the insurance clock haunted me still. Working early in the morning or late at night was like not working. Finding vivid facts, even letters, to enliven Ontario's history, justified my return to libraries on the campus. Yes, there was a deadline, but I felt safe out on my own again. It was like returning home. It promised to lead somewhere, though maybe not to textbooks next time.

Soon after graduation I had begun submitting work to *The Canadian Forum*; Northrop Frye, on the editorial board, encouraged this. Eleanor Godfrey, the editor through those years, became a good friend. She and H. A. Innis were the only two 'geniuses' I ever knew, each inimitable, unique. In early childhood Eleanor had been enrolled in the appropriate separate school, but set her will against continuing there. She balked at being taught at home, too, preferring to be read to by her parents or her sister. Their unavailability when she craved books one day, at the age of nine, forced her to try again on her own, and from that day on she read omnivorously. Qualified by home study, she was accepted at St Michael's College, but soon rejected systematized learning once again, and dropped out. Brilliant, politically astute, perceptive to the quick, with her sure sense of the absurd always on the boil, Eleanor attracted conversationalists who drew her into their circles.

In the *Forum* she found a counterbalance to such insanities as the McCarthy trials of the fifties. Under her energetic editing, public affairs and literature were alike given space. When I first submitted poems, Eleanor discovered that my current room was a few doors north of her family's apartment on Spadina Road. Her father was very ill, at home. When he needed to be turned in bed, at intervals, and only one person was at home, I could be available. Thus the contact became friendship.

When I rented that gable room overlooking Spadina Road's big old trees (there was a boulevard then), my plan had been to complete the Ontario history. But as men left for war, new jobs were opening up. Through contacts at the *Forum*, probably, I heard of an opening in the library at the Canadian Institute of International Affairs (CIIA). When they interviewed and accepted me, I asked for time to settle with Gage before committing myself.

I went to the editor there, expecting to lose some current salary. Had I done anything on the *History*, he asked. Yes, enough to hate breaking off, but I could not now meet his deadline. I showed him what was written, and a few references for later chapters, and he said 'The salary can become an advance, if you want to complete the book on your own time. We'll settle the final pay then.' That was more generous than I had dreamed possible. It spurred me on.

The Institute's office was then on Willcocks Street in an old house which was later renovated to serve as the University of Toronto Faculty Club. Thanks to wartime prosperity, the office soon moved to a bigger space on Bloor Street just west of Avenue Road. When the then information secretary enlisted, my work as librarian expanded to include the Information Services section of the Institute. The Royal Institute of International Affairs in England forwarded to the CIIA their regular 'Review of the Foreign Press'. Escott Reid, the Canadian national secretary, assigned to me the preparation of rewrites, edited down when necessary, which he then supplied to local newspaper editors. When the wartime messages came in from England at the end of a day, excerpts or summaries for the newspapers had to be done at once. It could be three in the morning before I went home. The office secretary often criticized me when I arrived late after such nights. Although Mr Reid made peace between us, I felt ill at ease that my advantaged position was resented by the office staff.

Pressures of all kinds – the work for Gage, poetry, the new job – must have built up, because when I left work one February at twilight, I astonished myself by walking southwest to the mouth of the Humber River. By then the tension was beginning to feel sloughed off, so I walked on in the gathering dark. Lakeshore Road was slushy but not impassable, I was carrying only a handbag, and, free of workday pressures, I felt energies began to rise. In the middle of the night I had to watch my steps around slushy drifts where a highway crew was clearing the road. But there was a reward – a shack serving coffee to the workers. They accepted my approach with some puzzlement but let me have a hot cupful. It stayed me until I walked into Hamilton in the morning, found a hotel room, and fell into bed.

Fortunately I had just enough funds to cover the room, a hearty breakfast, and a ticket back to Toronto. Once I was cleaned up, I went to work. The new president, later director general, John Holmes, was ready to 'terminate' me. They had tried again and again to reach me at home. Where *had* I been? I meekly outlined the night but could find no excuse for not telephoning to explain (though I knew I had needed to kick off into total freedom for a while, which any telephone call would have annulled). In the end I was kept on, with the condition that never again would I take off without reporting in.

In my earliest days at the Institute, A.J.M. Smith arrived in Toronto. He had begun work on his Canadian poetry anthology, with a contemporary section, and his initial invitation to meet was in order to introduce this project, his Montreal contacts, and his cross-Canada research. At his request I showed him some of my work. I found that we both responded warmly to the same poems, particularly cherishing those of George Herbert. For me, such shared enthusiasm soon got all mixed up with feelings for this person who also knew this choice, private world. Certainly my responses were whole-hearted, but when I learned that he had a wife in the U.S., I was heartsick. Looking back, I find the later deposit in memory is all good: once he called my parents' number in Ottawa while he was recruiting manuscripts there, found that I was home on vacation, and arranged to meet me.

To many in today's social climate it might seem strange that his marriage automatically put this man beyond range for me. My churchy background, they might say. But it was chiefly my parents' example of what marriage means that formed my own ethical standards. So when A.J.M. offered to take me out, it was on my terms – a walk! We took a local bus across to Hull where I knew the streets opening out onto a quiet country road I often explored. When we came to the lane at the end of the road, there was my surprise for him: Pink Lake, the clear waters deep in the woods. 'Did you ever swim here?' 'Yes!' 'Why don't we?' 'And walk back in wet clothes?' 'Why *any* clothes? There are lots of bushes to hang things on!' So we had a swim. Afterwards I found my clump of bushes no help as a towel, and sacrificed some scrap of clothing to dry well enough to dress again. The walk back to Hull and the bus home was buoyant, for me. He, I think, was tired by then. Although my diffidence was a new experience for him, I think, he accepted it in good part. I suspect he found more satisfying responses readily enough elsewhere.

A few years later I felt even more affinity and attraction for a man closer to my own age, a photographer for the National Film Board. We met through his friends, fellow employees at the Information Services. Finally, under the chestnut tree outside the Spadina Road rooming-house, he asked me to come live with him. Marry? Eagerly I asked it: 'How can you arrange your time so that we can go and meet my family?' 'I'm not the marrying type,' he said, with great assurance. A single life has its advantages. I never felt at an emotional disadvantage until a longing for children's company came much later, but I did sometimes feel the social stigma. ('*Mrs* Avison?' the receptionist, the Eaton's delivery service, or the telephone company would ask.)

Morley and Loretto Callaghan then lived in a duplex on Kendal Avenue. Morley tried to pair me with John Frederick Nims when Nims was at St Michael's College teaching English literature. But though Nims' wonderful sense of the absurd and his verbal wit made our companionship sparkling that year, he was Roman Catholic and I was not. And he already knew Bonny in his home town, whom he later married. A glimpse comes back: the beautiful dining room of the Eaton's College Street store one sunny noon hour; white tablecloths, two big bowls of leafy salad. Nims saw the caterpillar in his lettuce before I did. 'Well, well,' he said, 'a tiny person in a long striped wool bathing suit!'

Through Nims I had the joy of conversation with Father Flahiff (later Cardinal Flahiff). His presenting of Catholic doctrine shone out, illuminating the biblical truths I had been taught at home. The

Eucharist now means to me just what he then described (he read poetry, too!) I balked, however, at his Church's requirement of priestly absolution and, at death, the sacrament of extreme unction.

Through Eleanor Godfrey I became one of the habitués in her mother's apartment. The hospitable front room there is the locale evoked in 'New Year's Poem' (*Winter Sun*). Often the same group would meet in other locations. The Callaghans had regular Friday evenings, with Eleanor (later Eleanor and Bill Graham), Eustace (W.W.E.) Ross, a dour meteorologist as well as a poet, and his wife Mary Lowry Ross, then a *Saturday Night* journalist. They accepted me through Eleanor. The conversation was unrestricted, but everybody's wide, enthusiastic reading formed a constant. For example, Morley once mentioned a brief encounter with P.K. Page, whom he had met in Montreal. He made her shimmer as he spoke of her abilities. She was a new writer to anticipate. Sometimes the talk was heated, about foreign policy, or about some city council ruling where opinions differed. Loretto and I enjoyed listening, not a disadvantage, either, amid such gifted talkers, coming in whenever we had something to contribute. From Eustace I first heard of Imagism by pressing him on his passing reference to it. Loretto heard Eleanor asking for more about the Callaghans' earlier Paris days – something other than the recurring story of the high spot, the much-told episode about Hemingway, Scott Fitzgerald and Callaghan in the boxers' gym. Loretto filled in the picture: a Paris of days and evenings, easy hours in bars and open-air cafés. Her own impressions of the literati-in-exile of the 1920s were lively with side glances.

How strange it is that immediate events, friendships, work, beginnings of the editing jobs, all played across a ground-bass of the war. It dragged on. A friend, one of two assistants in the Information Service at the CIIA, lost her only brother. Bill Graham, from Winnipeg, who had met and now married Eleanor, would soon complete officers' training here and be sent over. Bill, too, had grudgingly come out of pacificism as news spread of life under Hitler. It cheered him, I remember, when the instructor at the Kingston training camp began a course by walking to a large window and pointing to an old fellow who was dragging a sack and spearing litter on the grounds outside. 'There, gentlemen,' he announced, 'is your employer, now that you belong to the armed forces.'

The pogroms had reversed Bill's and many other people's repugnance to fighting. For me too, there were immediate consequences. Both my brother and my brother-in-law were moved from stable peacetime lives: Ted was to settle with his family in England on some economic mission; Mary's Frank was sent from the National Research Council to a special assignment in Sarnia, because his graduate research had been in the ethylene oxide that was to be part of the war effort development of industry there.

For me, personally, war brought an opportunity to learn conversational German. I did already have some reading knowledge. There was a refugee in hospital here, threatened with TB and needing general care, who would exchange German lessons with me for English. Sigmund Laufer had only one surviving family member, his sister, who, he later found out when he returned to England, was safe and living in Israel. He and I have remained friends. We exchange greetings once or twice a year, and used to meet every summer, before his eyes failed, when he took a vacation from his translator's work in England to visit Canadian friends. Like me, he now lives in a seniors' residence.

Wartime gave news a high priority. Radio reports were vivid. Matthew Halton was not to be missed, especially after D-Day. At the end of every evening I walked to Spadina and Bloor, where the *Globe and Mail* was delivered. Several people would sit at the counter of a corner restaurant for a first, quick read, or to wait for the paper's late arrival. There I recognized Marvin Gelber, from a neighbouring house. We sat together so often that walking home together, talking about the news, was natural. He was a friend of Eleanor and Bill's too, included in the dinner-out celebration they gave me for one of my birthdays.

Two days stand out from that time, both associated with the old Park Plaza, long a pivot of interest. As students we had refused to admit it was bankrupt because of the Depression. The campus myth was that it *listed:* faulty construction had been discovered too late, so the building had been condemned! As things generally picked up, the hotel took on the opposite reputation: busy, genial, opulent, friendly.

The first of those memorable days began one morning when I stepped out of my rooming-house on Spadina Road and sank over my knees into snow. It was still sifting down, blowing in scarves from roofslants. To move meant heavy wading. Halfway to Bloor Street, somebody saw me struggling along and let me rest in their entrance hall till I could tackle the last half of the way. At Bloor one could walk in a single track trampled down by others on their way to work. No sign of streetcar tracks or, of course, motorcars. A valiant associate and two of our office staff struggled in. But telephones had to be kept clear for emergency use and there was no mail delivery. By 10:30 we were all caught up with our work, ready to close for the day with the rest of the city, but not yet ready to fight our way homewards. We did lock up, but then resorted to the old King Cole Room in the Park Plaza basement where beer was served, even to ladies if they had an escort. That morning of the big snow we were a jubilant collection of merrymakers, all in woollen sweaters, warm snowpants and high thick socks, many even in ski gear.

How far I had now moved from the minister's daughter model! I had not even a pang of guilt any more; everybody drank, some a great deal. The truth is, only whisky or gin overcame my uneasiness in circles where I felt I did not belong. Claims from hospitable friends on my wartime liquor ration helped keep me moderate.

The second association with the Park Plaza was a chilling one. Just as people remember where they were when President Kennedy's assassination was announced, so we all surely remember our whereabouts when news reached us of Hiroshima. For me it was out on Bloor Street approaching the Park Plaza corner. Revulsion for all human beings, myself included, was stifling. No wonder I just kept walking and walking all through my lunch hour.

Work with the CIIA came to an end a few months before the war was over. As in many such cases, I was expected to release back to a returning veteran the work he had before enlisting. Moreover, a man was more convenient for the Institute, since general meetings were held, after dinner, in the York Club or the Toronto Club where women were not allowed. During the war special arrangements had to be made to bring me in after dinner to take the minutes.

An oppressive period followed for me, with work as a lifeline. The Information Services had entailed editing of manuscripts. One member of the Board, Dr Alexander Brady, a professor of political science at the University of Toronto, asked me to make an editorial check of a manuscript he had ready for publication. I did suggest a revision here and there. There was very little to edit, but on one page he had repeated a word within a couple of lines, the word 'aggravated', perhaps. I had pencilled in a suggestion of 'irked' for one replacement. He looked up, alerted, inked in the change, and said delightedly, 'I have not used this word in the whole book!' Having a lovely simplicity about him – humility is not quite the word – he seemed cheered as he made little changes, and he recommended me to colleagues who also might need work tidied for publication. Accumulating references for an index, verifying the spelling and transliteration of foreign names, and many other such tasks entailed slow, meticulous work without electronic aids. (Computers then were huge, clumsy novelties, still under development.) But this kind of work provided me with security and flexible hours when I did not have a nine-to-five job.

I look back on one of my interim jobs with some amazement, and with affection. The Department of Political Economy, which was housed on the south side of Bloor Street in an old brick building which later became the home of the Royal Conservatory of Music, needed extra help one summer because the departmental secretary had been granted an extra month's vacation. I was brought in to cover part of that extra month of her time away. There was little routine work, since much of the mail was for vacationing staff. I opened what little there was and took important departmental mail right in to Professor H.A. Innis, the department head, along with letters directed personally to him. He was alone there for the sake of his own work: one manuscript was under way and a forthcoming book was at the University of Toronto Press in the final stages of production.

Sometimes he scribbled the tenor of replies to his own mail in short phrases, expecting a typed, elaborated version later. It was his usual practice. He explained that it was a habit necessary in major projects, when thoughts came fast and had to be recorded as clearly as possible without regard to grammar. Sentences had to be built later around these scribbled thought-skeletons. What I expanded for finished outgoing letters he signed without comment, once a day, along with routine letters (for which I had devised a standard form). As the days passed, he handed over for typing some articles to be tidied for this or that periodical. He was precise, but always kindly, when I misguessed a meaning.

There was an ongoing difficulty with his proofs from the Press that summer. Certain technical terms he needed, 'cooperage', for example, were not usual. When the book was completed, he had me buy a box of chocolates for the editor. His thank-you note recalled her repeated hyphenating, even in proofs, of 'cooperage', and he thanked her for her painstaking work and her kind 'cooper-ation'!

This unpretentious man could not repress and did not notice his continuous flashes of genius. Once he looked up, while dictating a courteous letter after a wartime flight back from Moscow. He had travelled the northern Great Circle Route, for miles and miles seeing only unrelieved darkness below, so that it was startling to glimpse any occasional tiny light. 'That must be what it is to be bushed,' he remarked thoughtfully.

During that time I moved back to Washington Avenue, the second of three extended periods of living on that street. Each time I rented a second-floor back room and each time the landlord came out on his porch to arrange my tenancy, handing me the keys and saying 'Try not to bother me again.' So I did not fetch him when the pipes froze occasionally, or even the time my back door blew off its hinges. We tenants hired our own help. Even so, it was not a bad deal. My room was small, but the screen-door opened onto a gravel roof over somebody's garage and this gave me extra space.

Evenings immersed in reading or new writing, with a percolator of coffee on the burner in the chill hours: this was the good life. Bed time retreated. To relax, I began to take late walks. The steady rhythm brought me home finally ready for sleep. This habit was safe any night I felt secure about it. If I felt any apprehension, I would stay home and resort to relaxing exercises instead. But I respected my sense of being quite secure out in the streets, an instinct that was only once tested.

That occurred along Bloor Street East somewhere, when a whooping car of boys slowed down, called out, suddenly swerved to the curb and grabbed me into the back seat. Oddly I still felt safe, or my voice would not have sounded so steady as I launched into the Rilke lines I had been memorizing earlier that evening. Line after line came to me. My German silenced these boys. They must have wondered what kind of loony they had in tow. They stopped abruptly, let me out and sped away. I wandered on, resuming my earlier preoccupations. Had I been edgy that night, my presence of mind would most likely have shattered, leaving me fearful of venturing out after dark any more.

JOBS ON CAMPUS

Washington Avenue was near the campus. So was my post-Institute day job in the Registrar's Office, University of Toronto. The war was still on, though nearing its end. I remember walking to work during double daylight saving time with the moon bright in the sky. (This was a device for saving electricity throughout the winter months, though I never could figure out how it did.) Early in the office morning, one memorable day, bells rang and hooters hooted: it was VE Day, the end of war in the European theatre. It was suddenly a holiday. Dazed, people wandered out of various buildings, the familiar pressure between news bulletins lifted, the sudden weightlessness an unnerving feeling, almost a physical unease. The staffs of the various offices straggled into the city, I onto a bus which also wandered hither and yon. The driver's random turns alarmed none of us. He promptly delivered anyone concerned about place and time; the rest of us had wandered afoot until a passing bus looked good – wherever it might go.

Somehow it was reassuring to set out for work at a regular hour, day by day. Most jobs offer some unpredictable reward, and the Registrar himself was its source in that office. Mr Fennell was a mathematician. Why had he accepted this appointment, when he enjoyed any opportunity to make the day's work into a teaching session? Perhaps he was primarily a deviser of systematic recording and weighing of examination marks to produce clear results as early as possible every spring. Would he have equally enjoyed devising a computer programme in a later day? His staff worked in teams of two, checking each other's work as they entered the final marks, course by course, in red ink from bottles, using nibbed pens. (When a drop of ink fell, we used paper blotters.) We had to strike the averages too.

Isabel Fraser, the woman I worked with, agreed to have lunch with me one day. My ice-breaking question was 'What books are you reading?' because I had seen her toting books to and from work. Her answer, 'Isn't that a very personal question?' somehow made me laugh delightedly, and we were launched on a friendship that persisted through many moves and changes for nearly sixty years. She and a sister teaching in Northern Ontario were soon all that remained of their family of six. Their parents did not long survive news of the loss of their younger son, an airman; then his older brother, a medical officer, was invalided home to Sunnybrook Hospital where he too died three years later. War losses can bond friendships, like mine with Isabel.

Isabel had already experienced being called into the Registrar's private office, bearing an exam sheet with marks all entered but not totalled, so she sent me off sympathetically when my turn came later. The Registrar held the sheet on his side of the desk, read off one series of marks, and wanted from me an instant total, sight unseen. He valued mental arithmetic, promoted by this method. One developed abilities under his edgy pressure! He was apologetic about his edginess, explaining that he had stopped smoking 'cold turkey', giving as his motivation the purchase of a set of silver flatware with the saved cigarette money.

One unhappy team member made an error in final totalling and checking. Unfortunately the incorrect total pulled down a student's average so far that he flunked his Honours course. He knew he had *not* failed the paper that had been marked so low. His parents came and protested hotly at the outer reception desk. The Registrar heard the raised voices, excused the receptionist whose polite attention had made those parents impatient until he intervened, and, with his air of authority, had the offending exam-sheet brought out from the finals file.

He spotted the error, took the outraged parents' full fury, apologized, promised to publish a correct result at once and to revise the student's transcript accordingly. Having accepted all of the blame and ushered the parents out, he returned, firmly closed the doors, and demanded to know whose initials were on the offending sheet. The receptionist told him. He strode off to his own lair, ordering the culprit to follow. The rest of us knew nothing more. Nobody was fired.

The receptionist appreciated his coming to the rescue. Several receptionists manned 'the desk'; it was often crowded at exam time and during registration. Behind it was an area of general work. Working among this large group of individuals was a new experience for me. Although our backgrounds were similar, our tastes and choices were often very different.

This was a happier situation than the first weeks had offered. My service had begun in the Registrar's Office typing room. For those strange weeks I was a typist in a square room with five or seven others, far enough apart to choose and shift our chairs for adjusting distance from the typewriter, but with that much space only. When I was introduced as the replacement for an ailing typist, the others were friendly. They told me about their friend's absence, likely to be a prolonged one, for she had been eating peanuts one evening, had choked, somehow inhaled a fragment of nut and developed TB. Their concern continued all the time I was there, and no doubt until her recovery – cards to sign, and hints that I, the new typist, was holding down her job until she was well.

The work was constant and steadily done until new work was brought in. (Of the content, I have no memory-trace; probably it was uninteresting to me and thus more easily typed mechanically for the sake of accuracy.) The chat among us five was easy during lulls in the supply of copy. The others were open to me, but their tone and preferred topics were an alienating factor. The other groups I had made adjustments to join had given me no handle on this new situation.

With immense good intention, but disastrous incompetence, I tried to play a role I could not sustain. It committed me to daily misery. To drop the role once I'd established it seemed a betrayal of the very likeable people here. To maintain it felt like slow rot, hollowness. The crispness of P.K. Page's 'The Stenographers' points up a painful contrast:

> In the felt of the morning the calico-minded,
> sufficiently starched, insert papers, hit keys
> efficient and sure as their adding machines;
> yet they weep in the vault, they are taut as net curtains
> stretched upon frames. In their eyes I have seen
> the pin men of madness in marathon trim
> race round the track of the stadium pupil.

The integrity of that poem helped me resolve to apply for release to some different work, with a vow never again to falsify relationships. This was the route that led me to the clerical section of the Registrar's Office, where the community instantly felt congenial. In that typing room, though, I had learned something I pondered for years: accruing education is isolating.

In the Registrar's Office, cross-currents and tensions abounded, not so much among the teams of two as between these teams and the large outer office where preliminary organizing of the work was done. The financial business was handled in one section, reception of faculty and students in another, and so on. Out of this daily interest came the core of 'The Agnes Cleves Papers', in *Winter Sun* (though the name, 'Agnes Cleves', was fictional).

It bothers me still to remember the tension, at first, of trying to shift gears at 5 p.m. (1 p.m. Saturdays) in order to live and write, the whole point of 'earning a living'. Changing from office to comfort clothes helped. Then I discovered beer. My flat roof was a good place for a case or two, and I'd be all set. 'Agnes Cleves' flowed with the suds until, one weekend, when I ran out of beer too late to fetch more, I found that words would no longer come. The experience alerted me never again to rely on anything but pen and paper. It helped me resolve to turn back and revise what had been written, a process that eased the way into continuing without depending on any external thing.

Evening time and weekend time began to be cluttered. The *History of Ontario*, the tag-end commitment begun at Gage's long ago and published in 1951, had lingered until this period. Freelance work continued to come. A way out of the pressure from work hours seemed to be opening. In any case, I was ready to risk free-wheeling, free of regular hours, for a while at least. Several professors brought me journal articles or manuscripts for a preliminary editing when pressures gave them no time. (Once at the Institute an historian had become infuriated by the changes I'd proposed: I found his prose style halting, and tried to make for better flow, here and there. I learned from him to test the ground with editing of this kind, before taking it on.)

Raymond Souster, back from the Air Force, was introducing us in Toronto to new poets who gave readings at the YMHA [Young Men's Hebrew Association], Spadina and Bloor. More than once the visiting poet and Raymond came back to my Washington Avenue room to share a bottle of wine, or have coffee. Cid Corman was one who maintained contact later, with postcards from southern Italy, or notes from Japan, or, in between, brief comments recommending new work from the States.

When soldiers, sailors and airmen like Ray came home, they were given latitude to re-enter civilian life. This city was growing and changing in temper and tempo. Industry, which had been geared to war production, was retooling for peacetime. Women who had known profitable wage-earning did not get jobs as easily now, so lost all but their new competence and self-confidence. Veterans were offered a choice of grants either for building a house on suburban lands, or for post-secondary education. One had to adapt to new conditions.

Many veterans who chose education but had inadequate school credits were accepted into an initial qualifying year, and I was privileged to teach such a class, Saturday mornings, on campus. It was enjoyable to lecture to receptive students, sound in judgement, willing to ask questions, determined to overcome prewar deficiencies in schooling and to use their education grants successfully. Some, on an initial brief essay, showed the need of extra tutoring in grammar, sentence structure, spelling. They readily agreed to extra tutoring after lectures, patiently learned and accepted correction. One, I remember, had not finished elementary school, but had matured in the services and was heading in a new direction. Years later when we ran into each other on the street, I learned that he had taken a history degree and gone on to a career in teaching.

Through my college friend Mary, or rather her husband Harley, I saw a little of the alternative grant (for housing). Harley Parker was an artist. He wanted some time to study but needed housing for his family, so he accepted land and money for a house, building it himself and using the construction part of his grant for study at Black Mountain College in the States before returning to teach painting at the Ontario College of Art. His house was a one-storey, creatively thought-out design: all utilities and plumbing at one end, with the kitchen at the front corner, the one entry wide enough for that whole section and easily accessible to the baby's room partitioned off at the front, and the main room with a huge work-cum-dining table, and bedrooms inconspicuously further back. The windows allowed good light without glare. Years afterward, when the family was moving to an old brick, semi-detached house in the Annex, one of the Parkers' sons asked: 'Are we going to *live* in this Renaissance pad?'

Willowdale was then built up mainly along the highway, Yonge Street. I loved the long trip out to visit Mary and Harley and baby Blake in their new house. There was the streetcar trip up to the city limits, south of Hogg's Hollow, then a second ride from there further north on Yonge. The stop closest to their house was almost in the country; indeed, the last part of the walk was through long grass in an empty field, a little copse, then finally to the 'Veterans' Land Grants'. Many of the neighbours became friends. Harley and Max Ferguson ('Rawhide')* were two who enjoyed each other's company and kept in touch even after moving elsewhere.

While work on the house progressed, the Parkers lived in an inexpensive flat, mid-town. Their first son was a baby then. I remember a visit one evening, when Harley was just completing a new watercolour. He held it up gingerly to show us, then gently propped it up to dry on the back of the bathtub. The tub was being used to rinse newly washed diapers, however, so when the painting buckled, it slid down into water. I passed just as Harley howled and fished it out, then called us both, jubilant, to see 'the effect': he had added the technique of watercolour wash to his repertoire.

Postwar excitement, ongoing freelance work, my own writing at home, the Registrar's Office job, and now the Saturday lectures to prepare and papers to mark – surely my college debt was paid off by then – all added up to a strenuous life. Health problems had surfaced from time to time, no doubt a consequence of that anorexia in adolescence. Now they continued, the first stage being a strange patch of time with few symptoms except much lethargy and feverishness. At work I had been given the name of Dr Lillian Chase, so telephoned her.

She came! 'Come, I'll drive you,' she said, after a brief examination. 'I want to make sure what it is.' She looked around the room while I got into street clothes, found a half-saucepan of soup ('Throw this out when you go down to the bathroom!') and finally, when I thought I was ready, she wryly suggested that a blouse would be in order over my skirt. She had me admitted to Women's College Hospital with rheumatic fever. Friends visited in merry flocks, standing either side of the bed. I learned then that you never position yourself at a bedside in such a way that the sick person has to keep swivelling her eyes.

---

* Rawhide was a CBC persona of Max Ferguson. His show ran nationally under that name from 1949 to 1961, though Ferguson continued as a broadcaster until his retirement in 1998.

That was a six-bed ward. We all became well acquainted. One woman had a visit from her husband from 1 p.m. to 2 p.m. daily (the only daytime visiting hours then). He would come in wearing his fedora, pull up a chair, lean over and kiss her forehead, sit and place his hat on the bedspread. She lay with her eyes closed. At the warning bell he would kiss her again, set the chair back, pick up and don the hat, and walk away. As soon as she heard the elevator come and go, she would lean down and roll up the bed so that she could rejoin our company, full of oomph. Did she play it that way to spare a laconic man from talking? Or was it unkindness?

We all took to another male visitor, come from Scotland. The day he proposed marriage to his ailing friend, we all busied ourselves with a magazine or feigned sleep. But when he had gone, we all came to and listened to her happy announcement!

When my fever finally stayed down, the doctor lectured me severely on Canada's Food Rules. Careless diet had undermined my health once; I should see to it that there was no repeat. She was a Saskatchewan woman, a good friend by the time I was well, and a resort for years. I telephoned her early one morning at about 3:00 a.m. a few years later, declaring that she had to take seriously some gynaecological symptoms I had tried and failed to interest her in before. Now there was bad pain too.

Surgery followed her referral to a specialist. That was a quick hospitalization, with a quiet convalescence, partly in Galt with my parents. While there, I found I could play into radio music with a penny whistle I'd come by somewhere. That led to buying a soprano recorder and, in due time, an alto one as well. When I was back in Toronto, at work again, the recorders brought me to the Conservatory. A specialist in early music there, Dr Wolfgang Grunsky, was new on staff. He welcomed an amateur, and taught me technique through lovely old airs and melodies, with exercises to warm up on, until I was ready to join a recorder group he had established. The highlight of that brief association was a fourteen-voice Palestrina piece, where my part was relatively easy as long as I counted my notes and rests as written. I say 'brief' because time was, as usual, too full.

Establishing priorities has been a lifelong struggle; everything and anything could entice me with unexplored possibilities. I was like the Godfreys' little dog, Rosie, looking out a window: how eagerly she strained to see and do everything the great outside world offered, her eyes glittering, the focus darting delightedly here and there, up and around. For a sensible human being such distractability is a disadvantage: recorder, and flute to which some of us in Dr Grunsky's group progressed, had to be deferred to an afterlife of infinities.

I was not the only one at the Registrar's Office whose eye kept straying to other green fields across other fences. One young man I remember revealed his range-finder abilities as we sat in the basement of Simcoe Hall reading completed exam sheets back and forth to check the final grades for graduation. At that time each diploma was painstakingly hand-inscribed by an old gentleman using calligraphy pens and ink. Our checking ensured that his copy was correct. But it was boring.

My co-checker, Eddie Klein, was a refugee who had been smuggled out of Germany just before the war. His English pronunciation was good because he read aloud to himself in his room, evenings. *'Oil for the Lamps of China,'** he said one day out of the blue, 'Isn't that a beautiful title?' I asked him if he planned to see the Far East some day. Without hesitation he replied that he was leaving the office next fall to become a medical student. Eddie did enroll, with eight dollars in his pocket. Somewhere he had access to a lab that produced a cure for athlete's foot (was it his formula?) which was eventually patented. That coup enabled him to pay back a loan and continue studying medicine. Ultimately he was appointed to the staff of a Boston hospital.

Like Eddie, I hankered to venture. The Saturday morning ex-service lectures were at Victoria College. There I ran into Professor Kathleen (Kay) Coburn, who needed someone to work occasionally as a researcher to speed her enormous job of preparing and editing S.T. Coleridge's manuscript notebooks for publication. She showed me photocopies of some of the pages she had brought from the British Museum, where she worked summers. The Coleridge work proved to be varied, scrappy at times, but very instructive.

Kay's office was a hive of activity. Her secretary worked on a

---

* The title of a best-selling 1933 Grosset & Dunlap novel by Alice Tisdale Hobart. A 1935 film of the same title, directed by Mervyn LeRoy and starring Pat O'Brien, was based on Hobart's book.

correspondence that had become worldwide, or from dictation as paragraphs of Coleridge text were ready for recording, deciphered and decoded, with all their marginalia. My work focused on Kay's queries, written clearly, sometimes without context. For instance she might need to find a couple of lines from whatever book the notebooks were discussing. It was easy but sometimes slow work to find the source in question, and to verify the words and punctuation.

What I enjoyed most was the range of subject matter. One verification involved going to the Pontifical Institute Library, the only place in Toronto with the particular books quoted or referred to in the Coleridge manuscript. Next, I was sent off to the Knox College Library with a few words of Latin and suggestions (from Coleridge's context) of three books from which they might have been taken. Grade nine compulsory Latin was all I brought to this task. I think it was the librarian who homed in on the bit to be identified. How dull such work has become by comparison these days, sitting at a computer instead of crossing campus among the squirrels and pre-empting august librarians' services!

Page proofs came when Kay expected, in midsummer. She had returned early from England to 'do' them at her island in Georgian Bay. She and Jessie Macpherson (Dean of Women at Victoria College) co-owned the place, built by aboriginal workmen. Every comfort had been installed. The fireplace was for beauty and fragrance rather than for needed warmth. There my Coleridge job reached apogee, reading aloud back and forth, as Eddie and I had done checking details in the old basement vaults, but outdoors here, sitting on the sunwarmed rock of the Precambrian Shield. Too warm? There was a private bay for bathing. Too chilly? A sweater and a workout in the canoe, Kay steering. She explored all my ineptnesses.

In response to the message that more proofs were being delivered, plans for hospitality slowed us down. When the editorial man from the Bollingen Foundation arrived, he was in shirt and tie, vest and jacket, a navy pinstriped suit with the pipestem pantleg then in style. A water taxi owned and operated by one of the cottage builders' tribe left him on the dock and swirled away. We were working outdoors at the time, and after introductions Kay put away the new proofs and invited her guest to join us as we worked. He got out a pocket handkerchief, poor man, spread it between him and the rock, and sat leaning with his knees up. The leather-soled shoes kept sliding forward on the rock. I am afraid that in her enthusiasm for northern hardiness the hostess let his discomfort happen on purpose. I felt for him, and openly mentioned, before lunch, how often my back ached from working without chairs and table.

Over the years I had many kindnesses from Kay Coburn; the difference in our temperaments, and drive, opened many doors to me. She knew, for example, that my private focus was still writing poetry. It was she who in the late fifties took the manuscript of *Winter Sun* to England and visited it upon Routledge and Kegan Paul, her publisher there, who in turn published it and circulated it here through their agent, the University of Toronto Press. Research questions for the Coleridge book made me a familiar figure in the University of Toronto Library and in 1948 a job attracted me which opened in that library's order department.

For the first and only time, I was almost snagged in a 'career'. Professors placed orders for new books, or rare books, for the library's collection. Some were eager for a first look when the shipment arrived, requesting a telephone call and a 'hold' before the inevitable delay of processing and cataloguing. I see vividly one specialist in Near Eastern studies 'popping in' to make sure we had not been trying to reach him. He was a little apologetic, those mornings. But who would not forgive him when at last the book arrived, seeing him positively bristle with excited anticipation. He defined scholarship, for me: to win through to excellence by years of archaeology, language study, deciphering ancient inscriptions, disciplined weighing of bits of evidence, respectful considering of other researchers' theories – and at the same time supporting his family by teaching. He brought his ponderous skill to undergraduates at a stage of their university careers when the subject was totally new to them, needing only preliminaries, and patience – all this from the zealot we saw in the order department.

The original University of Toronto Library was built into a grassy hill. You entered at the highest level. From the lowest, flush with a pathway where Taddle Creek once flowed, you looked up to floors and floors of dim-glassed 'stacks', the steel shelving of the collection, with irregular points of light here and there, where graduate students had turned on the lights of carrels.

The physical presence of those surroundings, with their many solidly built, carved, mellowing wooden tables, had fascinated me as a freshman. Now I was admitted to the mysterious depths beyond the circulation desk. I had heretofore known only the area where undergraduates waited for the books they had requested, shelf numbers carefully copied from an enormous cardex catalogue. Even the catalogue drawers had an aroma all their own. Yes, I know: computers have made all these processes immensely faster and more efficient. I nonetheless cherish in memory the cumbrous library I once knew.

Like the procedural meticulousness of catalogue and circulation desk areas, the reference room had its appeal. We haunted it because every book order had to be verified there. The old volumes themselves were personalities: catalogues from many of the world's great libraries, publishers' lists (current and forthcoming), *Who's Whos*, atlases. New book orders might be in other languages, with author and title in most cases – although occasionally a reference had been snatched imperfectly from a visiting lecturer's presentation and was sketchy. Fuller information, scribbled from book reviews or somebody's footnotes, was often hard to decipher. One of the special librarians, who did reference work there full-time, preferred to reign alone, it seemed. She was a short, plump lady, nearing retirement age, who often needed to consult the same shelf as one of us. It was not uncommon to feel her butt the haunch of the one working in close quarters at the same shelf.

There were six spacious desks in the order department. Facing us all, in front of the separate office of the librarian, Mr Stewart Wallace, was the desk of our department head, Miss Audrey Cordingly, a published bibliographer ('Tod & Cordingly'). Her systems were time-consuming – a cardex for all orders, progress reports on the back, each card to be removed only by a 'searcher' and re-filed before any lunch break or day's end. She assigned new orders daily, to each of us according to the languages we knew or, for unfamiliar languages, to a researcher she had trained to deal with them. She learned subject interests among us, and indulged them sometimes. One huge speciality was periodical orders: the foreign ones were difficult to search. There was a typist in Miss Cordingly's section, and a table for unwrapping exciting parcels or for filling orders or pasting in pockets.

The pockets-pasting was assigned to a young man whom Mr

Wallace had sponsored through some agency, Big Brothers perhaps. He was a quiet, fair-haired, kindly fellow, and easy to work beside. The shelves of arriving books-on-order were just behind him. Mr Wallace showed how seriously he took his responsibility for Brendan when this young man vanished one day. Part of his job entailed carrying boxes down the back stairs from our area. He came and went often, so when he left the department nobody realized he had simply walked away. The librarian instituted a discreet, then a very public search, but without result.

A month or so later I had occasion to be in the basement and, coming back up, had a smile from Brendan on his way down. Re-entering the department, I remarked to the world at large 'Nobody told me that Brendan was back!' An odd silence congealed around me. Through Miss Cordingly, the librarian had just announced his having received a message from England that Brendan had stowed away in the cargo hold of a merchant navy ship, but was found late in the voyage and handed over to the authorities. He reportedly claimed he was a Japanese prince, and his people needed him. The British hospitalized him, finally worked out his ID, but by then he had had a seizure and died. (Who could shudder at a ghost with such a friendly smile as I had seen?)

One of the senior librarians in 'Circulating' was retiring. We all delighted in her plan to travel right around the world now that the war was over: she had planned an itinerary and saved enough to do this extravagant trip in a leisurely fashion. But one morning in her first week of retirement, halfway into her corset, she fell dead. When seven of us went to the funeral home, planning to visit briefly on our lunch hour, we were surprised to be told that, since there were no next of kin, the funeral would take place that day if we'd care to stay. There was a chaplain for the establishment, and there were us seven. Sadness lingered around the circulation desk and in our department for several weeks.

Changes abounded when ex-service personnel swelled the student population: an addition built onto the old core building, our department to be moved, a new chief librarian and a new department head to be appointed.

Miss Cordingly had not mentioned any heart trouble. When she felt unwell one day, and asked the secretary to cancel a hair appointment for that afternoon, we finally suggested to Mr Wallace that he give her the rest of the day off. He not only concurred, but got his car from its parking spot and drew up in front of the library to take her home. I was asked to go along and stay till she was 'settled'. Her apartment was nearby. She went up the front steps on my arm, we turned and waved Mr Wallace goodbye. I took the key from her, unlocked the door, and she gratefully stretched out on her sofa. Before agreeing to go back to work, I insisted on telephoning someone to inform them she was here. The number she gave me was her doctor's. He said: 'I'll come. Stay till I get there,' and it didn't take him long. After examining Miss Cordingly, he came out to the hallway where I was lingering. 'When and where did this happen?' he asked. I told him. 'You mean she walked out of the office, and she climbed up the front stairs there? Do you realize you might well have killed her?' He ordered a nurse, telling me to stay until she arrived, and left.

Miss Cordingly recovered from that attack but died at home a year or so later. Her funeral was appropriate: in Grace Church-on-the-Hill, liturgical throughout, but with an oddly personal focus *just because* devoid of any life stories or reminiscences. The presence of her friends, and the quietness around the simple pronunciation of her full name during the service, was forceful, final and fitting.

'Where are you going for your holidays?' That is a seed of conversation among employees everywhere I've ever worked – that is, worked long enough to have earned vacation. The span of days off widens with length of employment. I had leeway enough, in the library years, to stump me: with no car, no cottage, no companion, I had to think hard. In those years Europe was out of bounds except to armed services personnel, or professionals who followed them during the period of reconstruction and rehabilitation.

Time to visit my parents came at 1:30 noon any Saturday: I could arrive at the library with a weekend case and catch a train to Galt after work. The bungalow there was the first house they had ever owned. Previously, churches had provided manses and grounds generous enough for the flow of guests and small groups entailed in ministry. Now retired, my parents had their own manageable place, with an extensive garden. They enjoyed it and each other, and for me weekends at home were welcome.

But a three-week vacation in 1954 opened new vistas. Somewhere in a periodical I had read about the summer school at Indiana University. They sent information and application forms, and I signed on for a class session in linguistics and a book-study seminar. It was exciting to need border-crossing ID and U.S. currency before setting off. When the date arrived, a change of trains took me into the concourse of Chicago's station, where everyone seemed to know where to find their connecting trains, how much time should be allowed for an early breakfast here, and where to find it.

Stepping down from the coach in Bloomington was an astonishment: it felt like a sauna. Occasional midsummer days in Ontario can be hot, but this was, to me, tropical, exotic. The trainman, the taxi-driver, everyone in the coffee shop called me 'honey'. Whether you asked for something, or thanked someone, the response was always a neutral 'mmhm' in a rising then falling cadence.

Summer students were offered lists of rooms for rent in town. One at a manageable price within walking distance, judging by the wall map, proved adequate for my stay. It was not air-conditioned but I adjusted to the climate somehow. Fellow students were solicitous nonetheless, because the other Canadian registrant had collapsed with heatstroke and had to be ambulanced back to somewhere in Quebec.

Linguistics classes began with a chart of phonetic symbols. We put simple statements down in this form, then checked our pages against what the instructor subsequently wrote on the blackboard. Next we were to write phonetically what he said. He sent me to the board to take down one passage, and frowned afterwards, then paused, then turned to the class and pronounced it 'a Northern Anglo accent rendering! You *do* come from the far north?' I did not say no, just mentioned Toronto, Canada. 'Aha'– he was right! Visual accent-reading must be fun, adding eyes to your ears everywhere.

The book study session offered options. My choice was Thomas Hardy's poetry. There were about fourteen of us, around a long table, in the first air-conditioned room I'd struck that day. The teacher arrived on the dot, in a light blue-and-white-striped two-piece suit with a crisp white shirt and white bow tie. He introduced himself: John Crowe Ransom. He was a poet I had read, and hoped to hear when I saw his name in the brochure at home. We were each to buy Thomas Hardy's *The Complete Poems,* recently issued, told to 'read it through', and were given a book of references to look at in 'our room' at the University of Indiana Library. One volunteer was enlisted to lead our next meeting, and the rest of us were dismissed.

The university library there had a smaller main reading room than the University of Toronto's. Instead, the space was used for a number of seminar library rooms, with shelves and one long table in each. The English seminar room, for example, had sections for each graduate summer course's material, with our Hardy section well marked there. No books could be removed from a seminar room; if the one you wanted was in use, you read something else until the user left for his next class or for lunch. It was a friendly and efficient system.

Our assignments were all the same as the first volunteer's: to defend, or promote, one poem. The rest of us were to challenge the choice by comparisons with another poem in our *Complete Poems*. Ransom's comments kept things lively. In the final session he thanked us all with a flicker of a smile, explaining that his own next assignment, from a notable publisher, was to provide *his* Hardy selections for their proposed new anthology.

The Indiana University campus offered options for free time: recitals in the music building, public lectures, etc. One lecture I had spotted on a bulletin board was an evening with William Empson. His *Seven Types of Ambiguity* had become a key critical book over the years for any English-language writer. Arriving early, I managed to find a good seat in the big lecture hall. Because newspapermen knew Empson as Chinese Editor for the BBC (he had taught English literature in both China and Japan), they smelled a story. Communism was arch-enemy number one in the States at that time, 1954, during the McCarthy era, when many prominent people in the arts were interrogated and imprisoned for leftist tendencies

Mr Ransom and Mr Empson were sitting on two straight chairs to the left of the podium, watching latecomers elbow past reporters at the door and disrupt a row here and there. Finally, Mr Ransom, in his powder-blue cotton corduroy suit, bow tie and white shirt, rose, welcomed 'the east and the west' in the audience, and, checking the shaking note in his hand, introduced this most senior Fellow of the Indiana School of Letters who had studied mathematics and English at Cambridge, taught in China and Japan, and was a critical writer of note to all English literature students. He then left the stage for a front row seat.

Empson stood, reached into a pocket of his loose pants for his notes, dropped some papers and other muddle, picked everything up, fumbled a little, then said: 'These are not pyjamas I'm wearing,' and, flinging his arms wide, 'This is my Chinese Communist uniform: this is what they wear for a Chinese parade.' Then he murmured an impressionist version of such a parade. Even in my good seat I found some of the words inaudible. Nervous laughter began and evaporated at intervals. From the pitcher on the lectern he kept pouring so crookedly that little would land in the glass and most on the floor. Was he drunk, perhaps? Someone behind me quoted a bit of Empson's villanelle 'Missing Dates'. I had liked that poem so much that his oddness seemed fitting: 'It is the poems you have lost, the ills/from missing dates, at which the heart expires./Slowly the poison the whole blood stream fills./The waste remains, the waste remains and kills.'

Finally, he owlishly looked us over. 'My topic was to be language and criticism, I know.' But this did not interest him, now that it was in his book. He would prefer a question-and-answer approach, if anyone had questions. But first, for four minutes or so, he wanted to tell us about going into the Chinese Civil War area because he needed a 'quiet place' to write his book on the Pastoral. What most interested him at the moment, he declared, was the indignity he had suffered at being put on oath before being admitted to the United States. He proceeded into a peroration on the U.S.'s puritan smugness, adding 'Every non-American is quite right to hate them.' At that point, any reporter who had not already leapt out to telephone in the reference to the Chinese Civil War, now plunged out the door. Certainly the Indiana University sponsors of the event would be cringing in advance of the press's likely crescendo of 'academic liberalism' sneers, and the administration's subsequent holding the English Department to account.

But before all was lost, we had forty minutes clear of Empson protestations. These were minutes of fine reading. There was an elegant, poetic translation of part of a Chinese opera, I remember. And before the intermission he told us about a British policeman who had worked with Chinese Communists all through the civil war, and was now in Malaya being paid to shoot on sight any Chinese Communist he spotted. I did not stay for the second half of the evening, the discussion period. Empson's stress had become infectious.

That was a strenuous vacation, but the university provided many comforts. Best of all was the extensive campus, huge unfamiliar southern trees, flowers, grass, well-kept paths, and a music building where many free concerts were offered by advanced students in the evenings.

One other holiday venture was at an opposite extreme. For some reason my vacation had been deferred until after the summer. October is a beautiful month, though. A friend of Eleanor (Godfrey) Graham offered me her family's cottage on Lake Erie near Welland, her childhood family home. Her brother-in-law would open up for me, if I would like to go. The bus would drop me at a year-round store, where he would meet me and lead the way down to the beach-front cottage.

Fortunately no one else got off at that stop the evening I arrived. We identified each other easily, he took my bag and led me down a gravel road and along a wooded path to the cottage. He unlocked the door, brought in wood, got the electric pump working, showed me the deck built off the living room and the screened veranda across the front, as well as the steep path down to the water's edge. He had already put in enough supplies for my first breakfast! When he left, I heard his car drive away. Traffic on that road was always light, off season. The cottages were strung out on a ridge above Lake Erie like a single-street village, all the way round to a point, far to the right. Trees concealed the view to the left. The silence was palpable.

That silence became a presence for my whole two weeks' stay there. I was conscious of violating it, mornings, when I lit a fire in the grate, waited till it caught well and could be banked safely, then ran down for a swim before breakfast, shattering the glassy silence in wait at the shore. Getting-breakfast sounds seemed friendlier. Since the sun had not come round to the veranda yet, I ate inside, tidied, and had five hours of morning ahead. The shelves held summer books, and I had brought others. Soon I was settled comfortably on the veranda with a blanket and an ashtray, all ready for the holiday high-point – undisturbed time to read when I liked, or write, or sit and think, without a 'should' under that sky. That is where silence found me again. Its presence had location, though I could not whirl around suddenly and see it. Striking of a match, turning of a page, offended it. We endured a contest of wills for long stretches on the porch, that summer.

Walking beside the lake interrupted one kind of aloneness, but even there the blank eyes of abandoned cottages watched the only movement in the wide expanse of sky and water. A sameness of surroundings mesmerized me, and the crunch of footfalls in drying sand alerted silence to dog me again. We did not become friends all fortnight.

One effect of this on me was a film of apprehension whenever daily activities subsided. In the evenings I would read indoors, with the friendly fire keeping silence at bay a bit. Sometimes the sense of a huge community all departed touched my fantasy and invited analogies. Imagine such a quiet read by the fire, full night now, and suddenly hearing a lone car door slam, and, yes, the crunch of footsteps approaching down the path! Of course the one lamplit building would draw a solitary man's eye!

By the time the knock on the door sounded, my heart was thumping hard. Well, if I could outface silence, I could face this. My tremulous greeting, when the brother-in-law stepped in, must have betrayed my fears. He apologized for not having warned me that the pump needed this interim visit. We then said goodbye, he told me to leave his keys at the store when I went up to catch my bus home, and I thanked him heartily for being so kind, indeed hospitable, in making this vacation memorable. But never again did I go alone into an unknown isolation.

Library staff would leave in clusters at the end of the work hours. Four of us lingered on the night of October 15, 1954, hoping the downpour outside would let up any moment. When it did not, and since we all lived considerable walking distances away, we decided to move, fast, to the coffee shop on College Street, and sit out the storm. That evening Isabel and I became friends with Oke, an Estonian refugee who had been working towards a medical degree until the Communists found more menial tasks for him (like me, he had entered exam results in the Registrar's Office and now worked in the library), and Ottilia, a refugee from Hungary. Finally we resigned ourselves to a soaking and sloshed our scattered ways home. As I was preparing a belated supper, my telephone rang. It was a friend, from New York. 'Are you all right?' I said that of course I was, why? Only then did I learn that 'Hurricane Hazel' had been causing the unrelenting downpour and litter of branches and twigs on the cement walkway past the campus.

After Miss Cordingly's death, the order department was expanded, relocated to a new wing, and temporarily placed under my direction until a permanent replacement could be found. A new chief librarian had followed Mr Wallace too. My interim duties were easy. Miss Cordingly's system, though cumbersome, was foolproof, and new staff members learned it and liked it. Otherwise they were free to devise their own work methods. One such 'method' did worry me: a worker's desk was covered with stacks of papers and books, her left-handed, close writing on the request slips she annotated being done at the left front merest corner of space that remained. I kept an eye on her orders, and was amazed to see that they were accurate and well-handled. Do all roads lead to Rome, given the wish to arrive there?

The chief librarian had a young son who, at birth, needed a complete blood-replacement. Of all the staff it was my blood which proved a match. As soon as possible, the hospital staff prepared me and the equipment for the process. I remember lying on a gurney beside the newborn in his protective shelter on a table near me. He was connected to my body by tubes. As my blood went into him, bright orange streaks appeared and faded, one after the other, on his skin. The effect on me was no greater than if I had been donating blood.

In a restaurant one evening some fifteen years later, Pat Gibson and I recognized each other. She was the older daughter of our doctor next door in Calgary days, and was now married to this same chief librarian! She declared she would invite me to her home in Streetsville when spring came.

So it was that father and son showed me around their garden one evening while Pat was preparing dinner. The boy wandered off and began practising golf strokes at the far side of the house. Suddenly, unintentionally, one of his practice drives soared our way. It hit me in the temple, painfully enough that I emitted an involuntary cry. The father strode back to the son and took him behind a corner of the house. After they emerged, we all remained engulfed in silence. Nobody mentioned the incident later when we sat at the dinner table. I felt reasonably all right by then, though.

Sixteen years earlier, my job as interim had very nearly become a promotion. When offered the department headship in a surprise summons to the chief librarian's office, I felt the dreaded career-status closing around me. Instead of demurring, I heard myself announce that in fact I planned to leave the library soon but of course I would stay until a new department head was appointed, and as long as I was needed during the transition. The librarian asked what I was moving into. Freelance work, to leave me free for writing, I told him. Fatherly counsel flowed: one could write evenings and weekends; one needed the stimulus of different work apart from one's avocation; my pension would be pitiful if I left now. I asked whether I could apply for a return of pension contributions as a lump sum, now. That would be a danger to your old age, he said. He was wise in all his words, but I took the lump sum when, in time, my replacement was trained and my final responsibility was thus completed.

The 1963 Vancouver Poetry Conference poets: Margaret Avison (top left), Robert Creeley (top middle), Allen Ginsberg (top right), Robert Duncan (bottom left), Denise Levertov (bottom middle) and Charles Olson (bottom right). (Avison photo – Family photo: courtesy of Karen McKim; all other photos – Credit: University of Manitoba Archives and Special Collections, Margaret Avison fonds, Box 1, PC151)

ESCAPING A CAREER

That move from the library was exhilarating and guilt-free. By dint of steady work for months, I had made up the time off with pay that the chief librarian offered when my father had a heart attack and I was needed in Galt. Now my privacy was rediscovered. I was free to read or write at any hour, or explore the changing city on random buses and long walks. I kept waiting for that inner compass to set the new direction. When I found Bible passages (for example, Jeremiah 18: 1-6) about being reshaped on the potter's wheel, I recognized the experience.

After a number of months of resumed freelance editing, and waiting, I moved my belongings to my brother's basement to be stored. (There my cartons got soaked in a disastrous mix of storm runoff and sewer back-up – evidence that discarding is wiser than hoarding.) The keys to my Washington Avenue room went back to the landlord, and in June, 1955, I moved into the big house on Bedford Road where I had been an occasional guest. There I would live on the third floor and work as a mother's helper for friends of the Grahams, Marion and Jack Johnson, two lawyers married at age forty, with four children, then aged seven, five, three and one. Any single woman who finds herself tempted, as I had been of late, to snatch babies from their carriages outside grocery stores, will recognize the power of the maternal instinct. For me, this new job was a relief.

Adjusting to different little persons at various stages of development took some learning. They taught me, bless them. As children will, they accepted my presence once I melted into the day's design by being there every morning and on until after dinner. When household duties kept me occupied, the younger two played nearby, the youngest still in a Jolly Jumper or a playpen. The three-year-old lived out his tin soldiers' fantasies, or climbed up a front-window armchair to gaze at the passing scene. I remember him turning, with a radiant face: 'Oh Mawgwet, I love buses!' The Toronto ones were red. We three went out every afternoon, they seeing, touching, marvelling at tiny weeds or blown leaves. Their receptivity was humbling, but on cold days I still tried to hurry them. Slowly I learned how infectious an edgy or apprehensive state of mind can be to children, and it was myself, usually, I had to discipline. When I didn't, they became wild creatures.

This family had a marriage agreement tied up with the wife's properties in France. Her family there had never met the children so Marion and Jack decided on a trip in early August, with me along to free their days for renewing old contacts and settling the *dot* [dowry]. As we crossed the Atlantic on the *Andrea Doria,* which in 1956 was to sink off Nantucket after a collision with the *Stockholm,* I just glimpsed England as a grey unevenness off on the horizon en route to Le Havre. One uncle lived in Paris where, on our first night, I approached a pharmacy, with many mispronounced words and awkward attempts at readable body-language (rocking a child, eating), until the proprietor and I smiled happily, he directing me, formula? no? canned baby foods? yes! Can opener, I learned, is *ouvre-boîte.*

Days in Paris meant a morning bench in some little community park, where nannies and young mothers sat reading or knitting while children played. In no time the four I'd brought were easy in French or in English, and knew which person to address in which language. On one of the Paris days Jack stayed behind so I could be on my own a while. I remember learning the Métro map, finding the Louvre, and the Left Bank, which Morley and Loretto Callaghan remembered so fondly. In the Louvre, overwhelmed with glorious opportunities but with so little time, I stood still and came to focus right where I'd stopped. By chance, before me was one sculpture, a stone ram. I forget his history and source. But as I gazed he spoke into me a quietness and wonder that ended greedy impatience. There I stood. To me he *is* the Louvre, all I'd hoped for. It was a chink of seeing that, I suspect, delighted me more than greater stretches of time could have provided.

As I emerged from the turnstile on the way home that day, an anxious tourist stopped me, carefully pronouncing the stop she wanted, not sure which branching walkway to take. I smile now at the picture of myself pointing, and saying confidently 'Par là, madame,' as someone had said to me earlier.

One of the mother's family members lived on a great estate on the route south. The elegance of their manner, their clothing – and their French – unnerved me. Happily, the children too were restive in the social circle their parents had joined, so we strayed together out across the lawns, up a rise, by a brook. It proved a good day until the little ones began to show how hungry they were. We returned, some of us plaintive by then. Goodbyes were said, then we stopped for supper at a country inn with a table in the back garden, and a formally dressed waiter who produced a high chair, seated the youngest and took our orders, including her with 'Et le petit personnage?'

There were two other centres where relatives were expecting us. Ecully, the next stop, was a small village near a larger market town. Since their children's sleeping quarters had not been prepared with me in mind, I spent the first night in the market town's hotel. There was a very early bus that would take me back to Ecully to help the children start their day. In the early light, we were a busful. Were my fellow passengers farm labourers? Or was there a factory somewhere nearby?

When the driver let me out at Ecully, a boy sent to meet me appeared on a bicycle, his white shirt already glued to his back in the warmth, carrying a long loaf of French bread hot from the bakery under one arm. He removed the shirt and slung the loaf in it, so his hands would be freer to bicycle slowly ahead, on our way 'home'. The home was near the village, stone walls all around, a high gate that was kept shut, a rambling old house with a Norman-style chapel building to the left of the wide entrance square, a glassed-in orangerie at the right, and glimpses of parkland falling away behind the house. Many people came and went, all friendly, probably all related. One daughter was about my age. She had seen me hang out diapers on the line one morning. Next day, before breakfast, she ran to me, gave me a quick kiss on each cheek: 'Bonjour madame, avez-vous bien dormi?' – then, explosively, 'Il pleut!' and she ran out to the line with me, then helped me drape my washing around our sleeping porch upstairs.

One Ecully afternoon stands out in my mind: in the courtyard miscellaneous kitchen chairs, a big wicker hamper, and all the women who were free then, myself included, peeling and quartering fresh apricots into various pots and kettles. Occasional talk. Plenty of silence, sun, sticky fingers – but they could be washed in the brook that ran through the park. The poem in *Winter Sun,* 'Stray Dog Near Ecully,' was partly about that afternoon, the women's idle talk 'reflected in tranquillity' some snowy day in Toronto, later on.

Our final visit was in the French Riviera, a small frame house back from the beach, with bitter memories of Vichy days (one could see the bullet pockmarks in many walls around the neighbourhood). The shore was a sandbox to end all sandboxes for the four children, who loved scampering in and out of the sea, as the sun dictated. We were oily with sunburn protection all the time, and gritty in the toes after the beach. For the first time there I saw nonchalant nude bathers; one large woman appeared regularly in an open-mesh bathing costume with bared breasts. Another novelty was eating eel for the first time there. I liked it – more like *eating* than picking snails out of their shells. (At a restaurant meal that summer lamb was offered. 'You would not like that,' Marion counselled. On other plates I saw it so rare it was still bleeding!)

At the end of the trip, back in Paris in somebody's van while the parents paid the last hotel bill and checked the boat-train times, the five of us devised a pastime. The seven-year-old began a story. When he broke off, his sister invented her own twist to his plot. The third, by then three years old, eagerly introduced a baker's truck. The baby, seeming to hang on to every word, was respectfully allowed to contribute too; she understood all words, but kept her counsel about what she could say if she chose. My turn, next, bridged the gap to number one, and so on.

On the trip home we struck heavy equinoctial storms. Even the nurse in the ship's playroom was seasick. I'd been given a form of Gravol combined with a wake-up drug by my Toronto doctor, but I still remember sitting woozily on the side of my bunk while the children, in their footed sleepers, used one slope of the linoleum floor as a slide, swivelled at the low wall, and waited for the floor to get steep enough to slide them back the other way.

We had dinners together in our cabin while the parents ate in the dining room. An embarrassing moment from that trip occasionally comes back to mind and makes me blush. The older boy was ready for his sleepwear, so he undid his serge shorts and stepped out of them. 'Pick them up, servant,' he said with a narrow look up at me. I did. But I was close to tears when I tried to tell his mother later. 'My goodness,' she said briskly, 'he's only a child, after all! He'd heard the stewards with the maids.' Insecurity can twist everything.

Back on Bedford Road in late September, whether Gauloise or good sense dictated it, I stopped smoking for the first (temporary) time. As Eisenhower said, 'I'll never smoke again. And believe me, if I do, I'll for sure never stop again!' It would be 1962 before I tried again.

The need to move on became clear at dinner with the family one night. I'd started a small cream sauce. 'What's that for?' the mother asked. She was a good cook. I explained that the little one would not eat her peas without the sauce; she'd only play with them. 'Nonsense! Freshly shelled peas are delicious as they are!' But the little one ate nothing, just rolled stray peas from her plate to the highchair tray, playing. It was a painful moment when my friend's eyes and mine met, and I knew she now needed to resume her full maternal role with this youngest child.

A French Catholic family, their First Communion celebration for the eldest, jointly with Eleanor Graham's son's, the two boys dashing up and down stairs with bath towels belted down so they could swish along like the Fathers: what other employment could ever have so widened my sense of what other people's families are like? This had been a recurring speculation ever since those walks in high school days past houses with Sabbath candles in the Friday windows, for instance, or the Finnish copper kettle beside an indoor window box on a hilly street just west of Keele.

Norrie Frye was a very considerate man, as well as a brilliant one. He kept an eye on many a student. Wondering when I was going to 'develop', he decided to stir things up. He proposed my name, as a poet, to the Guggenheim Foundation, and asked for a form on which I might apply for a fellowship. He sent the form to me along with a persuasive covering letter. I filled it out, asking for eight months in Chicago to read and write poetry. The request may sound modest; in fact, I wanted to stay within rail-range of Galt and my ailing parents. Eight months? It seemed a long stretch in an unfamiliar place, but time enough to organize decades' worth of poems, and do more and better writing, maybe.

This was the only time I ever asked for a handout on grounds of talent. It was drilled into us as children: *never be beholden.* My parents did in fact reconcile themselves to the grant as an honour, but for me, being a dependant those eight months was long enough, given my conditioned convictions and my uneasiness at being made somehow special, worthier of this bonanza than others who, I knew, were excelling in various ways, but unrecognized and certainly unfunded.

Embracing the opportunity was my reaction to some deadening prospect I saw or imagined ahead, at the time. Leaving the top floor apartment I had within my employers'/friends' house would have meant either scrambling for income and a new rental space, with no sense of direction about either, yet, or returning to my parents' home in Galt. I did return for a while, and found that families can be accepting, mine warmly welcoming.

To my parents' generation, a woman who did not marry had to be a teacher, a nurse, or a librarian to have security. Their perplexity when I left the library came to something like impatience when I broke the news of the shift to caring for one family's children. My father had said earlier: 'You may be a poet, but you don't have to contrive the dreary Grub Street life of a writer, not in Canada, with all your advantages.' I understood a father's perspective. But now something had come of the writing that was more practical, in his view: study abroad.

The early November afternoon came when we stood, three together, on the autumnal platform at the Galt Station, waiting for my departure, via overnight train from Toronto, for this new American venture. It was a cloudy day, with a cold, clear light that keeps the scene photographed in my memory still. Long after I'd caught my connecting train, when I was ready for sleep in my lower berth, we reached the border where an immigration and customs official boarded the train. My papers were ready.

The Consulate in Toronto had given me one anxious moment. The interviewer there would have preferred papers showing I had been accepted at a U.S. university, a straight student visa. But the truth didn't fit. She worked out her wording, took me through the conditions of temporary residency in the United States in preparation for my oath to honour those conditions, and as her last question in the rapid-fire recitation of formulas, she asked: 'Have you ever belonged to a Communist or a Communist-affiliated organization?' Memories rose up of the Young Communist League period. 'Yes,' I said, 'in the thirties, at college.' She gave me an exasperated look, then seized the pen she had dropped: 'Oh for goodness' sake!' she said, and signed the papers.

Now, in the middle of the night, my non-student status was alarming the border official. He actually suggested I exit the train at Detroit and, if everything were cleared up, proceed in the morning. In my nightdress? Would someone retrieve the luggage I had checked? I was flustered. The Consulate had been very thorough, I explained; they had assured me my papers were all in order. Wasn't there something I could do in Chicago, or later, at home, to satisfy border requirements? For some reason he decided that if I made a return visit to Canada within a certain number of weeks, taking with me another paper he would give me to be signed and stamped, it might all be worked out. This way, in time, it was.

In the Chicago station, over breakfast, I left my heavy bags in temporary storage until I found a room. The library and *Poetry* magazine were both on the University of Chicago campus, so I decided to find my way there. It turned out to be a direct trip on the El. There was a list posted, offering rooms for students, one of which I rented, then set out to find lunch and a few dishes, pots and other items for housekeeping. A neighbourhood Woolworth's had everything.

Fortified by food, I began filling a cart: dishpan, mop, cleaning cloth and so on. Apparently the manager had been watching me. 'You are a student?' I explained that I was a Canadian, on an eight-month grant. He too was Canadian, and beamed. 'I'll drive you to your room on my way to lunch. Where is it?' When I told him, he changed his tune. It was a bad address. Some blocks were safe; half of the block where my building stood was safe; my half of the block was no place for me. He would replace my cartful of purchases for me and bring me home to lunch where, along with his wife, we could plan.

I could not accept, but did promise to forfeit a week's rent and move out after one night, with plans to relocate in the morning. For that night, I wedged some furniture against the door, and placed objects under the window that would betray anyone entering that way. In spite of nightlong creaking and noisier steppings out in the hall, I did sleep fitfully. Nobody else seemed awake yet, when I gratefully departed the next morning.

Through the Travellers' Aid back at the station, I was given a short list of 'safe' rooms – all on the near-north side. The one I took was 'safe', all right. My landlady accepted only 'ladies', and imposed a curfew – 1 a.m., I think. My room, plus dressing-room with running water, had bars on both windows. In early days, whenever I ventured out, the landlady would emerge to help me with directions, or to satisfy the weary curiosity of a prisoner in her own home. Her fears put most of my destinations into danger zones where she could not bear me to risk going. The worst was George Williams College, in the community settled predominantly by blacks. (I joined a recorder group out there.) Had I heeded her caution, even the lively Polish area, within range for a good walker who relished new sights, would have been safe only at midday! But the comfort provided in her house easily reconciled me to her anxieties. No doubt some scary event lay behind to create them.

An American, whom I had met through my wartime interim appointment as CIIA information secretary, was listed in the Chicago telephone directory, or rather her Library of Foreign Relations was. When I telephoned, she responded with the instant hospitality I was astonished to find everywhere in that country. We arranged to meet for a drink before a dinner she was to attend; she was dressed for the occasion, and carried a dainty handbag, not the usual briefcase. It had suddenly cleared up after a sharp shower, I remember, as we walked past a major intersection with a small park at the corner. Before I knew it was happening, a thief snatched my friend's purse and took off across the park. She kicked off her high heels and gave chase in stocking feet, running faster than he did, hollering 'STOP THIEF' until he threw down the purse and fled for good. We resumed our walk, she with wet stockings again in her shoes, talking of other things. As in my Toronto times of night walking, where I was safe when I felt safe, this illustrated a confident woman's free range, in contrast to my landlady's fears.

Through the recorder-playing at George Williams College I met one group of friends. Other people I met through the *Poetry* office or in Chicago libraries became closer friends because our encounters were not organized. But the social aspect of my time there is best conveyed by an eighth-month party given at the private home of one player in the recorder group.

Open-hearted hospitality made that occasion easy compared with Canadian parties I had felt my way into, often relying on the first drink to untangle edginess until conviviality warmed everyone up. Here, easy friendliness on a shallow level made for a happy evening and, until the end, I did not realize that my leaving Chicago was the occasion we were celebrating. At that point someone spoke for the group, remembering good times on the snowiest practice nights, wishing me well, and, with sensitive probing, inquiring whether any of them might be able to intervene so that I could have my temporary visa extended while I made moves towards citizenship application. 'Oh no!' I protested.

But expressions of concern went on. If I had no visa, I would have to 'go back'. 'But I *want* to be back in Canada!' I burst out at last. 'My life belongs there. It's what I want, to go back now.' I can still hear the young man saying 'B-b-but you mean you d-don't *want* to b-become an American?' I could think of no answer but a puzzled 'No.'

That evening spoke for my sense of the place and the people, a superficial and therefore false sense, I knew. I had learned that it is risky to ask directions, when friendly response is more important to the Chicagoan on the street than accuracy in directing a stranger. Many times I went 'three blocks that way, turn left, and' found myself still lost. City maps, studied over coffee when street signs suggested I was closing in, brought me to my goal faster.

The American friendliness did ease routine matters, like cashing cheques and making purchases. But it became awkward again at American Thanksgiving. Nobody permitted me to enjoy my usual restaurant evening meal with a book. What would I, a total stranger, have added to their family festivity? Why would I want to be a part of it? But I offended three different groups that night by declining their invitations, miserably distracted from my own reading and from the lingering over food that normally preceded a good evening.

Often I have thought of those days when friends at home urged me to travel as they had, once the post-war 'reconstruction' period made travel again possible. To live in another part of the world and put down roots would perhaps open up a place, as eight months could not open up one American city in a short busy stay there. I knew that my impressions abroad would be as callow as they were in Chicago, and sensed that further 'travel' would frustrate real discovery. My own city, where I find myself – not a sought-out city but the one where, it seemed, circumstances placed me – my own city is still undiscovered, and yet it has slowly unfolded its map to what a person needs of a place, my own map, here.

Every morning, then, I worked in my North Side room, fishing one poem at a time out of a dunnage bag's worth of accumulated poems. Some were not good enough to keep, but did become the starting point for revision, or triggered new writing. Much went into long-term discard; I threw away very little, in case something still had a spark and might ignite on its own if I didn't dishearten myself by bearing in mind its present blurriness.

On the whole, it was fun. One day in early winter, when I left after lunch for the usual afternoon in a library or for an exploring walk, I was still so bemused that I went into a bar, ordered some coffee, or a drink, got out pen and paper, and slowly wrote a fairly finished version of 'Snow' ('The optic heart must venture …' *Winter Sun*), although I am sure the impetus and the words came as a surprise, unrelated to my morning's work, the book I was currently carrying, or anything on my walk downtown. It was an exhilarating experience.

Instead of a planned afternoon at the big public library, I sped out to the *Poetry* office. Sure enough, Frederick Bock was there, proposed dinner together and followed that up with a peaceful drink in a couple of bars, one where a hypnotist did a performance that made mild fun of his volunteer victim during the trance. That was our reason for moving on to another place where Frederick knew there was good jazz. Whether I showed him my new poem I cannot remember, but most writers in the first flush need to know it is there for somebody else, so probably I did.

The wealth of libraries in Chicago delighted me. Some of them were clearly too specialized for my 'research' – really just a reaching out for the stimulus of new ideas. The Crerar Library, for example, was on my map. I advanced on it with resolute aplomb, but floundered when I found that it held scholarly books on subjects I knew too little about to justify a request. However, I did fill out a slip for something that, on the catalogue card, sounded vaguely botanical. At least I might glean items for my letter home: my father was an enthusiastic gardener. Out of *that* plant-studying afternoon came 'Not the Sweet Cicely of Gerarde's Herball' (*Winter Sun*).

Such high points, plus the Art Institute visits, were typical of my days in Chicago. Afternoon walks often took me past the Moody Bible Institute, which would have yielded treasures if I had not then been stoutly anti-evangelical. Knowing that Moody, Dwight L., had been somewhere high on the list of evangelists made me suspect anything with his name on it. The Bible Institute's red-brick bulk brought to memory my father's stories of church services in his youth. Visiting evangelists, in teams of two, tried to emulate the Moody & Sankey (musical evangelists) team of their own boyhood days. But they pressured people, my father felt, without true fire. He admired a choir member called Kate Brown because, though she was conspicuous in the front row of the altos, she remained seated when everyone else in the church stood, at the big man's urging to do so, to affirm their renewed dedication. Because of this early context, evangelism suggested a faddy enthusiasm to my father – an offence to solid, considered faith. In the Moody Institute I might have found some of the early jewels of Christian faith I learned to look for long after Chicago access was closed to me. I regret missing the biblical expositions I might have enjoyed there on public occasions.

For walks in wind and snow, Chicago is glorious. Big city that it is, as Sandburg celebrated it, nevertheless the power of windstorm and snowstorm, that winter, was its true shaper. Men make machines to plough through some snow in some areas, good for some storms. But windstorms? It was a relief to find ropes, tough seamen's ropes, on Chicago main streets, so that you could move hand over hand, from shelter to shelter, against a gale.

Frederick marvelled at my whoops of joy amid the din of such outdoors days. For him, to endure was the objective. Bit by bit I learned why. With encouragement from his brother, who had gone into the family's retail furniture business, he had planned to come to Chicago when he graduated from the University of Iowa. But illness had struck their mother, then their father suffered a severe stroke, so Frederick spent several years nursing them, at home, until both died. Now Chicago! *Poetry* magazine had welcomed his contributions and offered him an editorial post.

Not surprisingly, his years at home had left him tired. He sought out a doctor who began a series of tests and physical examinations. The outcome: a diagnosis of Hodgkin's disease. At the time, this type of cancer was not manageable, as it has since become. Frederick himself made a contribution to the research that was looking for new approaches and improved therapy. Steep medical bills would have strained his resources, so he accepted free hospital treatment in exchange for submitting to experiments that the cancer research team would devise in hopes of helping him, and subsequently others. He entered the process as a new avenue of exploring, out in the big world.

Over the years, there and, largely, in New York later, I witnessed his ups and downs; one side effect was abrupt premature aging (withered skin and thin hair). The counteracting drug gave him soft brown hair again, a boyish face, rosy and smooth of stubble. And through all the changes, his real self grew stronger, his sense of the absurd livelier. In those Guggenheim months, he told me his diagnosis only to explain his disappearings into hospital. We talked about our work, or our reading, or listened to jazz, evenings.

At Iowa, Frederick had taken a course in 'creative writing'. This was the first time I had ever heard of such a course. It was an introduction that jaundiced my opinion. Why? First, because Frederick would show me a new poem – in the first draft stage – an impulse I recognized, with delight. No later touch seemed needed in most cases: his impetus was strong from line one to the end. But then, as instructed at Iowa, he began picking at every punctuation-mark, every word, testing every cadence, worrying over every consonant, until I felt that his poem was being needlessly battered.

When I wrote 'Butterfly Bones; or, Sonnet Against Sonnets' (*Winter Sun*), the rigorously disciplined Iowa poets were in my mind. Their individuality was worked out of them, somehow. I saw the process, from the joyful 'first drafts' Frederick showed me, to the colder, surer final versions – although 'final' is inaccurate. He never was satisfied with his finished work. From New York, in Brooklyn, even in the manuscripts Frederick left after his death (now in the University of Manitoba Archives)*, the ongoing tinkering was evident.

Probably I do an injustice to later creative writing courses by closing down on their potential from this one experience. Poetry writing in my early days was private, unimportant, permitted the way diary-keeping is indulged. Spontaneity, first glow, maybe show a friend in the first flush of writing: an enjoyable event. But the page was soon out of sight – saved, mind you! – and the rhythms of real life took over again. Not a fraction of the resulting dunnage-bag proved worth polishing and offering to unknown readers. That sorting, in Chicago, was perhaps all the more prudent because of Frederick's disciplined revising.

Back to Toronto I came with a completed manuscript and no plans. My long-suffering friend Isabel had a gable room available as part of her new apartment in a ramshackle old house on Hazelton Avenue. She had used that room for storage when she moved in, but

* Bock papers are also archived at the University of Iowa and York University.

now cleared a space for me to sublet until I knew my next step. There was a big chestnut tree in bloom outside that gable window, and space for a desk there.

Late that spring (1957), at lunchtime, in the Royal Ontario Museum courtyard, I was hailed by Professor McLuhan and brought over to join him and the Fairleys. Margaret Fairley was looking for Canadian poets to work with a friend, Mrs Polanyi (Ilona Duczynska), on a Hungarian poetry translation project. I did not need the language, she said. Intrigued, I agreed to start the work in my new room one afternoon later that week.

Through Ilona and Karl Polanyi, I first learned what a European 'intellectual' is. Never have I worked with such rigour as on the many, many evenings, weekends, free hours now. Ilona had prepared the raw material on which 'her Canadian poets' could base their translations. The work had been well done: a text with a widely spaced Hungarian original above, and a very literal word-by-word English version, in different ink, below. To approach these pages, one needed the historical context and some knowledge of the poet. Ilona knew, and could communicate this information vividly. But it ate up our time.

Then I would read through her first version of the poem, trying to get clear the colour and feel and associations for her bald, literal meanings: 'stone' – was that a cliff? large liftable stone? mason's cut stone? boulder? Next, the ear: I stared at the unfamiliar Hungarian words and listened as Ilona read and reread. In the end, this was not adequate; she made tapes of the Hungarian texts so that I could check the interplay of sound and sense over and over again as I worked. Our first session in the sublet room led to many more there, and later in the Rouge Valley cottage where the Polanyis lived.

Work so novel and growth-giving was good, but did not pay. For a time I sold books in the Avenue Road shop of the Park Plaza Hotel. Fortunately the cash register in those days was as straightforward as a poke-and-crank adding machine. Parcelling was another matter. One shelf of Penguins proved popular; these were small softcover books which slipped easily into one size of small bag. Wrapping the hardbacks was more of a challenge. Finally, with practice, I learned to get paper and tape around them without obvious fluster.

One of my customers was Kay Coburn. She showed no surprise to see me in this new guise, but contacted me soon afterwards with a proposal. The editors of other Coleridge volumes were bringing questions to her, as general editor. She needed to use my earlier experience with ferreting out quotations and references – any hours I could find. Gradually we worked out times and, since her work paid better than retailing, I left the store before long.

I enjoyed juggling work times to keep both balls in the air, for a while, but the translating eased off, in time, and the Coleridge assignments were irregular. For income's sake I was open to a new project that a friend of the Godfreys proposed: ghost-writing an autobiography for Dr I. A. Wolinsky, whose arthritis had frozen his neck and arms, leaving him gloomily stuck at home at an age when he had expected to work for several further years as a surgeon at the Toronto Western Hospital. His concerned children pooled their resources to pay me monthly for a set time if I would spend mornings with their father, encourage him to tell his stories, make notes and work up a book manuscript.

The initial visit to the parents' home was all it took, on my side, and the doctor also seemed willing to give the project a try. Through that snowy winter I relished the walk west seven blocks or so, Mrs Wolinsky's welcome at the door, the cup of tea she left her husband and me 'to warm up on' and, often, an unscheduled lunch after my time was up, if the note-taking that day had gone well. At the sponsoring family's request I took a draft manuscript to the Macmillan Company office; an editor agreed to glance through it and made an appointment for us to meet in two weeks. Thus it came about that there were two books published in 1960: *A Doctor's Memoirs*, by I.A. Wolinsky, and my *Winter Sun*.

Ever since returning from Chicago I had tried to find a publisher for the poems. Every writer knows the rejection slip routine, poets particularly. The fifties were not a prosperous time and poetry never did pay enough to help a publisher stay afloat. I still remember one rejection, gratefully, because it was not just a printed form. It said: 'This book is too modern to make a book of traditional verse, and too traditional for a book of modern verse.' My response was: 'I write what I write' (adapting Rivera's 'I paint what I see', the artist's response when Nelson Rockefeller tried to dictate the subject for a newly commissioned mural).

Kay Coburn knew of these attempts to publish. She befriended my manuscript, asking my permission to 'place' it in England, if she could. Her next trip was soon: she needed work time in London to consult manuscripts in the British Museum and to do peripheral research. Hence the Routledge and Kegan Paul publication, at last, of *Winter Sun*. Their Canadian representative being the University of Toronto Press, copies of the Canadian edition began appearing here.

Would the book ever have surfaced without intervention from a known scholar? Now in twenty-first-century Canada, published poetry abounds. Overabounds? The readership shows no comparable expansion. The abundance of new books may now make the pendulum swing back again. Perhaps the popularity of poetry readings in little bars and coffee houses will shrink the demand for a book at home alone under a lamp?

For my father's sake, I was glad that I had a published book to take home. He respected a book. If my strange way of life had been a worry, a book printed and bound and being sold was solid evidence of stability, of good sense in my lifestyle, somewhere. Because by now his health had become precarious, I would catch a train to Galt sometime each week in order to do grocery shopping and help Mother keep the household running comfortably – and to keep the garden from distressing those two who had built it up to a lovely profusion in midsummer, with some new emphases in the earlier months and the fall.

When my father entered hospital for surgery, we three children all gathered to support Mother. The family doctor gave him a choice: 'You have cancer, Dr Avison. At your age it will likely be slow to develop. You might just enjoy the time you have at home, and later on we can help you tolerate the disease. Or we could operate now, remove the growth and learn whether we've been able to limit its spread, for a while at any rate.' 'I have never had an operation,' Father replied. 'I'd like to take that.' When he was sharing a hospital room, he and his roommate enjoyed each other. And he was surprised how easily a person 'goes through' the symptoms and miseries he had only witnessed over the years, as a visiting pastor.

He confided his one worry to his physician: 'If I am in bad pain, I don't know how I'll behave, and, for Mabel's sake, I don't want to carry on.' The doctor reassured him with the statement that by his age he had already hit the peak of his pain-tolerance and had never 'carried on'. 'If it goes beyond the tolerance point,' he continued, 'the nervous system cuts out so that you feel none of the pain.' (Was this really true?) Father was relieved, and he never did 'carry on'. Once, in his room at home, I saw a tear cross his cheek onto the pillow. He saw me see it. 'I'm all right. It's just that I was thinking, I'll never play lacrosse again!'

For his sake I was glad of the announced honour: 'A Governor General's Award!' he said happily. Being singled out, though, name in newspaper, prospect of a dressy public event, stirred up mixed feelings in me. The anchorage of reassuring my father (about the point of my haphazard occupational choices) did help. Gratified: that was another good reaction – for every writer assumes a co-creating reader while in the flush of composition, but learns to be content on the whole with one, or two, who will read the newest poem in manuscript and probe when they're puzzled, and finally admire what they hold in their hand – out of friendliness? because the writer's need seems urgent? or simply because communication is a value, whatever form it takes? For this process to continue out among total strangers underlies the pressure to publish. The award meant, then, that somewhere unknown readers had received and were reading my long-delayed book.

A second reaction is regret at the discomfort, well remembered from public school sports days, of defeated losers and the one winner's rotten awareness of a friend's finding the losing hard to handle. Events established that I did not cope well with this situation among acquaintances, whose congratulations I gracelessly shrugged off in embarrassment; the public unease became acutely painful in Ottawa, where a medal and a citation (no cash award back then) had to be formally presented among various grandees and *littérateurs* speaking little English, the language being the last shred of identity I could cling to.

An elegant invitation came in a formal letter, with an RSVP form making acceptance simple. A second committee packet gave details of events of the day appointed – essentially when to turn up where. My sister and her family invited me to stay with them. My work hours at that time were happily my own to schedule, so it would be the day coach by train, not the sit-up-all-night trip. Mary and Frank inspected my wardrobe on the evening before the ceremony, approved and improved details, and encouraged me in my growing nervousness. Frank, who was a National Research Council civil servant, assured me that officials would guide me through it all.

So I set out from my sister's early the next afternoon, trying to distract myself with fellow bus passengers' comings and goings or an idle flipping through of a newspaper somebody had left behind at her stop. It was a soothingly long way. We'd planned it so that I would arrive early. They'd given me clear directions to a second bus from downtown. Oodles of time to stew!

A small coffee-hut caught my eye – stools, counter, coffee-maker, tray of buns and cookies, one shirt-sleeved proprietor behind the cash, and one small TV facing the stools. A space-launch was on the TV screen. I easily joined the excited talk with a couple of others watching – one courteously switched to English for my sake. At the hour of doom, I felt warm-hearted and hopeful, catching the right bus easily.

The driver let me out on the roadside at the driveway into Rideau Hall. In my good shoes, I stumbled now and then on the gravel driveway. A doorman guided me to a cloakroom just off the entry. When I reappeared I was ushered to my place where, with a surge of genuine delight, I saw that Anne Hébert, herself, would be seated at my right. We exchanged nervous smiles. I watched the others being led up to where I would go to be offered a handshake and a brief conversation with Governor General Georges Vanier. When my turn came, the medal was presented with congratulations, as was a beautiful leather-bound copy of my book. Thank-yous murmured, I was ushered over to a different seat to sit with relieved others.

A stand-up reception followed the ceremony. Trays of wine and goodies circulated, but every time one of us was about to sip or bite into something, a camera-man's 'excuse me', and flash, interrupted. The Governor General stood among us; I could not concentrate on his conversation, for Anne Hébert and he spoke in French, and I was tongue-tied in either language every time someone courteously included me. I endured until dispersing seemed in order.

By the time I was back in my outdoor clothes, everybody had been whisked away. Ah well, I knew the bus stop. My knees as shaky as my good shoes in the gravel, I managed the walk out the driveway to the bus and the trip to the Hotel Chateau Laurier, where I inquired about the room where before-dinner drinks were being served, found it, and arrived just as the bar closed and guests were being led into the adjoining dining room. Not again! I snatched a drink from the last tray being carried away, downed it in a gulp, and followed the others into an elegant narrow room sprinkled with dutiful civil servants and the few awardees, distributed singly or in couples.

Wine glasses and water glasses were filled. The first speech was a formal welcome, I think. I cannot remember who sat on my left or right, halfway down the table, or any of the initial talk. Whenever a food waiter came, a wine server followed. I was too nervous to cope with the various dainties, though I did try to do as others did when I could make out what they were doing. The wine helped. In fact, by the time the toasts were made, and the several speeches, I was blissfully unconcerned.

Others around the table, I believe, froze with dismay at one point. One of the long speeches about the initiating of the Governor General's Awards got lugubrious in tone, because a civil servant who had just died, whose name and fame I really did respect, was included in the history, with a hushed word or two of tribute. I laughed out loud! Impossible ever to explain the elements that came together to provoke that minor explosion. When I was finally free to leave, I wrapped up for the street and the bus trip back to Mary's. The children were long asleep, but Mary and Frank fed me toast and coffee, and let me talk myself down, and it was all over.

I am not pleased to have to confess my gauche, unappreciative, my awkward, yes angry attitudes that day. I wonder if any other writer has ever been so apprehensive as to behave inappropriately and mess up his high moment. The experience forewarned me to go with a friend in 1991, when *No Time* was given the award. I found the experience much different. Perhaps subsequent planning had even taken my duck-out-of-water day into account. Or perhaps it was I who had changed.

Reflective after Ottawa, I was in an unsettled frame of mind. My father's death was clearly on the horizon. Mother, blind and alone, miles from shopping, the prospect of my moving to Galt, perhaps finding work in Preston or Waterloo but having to learn to drive a car: certainly a significant shift from my daily life's old axis seemed inevitable. The prospect was stimulating in some ways, but unnerving, like the morning after a minor earthquake. The familiar assignments continued, one of them casual hours when fresh proofs arrived from the Bollingen for the ongoing Coleridge project.

One day I was reading in Kay Coburn's office when other duties involved her with a visitor there. She asked me to take the copy and proof sheets (books were still typeset in those days) and find a corner downstairs in the Victoria College ladies' cloakroom. There was space at a large table; one or two women were reading in easy chairs near the window. It was quiet even when students came and went (the washroom opened off this large room). Soon I was concentrating as well as up in the office.

And then I became aware of someone standing silently right across the table. Forced to take notice, I looked up and saw black eyes intent upon me, in a little face with lurking mischievousness in the features. She *was* waiting to speak. 'Do you know the joy of knowing the Lord Jesus?' she asked. I was exasperated. 'I know the theory. And, as you can see, I am busy,' and I returned to my work. But she did not leave, and my conscience became uneasy. I was not naturally unkind, I told myself, and need not have been so dismissive. So I looked up again, expecting her to look downcast. But her face shone! 'I never *have* been beset by doubt!' she said admiringly. Then she wrote an address on a slip of paper. 'There are services every Sunday evening at this church,' she said. 'Come and see if you like it.' I accepted the address and she left.

The location on her note was only a few blocks from Washington Avenue. I had moved back there, to an identical room in a different house along the block. (My friend Isabel had taken another apartment by then, the hippie sixties having hit Hazelton, changing it from a shabby backwater to a Bohemian cauldron of excitement, thus bringing about some hubbub and steep increases in rent). A diary-entry* from November 6, 1962, describes a strange experience I had in this new Washington Avenue room:

> Woke at 6:00 – mouse-rustling? I went to the roof-door, expecting a small-sized bird tugging a paper-bag, perhaps, or a miniature squirrel, but saw nobody. A scarf-silk blue began, red-eye sun, & it dawned that the pear-tree – to date green but sere – was losing its leaves, as one event. No breeze.... A cold air, the sun rising, and by 6:45 the tree leafless, although I believe I wakened for the beginning of this rustling demission.

---

* No diary is listed in the University of Manitoba Avison fonds, and no diary has turned up elsewhere.

Sunday morning, late, was party time for campus habitués, and I often passed that church at Spadina and Harbord on my way to some graduate's quarters, usually with the bottle one contributed when possible. The entering flock I passed seemed to me quaintly, or over-carefully, attired – a new breed, unlike the United Church faithful I remembered from my father's church thirty years earlier at a time when most people had been automatic churchgoers.

Perhaps the idea of a stalwart minority, be the current culture what it may, became intriguing. Two years after the ladies' lounge episode, I finally mounted the stone steps and entered the big doors of Knox Presbyterian Church. I brought my own tiny Bible, and chose a place to sit in the centre section, about a quarter of the way down. It occurred to me that here were the people I had known in public school, as distinct from the exclusively academic group I had been working with for years. For months I came and went, reading the prophecies in the Book of Ezekiel when proceedings did not engage my attention (a literary equivalent of Picasso, in ancient times!).

The sermons merited a respectful hearing. 'Dr William Fitch', the bulletin said: his doctorate in the humanities was from Edinburgh University. The youngest of several brothers, as I later learned, Dr Fitch had the warmth and liveliness that come of being well loved in childhood. He unravelled passages of Scripture, making the context clear, and he focused with forceful conviction on the relevance of his chosen text, in language that was lively and precise. One of the Sunday morning party group ran into me in the library and asked if I'd been away. No. Where *had* I been? 'I've been to church.' 'You've been to *what*?!' Another unnerving shift was being felt, in relationship.

At the church, I came and went alone, happily unchallenged. Once when the minister shook hands at the door, he gave me a direct look and greeted me too, without asking my name. Finally, leaving the service one time, I stopped a woman outside and said: 'I keep hearing about faith in there. You people have it. I don't. What am I supposed to do?' She suggested I make an appointment through his secretary and ask the minister. In due course I did.

Dr Fitch tried to pinpoint my question. Did I know … historical, textual, Old Testament backgrounds? I did. I explained my upbringing. 'Your questions are not for information, then,' he said. 'Go home and read and reread the Gospel of John – daily.' This I dutifully did, first thing each morning. The text was to me like shapes and colours that conveyed little meaning until I had plodded along for thirteen chapters.

Early on the morning of January 4, 1963, dressed for work as usual, I read on. 'You believe in God, believe also in Me' (John 14:1). I did believe in God. Whoever had spoken, the 'Me' – it was not visual, but not a mere feeling – that Person was impingingly present, before me. Not even questioning this strange visitation, I spoke: 'If I believe in You, You will take over. I'll believe, but oh, don't take the poetry. It's all I've got left.' An ancient poet describes the confrontation: 'Put me in remembrance; let us contend together. State your case' (Isaiah 43: 26). It infuriated me to feel that my 'case' was weakened and about to crumble. Finally I hurled the Bible across the room and said, 'Okay, take the poetry too!'

I think I expected to lose my identity then. But what happened was odd. On the cleared desktop, what looked like iron filings appeared, all joggled about, until they began to arrange themselves in a design – angles, arcs, curving lines. After a few moments the desk was its plain, old surface again, cluttered with papers.

With a glance at my watch, I firmly stood up, collected coat and bag, and left for my daily assignment, resolutely blanking out the morning's events. But the new direction declared itself bit by bit. My five senses were noticeably quickened. Creative ideas abounded. I appreciated friends afresh but, to my surprise, I found I could side with an unpopular spokesman, if necessary. In fact, a new design had come into my life, like that iron-filing display taking shape on the desk!

Moreover, the morning after that initial experience of Christ's presence, my scripture reading was broken into by the need to write a new poem. It came fluidly, arriving at a first draft without blots or second thoughts. It was 'A Story'. More and more poems piled up over the months after that, and, astonishingly, when Denise Levertov telephoned from New York's Norton Press, I had enough for *The Dumbfounding* (1966). Norton wanted to shake off their identity as publisher of only technical and scientific works, and had asked Denise to assemble six poets' manuscripts they could put out under their imprint. When she asked me for a manuscript, I warned her that these new poems were not like earlier ones, and that she might not like the emphasis on my new-found faith. She wanted them anyway. This opened new ranges in our subsequent correspondence and, whenever we met, in our conversation. (She did not mind the change.)

In the days when the Presence first became real to me, any minute might bring a new discovery. Once, on some job, for instance, I was asked to take the minutes at a crucial meeting. With my amateur version of shorthand, I concentrated all morning on the verbatim report. When the participants took their break at noon, the chairman asked me if I could have a transcription of the minutes ready for the afternoon session. By the time I had typed my notes, I could barely wash up and sharpen pencils before the group gathered again. On his way in, the chairman asked me for his copy and soon we were all off again at the same pace. Pangs of hunger, or the onset of self-pity, made me inwardly reach for help and I was suddenly pleased to think 'I am fasting, and I can offer it as private praise.'

The days and weekends were unpredictable in this period. As much time as I could free from earlier commitments, I spent in Galt. Mother did not drive. Shopping was possible by bus without losing too much bedside time. Now that my father was really ill, he was quiet in spirit, uncomplaining, and frighteningly patient. He still cared about his garden: whenever I arrived, his first request would be for me to deal with the trees and plants, whichever most needed water.

A Dutch woman was helping Mother with housework. Her husband had been an organist in the Netherlands but, as immigrants, he and his family cheerfully took on whatever work could be found. One son, Dick, became a stalwart friend of my father. He would come over whenever he could, step out of his boots at the door, stand in sock feet at the bedside, just off the front hall, and take orders for urgent requirements in the vegetable and flower gardens. Only the blue spruces and the shrubbery were left for me to do – the three-pail drink, poured from the slope above the old tree to 'open the ground', gently first, and then to fill the whole root area. The nesting robins got along without our help, just outside my father's bedroom window.

My parents knew that many weeks earlier I had accepted an invitation to participate in Warren Tallman's Vancouver Poetry Conference. No, they counselled, don't cancel it now. And come back with new things to tell us about the West Coast. It will have changed since we last saw it. I let them persuade me. The conference was designed to introduce new American poets in a venture parallel to the Toronto series Raymond Souster had organized after the war. Irving Layton happened to be seated beside me on the plane. We had often met at events, or as fellow guests in someone's home. Now, one on one, we felt friendly, but ready for private space and for quiet through those hours aloft. There was no need to talk.

How vivid is that flight in memory! At takeoff, unbidden, came the metaphor of my father's approaching takeoff, a more exhilarating one, for he would not be crashing, or arriving at any airport, but out-distancing earth and sky to reach his destination. I wonder if it's true, as I felt then, that to such a person, who does not fear death, there is nonetheless a kind of nervousness at doing something radically new, without fellow venturers, without any credible rehearsal.

It felt chilly at the Vancouver airport. The student residence at UBC, where I was billeted, seemed to me insubstantial and draughty. But I had packed warm clothes, remembering that the climate there would be a happy escape from the summer heat at home. My hostess for dinner that first evening was Professor Helen Sonthoff. The other guest was Jane Rule, from the United States, who later became a widely read Canadian novelist. In hindsight, the evening blurs a little because of the time difference – it was already my Ontario bedtime. Helen understood and drove me back to the residence before the hour was really very late.

Fortunately the first session, next morning, was mainly an outline of the programme: open discussion sessions among the invited poets, seminars offered by some of the guest poets (I was not required to do anything except attend, if I chose, as an auditor), then one evening's public reading by each poet from his or her work, followed by questions and comments from the floor. The guests were briefly introduced, packets handed out, and that was all until the afternoon.

That first day, it may have been, I was driven into the city for a delightful coffee with George and Angela Bowering. Her feather-touch of wit, the gift of listening she showed that day, our instant ease with one another, were unusual, peaceably low-keyed, an established human contact amongst all three of us that would remain undemandingly lively over miles and years. Contact with George survived Angela's death, which inspired 'Bereavement and Postlude' (*Momentary Dark*).

To this day, I quake to remember the start of the solemn panel discussion. There we sat on a large stage, with a theatre-sized audience of conference registrants. This first free-for-all session took place with only part of the U.S. contingent: Olson and Ginsberg had not yet arrived (if I remember aright). A registrant put this question: 'What makes a poet's language distinctive?' We all fell silent, trying to pin it down, then attempted answers. *Not* just affection for words, which is common to all good writers; *not* necessarily a matter of cadence, formal structures, rhythm. The answer that came to me, forced out of minutes of dismissing options, was new to me too: 'It is saying "I am here and not not-there".'

Robert Creeley instantly identified with the formulation; this made later informal times among that platform group less strained for me. The Americans were old friends whose conversation was in a context of many prior explorings of ideas and literary discoveries. I was aware of being separate, Canadian, more formally dressed, and often in awe. The great gain from such discomfort was the fact that Denise Levertov and, oddly, Charles Olson, perceived this. They often manoeuvred me back into the circle of talk, inconspicuously.

Each invited poet at that conference was booked in a large auditorium for a solo reading, to which anyone could come and, as I saw at the first reading I attended, many people did come. Professor Warren Tallman, the organizer, had his own following on campus. In addition, he had arranged good publicity for public events during the conference. Between sessions and at mealtimes, the talk among ourselves made it evident that Robert Duncan and Denise Levertov were intrigued by current ideas that somehow bothered me.

> And when we are deserted there,
> when the rustling electric has passt thru the air,
> once more we begin in the blind and blood throat
> the African catches; and Desdemona, Desdemona
> like a demon wails within our bodies, warns
> against the towering Moor of self and then
> laments her passing from him.
>
> Robert Duncan, 'An African Elegy'

Or

... working in words I am an escapist.... But I want every part of the actual world involved in my escape. I bring the laws that bound me into an aerial structure in which they are unbound as outlines of a prison unfolding.

Robert Duncan, *Bending the Bow* (1968)

All this seemed free-wheeling and speculative; was it the sixties ethos, or the 'post-Christian' climate? In any case, the prospect of including 'The Story', clearly based on a familiar parable of Jesus, and 'The Dumbfounding' in my solo reading which lay ahead, made me defensive in advance.

Only eight months earlier, my stance had been theirs. The shift in reality, that January 4th morning, was merely a first step, not one I took until the living Jesus drew near, past evading. I knew by now that one normally proceeds differently in conversion, first repenting, then receiving forgiveness and embracing new life as a believer. But it had not been so, for me. Believing in Jesus now unfixed all my prior values. They began to shift backwards – like those iron filings on the desk. The Bible newly speaking to me, too, gradually gave me my first clue: 'repentance' involved recognizing that the 'morally good person' (I'd thought that described me!) was shown up by this Other One, this humble, lovely Person. A truer picture was emerging. The truth was given gently: at age forty-five, any radical all-at-once revelation might have unbalanced me. Therefore, now in Vancouver, I was not equipped to defend the faith, only to testify to it. What I did not realize was that, in those unsettling sixties, young people were finding a new, sometimes frightening, freedom, so the timing of that conference made for a surprising receptivity, open to my new awareness too.

Charles Olson, the senior poet among us, would not hear a *no* when he invited me to a good meal before my reading. He urged me to accept a bit of brandy with my coffee. It would help, he claimed. It didn't hurt! I read from *Winter Sun* that evening, and from *The Dumbfounding*. The audience seemed friendly. Outdoors, after the event was over, Allen Ginsberg came out to the crest of that UBC entrance-hill, and greeted me out of the darkness. His words I cannot remember, but I felt that he had received my reading with a generous heart. This sent me home to the dormitory in peace.

The next morning I was just assembling my backpack for the day's events when Helen Sonthoff knocked on my door. 'There is a message for you to call home,' she said. Mother simply said: 'Wilson (my father's name) has died.' I said I'd come back, and Helen helped arrange the flight, my excuses, transportation to the airport, even the final details of my packing. The plane went to Toronto, of course. I decided I'd figure out the quickest way to go on to Galt. But instead, the United Church minister of my parents' Galt church was waiting at the airport to drive me home. He and my father had read and exchanged books over the years, enjoyed talking about them together and respected each other. His wife had gone to stay with Mother until we arrived.

Mother told me how it had been. 'He got up and shaved, put on his clean underwear and a shirt, then went back to lie on the bed.' She offered to bring his breakfast, but he said, 'You eat and then bring your tea in here.' She was sitting on the side of his bed with her tea when he breathed out suddenly, his head rolled to one side, and he was gone. 'I was almost ready for it,' Mother said. 'Often at night he'd be so still that I'd reach over to see whether he felt cold.' My father had wanted no more hospital time. The doctor said he was within ten days of needing a stoma, for breathing; but his heart gave out first, so he had his wish. It was a family funeral, before notices were placed in Ottawa, Toronto and local papers. He had written out the funeral service: scriptures, prayer. The minister who met my plane carried out his instructions. My father was buried in the Toronto Necropolis, in the city where he was born.

There were quiet days in Galt after the rest of the family left: one morning with a lawyer since the estate was small and the handwritten will carefully explicit – house and (joint) bank account 'to Mabel, my wife'. But there was no direction about the wall of books in that study with the fireplace. When visitors came, and many did come from former churches in Guelph, Toronto, even Ottawa, Mother invited each of them to choose 'any of Wilson's books' they would like. The local minister was given first choice: he took one, but asked to be given any residue for his church library. We put the house up for sale, and began sorting and clearing out.

Mother set the schedule, methodically. She knew when it was time to book the moving van, coordinating the date with the rental of a two-bedroom apartment my sister-in-law had found for us. I had sublet my Washington Avenue room to Mrs Polanyi's son-in-law, then a graduate student in History at the university. He happily agreed to keep the room. Arranging my final move-out was simple.

Was everything happening *to* me, not by mutual consent? No. I had been full of schemes for keeping the Galt house, earning locally, remaking life there. But Mother was definite. She knew that I had applied for graduate school in October. Foreseeing the need for new teachers as the 'baby boom' generation entered post-secondary schools, the provincial government was offering a deal to graduates with a B.A. who could pass a qualifying exam in their field, mine being English literature. Ontario would help with fees in return for a qualified registrant's commitment to teach for at least two years in an Ontario university. Ambitious for me as always, Mother opted in, as it were.

Only on our last day in Galt did I note her own way of dealing with one loss by embracing another: the loss of the only home privately chosen and loved in my parents' married lives. Indelibly vivid to this day is her erect, forward-looking body language in the car, as my sister-in-law drove us away for the last time. The lingering look back until we rounded the hill corner was mine. The For Sale sign was still on the lawn. (It comforted me and perhaps gratified Mother when, before long, young Dutch neighbours became the new owners.)

The piano mover was to put Mother's piano into the new apartment at Avenue Road and St Clair; I was left there to supervise this first stage of the move. The main load would arrive the next day. It was intriguing to prowl those hardwood floors, from room to room, examine the empty shelves in kitchen and bathroom, eye the high narrow windows (it was in a half-basement at the quiet back of the old building) and finally sit, somewhat disconsolately, against a bare wall. The piano arrived finally, and I went on to Ted's for dinner and a night's sleep.

Nest-making was left out of my makeup. A workplace was all that a home had ever meant to me before now. But Ted and Ruth knew how to accommodate Mother's preferences, and soon made the new place habitable. We were still emptying boxes of linen and crates of dishes and kitchenware the morning of the Ontario qualifying exam.

I arrived at the exam hall in time to find a crowd in the courtyard outside, humming with tension, many of them desperately checking this and that in notebooks or in their copies of *The Oxford Companion to English Literature.* I was glad to have allowed barely time enough; I felt like a sleepwalker. When we were admitted, divested of whatever we'd brought along, and given the examination papers, my chief feeling was relief to be sitting down for two hours, or whatever length of time it was.

When course work is far back in your past, you are probably just as well to feel detached and submissive to a peculiar process. The true-false questions were fortunately optional; even the law of probability would not have helped me enough there. Some of the essay questions hinged on periods and books I did recognize. Getting marks on exams had been dishonest because I could always string a good line, with enough specific content to pin down a flow of the pen here and there, suggestive of ampler illustrations at the ready, given time. Examiners must early become aware of students' vagaries. My hit-and-miss method of coping with scrutiny is consistent with my jackdaw ingathering of learning in post-student years. In other words, I was not a scholar.

Mother and I jointly paid for the new ménage. Our advertisement for daytime help emphasized 'to read to, and prepare lunch for, an elderly lady'. The person who applied and stayed for years (Mrs McCormack) had been widowed in Belgium when Germany invaded, had somehow reached Canada, ultimately married a doctor here, but was now again a widow. She read tirelessly and well. There were breaks for conversation, I am sure. Preparing lunches for two would have been my job, but Mrs M. had had surgery for stomach cancer and was restricted to a mixture she brought and stirred up for herself, while Mother had a sandwich and soup. The two of us had dinner at day's end.

Deer Park United Church was just across the street, and Mrs Stanley Russell, who lived in a front apartment, asked me to help her over on Sunday mornings. Her husband's death had clouded her memory, perhaps. I remember her muttering, as she clutched my forearm, 'Just look at their heads and the names will come.' It seemed natural for Mother to become a member there. In the evenings I went back to Knox. When Mother confessed that the centre-aisle architecture, cold stone, and lack of friends made her wish she could feel more at home in Deer Park, a friend at Knox offered drives if she wanted to come. Dr Fitch made her welcome on the first visit, people who knew me introduced themselves, and she was comfortable there.

ACADEMIA

Evenings would have been long for Mother if I had buried myself in books right after dinner. Her bedroom was just across the hall, so at intervals I'd read aloud some assigned text. Edmund Spenser became her favourite. I remember once puzzling over a reference in 'The Faerie Queene', having lost track of a minor point. 'Oh! You remember: it's that part about Britomart, earlier,' Mother prompted. She was right!

That whole first year was a pleasure. The Spenser course, which appealed to my ear, made it glorious fun, but for that very reason I found it hard to read Spenser for content. His rhythms, the shape and sound of his words, so dominated that it was like examining embroidery work from the wrong side. The sounds convinced me that Spenser must have had a space between his two front teeth, and unconsciously enjoyed the airflow over his lips as he read aloud or spoke his lines for the pleasure of the sound, as poets still close to troubadour times may have done. (This is speculation, not scholarship!)

Meticulous detail, with a somehow detached delight, marked Professor Endicott's approach to John Donne and Thomas Browne, especially *Urn Burial,* in another seminar that year. He led our small group at a light fantastic pace, helping to establish for us the historical context (much of it Church history), ornamented with lively anecdotal accounts of the bishops (often subjects of a poet's dedicatory verse, sometimes even patrons of a writer). In that group was an earnest Anglican youth doing prerequisites before studying theology towards ordination. He intruded his theological preoccupation into literary discussions, thus heightening our sense of what religious persecution had been like in the past. Donne, we learned, had been brought up Roman Catholic, but, after his brother was imprisoned and died far too young of 'prison fever', deliberately became an Anglican. 'Too much death' was his sage explanation. (Bunyan must have had a hardier constitution in his day.)

Professor Endicott had lived in China and England, his Canadian parents having gone as missionaries to the Far East. Some glancing information led him to mention this background. Years later, through friends of my parents, I met his brother, Jim Endicott. He owned a cottage in the Kawartha Lakes and, one summer when as usual I had no holiday plans, invited me to his private island resort. I remember Mr Endicott waiting for me at a dock. I recall his courteous help when I stepped down into his boat, and our swift, noisy arrowing across to another dock – his 'camp'. There I met his wife and another visitor, a young Chinese lad.

Everybody was welcoming, but I was discomfited because most of the people were bare naked. 'Here some of us enjoy nudity,' Mr Endicott explained, 'but it's optional. Just do whatever you choose.' Even just contemplating afternoons sitting naked on the grass or rocks, chatting or sharing a meal, unnerved me. I put off 'until the morrow' any decision whether to try to fit in or to flee in fully clad anonymity. My host was every bit the same gentlemanly, friendly enabler next morning when he steered his launch across to the dock near a bus depot, and helped me find out what time the next bus would come.

Miserably embarrassed by my awkward discourtesy in leaving, sorry that my thank-yous sounded so hollow, stiff to the core with unwelcome rigidity, I nonetheless did not regret leaving. In my adult years, I have found that any major impact takes weeks and weeks of inner shifting and adapting – accomplished willy-nilly, and irrevocably, but not by any directing or managing recognizable as mine. (In this instance, the question of adjustment to nudists' ways never again impinged, nor has been made.)

We studied the Romantic poets in another course that first year. It was a seminar with Milton Wilson who later encouraged me as a poet by including my work in his anthology *Poetry of Mid-century 1940–1960.* The sounds of Romantic lyrics, by contrast with sixteenth- and seventeenth-century poetry, again preoccupied me and led into my M.A. thesis. When I read Byron's *Don Juan,* with its jolting shift away from the lyrical mode that had marked the period generally and his own early verse, I was fascinated. What had come into his verbal culture to create this break with tradition? Since the newspapers of the day had begun to report society's scandals about him, I decided that Byron must have read at least some of them, picking up journalese with a natural ear that affected his poetic style thereafter. It was fun speculating, but giving evidence in support of the thesis meant hours with microfilm of nineteenth-century English newspapers that jiggled on a black screen and gave me eyestrain for weeks.

Saddled with increasingly deadly studying and essay writing, I hung on by finding a balancing focus. Knox Church was supporting a downtown mission, Evangel Hall; I volunteered there during my free hours. It impressed me that the Superintendent and his wife, both young and even farther in background from inner city life than I (from my brief contact with the poor in Calgary days), chose to live among the welfare families, raising their children, who were born while they worked there, in the same streets and schools. I learned that coal delivery was much slower when the order came from a 'bad' address, and that grocery prices were higher, but quality lower, in such an area.

At first I helped sort clothing sent in from churches. In time I met people who came to the worship service at the mission, and I attended a Bible study with them during the week. It was a breath of fresh air after the campus, helping me to persevere toward my promised two years' teaching-in-an-Ontario-college. I began praying that, for Mother's sake, it would somehow be a *Toronto* college, and it was: Scarborough College, University of Toronto. But first there was more course work and then five successive days of written examinations, from Beowulf to Modern English literature, and an oral examination which focused on the thesis interest, though not exclusively.

The Milton course with Professor A.S.P. Woodhouse was a primary objective in my second year, and I was early in registering. But that was the year Professor Woodhouse died suddenly. He had been a pivotal figure in University College's English Department, attracting students from abroad and giving the University of Toronto English programme widespread recognition. His loss was felt keenly in wider circles by many scholars, as well as by hopeful students like me.

By the time his registrants knew they had another major course to find, most of the graduate seminars were full. As a last resort, with Kay Coburn's work in mind, I managed to find a place in a new, young Coleridgean's seminar: he told me that he had done two Ph.D's in a notable English university, and that he was 'in Mensa', the group of people with identified, tested high intelligence quotients. (From World War II experience, I knew there were many equally bright but more modest geniuses out there, whose verbal skills may not have been up to the standards of word-oriented IQ tests, but who excelled in original conceptions or in practical application of them. Harley Parker had highlighted this, and other artists in his circle told lively stories to establish its truth.)

It will be clear that I found the Coleridge course disappointing! In fact, throughout a year's meetings, S.T.C.'s prose, lectures, poems, were never once touched. We were assigned endless reports on 'secondary sources' – books and articles *about* Coleridge, *about* his influences, etc. When we pressed for an escape back to the actual texts, the professor read it as a revolt, and marked us all at the same, lowest possible, passing grade.

An 'outside minor' was required of us, a course outside English literature, preferably involving a new language. Again my plan was first-rate but did not work out. With the encouragement of a lively young professor of Classics, I had decided to launch on a doctoral thesis examining certain figures of speech in translations of Homer from Alexander Pope to Richard Lattimore – a thesis on poetics, but by a back door. The professor would design a private, one-year course in which I could pick up enough Greek to deal with Homeric figures of speech. (I had already had some private tutoring from a recent immigrant from England who responded when I ran a newspaper want ad for such help with learning ancient Greek. That was all I could build on now.)

But my prospective sponsor was snatched by sudden death, a heart attack. The news horrified me when, one morning, I found the whole university in shock. Nobody else in the Classics department would back such a thesis unless I did several years of prerequisite Greek. I began to hope that a thesis might be evaded altogether. This pleased me. The kind of free-flowing prose I had trusted in while writing the initial qualifying examination would not do in a doctoral thesis. There, every proposition would have to be pinned down by solid, assembled evidence, amply anchored by footnotes. All scholars go through this once, before working through to the freedom to write well, enjoyably and still authoritatively, but it would have been a torment to me, as a writer. The Ontario Government's subsidy could be earned without the thesis, so I eventually abandoned the idea of doing one, and thus of earning the doctorate.

In fact, in the Sargasso Sea of preparation for comprehensive exams and the oral, the final course, my 'outside minor' turned out to be a bright spot. I chose Old Norse. The students who arrived for our first meeting were congenial, and we learned that a visiting professor from Denmark, Herman Palssohn, would be our instructor. He was young, he wore a burgundy vest under his blazer, and he said we would *read* the Old Norse text we had been assigned! (Not a word about learning this new language's distinctive grammar, etc.)

We turned to the page number where an Edda began in this alien-looking text. The young Dane flicked on a tape-recorder: a deep-voiced Icelandic man, solemnly reading our text, was careful while laying the plot's groundwork, and gradually became passionately involved in later dark, murderous doings – as we did too, reading fairly easily thanks to his beautiful identification with the words on our pages. (Some knowledge of German was a help to me in following the Old Norse text.) We came away from this first exposure delighted with our good fortune.

As the young Dane described the cramped winter bunkhouse, with a crowd sitting along the lower bunks, one flickering lamp, and the storyteller 'reading' the tale, we learned to picture sagas at source. The silent listeners caught the rhythms and began to sway backwards and forwards in time, just a bit, then more and more energetically while intensity built until all were rocking vigorously, as the reader's pace quickened and his voice throbbed. This deep listening influenced a *Momentary Dark* poem called 'Songs'.

There came a day when all of northeastern North America was plunged into darkness by some hydro mishap, affecting New York City and Toronto alike. We were deep in Old Norse when it happened. While we waited for the lights to come on, the professor told us about the bunkhouse audiences. But when the lights still did not come on, he asked the student nearest the classroom door to open it and stand with his free hand out: then each of us was to find the hand beside us and follow the leader around the table, out to the stairway banister. It was three flights down. We negotiated together, down, out the door and through the campus to Bloor Street. An exhilarated student in a white leather jacket was directing rush hour traffic in the middle of the Bloor Street–Avenue Road intersection. Since Mother was in the dark both with hydro and without it, I didn't need to worry, calmly caught a bus and was home at the usual hour.

Preparing for the written comprehensive examinations and the oral would have been dreary had my months of review and study not taken place on the same lower level of the old University Library where bp Nichol was 'stack-boy'. His job was to reshelve returned volumes from endless carts brought down from the front desk. We met as fellow poets, and played the days away (his version appears in *bp Nichol Comics* and mine in the written interview with Sally Ito, in Tim Bowling's *Where the Words Come From*). One thing I learned from graduate school: enjoyment must be part of work, or it's essentially a waste of time. For me, that is. If things don't light up some way, they die on my page, my pen runs dry, and the discarded pages prove not worth rewriting or revising.

In those graduate years, one fellow student stood out. Peter Such met me in front of Hart House, in shock, the day President Kennedy was shot, and shocked me in turn with the news. He is a man I had liked ever since a recent late autumn noon hour when students were spilling out of doorways, and the sudden thick first snow that was falling had already furred over grass and walkways. White everywhere dazzled us. One African exchange student stood on the path, aghast. Peter leapt into the little drifts, shouting jubilantly: 'It's snow, you black bastard!' and began a snowball fight with him that both relished. Peter's English childhood made him free of race consciousness, and the African became one of his friends.

Peter groaned under the degree requirements though he grimly persevered to the end. 'You've got some tank of gas the rest of us haven't,' he said one evening. 'What is it?' I tried to explain that my priority was Christian truth: because Jesus mattered most, He put everything else into perspective, and helped me cope. 'You didn't strike me as blinkered,' he commented, withdrawing his interest. But then he came back to the fact that I used my study time placidly while he stewed, resented, resisted, even though he knew this wasted energy. 'I can understand people having faith because of the good bits, but ...' Then he mentioned the war years, walking a curb in London alone, longing for his dad to be back.

I had raised the same caveat decades back, when Nanny, my father's mother, would sweetly portray the Lord in terms of His handiwork in flowers and songbirds and trees. 'Yes, and how about the rest? Hurricanes, the thirties drought, famine areas, floods?' Thanks to the thoughts Nanny quickened, I'd been preparing a long time for Peter's yes-but.

An omniscient God knows good *and* evil – as man chose to too, in the Garden of Eden. An omniscient God comprehends, encompasses, the evil as well as the good, but, unlike us, He knows how and at what moment to cope without interfering with our interim strategies, or our shared responsibility for most of them! If Jesus went on relying on God as His Father in the face of people's murderous stupidity about Him in His days on earth, it made simple sense for me to rely on God for getting through the graduate school's hoop-jumps, since they stood between me and the ultimate goal of teaching (and earning a living). By the end of the conversation Peter was still restive, but he was guardedly friendly during the rest of our student days together.

Poetry, I was concluding, was a poor vehicle for what is called 'apologetics'. I tried to remember Peter's reservations when something moved me to write as I read a passage of Scripture. The passage might stay with me through days, and assertively gather new facets, until writing a poem was the only way to be clear of it. Such poems can have an angularity that comes of awkwardness and inhibits the proper sense of collaboration between reader and writer.

Priorities that put schoolwork into perspective came naturally to me as a student over forty, even making the work an escape from confining duties, whereas to young candidates who were continuing straight on from their undergraduate years in the same academic buildings, such priorities were no longer fresh. Dogged disciplined work had to steady them in rebellious moments. For me, it was almost all pleasure. Being in the library daily, I let myself be tempted. This note turned up among stray papers from those days:

> Books sometimes fall off the shelves into my hands. On my way to the section of shelves where I was supposed to collect an addition to my carrel-shelf collection, a low-voiced title stopped me: *What to Listen For in Music.* The writer was Aaron Copland. Oddly, tears came to my eyes at the thought that a composer of his stature should reach out, not to other musicians but to an outsider, the kind of person who is caught in a concert audience as part of some social obligation and feels it's all over her head. Copland encourages people to believe in their considerable innate ability, and to discover that music can enhance all that they already are.

There are risks in indulging in random reading. When the time came for the Comprehensive Oral Examination of me, alone, with three faculty specialists asking the questions, I found I was answering 'I don't know' once, twice, too often? 'Matthew Arnold on the Anglican Church?' is one of the questions that stands out in memory as a block of blank cement before my eyes: I had never read him on that. No use faking. By a squeak, those three professors kindly gave me a pass.

Afterwards as I walked towards the coffee-shop, the sidewalk under me felt like a trampoline. At coffee I met the candidate who had preceded me and who was in deep gloom. He too had been pinned down on facts that escaped him, texts he'd skimmed, or neglected, among the six centuries the questions could cover. But the examiners had deferred him; he would have to repeat the oral. He explained that it was because some questions stumped him and he had tried to fake the answers – the wrong way for a future teacher to deal with a classroom situation, hard though it may be for a teacher to admit to a student 'I don't know, but I'll find out and answer you next time.' This may not be relevant to an autobiography, but it stays here as a tip to doctoral students facing orals in another day.

Some moments stand in memory in their own right, distinct from the person or persons incidentally participating. Lloyd Haynes had been a familiar part of our undergraduate English group. Because of the Depression we were small enough in number that we all knew one another. Many years later, around the time I was teaching at Scarborough College, I was startled to see Lloyd at the door one evening. 'Can you give me half an hour or so?' 'Come in.' 'No,' he said, 'I brought the car. Can you come out for a little while now?' Mother was in bed and agreed to the idea. I fixed the telephone, so she would not be tempted to get up and answer it, and left.

At the waterfront, in those days, there were wooded grassy spots, small drive-in parks. Silent still, Lloyd opened the car doors. As we stood at the water's edge his introductory words were unemphatic. His only brother was needed to work on the family farm which was to be his one day. All the family had supported Lloyd's plan to use some of his savings to attend college, but when war broke out and his brother signed up, Lloyd had to take over the responsibility at home, suppressing hopes – not for a graduate degree, but for singing lessons! 'May I sing, this once? Now?' A nod was all he needed. In a fine lyrical tenor he went through a short repertoire of European art songs, folk songs and a modern one I cannot now identify.

Those electrifying few minutes rose and somehow enwrapped themselves then and there – for him too, I hope. Timeless moments of non-relational preciousness are rare, but enduring. Even writing this renews the living memory. We went home, quietly thanking each other at the same moment, and so laughed and said goodbye.

What happened the rest of the way, Lloyd? Farming? I still remember you stoutly declaring your love for every field and lane and fence-edge of that farm, but grudging the loss of a few scraps of time, in a busy season, to pause to notice a weed here, or a mingled fragrance there from a ditch just over the fence. 'In farming,' he said sadly, 'it all has to come down to every last penny, to the money.' My mind went to very gifted young writers who gradually seemed engulfed by 'business' when they had a young family depending on their earnings. Women writers in those years could better protect their privacy and their time.

It was a relief to finish graduate studies, 'all but the thesis', doubly so to be accepted on the English Department staff at Scarborough College, 1966. Twice a week I had to travel from St Clair Avenue to the downtown campus to catch the 7 a.m. special bus for the College. It made several stops along the way and would be filled long before the final stretch. Once, a female student passed out before we reached the last pick-up spot, standing safely wedged in an upright position and only perceived to be unconscious when she crumpled to the floor as other students began to disembark at the College. 'Morning Bus', in *sunblue,* was written on one of those early morning trips, on a note page balanced atop a pile of books on my lap.

The role of assistant professor was not mine for long enough to become really credible to me, although students seemed to identify person and role, as freshmen will, for whom everything is unaccustomed. The lectures in English 1-a, in an amphitheatre, called for careful planning. To drone on for an hour? Surely not! When towards the beginning of an early class someone asked, 'Will this be on the examination?' the reason for harassed note-taking became plain. 'I'll work out what you will need to remember for sure and put it on the board before class. You can copy that down for study notes. From then on we will be free to enjoy our text and explore it,' I replied.

The listening became different after that. In one Spenser lecture, I remember, I chose a few lines to read, to pin down the talk about poetry that classrooms engender. Electricity sparked among the listeners, palpably. 'What struck you all, suddenly, in that passage?' I asked. One word: 'shame'. What it meant to them had to be fitted in with what it meant to a Renaissance reader or writer. They talked it out a little, and then we could return to Spenser's text. The silent intercommunication when students react unpredictably must be heeded, or misreadings are inevitable. That morning taught me something about the poet's poem and its reader.

English 1-a was split into two amphitheatre-filling sections; therefore every lecture had to be repeated for the second group of students. One dreary session with group two taught me another lesson. As someone remarked in the astrakhan apple season, the first bite is best. The first apple is so good that you reach for another, but the second one will not be the same! A rejigging of material was the only way to meet 1-a's second section.

Seminar groups with first-year students were an eye-opener to me. After we introduced one another around the small table at our first session, I handed out copies of Marvell's 'Garden' so that we could explore it together. Each student, in turn, was to read aloud one stanza. This turned out to be a torment and an unforeseen embarrassment all 'round: many poor readers were exposed – all but two at that table who had been lifelong bookworms and therefore had suffered as browners. The others had full high school credits but had never been read to as children, I suspect, nor had they been required to read aloud at school. We kept at it over the weeks. They gained confidence in an unthreatening group, began to develop fluency and to read for the ear as well as the eye.

People have deplored plagiarism among university students. I did, too, at Scarborough. One young man came in, by appointment, to receive his essay and term marks. I had been dreading that meeting. He looked hopeful! I picked up his laboriously handwritten pages and asked him how he could expect a mark for someone else's essay (one I had recognized from its style, and easily found in the Scarborough library). He was indignant: 'It said all the things I'd thought as I read the text and could not express so clearly!' The innocence seemed genuine. I offered to give him an oral exam, then and there, and he earned a legitimate mark by remembering the text well and answering my questions in his own words. I found it helped students to write their own essays when I suggested that they find someone (not the teacher!) to write *to*: read and think, and then write as if to a younger sibling who wanted to know what they were studying.

That young man was not part of a different seminar group who sat grim-faced, with folded arms, one day when I came in. 'Please open to page so-and-so.' Dead silence. I waited. 'Have you a spokesman?' Someone blurted out that they didn't want to 'do that old book'; they wanted to talk about something that interested *them*. 'What topic had you in mind?' 'Well, for instance, *Catcher in the Rye*.' I asked whether we should go on to *Franny and Zooey* etc. too. No answer. I agreed that we should talk about what they had chosen, but said I had no need to introduce something they had already discovered themselves. What would we say about the book? Did anyone have any questions or comments? The rebellion dissolved, as did that session, but next time we went on with the course they had paid to take.

The brightest light in that group sat looking remote when we got back to work next day. He stayed behind afterwards. He was sorry, he said contritely, but he was withdrawing from the college and going back to his home in Northern Ontario. I asked whether there was illness in the family. He almost broke down when he replied 'No. It's just that the first snow fell as we sat here today, and nobody else noticed.' He was responsive not just to the natural world but to ideas and literature as well, and I felt confident that he would find his own time and place to resume studies somewhere, if not in a big city.

In contrast to that freshman seminar a fourth-year group excelled; in their own way, they kept me and one another interested and learning. In the 1960s, to 'prescribe' texts was to invite rebellion. These students wanted to create their own courses within the generous limits that the final examinations then permitted. It was no use, I could see, to impose preordained outlines, the very issue they delighted to protest. Fortunately, they invented a course that worked both in their interest and to their liking.

The seminar was to address one question, through both fall and spring terms of this graduating year: what is a poem? They let me work out with them the structure to be followed. Each week one student would offer a definition of a poem, basing it upon one text he had chosen from the assigned anthology. The other students would have a week's notice, so that there would be a common basis for discussion. Then the definition was to be tested by finding other poems it did not fit, not quite or, in the case of extreme examples, not at all. One volunteer agreed to lead off at the next seminar. And they all prepared by reading the same text. They read to get 'marks' for participating, and to focus on the piece they might choose to offer, in turn.

The definition was to be built upon the unchallenged elements in each presentation, which would be further refined and developed as the year went on. Most of the sessions were lively. At the end of the spring term, they decided: 'A poem is that creation, in words, that requires the same energy from the reader as from the writer' – my paraphrase, probably, but their conclusions tended that way and were carefully framed.

One name had been on my list for this seminar all year, but no one answering to it appeared. The college registrar's records showed him as a fourth-year registrant. His fees were paid up to date. He had even asked the office to have application forms for graduate school mailed to him. After inquiries at the office and consultation with the English department head, I left pressures about his non-appearance up to them. As a result, the student sent in a cassette of his readings and critical views of the anthology, to cover the whole year. We have all skipped classes at times as undergraduates, but this was exceptional. I left his mark up to others, and he did go on towards a master's degree the next year! The sixties were unsettling, but colourful!

Scheduled lectures and seminars left wide margins each week for preparation, marking, meeting students in interviews. Another English teacher drove back and forth; she offered me a ride back into the city some afternoons whenever our timetables permitted. Even though Mother had a pleasant companion those years, and was in reasonably good health, it was best to work at home and to be accessible at need. Twice a week, however, there was night school which kept me out until 11 p.m.: teachers working toward a degree or upgrading, motivated, on the whole, but jaded after a day in their own classrooms; and a few other adults working for credits towards a degree, interested and interesting to meet.

This new audience kept me fresh for the lectures. But another hour loomed ahead. The discussion part became hard to move along with people less venturesome than the young. In desperation I asked for, and was granted, a helper for the second hour's work; he was given some title – Lecturer? Assistant? He was a steel worker, a tremendous reader, who had availed himself of lectures in St Catharines but never sought a credit or a degree. The very terms were foreign to him.

How did we meet? Probably in libraries, usually standing to talk, for characteristically he moved from foot to foot, restless always, with a self-deprecating smile hovering around his lips. His intelligence was electric, original ideas sparked away at every brush with him. To my relief, he felt intrigued by the Scarborough night school challenge, and the department accepted him. The pay was nominal but welcomed by him at a transitional point in his life.

His first move was to create two sections for the non-lecture hour. He gave out half sheets of paper and asked that everyone sign them and write *one or two words* indicating a place where they liked to be or an occupation they enjoyed. Halfway through the lecture I asked whether the papers were ready, then he collected them and sat poring over them in a back row of the amphitheatre, arranging and rearranging, until the end of the first hour. By then he could read out the roll for each section, based on the mingling of personalities he thought likeliest to work well together. The students were amused by his method, but impressed to find it really worked. He stayed all year, then vanished again, though at intervals he sent me a page or so from something he was writing, prose pieces as arresting as his initial conversation had been when we first met. Somewhere about the world he must be quickening people still, for he was much younger than I.

The experience of meeting students, expanding my horizons from lunchtime conversation with other teachers, and working under a congenial English department head, Professor Margeson, made Ontario's two-year assignment a pleasure, on the whole. One faculty wife turned out to have been the child with the Pekinese whom I had entertained under the caterpillar-infested grape arbour when we first moved to Ontario in 1929! She and her husband had pioneered the tracing of the monarch butterfly's migrations. I suspect she had long forgotten our early uncomfortable encounter, if she had even noticed anything but awkward first approaches at the time. I did not mention it!

The Christian students had a campus group. They asked me to serve as staff sponsor, having heard that I was a believer. The effect among my associates was intriguing: challenges and taunts once or twice when table talk touched on the 'why' of tragedies and evil in our midst, and injustices, and 'those awful TV evangelists'. Or sometimes a pounce for a biblical reference someone needed for a lecture under preparation, for which I would usually have to resort to a concordance. One English classicist, an Oxford graduate who taught ancient history, became a friend through sharing the drives back to town on early afternoons; she loved to bait me. The story of the prodigal son, for instance: 'The father of those two sons always strikes me as a bit of an ass!' she would say. We were each declaring a cause, to each of us one that needed no defence, so that all such lively moments sparked and faded out.

With the Christian student group it was easy too, for they had their own executive and needed a staff sponsor only in order to be permitted by Administration to put up posters, invite speakers occasionally, and call regular meetings. The mix of spiritual fervour and hormones was indeed heady. My 'counsel' was chiefly to alert them to dates for their events which would conflict with other College plans. It touched me to see their maturity. At the end of my first year at Scarborough the elected incoming president and secretary became engaged; when we returned for the fall term, they had broken up. But they worked selflessly together on the executive through that whole term, overcoming tension early by strict attention to their responsibilities.

If word of my evangelical sympathies became common knowledge to my students, there was no indication that it troubled them. Perhaps because they knew, they brought occasional off-topic questions into class discussions, and enlivened the atmosphere. My sympathies became clearer, to those who noticed, when *The Dumbfounding* was published during my first year there.

Life in academia was not attractive to me, long-term. Gradually I saw that I had exhausted my scholar's resources in the two years of required teaching. They had been lively, but I lacked the academic fat for long-term sustenance, or the drive to keep up research on new topics, write the thesis, and finally fit into the groove. Perhaps, though, there is a place for two-year invasions of campus by outsiders with something to offer for that length of time, and with a liking for students.

EVANGEL HALL

Since my academic salary had far exceeded my expenses during the two teaching years, more involvement at Evangel Hall became an option, made possible in 1968 by the Presbyterian Church in Canada's Home Missions budget. As a volunteer from the time I joined Knox Church, I had learned to respect Howie and Esther McIlveen, the couple who took over as new superintendents. They had taught me the Toronto reality that resembled the New York City reality Dorothy Day exposed herself to, in heart and in day-to-day living. She was co-founder of the Catholic Worker Movement. (See *The Long Loneliness*, her autobiography.) Like the McIlveens, she lived among the people, as one of them. Earlier, I had been receiving her newsletter.

When I think of Evangel Hall in those days, I remember the huge blue cross jutting out over Queen Street from the entranceway, the wood-framed blackboard with news or announcements in the display window, and the regular 'staff', culled from transients and drop-in visitors. Jim Mulcahy, for instance. He ruled supreme in the second floor kitchen and worked with us preparing the supper sandwiches served every night to a full 'congregation' who suffered through the 'Grace before Meat' before enjoying the food and hot, sweet coffee (with condensed milk) in time to reach shelters when they opened their doors to anyone willing to risk sleeping there.

Jim it was who made us our staff lunch. We always hoped it would be plain, not one of his dubious concoctions; he had once been cook for a lumber camp. One morning I arrived almost late and was busy at first, but when a chance came I went upstairs for coffee. 'Not yet,' Jim said, 'it's only been boiling ten minutes.' Whether the deposit was ever scoured out of the big metal coffee pot, we did not ask. Jim was one of us for years. One night, on his way home, he was run over and killed instantly. The kitchen at the Hall didn't seem the same place for a long time after that.

Another constant stimulus those days was Bill Kernot. Bill had grown up a Cockney. 'I began drinking as a boy in London,' he remarked. 'My mother would send me out for a mug of ale, mornings, to get her going, and I'd lick the foam off it carrying it home.' One never knew whether Bill was being truthful or just creative! He had lost an ear to some sort of violence, and never said how or why. A prosthesis had been made that few people knew about. At a whim, he would alarm someone by plucking it off.

Bill was very bright, but too small and frail to help with many of the cleaning and chair-moving jobs other volunteers did. Instead, he found his own niche. Every day he would labour all morning with coloured chalks and an eraser, preparing his 'thought for the day' to display on the blackboard in the storefront window. Since Evangel Hall was a mission, Bill drew his 'thoughts' from a large Bible. He searched, at random it seemed, for something that would both tickle his fancy and pass muster, delighted when he found one like 'I will come like a thief in the night!' If a try was rejected (he sometimes picked to tease), he would wash his blackboard and get back to work, persevering in spite of the punishment he had given his body for so long.

One day Howie McIlveen spotted a stranger out on Queen Street and encouraged him to come in, for he seemed unlike the long-term drinkers. Jack was from Norway, had come to Manitoba, married there and run his own butcher shop. When his wife died he took off and ended up in Toronto, disconsolate and sodden, outside the Hall. Simple friendship, a listening ear, helped him recover his dignity. Long after I was part of daily life at the Hall we kept in touch through the Sunday services. Drinking was never again a problem for Jack. It had been his way of crying out after an overwhelming loss.

Jack lived in a subsidized apartment in the nearby housing development where he once treated me and my friend Joan Eichner (whom he knew through her hymn-playing at the services) to a Christmas dinner, beautifully prepared and presented. We asked him to tell us about his years in the northern part of Norway. There were rocks like shelves, for drying fish, he remembered, and newly washed linens could be kept white by draping them over great boulders in the sun. Taken in, they kept the smell of sun and sea.

The McIlveens ultimately received a call to a congregation in British Columbia, so reluctantly separated themselves from people and volunteers at Evangel Hall. To my contented sense of belonging, underwritten now by a Presbyterian Church in Canada Home Missions appointment as 'women's worker', I became a full-time staff member under the Rev. George Cunningham, the new superintendent. He had served congregations in the Maritimes and in Scarborough, where he and his family continued to live after his work on Queen Street began. Ruth, his wife, was pianist for the services on Sunday as long as she was able. And then it was Joan who played the hymns in those quiet 7 p.m. services. Mr Cunningham became a good friend to us both.

Women's work, children's and youth programmes, men's programmes and 'drop-in' contacts were all part of Mr Cunningham's responsibility. His daily, brief staff meetings were more for prayer than for instruction. Staff lunches were times for sharing information. Enormous buoyancy entered any situation when he was around. He was unlikely to intervene, but good at setting limits whenever we consulted him with a problem. Help with food was permitted only once per month per family: how could I make this clear to a shy Native Canadian wife asking, urgently and too often, because, as she finally explained, hospitality was her people's way of life, and when more and more of her people came to her door, once word got out that she had a roof and a stove, how could she help them when once a month she received only enough for herself? Other agencies existed, but would any aboriginal refuse another her hospitality? Never! Only their own people could be trusted. She knew the Hall and knew she could ask people there to help.

For me, the widening awareness of networks of help revealed my city from a new angle, full of unexpected, hidden jewels. Toward closing time one afternoon the door opened on a forlorn woman. Or child? She held a paper shopping bag, and walked with a limp, a steel brace and a thick-soled boot on one leg. She sat wordless at the desk inside, looking dazed rather than upset. At last she explained: 'The dogs have eaten my ma.' Several uptown apartment dwellers who liked large dogs found it best to pay her mother for daycare until, at 4 or 5 p.m. after work, they were free to walk the dogs before going home together. Doreen had seen some dogs snarling at her mother, so fled the public housing area and the other witnesses – who I hoped had called the police or a security guard – and 'left home'. Her bond with her mother was close enough, but frayed by perceived neglect on one side, and, on the other, exasperation with an irascible, handicapped child. She now presented herself to be looked after. Investigation proved her story exaggerated, though the mother *had* been taken to emergency where she was still waiting for treatment or admission.

One central social service agency suggested, as a temporary solution, 'Winnie Hunter's', a name *not* on my list of resources. Nevertheless I dialled the number I had been given, spoke to Mrs Hunter herself, and she simply agreed! 'Bring her here in time for supper if you can.' One of Winnie's girls had found a job and a new rented room, and would be leaving later that week. Meantime, Doreen could have Mrs Hunter's bed. For *her*, there was a couch in the adjoining front porch. We found the semi-detached house on a short street running east off Yonge, near St Clair Avenue. Seven or eight girls usually shared the space. Doreen was made welcome and sent to the downstairs washroom to soap her hands in readiness for supper. Mrs Hunter gave me a small information sheet about the house and told me not to worry, promising to report by telephone before noon the next day.

A week later I visited again. Doreen was nicely dressed and seemed cheerfully at home. She proudly recited a number of verses from John 14 that she had been given to memorize. Winnie had a piano and was teaching Doreen 'her notes', she told me. It had become a permanent placement! The injured mother took off, apparently, when she was well enough; whatever efforts the agency or Winnie made, the family bond seemed to remain tenuous. Doreen grew healthier. When winter came, a social worker was firmly instructed by Mrs Hunter to see to it that some kind of waterproof protection would be provided for Doreen's thick-soled boot and for the normal one as well, both usually soggy through the winter. Good clothing hung in Doreen's cupboard in a room of her own.

The funding remained mysterious to me. Some of the girls were likely receiving government disability grants. The daily expenses for groceries, medicines etc. were certainly supplemented by Baptist funds. Winnie explained that she had been a missionary in Africa until her husband died, and had learned to 'live easy with difficulties, trusting the Lord'. For example, when sudden nightfall had caught her alone in the jungle on the way home from a sick call and there were probably wild animals roaming, 'I just lay down on the roadway, well away from their drinking hole, I hoped, and asked the Lord to watch over me, and He did.'

When Winnie had pneumonia, there in the little house she had intended for her husband's years in retirement, she lay untroubled, directing the older girls to keep the house running until she was better. And she did recover, sensibly resting as long as her doctor advised, but in charge throughout. This service to the community had no official status, but it continued to fill a need in the city over many years. It was a privilege to have met such a person.

Acute needs were easier to handle at the Hall than programme events. A group of volunteers made possible a Sunday morning programme, but nobody dreamed so many children would stream in when we opened the doors. The parents, sleeping late at home, put the children out to play, winter and summer, for the sake of quiet indoors. We learned to use up their energies early by permitting floor hockey on the ground floor of the Hall, with food upstairs to keep smaller children out of harm's way. By 10:30, staff and volunteers gathered their classes and settled in upstairs rooms for Sunday school proper. The youngest children then came down to ground level to enjoy a puppet show or storytime, followed by a short prayer, then crafts at little tables, well-spaced, with crayons, coloured paper, kindergarten scissors, etc. supplied from a circulating food cart as needed.

I remember one prayer time after a Joseph story, when a little fellow said, 'Please pray for my head.' I did, then set him at an art table and telephoned his home, grateful that we had registered these children. 'I'll be right over,' his mother said. He had been struck by a car a few months back and she knew what Sick Children's Hospital had told her to give him for pain, and how long to hold him down quietly until the medication worked. Years later, on a return visit to the Hall, I heard that same boy, now a weedy, dark-haired teenager, reading the New Testament lesson at a morning service.

How grateful I was now for my nursemaiding experience where I had been prepared, a little, for this immersion into impromptu child-care activities! In Chicago, to keep my feet on the ground in those heady months of poetry and jazz and new friendships, I had volunteered at the downtown 'Y' daycare for a couple of late-morning hours weekly – another unforeseen preparation for Sunday mornings now. There I had observed how normal children avoided, even excluded, anyone who showed symptoms of emotional or psychological trouble. It seemed self-protective, not heartless. In Toronto, too, odd behaviour usually meant isolation, the exception being simple retardation: fetal alcohol syndrome was then an unfortunately familiar part of growing up in the Alexandra Park area.

Through the Sunday school, contact with community ladies became possible. When volunteer drivers offered to take the children on a picnic some Saturday afternoon in late spring, I used the occasion to communicate with their mothers, sending home with each child a notice which I would later pick up, signed, if the mother gave consent. All waited to sign until I appeared. To each mother I extended an invitation to attend the ladies' midweek group, *upstairs* in the Hall (ladies dreaded getting mixed up with the late afternoon lineups of men at sandwich-and-coffee time). A number of mothers already knew the Hall as a resource in the last days before welfare cheques came for another month. As we talked at their kitchen tables, they found the proposed *selling* of clothing (prices 5 cents to 70 cents) at a bazaar day, with prospective group members acting as clerks, would permit them to do their own shopping up to $2.50, before the doors opened. This event established a volunteer role for the helpers, who became the nucleus of our new group. The sale became a regular feature of those years at the Hall. The men learned to respect the reason they had to wait until after clean-up that day, except for necessary private sessions with George Cunningham or his assistant, Bill Kerr, who could keep a one-on-one office space available, in spite of the ladies' being all over the drop-in acreage on a sale day.

For Bill Kerr, this ladies' day must have been a relief. He bore the brunt of the constant pressure of men needing a sweater, needing a coat, needing underwear, needing cash to get off the street and to get 'an address' so they might qualify for welfare or disability income. He knew some of them and wanted to be encouraging. Even with the habitual drunks he had become patient, hopeful on the basis of a fine training course he had been given by an agency staffed with experienced specialists. The local Alcoholics Anonymous group developed out of his contact with them.

Nevertheless, he found the incessant demands oppressive. Even harder to bear were the endless devices the men used to present themselves as basically sound citizens, with self-contradictory versions of why they were temporarily in trouble through no fault of their own, deeply grateful for the good work of Evangel Hall. Some even professed devout faith, echoing words learned through the prayer before evening sandwiches and coffee.

One day at our staff lunch somebody mentioned walking her dog, evenings, finding it to be a wonderful way of shaking off sadness for the people she had spent the day counselling (she worked with the young people's group who used the building evenings, but many an afternoon too she had visitors and small planning sessions with local teenagers). Bill Kerr enthusiastically endorsed her preference for dogs. He turned the conversation to cats, though, the only pets his wife and daughter wanted. A dog, Bill remembered, would follow you, learn to stay with you, obey you, show loyalty no matter how uncomfortable circumstances made him on ill-judged outings. But a cat doesn't care what you want or where you are. If he wreathes around your legs and makes up to you, it's only to be fed or given a treat. Cats see only themselves, ever! Poor puss at home: he or she was not the one Bill railed against; it was only the daily softening-up tactics of the endlessly needy.

With the women, the clothing sales obviated the stress that Bill experienced. True, dresses and coats given as donations to the Hall tended not to be in large sizes. Even nightwear was skimpy for mothers needing ample flannelette gowns. But what was there was offered. It gave new hope for next time, even when this time nothing would fit. Elsie, one of the Evangel Hall staff members, was observant enough to forestall discouragement; for a woman who found nothing that fitted, she resorted to supplies in the basement: a warm throw, perhaps, or a pretty teapot and a couple of cups, so that most customers could go through the cash with something nice after all.

Visits in the Sunday school children's homes, and bazaar days, soon meant that the traditional ladies' midweek group grew and grew. The earlier members were a well-established circle who had known one another over years. They knew the hymns, respected the Bible-study routines, knew the outings they could look forward to, had the right etiquette when tea and cookies appeared (there was always the chance that some donor had brought good supplements to our biscuit tin).

But now I discovered my lack of training afresh. Until new contacts had been made, I had accepted, unchallenged, the ways familiar ever since the Rev. Mr Koffend's time, when Alexandra Park was newly settled by immigrants from England. His fervent love of the Lord touched every group formed then. The established circle of ladies attended various churches for family weddings, funerals, feast days: Greek Orthodox, United Church, Roman Catholic, Pentecostal, Salvation Army. Denomination was never an issue. Mr Koffend's spirit blessed all the work he left: because he had made the Bible central, people continued to accept prayer and Bible study groups, remembering him under every new superintendent. Esther McIlveen's imaginative introductions to a parable would draw people into the story, then into her teaching, once the terms were clear. What I liked to start with was the text of the story as written: picturing who was speaking, where, who stood or sat listening, then imagining ourselves as part of the crowd. This called forth fresh awareness that Jesus *knew* we would be hearing today, far away from the Bible lands, speaking English not Aramaic. For Him we were part of the written story, but centuries later, and invisible to the ones present around Him. This teaching device had two consequences. It was intended as an unthreatening approach; if you simply sat there you were included, could listen, but need not dread having to say anything. And it served to teach the old-timers patience. Some of the older ladies found it hard to accept the newcomers, many of them new to Bible reading, some likely to snap cigarette lighters and reach for ashtrays. Established members had to put up with husbands and children at home whose drinking, smoking, defiant, often abusive ways had made our Wednesday afternoons a haven of peace.

One member, a twenty-eight-year-old with the mental age of about twelve, but possessing a simple faith that what she had been told was trustworthy, kept the group from splitting apart. Both groups accepted her. Her living faith made her ask about meanings of words in what was read, or beg for what she called 'a for instance', an illustration that would clarify the text. The answers and the discussion, as we felt our way together, encouraged the new young mothers, and challenged the old-timers who may have accepted formulated doctrines too long to think them through.

It was my disastrous dinner party for this group that completed the bazaar-day ease we had not felt in our study sessions. The ladies came at midday, as invited. I ushered them into a room full of wooden chairs; the table would be down the hall. I perspired over steaming pots of potatoes that were cooking much faster than the rest of the meal, going back and forth to explain we'd soon be ready. On one trip, seeing the ladies sitting back against a wall right around the room, stiffly correct, I cried out 'Oh, and I have a box of decorations here but I forgot to fix up this room!' They came to life. 'We'll do it!' And when I mentioned my dismay that part of our dinner would be ready before the rest, two of them simply followed me back to the stove and coped. In my moment of panic, their unease and mine were one. We were on easy eye-level, at last. The guest cooks *were* helpful, the front room was duly brightened for our coffee time after dinner, and we had made a new start together.

One morning's mail brought a request from a far uptown young people's group who had voted to spend a weekend on some project for the Hall that would involve them all personally. Mr Cunningham knew of a campsite with a lodge and good cabins by a small lake not too far away. How about a weekend for the mothers and children, with the young people to help? We explored the cost, and the sponsoring church found ways to raise the major share of it. Excited planning was not just on their side. The ladies in our group were enthusiastic too. The sponsoring church found drivers to take all their young people to the camp early on a Friday afternoon. Our staff, children and mothers followed later in hired buses.

It was cheering for the mothers to learn that they would be free of child care all day, taking over from the 'babysitters' only at bedtime. The campsite was lovelier than I had dared to hope. The bus became very quiet as we bumped over tree-roots, under deep shade, on the access road from the highway. When we arrived, the awed mothers and the squealing children were an odd contrast. Fortunately the 'babysitting' group of young people was waiting when the bus door opened, ready to prevent a rush of eight-year-old ruffians straight to the water. Using whistles like school sports teachers to get the children into groups, they marched them off, as we adults looked on in amazement.

Three highlights stand out for me from that weekend. First, the hours after a good meal when the mothers relaxed on sofas or lounge chairs in the friendly ground-floor common room, with windows and doors wide open to the fresh outdoors and the veranda chairs, and the distant fading-away of children's voices, off on an adventure. Second, the little girl on the bus going home who sat beside me, on the window side, playing with a very small doll and some scraps of cloth she'd come by at a crafts session. 'Here's how we do,' she'd say. 'First, we has a smooth white piece, then we has a soft piece at the top, *then* we puts another cloth, all smooth, and on top of that another darker piece. Then we turns it this way so you go here, your head on the soft piece, and we pulls up the cloth over you.'

Third: Barbara, one of the ladies who attended our group irregularly on Wednesdays, and once came after she clearly had been beaten, still bruised more than she meant people to notice. She never explained this, or her off-and-on attendance, and kept to herself on group outings. Here it was good to see her go down to the lakeside the minute the bus let us off at the campsite. She spotted a rowboat upended on the sand, flipped it over expertly, picked up a can to bail with and both oars, shoved off, stepped in and was afloat. She did not try to go anywhere, but simply used the oars to correct any sideways drift, or to keep out of the shallows, happy to be untroubled out there on the water, at peace.

In my mind, there was a background to this picture: Barbara's home, when I visited her there. It was lunchtime before I left. I watched her use a large, clean empty can as container on a hot plate where she heated a small tin of soup for her children's lunch, and her own, if any were left. The table was an ironing board, with two spoons set out on a clean towel. She showed no dismay or embarrassment that nobody had a chair to sit on. (She and I had been sitting on the family's bed.) In her eyes, and she hoped in mine as well, standing was best, given the height of that lunch table. Her husband's workshop was below. She said, simply, that he sent out for his lunch, presumably giving himself a more generous allowance than he gave his family. I had met him on my way in, a well-built, dark-haired, rugged-faced man, with something about his expression that explained Barbara's bruises. His family tradition had made him think of his wife as a chattel, I suppose. The children grew up with two very sharply contrasting parents, neither one likely to be able to ease the way for them!

Yet at one women's midweek meeting, Barbara slipped a piece of paper into my hand – a poem she had written about the first signs of spring. The rhythm and most of the rhymes were unforced. Yes, it echoed the style of greeting-card verses, but why not, since she had read only those. It was clearly her own poem. From then on I tried to lend her things like small magazines, books with poetry and prose interspersed, a discarded high school text of poems. Having defined herself by appalling boundaries, she saw these offerings as tantalizing but from another world which was out of reach.

The next time I saw her it was in the Queen Street Mental Health Centre. Towards the end of her stay there, when we were walking out under the trees in the Shaw Street corner of the grounds, she showed me a few more poems. Later she gave me a tour of the hospital common areas, then led me past a TV blaring in an empty anteroom into a spacious area where there were cubicles off to the side with patients' beds, towel racks, dress hooks. She seemed peaceful there. We sat on a sofa, not far from a thin, quiet woman holding a magazine on her lap, unseeing. Barbara introduced us, as though hostess at a morning coffee party. But the woman started up suddenly, ran to the sealed window and smashed through the pane with her fist. A ward-nurse sat facing the window, writing up reports. She barely looked up as Barbara found a broom and swept the broken glass against the outer wall, but not until she had torn a piece off her blouse and made a tourniquet to stem the bleeding from the woman's arm. In this setting too, her human dignity shone out, in spite of the low clouds that kept gathering over her life.

In negotiating access to the wards as a regular visitor, I had met with the new director of the hospital; this was the period when medical specialists were put in charge of Ontario hospitals – a period of immense, but costly, improvements that did not last. (In Queen Street, for example, a new indoor swimming pool, very unobtrusively supervised, had clear therapeutic value to the patients for the period it was in use and kept up to standard.) One day, a telephone message came for me at Evangel Hall from this director. He said that a poetry group had been going on for months under a volunteer, a retired teacher, a man the patients had come to count on and seemed to enjoy. But that man had suffered a serious stroke, and the director said it would help the members of his group if a new leader could be introduced as an interim substitute.

Clearly the attendants scattered among the patients in the poetry club had relaxed their listening minds, though not their vigilance; they had been present, but they were unable to tell me what the leader had read, or how he had kept the patients' interest. Therefore at my first session I flew blind. I had brought in a few thin anthologies, a selection from my own books, and whatever I'd carried that morning to read on the bus to work; this would be fresh, at least for me! It added up to a modest pile of reading material. To break the ice, I turned to some Canadian nature poets to read aloud, and left the pile of my books on a small table in the centre of the group, inviting anyone who so chose to read quietly for himself, or read aloud to us all, using any of these books during the hour.

One man fumbled among the stack and then, rejecting what he found, stood at attention and with great fervour recited 'Rule Britannia' from memory. But he subsided and listened reasonably enough afterwards. Some patients leafed through what they had picked up, but no one else was launching into reading, so I did. I had brought a copy of the Middle English poem, 'Sir Gawain and the Green Knight'. It must have been early winter with Christmas in the air to explain that choice, although the plot likely would catch and tantalize a listener's interest at any season. Poe's 'Annabel Lee' held them too, some of them stamping where they sat, keeping the rhythm, on the second reading they asked for.

To my amazement, in a later week of this venture, someone asked to hear, again, the poem he called 'the jolly green giant'. Fortunately I still had the book with 'Sir Gawain' in my backpack. Another man asked me to read Blake again, weeks after I had read it, 'the one about the lily'. He was remembering, in Part I of 'The Book of Thel', the opening lines of stanza two, or at least he accepted that as what he wanted when I read it again. The experience of these weekly sessions challenged my assumption that real poetry has increasingly become a minority taste. What has made it seem inaccessible to 'ordinary' people? Capital-E Education? Capital-C Culture? Those in the hospital's poetry club were from various backgrounds, but I learned when I asked about poetry in their school texts that many had public school credits at most.

I cannot remember, now, how long this assignment lasted, or why it was finally discontinued. But I do remember the last day. As I arrived, the nurse in charge told me that this was a special morning for Gavin, a highly literate and responsive member of the group, because he had now recovered enough to be graduated to outpatient status. The first step had been agreeing about his choice of outside lodgings, where he would begin his new life and his initial 'job' (on subsidy) which meant attending programmes at the hospital from 9 a.m. till 4 p.m. until he was ready for more independence. Since the whole group was waiting, I said nothing to this man then, but on the way out I paused at his chair to wish him well.

Before my words were all out, he glared, blurting 'Don't you know I'm the seventh son of a seventh son?' and suddenly grabbed me around the neck in a vise-like grip. The attendants took control, and explained, in his hearing while he quieted down, that moving out of a protected environment after such a long time was often very threatening for patients. After Gavin had left with the others for lunch, I asked what happened on weekends, if 4 p.m. till morning was that difficult for daycare patients to handle at first. 'NOTHING!' In a further conversation with the Queen Street Hospital medical director, I learned that the number of suicides over weekends proved how hard it was for those patients to endure even two days outside the hospital.

Mr Cunningham and I talked over a new idea of planning special weekend events, if we could staff them, to help people pass these free hours safely in our area of service. He co-opted Presbyterian church congregations, asking for people with cars to pick up passengers at the Hall (daycare patients to assemble there on their own initiative), then bring them back again in late afternoon. He worked out staffing and proposed a programme of Saturday picnics or other outings. Simply making a few extra sandwiches looked after the midday meal, along with a bag of fruit and any contributed sweets which could be diverted from weekday supplies to supplement this Saturday lunch. The youth team hauled out equipment for quoits and croquet, and offered a softball and a bat as well.

On several of those picnics, or on cold days between seasons, we chose parks that provided roofed, protective, buildings. Again and again we saw how quickly the men relaxed in a contained area, enjoying fresher air, longer perspectives, trees, even flowing water in season, a chance to take off their socks and wade. On the last picnic of the season, in a year when Thanksgiving was late, we had a special treat: pumpkin pies. I remember getting them down from the fridge at the Hall, putting them into boxes, carrying them carefully onto a bus, and, after the sandwiches, preparing to cut them in pieces to serve. But when we lifted the wax paper, we saw that they were *all* furry.

Mr Cunningham sent a car for ice cream instead, but our restless picnic party strayed before the new dessert arrived; indeed one of the men went clear out of sight. Everybody else, ready to go home, had to wait while we took turns looking along the banks of the Humber till he was found. Finally everyone had been driven home, the remaining supplies unloaded at the front door of Evangel Hall, the drivers thanked and the clutter sorted, inside, to be put away. Mr Cunningham hoisted the games up into a high cupboard in the back office, straightened his back, and suddenly laughed boisterously, as only he could laugh. 'Well, Lord,' he said, as he subsided, 'we blew that one!'

The release to my own weariness was instantaneous. It lit up a memory of an earlier release, when the McIlveens were in charge. At lunch one day, either Bill or I had been exploring our reactions to the word 'needs'. One particular family had been reported to Evangel Hall by other agencies: securing help from multiple sources on the same day comes to light that way. Having been forewarned, the receptionist stalled when this family appeared for 'help'. The mere hint of a refusal touched off in them an outburst of abuse, vituperation, fury. The superintendent took over, got them alone, and talked them down somehow, so they were civil by the time they left. He recognized that, because they felt like 'losers', rejected in life from the outset, they preferred to play the role of the unjustly treated, rather than admitting to poverty and genuine need. Even grudging offers of help, not to mention denial, could then be taken as intentionally demeaning.

Perhaps this was the occasion that gave me the idea of going to the city office, one morning early, when people were lining up for 'welfare' (formerly called 'the dole', then 'relief'; by the time you read this, some new euphemism will likely be current). When I arrived, there were already some fourteen people ahead of me. We were fairly silent as we waited, shuffling ahead as clients were admitted one by one. Nobody recognized me. A resigned but friendly attitude was common, with the exception of one lone mutterer signalling her isolation. Nobody complained about the slow progress toward their turn, though everybody's feet must have hurt, that sultry morning, as mine did.

When at last I got to the window, I explained that I was not a legitimate applicant, but had come in order to learn how to identify with the experiences of the welfare contacts from Evangel Hall, and now I was ready to leave. Instead, I was instantly offered admission to 'their' closed-off area so I could sit down there and observe further. Not wanting to change roles, a point which the harried workers understood, I refused and left, but with a useful list of names of staff I could contact at need in order to speed any further communication.

Such contacts, and the home visiting, made me more and more enjoy the downtown sidewalks and storefronts. Two 'Sketch' poems in *sunblue* (one subtitled 'A work gang on Sherbourne and Queen, across from a free hostel for men' and the other 'Cement worker on a hot day') reflect that time. In the same group, another 'Sketch' ('I as a blurry') evokes the quiet of the apartment I entered at the end of the day, where Mother waited. On summer evenings we would walk out to the tree-deep street behind the building. (There, I discovered, lived my graduate student friend Eric Wright, now busy producing more crime novels like the ones I had already read and relished.)

The quiet evenings gave an opportunity to learn what the day had taught. Seeing how I was received as one with the welfare workers, after having been accepted in the lineup as one with the applicants, reminded me of the women's group activities. Just west of the swimming pool at Dundas and Bathurst Streets, we noticed a new Toronto Public Library branch. In fact Audrey, a member of the group, first mentioned it. One afternoon our programme included a visit there. It was astonishing to me to see how happily the ladies scattered around the bookshelves, looking into a book here and there, some finding a chair and lingering over their choice.

When time was up because the mothers had to be home when school was out, I told them to choose one or two books to borrow. A card cost ten cents; I had inquired and was ready to lend the sum to anyone who hadn't come prepared. They hung back, until one woman explained: 'The librarian said we could take books out, but she doesn't know we're welfare.' They thought that disqualified them! In a quick aside with the librarian I reported this new imagined instance of being rejected. She very warmly spoke to us as a group, urging books upon us and explaining how to sign up for a temporary card, so as to receive the permanent card next time. 'All we need is your name and address,' she said. 'This library is "public", meant for anyone in Toronto.' Reflecting on that library visit, I learned that correcting my own background biases had to become a continuous process of noticing and adjusting for slippages! I was 'one of them' only as I was *myself*. As, for example,

Miss Emerson, a regular visitor to the Hall, was *herself*.

My first memory of Miss Emerson evokes as well that of a selfless man, the Rev. George Lowe, who brought his car to help out in one of Miss Emerson's constant moves from one rented room to another. (He was one of her uptown resources because she sometimes worshipped at Knox Church.) Miss Emerson had two cats in her arms. We carried her worldly goods out to the car in a few shopping bags as she supervised, directing Mr Lowe at the last minute to bring out a vile-looking basin of dear knows what fluid. This was to be put on the car floor, in the back seat. Mr Lowe managed not to slop any onto the floor. Now that all was in order, he opened the front door for Miss E. with as much unconscious courtesy as if she were a royal visitor.

Such natural ease was more than the members of the ladies' group could manage when Miss Emerson appeared on occasional Wednesdays. She felt their unease. Likely for that reason, her visits to the Hall were to staff members individually, usually to me. The purpose was often unclear. Certainly, over time, she struggled to convey the person she knew herself really to be: artistic, with some background in a respectable dance troupe in California. Glimpses of her capacities seemed confirming. How she ended up in Toronto remained a mystery to me. Her mental confusion was not caused by alcohol abuse, I concluded, although one of the moves, farther east than my district so that I never visited her there, was to a 'private convent', her one co-resident being referred to as 'Reverend Mother'. Miss E. respected this 'Reverend', but also envied her because 'after we have our devotions, she gets to finish all the wine.'

For safety and for protection, rituals seemed necessary to Miss Emerson. Because some danger lurked at every threshold, she had learned to outwit whatever or whoever it was by always entering a room with a dainty little hop. Nostalgic for some other life which seemed to have included tennis and badminton, she once told me that she never played sports any more. 'My cats play all the time, though they're tomcats, as I found out. But we learn to turn men into women and then they're all right.' (I guess she meant the cats had been neutered.)

A rootless, marginal existence, those years, contributed to Miss E.'s confused mind. When Mr Lowe found her a protected residence in her early 'retirement' years, she emerged much as she had portrayed herself, although, alas, now subdued. Perhaps the above record of a difficult period is distorting. 'Flash-backs falsify the Past:/they forget/the remembering Present' said W.H. Auden in 'I Am Not a Camera'.*

We often saw Rose at the Hall, invariably with Peter, her eldest, and a little cluster of lively younger ones. Rose was mentally limited, but had that clarity of eye that made early psychologists define one category of the disabled as 'the innocents'. Her visits were not for clothing or food, though she might absentmindedly accept something Elsie, unasked, would bring up from the basement supplies. For the first few minutes she was there just to warm up or cool down (depending on the season); *then* she would waken to the fear that had driven her here. Social workers kept inspecting her place, uneasy about her ability to provide a responsible home in spite of her genuine devotion to her brood.

One terrible morning she was almost incoherent. They'd threatened to take her son Peter into foster care because her boyfriend had been with her overnight, too close to Peter's cot. 'They ought to know,' she cried, 'that I love Peter, I protect him – that's why I have always lived so moral!' Her protest was indignant, although to any observer the racial variety among Rose's children might excuse the workers' misreading. Heart-whole. Heart-breaking. That was Rose. What was it that drew unstable people to the Hall? We offered no 'therapy', just a restful interlude of being accepted.

Part of accepting Rose for who she was involved conceding to the social workers a justified concern for the children. Was her place too crowded? Did she feed them only fast food? Again and again, when foster care was threatened, we could testify to the bond of genuine love in that family even though, in her drivenness, Rose trailed the children endlessly about the streets. (Long after my days at the Hall, on a midtown street, Rose and her grown children passed me in the same familiar little procession. She was intent on some objective, and I did not greet her.)

A strong, stable Ukrainian mother in regular contact at the Hall was also intent on a child's needs, although her child, Maria, was now

---

* W.H. Auden, *Collected Poems*. Ed. Edward Mendelson. New York: Random House, 1976, 631.

an adult dodging her mother's visits 'for the good of all concerned'. Maria was an alcoholic. She said so, flatly, the first time we met. Like her mother she was highly intelligent, independent and uneasy. I visited her, with her prior consent, while she shared rooms – and drinks – with an amusing, articulate man who seemed less addictive. They were fond of each other, but when her mother did visit, Maria felt ashamed. That ménage broke up.

Mother and daughter then came to Wednesday meetings together for a time, until one day the mother, alone, both angry and frantic, reported that Maria had vanished into a new bout of drinking. It was Bill Kerr who finally found her. One of the men in a 'wine house' (someone's rented room where drinking 'friends' converged until the landlord finally put them out) appealed to Bill to come and rid them of a woman there whom they were finding unmanageable. Bill carried Maria out, alarmed at her emaciation and bad colour. Because he had another appointment that afternoon, he called me from Emergency to see if I could wait with Maria until she was seen by a doctor.

I telephoned Mother: 'Make a sandwich for yourself and have tea (she was still able to do that), and don't worry if I am so late that you're asleep when I come in.' Indeed it was after midnight when Maria's turn came. The intern on duty saw that her symptoms were serious, although it clearly exasperated him that she had so mistreated her body. He admitted her, finally, but said to me in her hearing: 'Why waste your time on someone who clearly isn't worth it?' I hope he saw Maria again after her care and treatment; it would have answered his question. Her mother was relieved to know she was safe, the several weeks' hospital care restored both of them, and many months later they were still living together, successfully, partly supported by a craft skill at which Maria excelled.

During my years at the Hall, I sometimes jotted down a poem on the bus trip home, to be revised later, in the evening. Some of these poems eventually appeared in *sunblue*. Evening was also a time for reading aloud to Mother who had an appetite for everything she felt she'd missed by not having more schooling. This reading was all the more welcome because she was inhibited from playing the piano in our apartment. The acoustics worried her. She heard every heel-tap in the apartment above us and therefore feared that her piano must be too loud for the tenant overhead.

Once again Ted's wife, Ruth, came to the rescue. The apartment buildings at Lascelles Boulevard were relatively new. Ruth had friends who were contented there, and a ground-floor two-bedroom unit was available. This move, in 1969, was simple: no sorting or discarding was necessary. In the early days we loved the big old trees in the courtyard with its goldfish pond. (Later it deteriorated until only the cement basin remained.) For the sake of reading or writing on the bus, I still travelled the slower route home up Avenue Road. The new apartment was properly soundproofed, judging by our unawareness of neighbours. Mother enjoyed hours at the piano there. One evening, as I went out, I was surprised to see four tenants sitting on the steps at our end of the hall. They had heard Mother playing as they passed our door and wanted to listen until the piece they recognized ended. They signalled me to say nothing, so I said nothing. Let the superintendent tell us if anyone complains.

Before the move to Lascelles Boulevard, a teacher temporarily in Toronto had begun to lead a Bible study group in our other apartment. We enjoyed the variety of people who took part. Only the leader had to come prepared; the rest of us took turns reading aloud the passage she assigned, then she supplied essential background facts and directed our explorings of the passage's meaning. Some of those who came were brought by the leader; they, in turn, would bring someone else along for one session. Many chose to come back regularly. A few were my friends. This group continued comfortably in the Lascelles apartment, for Mother's bedroom was at the end of the hall and she could retire early if she wanted to.

One session stands out in my memory. Participants' backgrounds were diverse, as were our preconceptions, so we were each asked what we meant by the term 'Christian'. Our varied responses puzzled a nun in the group who said, when her turn came right at the end, 'I'm sorry, but none of you are Christians, since none of you were baptized in the Church.' The group continued for years, even after another move, to a friend's nearby apartment, when Mother was permanently hospitalized in the early eighties.

As Mother's age began to take its toll, I grew increasingly conscious of end-of-the day crises at Evangel Hall. These involved time-consuming action to shore up shaky situations that always seemed to come to light late in the day. Once just at five o'clock, a woman appeared in a state of terror: 'I've been shown the door,' she said grimly. She was bruised and worn out. She had lived on the street years earlier, she told me, but now she jealously guarded her independence and the new status it gave her. The telephone numbers I used in such cases rang in empty offices, or to empty offers of a place on a waiting list. What about tonight?

The woman finally asked to use the phone 'to call Gerry'. Apparently he had a room available, but I was mystified by her threatening acceptance: 'None of your cracks! I need the space, and when I present myself, the Church lady will be with me.' En route she explained: 'It's a cathouse; but he knows I can make trouble for him, and for them, if he breaks his word.' We walked over together to the big brick building I'd often passed, innocent of what paid the rent for those many second storey rooms. When we arrived, it was plain that the woman would be given what she wanted, on her terms: clearly she had an old score with 'Gerry' that left him cowed and in her control, although not a control she wanted to exercise except from dire necessity.

That evening, going home late, I was bothered by an awareness of dark, stark truths, new to me but probably enmeshing and overshadowing the lives even of some in 'my' ladies' group. What lifted my spirits was a visual memory of seeing myself as they must see me. Once, as I was playing recorder in an idle interval at the Hall, Elsie came up from the basement storage room with a jacket for one of Mr Cunningham's clients. When she saw me with the recorder, her expression was amused and mildly condescending. 'Oh *Margaret!*' was all she said, but it spoke volumes.

I walked buoyantly around the streets, associating them with my happy early years in the impoverished downtown area of Calgary: the Jewish stationer's where I went for my pens and pencils; the laundromat, where people were companionable when I spent most of a day working there, washing the bedding from the Hall's lower storage shelves after a sewer had backed up; the hydrant, which a work gang unscrewed to produce a great gush of water for soaking their heads and drinking on a hot day, and which they managed with great effort to cap again; the beginnings of the Kensington Market, farther afield than I had occasion to go on Hall visits, but I went anyway. One hot summer evening, I saw how residents there coped with the heat: a father sat reading the paper, propped against a tree trunk in a little park, his children asleep on quilts around him; another family was gathered around a tablecloth on the grass, having their evening meal outside. No doubt I became a familiar oddity to them over those years.

One evening I was very late leaving the Western Hospital's Emergency: I forget who needed sponsoring that time. It was dark on Dundas Street's south side, where the sidewalk is overshadowed by the fenced-off housing apartments to the south. The one other pedestrian in sight, a man, was staggering towards me, burly and dangerous-looking. I regretted my bank visit earlier that day ('You've asked for this!') But as he drew level with me, he simply mumbled 'Pray for me, mother!'

Those late nights were hard for Mother too. Her companion was hired to stay until 5 p.m. Supper, and my company, came next, preceded by a time at the piano. When I didn't come, and didn't come, she would go back to her room and lie down, patient but undoubtedly trying not to worry. I felt deeply involved in the work at the Hall but my time there was coming to a close for three reasons: increasing concern about Mother's unpredictable hours alone; the fact that poems (towards the *sunblue* collection) lay unedited and disorganized; and a conflict that had developed between the superintendent and the sponsoring church over need for a summer camp – a conflict which caught me in the middle. My sister in Ottawa had already suggested that Mother should visit her family for a time, so when, out of the blue, the University of Western Ontario wrote offering me fall and spring (1972–73) terms there as writer-in-residence, I consulted Mary and Ted, then talked to Mr Cunningham about accepting. Burning bridges was not easy, but it felt right.

Margaret with Sunday school class at Evangel Hall.
(Credit: University of Manitoba Archives and Special Collections, Margaret Avison fonds, Box 1, PC151)

LONDON, ONTARIO

London, in 1972, was new to me, in spite of childhood's 4 a.m. trips to the market there. Two cousins from that farm lived nearby, Jean in St Thomas and Betty in London, not far from the university. Betty wisely counselled me to buy myself proper gloves for the reception the English Department would give to welcome me. I promised to conform. I spent a night or so in a small hotel, looked for an apartment and scouted out a riverbank path from downtown to the university. Why wait for a bus to go a walkable distance, especially when the walk could be along the river rather than through the business/insurance district?

The room assigned me in the English Department was deeply quiet, with leafy windows and bookshelf space left for me by the usual occupant who was on sabbatical, out of the country for the year. Back downtown I went to the London Market where there was a community bulletin board with apartment listings. I bought some good local apples and investigated the small unit offered for rent by the shoe store, which opened on the street at that time, but was part of the sprawling market building. The unit was up a double flight of stairs, furnished, clean, available, far from living quarters for the campus and the business district: a welcome retreat. I paid the shoe store landlord a month's rent and moved in.

Now the river walk seemed much closer. Starved for the natural world, I dodged pavement in London, and found lovely quiet places with wild grasses, scrub, running water feeding down towards the river. In *sunblue* there are two reflections of that river walk: 'March Morning' and 'A Lament'. Unscheduled office time gave me leisure for banked-up energies, welcome after the recent, disciplined years.

What was expected of a 'writer-in-residence'? When I asked at that English Department reception I was told it was up to me how to interpret this novel appointment. In the stress of meeting colleagues, acclimatizing to a new campus and faculty, and still dizzy with the decisions and the moving of those days, I dared not accept any drink but ginger ale, although every choice of wine and liquor was circulating. My choice that day, for that day, had unexpected consequences. One person high in the University of Western Ontario administration and one faculty member each later invited me out for a private lunch, to find out how I had managed to stop drinking – each nerving himself with straight rye in order to inquire. Some impulse made me describe my work at Evangel Hall, where alcoholics on the wagon needed to be spared the tempting smell of liquor from someone on staff. And I explained about the Alcoholics Anonymous group there, where anyone was welcome – and anonymous.

The administrative officer who talked with me, at that private lunch, gave me his number and asked me to seek out, in my own name, a meeting in a London district where he would not be recognized, and go with him the first time. How he fared after that initial A.A. contact, I do not know. While I was debating a consistently abstemious year in London, a sponsor of the Intervarsity group invited me to meet the executive – and served us sherry before dinner! For some people, a Christian's distinctiveness is compromised if he or she 'drinks'. For others, faith in Christ is hindered by giving inquirers the impression that Christians are spoilsports, ascetic to an unhealthy degree. I won't tell how I resolved this puzzlement in my time at UWO.

I should add here that, in my youth, the Women's Christian Temperance Union tried to condition a new generation to break away from the appalling alcoholism that 'gentlemen' had tended to fall into, in the dismally primitive and demanding pioneer Ontario experience. Children, and I was one of them, were given temperance poems to memorize, and urged to 'take the pledge' never to 'touch alcohol'.

Finding a church before my first Sunday in London led to further walks in different parts of the city. That first Sunday I attended a nearby Brethren Assembly because three members of the denomination (one in West Toronto, one in North Toronto, one in Scarborough) had impressed me with the mature, informed, natural ease of their statements about truth. I had not known that there was a 'narrow Brethren' kind of chapel, nor did I sense any unfamiliar note in the teaching that first Sunday. But it was not as welcoming a congregation as the ones I had visited in Toronto. An elder confronted me on my way out: 'You cannot come here without covering your head,' he said. I am ashamed to say that I hit back: 'And you have to shave my head since I did' – a second legalistic misreading of Scripture. Where to go the next week? From walks, from local papers, I decided to start wherever there were two services on Sundays. A small Pentecostal

Assembly near the campus ended my search.

In the process of finding a church with Sunday evening services, I did much walking. Once, after miles on the sidewalks and deep in the working-class area of London, I came upon a movie theatre advertising a re-run of *M. Hulot's Holiday,* a film which enchants me afresh every time I see it, though revivals are too few and far between. The seats were uncomfortable, the place shabby, but I sat happily through the feature I'd come to see. When the lights came up at the end, I saw only one other person in that matinee audience, long legs sprawled out into a far aisle further forward, and recognized Don McKay, the poet, then professor of English at UWO. (He did not see me.)

One morning soon afterward, my telephone rang before 7 a.m. A professor with strep throat. Would I take his 9 a.m. class (Renaissance Poetry) – just that one class? It was too late to ask administration to substitute someone for him. 'Do anything you like for the hour,' he said. He did tell me what their anthology was, and I managed to borrow a library copy en route that morning. For me, it was the Scarborough Marvell seminar all over again. But I did not teach, unsure of the context and how the professor would have fitted it in. We read and talked about a poem or two. Just fun, for an hour, with most of the students polite about it.

More fun was a special class where I had been invited to speak for an hour as writer-in-residence. The theme in my mind was that of easing readers of poetry away from a determined good will, a setting of the lips, an uncapping of pens, a 'ready to attack' mindset developed during high school to prepare them for 'theme, style, meaning of' examination questions. What I read them first, from the opening of 'The Apex Animal' (*Winter Sun*) were the lines about 'A Horse ... – rather, the narrow Head of the Horse ...' adding that to 'explain' this I had, the night previous, written a new poem. Then I read 'Strong Yellow, for Reading Aloud' (*sunblue*), where the student's questions come in with the old anxiety which is clearly blocking his receptivity. The grading of English papers, the setting of examination questions, have to be fair to gifted and dogged students alike. Teachers inevitably find themselves harnessed to exam paper questions for the sake of their students. And so now I regret writing that flippant, mystifying kind of mockery of teaching that makes 'a poem' something to explain and analyze. *Caveat emptor.*

In my London apartment, I could revert from a public to a private person, and there write uninterrupted. 'A gizzard and some ruby inner parts' (from 'A Lament' in *sunblue*) restores a memory of just that, on the river's footpath. The Clydesdale 'painted, /with real mural eyes' ('Strong Yellow', *sunblue*) watched me whenever I was entertained in a certain good downtown dining room. From that apartment I could live an everyday life, enjoying the neighbours I met in the nearby laundromat and the apple seller in the market downstairs. It was even intriguing to lie on my side of the wall when, around 11 p.m., the many Chinese students, who were fellow tenants in that warren of a building, gathered for a communal dinner next door, after their evening's studying. I learned to sleep untroubled – just as I did in a subsequent apartment, right over the Toronto subway tracks, when the rhythms of alternating clatter-past and silence trained my ears to inattention.

Until UWO invited me for this work, I had never heard of the position 'writer-in-residence'. Remembering Gladys Story's powerful influence on me, in that one grade nine term so long ago, made me feel tentative about taking on the role. 'Your manuscript one day before your appointment': I printed this for the office door. Under the words I squared off a timetable for morning appointments. Would anyone follow the trail to my corner and sign up? At first the mornings were free for my own reading, a chance to put flesh and bones on titles and authors which were heretofore nothing but wistful scribbles on scraps of paper, collected in a bulging envelope. But gradually the papers and notebooks – and one hand-printed chapbook – began to arrive.

Most of the writers were glad of a reader, as we all are. Show me anyone with a fresh story or poem who isn't eager to preempt time with a trusted friend and insist on a reading, then and there! Whether my comments as writer-in-residence should or could help or hinder, neither they nor I knew. One of the submissions was given me by Stan Dragland, a professor of English there at that time. (He later moved on into writing and editing full-time: his meticulous editing challenged me continually in the final stages of *Concrete and Wild Carrot* and *Momentary Dark*. In UWO days, of course, we did not foresee that future.) Stan tells me now that he was bracingly jolted by my cuts from his work; he failed to sense my insecure efforts to *earn* the enormous salary that year, the largest salary of my forty working years.

The students who submitted work seemed to survive our interviews. When two people are vulnerably present, each probably reads the other's body language and facial expression more intently than they listen. I know that I helped some of the writers to the next rung, towards confident realization of their intention with a poem or story. Some received comments on rhythm, for example, with suggestions about how purposeful interruptions in a flow can guide a reader's responses. With others the writing ability seemed more limited, fun for celebrating private occasions. The time with them was friendly and happy. Stories are not an art I can practise, though *reading* good stories is some basis for assessing those of young writers. With these I could help chiefly by reporting myself as a reader, how I had felt at this point or that, what kept me expectant and reading on. Good prose I could delight in, but only minimally help someone towards developing it when it was faulty. Tentativeness is no small advantage with young writers. In some cases a definite comment on a line in need of revision was unacceptable, though justified, if the young writer's personal and artistic investments were still mixed. But only one young man, the chapbook submitter, made it clear that an appreciative reading was what he wanted.

Fortunately, there were submissions I simply enjoyed, interviewees who were instantly on the same wavelength as mine. Polly Fleck was one, wife of the chairman of the English Department. She had written a very original fantasy, overcrowded in places, perhaps, by her imaginative energies. Another was John B. Lee. I can still see him the day he came in, glum, unfidgeting, guarded against nonsense. He had told me he was dropping out of UWO – warning me off, I felt. He claimed nobody liked his work when he read it at home, on the farm. But it was arrestingly good. He knew I valued it for what it was. From that time on we have been in friendly contact, and his published works are by now enthusiastically welcomed by many.

In later years I learned that a writer-in-residence usually gathers together a small writing group in which mutual criticism is responsibly monitored: writers thus help other writers over the humps. I was prejudiced against such groups because of what I had learned in Chicago, through Frederick Bock's poetry, about creative writing techniques taught at the University of Iowa. Frederick worried unduly, over-revising, it seemed to me, seeking to 'load every rift with ore'.

Subsequently I kept reading other young poets whose styles were too similar, so that one could identify them, accurately, as products of the same Iowa group. Does the pressure of an 'authority's' influence inhibit a young writer from coming into his own voice, learning to write by his ear? Does a restricted model over-influence someone, inhibit his openness to wide reading and discourage his echoing of current enthusiasms – an enjoyable stage of learning?

There were no writing groups in my early years, apart from unscheduled events when Earl and Esther Birney invited Miriam Waddington, who dragged me along; the 'event' might be an Irving Layton visit to Toronto, with the current mimeographed magazine from Montreal. (My copies of these were placed at York University when I cleared out our Lascelles Blvd. apartment.) Irving's ebullience and indiscriminate enthusiasm about his latest sheaf of poems carried those occasions; we listened for the best poems, moved and delighted by these. Discussion was just like the intermission talk at a play or concert, inconsequential. Therefore it did not occur to me at UWO to suggest a creative writing group.

At UWO the high point was Stan Dragland's announcement that he had found an old hand-cranked press in the basement Belial Press area, and a compositor's font of letters, figures and ornamental pieces which delighted him. The press was in working order, inked and ready to run – for what? Why not for students' poems? My name for the project was *The Pom Seed* (remembering that joyful mess on a hospital bedspread from my school class's gift of a pomegranate in a basket of fruit!)

Student contributors and I signed up for shifts of cranking out the pages, once tireless Stan had set the type and looked after the inking. Morale was high. Seeing their work in print, and watching people reading the magazine around campus, gave the writers satisfaction, and enough distance to re-evaluate their own poems. I do wish my copies of that first year's magazine had survived later moves.

London snowfalls came as a gorgeous surprise that winter. They were frequent and abundant and so white, after Toronto's winter grime. Being a non-driver, I was, at first, puzzled when friends with cars seemed to be cautious about driving out of town in bad weather, for I had never seen the whiteouts sometimes encountered on the highways around London. When I travelled, it was by train – for example to the family Christmas in Ottawa, or back and forth to our Bible study meetings in Toronto, now held in a friend's apartment.

In May the university community drained away. Those months had been a welcome change from the routines to which I would now return.*

---

* On February 10, 2005, Maclean Jamieson, one of the editors of *Applegarth's Folly*, a London, Ontario-based literary magazine, wrote to Margaret concerning the 1973 publication of her poem, 'March Morning in London, Ontario', sending a web address for his memoir of events leading up to its publication: http://webhome.look.ca/~sinuhe/Avison.htm. Margaret replied: 'Thank you for recovering such a good patch of the past for me and refreshing my old memory about that good experience we shared at UWO long ago.' Recent attempts to bring up the website have failed. Margaret's print-off of the article will be stored with her papers at the University of Manitoba Archives and Special Collections.

Margaret with birch trees.
(Family photo: courtesy of Karen McKim)

CBC ARCHIVES

My high school and university friend, Doris Mosdell (now Sangster), worked at the Canadian Broadcasting Corporation. She had been on the staff there for years, doing on-air movie reviews for a period, as well as condensing novels for a regular radio reading programme. Since she was trained as a library cataloguer, she now, in 1973, had a full-time job in the CBC Archives. Before computers, CBC programmes were analyzed in detail by human auditors, then indexed for quick retrieval of items for use in sudden news crises. A cardex was made by the cataloguer from summaries written by auditors. On my friend's urging, I applied for an auditor's job, was accepted and joined the CBC Archives in its old warehouse building on River Street. The nine-to-five job balanced well with my home responsibilities.

The old discs, now copied onto tape, which we audited (a row of us, with tape-reels playing above our typewriters), were stored in metal stacks like the ones bp Nichol and I knew in the old University of Toronto library days; I enjoyed having to go in there to retrieve or refile. Routines varied according to the pressure of sudden demands from the newsroom: 'Give us context!' Using the catalogue as a guide, we would search for relevant items, then flag rushes for the technician, who would then prepare a clip for the broadcast people. The technician and his family, from Newfoundland, were determined to stay only until the oldest child was of school age, then return 'home'.

All the staff members in Archives were distinct individuals. The work tended to be solitary, but on occasion there was a party – for a birthday, say, or for relaxation after a news crisis and the resulting pressure to provide tapes of context materials. Once, a sparkling conversation touched on 'redneck Southern Baptists', and drifted into gentle mockery of 'Bible-thumpers'. It was awkward to have to say 'You'll be embarrassed if I don't say it, and I'll be embarrassed if I do: I trust the Bible's authority, and learn from preachers every week.' They heard in the spirit in which I meant it. I knew that because of the way they warned me off the brownies at another party: 'We've put marijuana in them.'

Of that job, I remember two special days: one, the morning when, to my complete surprise, I found 'we' were on strike, so I thanked the picket person and spent the morning at the Beach, beside the water; the second, the off-hour when the park where I often ate lunch was shimmering and fluttering with pre-migration monarch butterflies. That little park also drew residents of the area, friendly with the school crossing guard whom they all knew; by choosing the earlier lunch hour, we tried not to preempt the break this official took once the children had gone back to school after lunch. Peripheral employment provided by the large CBC building furthered mutual tolerance too.

Walking around the area at midday was my preferred breather. Thus I stumbled upon St. Paul's, a beautiful Catholic church, now a basilica, on Power Street. The painted figures for the Stations of the Cross were set in eye-level niches all around the sanctuary. It was a beautiful place to sit until quiet settled in. Neighbours were close in that part of the city. One noon hour I found an unusual number of parishioners at prayer when I went into the church: the radio that evening reported a local child's murder. No wonder I had felt like an intruder that day, the only time I ever did. Perhaps the inner-city Calgary of my childhood, the Toronto Junction streets I walked in during the Depression years, and the friends I had met at Evangel Hall, made the area around the church and that old CBC building feel friendly.

The hours fitted my home responsibilities. The steady care Mrs McCormack had given, in spite of her illness, was never quite duplicated by any subsequent helper. A period of interviewing applicants attracted by Help Wanted advertisements (for 'a companion and reader, days, for an elderly lady') showed me I was not as discerning as I needed to be. Although I explained that my job required punctuality, making prompt arrival of the companion essential, this expectation was, in experience, unrealistic. Then when I came home unexpectedly one day, I found a person whom I had hired (she had wanted to read aloud, and seemed friendly) slumped in a soft chair. She had clearly been inert for a long time, and Mother was still in bedroom slippers, hunched up in her chair as though in hiding.

Twice – the above was the first time – I fired people, though it cost giving them their week's pay to avoid trouble. The second time I had thought the person would be a long-term solution. She was tallish with fine features, well-spoken, neat – but when I would go through Mother's closet collecting laundry, it seemed as though things were missing. They *were.* One evening when we were to have a visitor, I went to get Mother's pretty new dress that I had hung up in its covering tissue paper the weekend before. That too was gone. And at bedtime (when I often read Mother one of the letters from my father which I'd saved in packets over the years) I found a packet missing, not anywhere I searched.

Later that evening I called my brother's wife. She said 'Ted came home late and is just finishing dinner, but then we'll drive right down!' She found the street address of the companion and we went to her apartment door. I will never forget the woman's eyes when she saw us there, deeply unhappy, with no defensiveness, almost relieved. 'I know,' she said. 'I knew that dress was many sizes too small for me. I can't help it. I am a kleptomaniac: I *have* to take things, and afterwards I hate what I've done and throw them away. You'd better call the police.' Of course all we did was fire her, and finally persuade her to take the balance of her week's pay. It was good to have Ted's backing, personally and financially.

For a time, an unsettling number of plausible companions came and went. Then a solid solution shone out, a woman who enjoyed books, read well, liked Mother, had a maternal interest in fixing up the lunch table so it would tempt Mother's appetite, and so on. It was all the more surprising, then, when after I came in from work one day, I found that my footsteps clicked everywhere I stepped in the kitchen. I scrubbed that floor and a few bad spots on the hall and dining-room carpets, then tried her telephone number. She answered. 'It was sticky …' I began, but she broke in: 'It was a disappointment. When I was preparing lunch, I somehow dropped that jar of honey. I did try to clean up the glass pieces …' Probably I made an aggrieved response, though I did want her to continue as Mother's companion.

But about ten days later, her son telephoned early in the morning. She couldn't come, he said. I began to splutter that it was late to be telling me, and was she sick so suddenly? 'She is in the hospital,' he said. 'She has cancer. She knew someday it would come to this.' The boy was in grade thirteen, an only child, his father having died when he was seven years old. At the memorial service not long after, it was a comfort to meet one of his high school teachers, a man who had taken an interest in the boy; he would know best what could be worked out in the tiding-over period.

'Tiding-over' covered our situation at home, too, for a time, especially when rush hour traffic slowed the Queen streetcars heading to Yonge Street. There the subway trains were frequent but jam-packed; each stop was prolonged as passengers tried to get off while crowds pressed at the doors to get on. Travelling to and from the CBC job took too long. When an elder at Knox Church asked me whether I would be interested in helping with Mrs Lillian Dickson's work, lights went on in my spirit. Mrs Dickson had spoken of her 'Mustard Seed' work at missionary conferences with such direct, factual, absurd and poignant particulars, that I was indeed interested. Resigning from the CBC I do not remember. Certainly I used my accumulated days off to prepare the manuscript of *sunblue*, poems collected from 1966 on, and to hope I might be accepted in this new job which was near enough to our apartment that the weekday nine-to-five might be manageable.

Author photo (Newsome Photography)
for *Winter Sun/The Dumbfounding: Poems 1940–66*
(McClelland & Stewart, 1982).
(Credit: University of Manitoba Archives and Special Collections,
Margaret Avison fonds, Box 1, PC151)

MUSTARD SEED MISSION

The job interview took place at the Toronto office of the Mustard Seed Mission, which was in Forest Hill Village at that time because A.J. Stewart, the secretary, had been living nearby when it was set up.* There was a flight of stairs to the second storey, which held three other offices – for a dentist, a medical supplies agency and an insurance company. Whenever the insurance broker needed privacy with a client and I was alone in the office, his wife became a friendly visitor. I met the dentist and his nurse only once, when for the first time I felt a sharp pain in my jaw while chewing something at lunch. I put my palm to the place to comfort it, an instinctive gesture, and felt an alarming swelling, round as a Ping-Pong ball but larger. The dentist laughed: 'It's backed-up saliva, that's all.' He could make a puncture, from inside, to drain it, but he assured me that it would drain by itself before long. It did. I think of him gratefully on every recurrence, fortunately wide-spaced.

Initially, I was not alone in the Mustard Seed office. Mr Stewart was in charge. His wife, now my good friend Addie, helped him by opening mail, typing receipts for donations, and keeping a special file of letters and reports from Mrs Lillian Dickson, who founded and was the *animus* of Mustard Seed Mission (in Taiwan and Indonesia). But both Stewarts needed more freedom for their varied interests and duties elsewhere. Mr Stewart knew me as a member of Knox Church where he was a senior elder. I learned later that he had considered interviewing me, but first asked a mutual friend whether I was well enough organized to manage an office (his assumption being that anyone who wrote poetry might be unreliable in this regard). He did not know that orderliness had always been necessary to me in earning a living.

It was kind of him to pursue the possibility just when I needed work nearer home. (Mother was known to the Stewarts because she came to church with me as long as she was well enough.) Addie's presence as my trainer created a comfortable ease with her husband as

---

* See 'It bothers me to date things "June the 9th"' in *No Time*. The poem's dedication reads 'for A.J. Stewart (who died June the 8th)'.

well. While she showed me Mrs Dickson's books, the file for letters from Asian children to be redirected to their sponsors, and photographs for use on Mrs Dickson's next speaking tour, Mr Stewart interpolated stories from his tour of the work on the other side of the world, when Addie was left to run the Canadian end alone through those many weeks.

Mr Ling, Chairman of the Mustard Seed Mission Board, came to the office that first day. In time I would come to respect deeply his wise counsel. Addie took me down to the nearby coffee shop which was to become our retreat whenever a board meeting took over the office. By the end of the day, the job was mine, and I was free to go home early enough for my first walk through the tree-shadowed residential streets near Upper Canada College, with lawns and gardens maintained by landscaping crews who brought mowers and clippers and hoes and such things in ungainly trucks. The houses often looked closed up, their owners wintering or summering somewhere else.

As I walked those streets I remembered a remark Mr Cunningham had made one evening, as he drove me home through them from an Evangel Hall event: 'This would be a fastness impenetrable to any door-to-door visiting venture.' I often felt tempted to test his pessimism by knocking on one of those doors – without any clear notion what I would say if someone did happen to be in residence – but I never tried it. Instead I enjoyed the lawns and gardens on the way to and from work. In winter months the beauty was in evergreen shrubs and trees, ironwork on porches and gables under puffs of snow. Toward the traffic light for crossing Avenue Road, smaller homes drew closer to the sidewalk. It was that Avenue Road crossing, or rather the sky over it, that I associate with writing 'Kahoutek' (in *sunblue*). Toronto is full of places I associate with individual poems.

At age ten, somewhere in western Canada, Mr Stewart had begun work as an accountant. From that time he worked on without schooling, glad, as one of an immigrant family from Scotland, to help support his family and to fund the music education of his brother. It excited me to learn that this brother was Reginald Stewart of the Promenade Symphony Concerts (1934–41). His was the first orchestra I and many other Torontonians ever heard. The ticket price was minimal for a narrow bench in Varsity Stadium, on Bloor Street West at Bedford Road. Reginald Stewart needed no curtain rising, no complex lighting effects; he did it all himself, clad in an elegant cape that flared as, baton in hand, he swept in and leapt to his podium.

The original source of finance behind all this, A.J. Stewart had repaired his deficit of institutional education through lifelong reading. He remembered what he read. He had memorized the poetry he liked. His deference to me with my M.A. bothered me, for I was finding him more learned than most of my professors! When the day's office work was cleared away, he sometimes talked, giving me a glimpse of his experiences. Before I knew him, I used to browse happily in his downtown bookstore, a Christian bookstore with a solid reference section, well-marked sections of standard works, and a shelf of tempting new books near the door. The store was filled with browsers and customers every time I visited, little thinking that one day its proprietor would be elsewhere and my employer. At downtown rents, that store must have been a labour of love, with long hours and agonizing bookkeeping to stay one squeak ahead of expenses.

In due course, A.J. and Addie entrusted me with the work at the Mustard Seed office. The day would start with opening our box in the St Clair Avenue post office, stowing the mail safely for the walk to work or, if Mother's helper had been late, for taking public transportation in order to open the office in time for telephone calls. The work was supported by individuals from all parts of Canada who had attended meetings where Mrs Dickson spoke and showed slides. Her 'tours' always precipitated a crisis time in this job, but an exciting and stimulating one. Dates and hours of meetings had to be arranged, bookings urgently proposed here and there to avoid dead time – all this apart from scheduled meetings with the board. Trains and planes were arranged by Mr Stewart whenever distances were greater than he and Mrs Dickson could travel by car. For local meetings I would have the good fortune to travel with her by taxi, with a trunkful of books for display along the walls of the meeting room.

Who was this Mrs Dickson whose books were produced in the early years around the edges of full-time administration and homemaking? Picture a woman small in stature, shoulders and upper arms surprisingly strong-looking, hair with tight curls impatiently controlled by brushing down with water at need, a round puckish face, and sparkling eyes darting here and there, missing nothing. Once, in a taxi to a meeting where she was to speak, she turned from the car window to exclaim: 'The young women wear their hair long and loose-flowing now; it looks pretty on them!' Or, 'Nobody here wears dresses!' The pants so popular during this era would have been a boon on her hair-raising journeys in to Taiwan's 'mountain people', the island's aboriginals.

Her husband, the Rev. Dr James Dickson, built on the mission work of the Rev. Dr George Leslie Mackay in northern Taiwan (Formosa), teaching seminarians and training Taiwanese Christians to plant churches and fan out with the Gospel wherever there were towns and cities. He yearned to go to the aboriginal areas himself, but rightly judged that the required language learning and time-consuming, rugged travel, would mean taking on too much. His determined wife, sharing his vision, was already venturing into the city streets, singing with her accordion and preaching when a crowd gathered. She had her ménage ordered, with helpers who would cope in her absences, and, at age forty-six, began her work up in the mountains with the local tribes.

I have seen Mrs Dickson's absorption in the world outside herself. It is easy to picture her stumbling eagerly into mountain fastnesses, crossing chasms spanned by rope bridges that rise and fall with every step, and without handholds. The people she reached there became dear to her heart. In her slides and display photographs, we saw some of 'her' mountain people who had become teachers, childcare workers, nurses or sometimes missionaries bound for other Asian peoples, carrying the message of new hope, and opening perspectives on life here and in eternity.

All this stimulated me as a participant in my church's 'visitation evangelism' venture which began in 1978. Joan Eichner, my close friend, coordinated the programme. Every Sunday, visitors and members alike were invited by the minister to sign their name and address in a 'friendship pad' which was passed along each pew. Thus regulars met newcomers, and, from the collected new names, Joan made up a list of people who might welcome a visit. One of my volunteer jobs was to telephone these people to try to arrange Tuesday evening visits by trained teams from the congregation. Joan sorted out who would go where according to the results of my preliminary telephone calls. These calls were often cordial, even when a newcomer preferred not to be visited.

Our training was based on an established model of 'visitation evangelism' learned by some of our initiating members at a seminar in Cincinnati. Our visits were made easier when people knew in advance that we wanted to become better acquainted, and that we would be reading from the Bible with them. According to the Cincinnati manual, only certain passages of Scripture were to be read, with any comments on these strictly limited to the emphases Greg Scharf helped us see as central. He was one of our ministers, a gifted scholar who in later years became professor at a prominent American theological school. His training made the VE programme, as it was called, a benefit valued by all team members.

I now realize that the chosen emphases too easily became rigid formulae in our presentations of the 'good news', but I was then relatively young in the faith. Guidelines were necessary. Sometimes their very clarity awoke a warmth of recognition from a Christian in whose home we had gathered. Such visits made real to me the concept of 'oneness in Christ'. Guarded agreement, with some embarrassment, was a more usual response when we closed a visit with these readings and prayer. A few times we faced challenging questions. A graduate student in bio-engineering, once a choir boy in an evangelical Anglican church, carefully edged around his current difficulties with the faith. I felt sure of his strength in science and was convinced that, one day, he would also be strong in the knowledge that covers ranges beyond reason.

One visit was poignant, unforgettable in fact, and still causes me pangs every time it comes to mind. It was to a young intern at Sick Children's Hospital, a man from England doing graduate work in pediatrics. He said he had believed in Jesus and looked to God for strength and help, but now he was shaken. 'What do you say to the parents of a five-year-old who has died, when they ask "Why? How can God allow this?"' I can't remember my words that evening, but I do remember realizing that they by no means reached this sensitive man on a human level. It was not an evening for theological discussion! The poem 'When Their Little Girl Had Just Died' (*Not Yet but Still*) came out of this visit.

At Mustard Seed I was discovering that I enjoyed the business details that accrued after each of Mrs Dickson's meetings: the collected contributions to be sorted and counted and reported to a sponsoring church, the bank account balance to be verified. Mr Stewart did the final report showing costs to Mustard Seed and funds raised for Mrs Dickson's work. My part, listing cheques, counting bills, sorting and counting and rolling the slush-heap of coins, forced me into new games. We had an old manual adding machine, operated by entering numbers and keeping the roll of tape unjammed. The tape held the record I clipped to the final figures for Mr Stewart to work on. The tape would balk if I made entries too quickly, so I began to make the mechanics of slower entering less tiresome by checking my own total against that of the tape. Mr Fennell's tests in the Registrar's Office had developed my capacity for mental arithmetic. Once, I triumphed over the machine. Noticing a discrepancy between its total and my own, I re-ran the figures and found mine vindicated. The fun ended there. Mr Stewart smiled when I crowed about this, and quickly ordered a new machine.

Gradually I found the lone hours at work a good counterbalance to my after-five responsibilities. Despite the immense kindness of Ted and Ruth's doctor, who made house calls unasked, as though for a casual visit, Mother had grown frailer. I saw that Dr McCulloch would observe the pulse in Mother's neck while she was unaware. He prescribed vitamins – and, very reluctantly, a sedative because Mother closed her lips against the tablespoon of brandy he had ordered for bedtime. 'I took the pledge as a child,' she said firmly, 'and I'll keep my word!' Ted's mortal illness from inoperable cancer was already looming over us, but she denied any hint of it, ultimately even denying his death. Dr McCulloch went along with the denial, but when she suffered heart failure which left her immobile, he could no longer fend off hospital life for her. I hated having the ambulance tote us off, though I was more reconciled when the attendant, checking Mother's pulse, asked the driver to sound the siren. The emergency doctor who examined her let me present the family's written consent to her own preference, which she stoutly reiterated even as she lay on the gurney: 'DNR [Do not resuscitate] – no special measures'. Ignoring her, the intern simply explained to me: 'This is a treatment hospital. We treat your mother, or you take her home.' And he ordered a life-extending injection which meant several years lying prone.

If nightly hospital visits added a dimension to the day, at least there were no more frantic 7:30 a.m. telephonings to replace a companion who had cancelled that day, or permanently. It must have been a relief to my friend Joan, too. Her car had made grocery-shopping possible. As long as Mother was able, Joan would also take her out for drives. A turn off the Bayview Extension onto Pottery Road towards Todmorden Mills once prompted Mother to exult in being 'out in the country again'! We did not refute her assumption. (Todmorden Mills had precious associations for my father. *His* father, John B. Avison, had served a parish there before he died of tuberculosis in 1882 when he was just twenty-nine.)

With Mother now hospitalized, I could not carry the rent for Lascelles, nor did I need two bedrooms. My precipitous move to Fellowship Towers Seniors' Residence might have been a bigger chore had not a business couple with a truck come to see if I had anything to sell for a second-hand furnishings and cottage-needs business they ran west of Toronto. They took everything worth keeping that I had not designated for my one-bedroom apartment at Fellowship Towers, even kitchen utensils! Then a friend who taught in the department of English at York University selected some books and papers for the library there. Everything else was earmarked for my new place. Moving day was a scorcher in mid-August. Mary and Frank, here from Ottawa to help organize the new apartment, and visit mother in hospital, campaigned for an air conditioner, asap!

Strange as it seems, there was still time for the weekly Tuesday evening visitation evangelism sessions. 'Cold calls', for which no prearrangement had been possible, were occasionally disheartening. One of these turned out to be to an Inuit, lodged up the stairs from a street door. After we shouted up an explanation of why we were there, he fetched his coat and came down. He led us across the street to a small café where he ordered a hamburger. One of our team members ordered pie, and we all sat over coffee. This northerner had been delegated to negotiate for his people here, but hoped to escape the city soon. He spoke respectfully of an Anglican missionary in his area, but I felt that our social conversation was unsteerable into any talk about the Christian faith or how the Bible fitted into the whole.

One astonishing visit involved a long drive into the northwest suburbs of the city, to the home of an Asian family who had been signing the Friendship Pad and had accepted our offer to come. Several of them met us with courtesy but few words. We were never sure whether they understood much English. They sat in a semicircle facing the two chairs set out for us. Then the hostess, beaming, slipped out and returned with two large plates on which lay two hot king crabs. No implements. No napkins. We ate. The lady of the house, smiling again, removed our plates and returned with two others, each holding a hearty square of white, iced cake: 'We cook Canadian too, for you!' We ate solemnly while the semicircle watched, nodding encouragement from time to time. Then poor Greig Brown, the visit's leader, handed around New Testament paperbacks and struggled through a heavy presentation from Romans. Amid smiles, we at last bowed our way out. Whether our host family ever returned to church, I do not know. If they did, I never spotted them.

Another visit, to a comfortable home on a leafy street west off Yonge Street just within the northern city limits, promised to be more congenial. At first it was. After we had been made welcome, but before our conversation had more than warmed up, a miniskirted girl with overdone eye makeup and spike heels clattered into the house, removed her jacket and scarf in the hall, then banged her way upstairs without a word to anyone about the young man who had also come in and followed her up. The parents gave us the heartbreaking explanation: this only child was a diagnosed schizophrenic, unreachable and unmanageable on bad days, but nevertheless released from hospital into 'home care'. No part-time nurse, not even a psychiatric social worker, had any further help to offer, and the parents were frantic in their concern that they would soon have a pregnancy to face. We listened a good while, wordless, then left.

Some students in a third floor flat on Robert Street were candid and curious. We gathered that their earlier experiences in Sunday school, and homesickness in the big city, had made church seem a friendly possibility. They listened to the Bible reading when we got around to it, but they were evidently just entertaining any and every new idea, excited by the prospect of learning new viewpoints and cataloguing each as mental equipment. Speaking of the Person of Jesus was out of bounds with them.

We visited many like them, in rooms within walking distance of the campus – students who hailed from west coast to east coast, from Australia to China, all of whom had come into the church looking for company on cold, lonely Sundays. They stretched our stiffly prescribed presentations, gradually forcing us to be more flexible and to listen better.

On 'cold calls' to addresses within walking distance, where no prior arrangement had been made, it was exceptional to find a single-family dwelling rather than a range of rented rooms. The Rev. Dr Alex McCombie led one visit to a new homeowner from out of town who was supporting his young family as a construction worker. He remembered a little of the Bible from childhood, listened to the reading at the close of our visit, pondered Dr McCombie's questions, and responded with sudden joyful faith and willingness for life-commitment. The two men, visitor and visited, bonded in acknowledged unity and arranged to meet for further Bible studies in the weeks ahead. Seldom had follow-up been built on such a firm base.

My daily visits to Mother, now on the Riverdale Hospital's chronic care floor, were different from visits to her in the Wellesley Hospital. There, Mother had been in a good cardiac ward. Ted had been a member of the hospital's board, Ruth was still buyer for the hospital's gift shop, and their daughter Joan was a Wellesley nursing graduate who had worked in Emergency there. The comfortable stay there was also partly owing to the kindness of the hospital's social worker, a thoughtful, slow-spoken man, who resisted the medical staff's designs on Mother's bed for active treatment. He knew that I came daily from work, staying until lights out, and therefore he delayed a transfer, hoping to find a chronic care opening which would be within my range. At last a move to Riverdale (now Bridgepoint Health) became possible, just a quick transfer-ride for me by public transportation. This man, retired, must have lived in my district, for I sometimes met him out strolling. We smiled when we passed each other, remembering.

The particular surroundings of Toronto landscapes are knitted into human experiences. I associate the Wellesley Hospital years mainly with 9:30 p.m. icy winds in January and February, no sign of a bus coming up Sherbourne Street or along Wellesley. Ice and occasional menacing strangers made walking after dark unsafe. By daylight, though, the walk to the hospital was welcome, a diagonal route through an area of old houses, quiet streets and old trees: this became a new familiar area for me.

Even better, the Don Valley was a daily refreshment, both approaching Riverdale Hospital and, in glimpses, going home. There were moments free for stepping off onto the grassy hills, when Mother was being washed and turned, and these stimulated my sense of space and my ear for birdsong. At that time, Riverdale's seventh floor was for chronic care cases. The nursing station was at the core of a circular corridor of rooms. Care was heavy-duty, a steady pace from the first bed right around to the last bed, by which time rearranging the first bed was again necessary. 'Rounds' indeed.

Mother's was a four-bed room. Opposite her lay a snowy-haired, calm-faced woman, unmoving. Her grandson came daily and unnerved the nurses and us visitors by pulling the curtains around her bed and disappearing behind them. Beside Mother was a spectrally thin woman who muttered inaudibly, or sometimes wailed. Sometimes she gestured with a distracted waving of arms. Opposite her was an entertainer of anyone who cared to take notice. She manipulated her wheelchair back and forth between the beds but never through the doorway: a threshold was some sort of barrier she feared to violate. She spoke in a southern accent. Her accounts of earlier experiences were clearly delusional – things happening or about to happen, in a context of groves and harbours and old houses and gateways and guardedness. Menace lurked, but keeping within limits gave protection. Workplace talk about success in jobs, and unfair blame from a thin Uncle Somebody who haunted several of her tales, built up a portrait of a woman who was no victim but a minor character in a fantasized business, or in some local social setting, with opulent living in cities. She was a wonderful storyteller with an uninsistent clear voice, directing words to no one, just to the world at large, as long as she was awake.

Mother spoke little by then, never sure whether the words in her mind would be compassable on her tongue. Sometimes alien sounds blurted out and distressed her. She liked having her hair brushed and tied in ribbons on either side of her neck. By day she preferred to wear her own blouses, or sweaters when it felt cold. I read to her sometimes, for my own sake as well as hoping she would like it. Supper trays were a big event. I fed Mother and sometimes the spectral lady as well, for she seemed to ignore the tray, and the nurses' feeding time was not equal to the need. Collection carts returned quickly, in time for kitchen staff to clean up during their shift, so many a tray was collected untouched. When the others in the room fell silent, on in the evenings, I would watch the mice run about. They came up through the air vents, the nurses said.

When a whirlwind of nurses would arrive in Mother's room to attend to the patients, I walked around the circle and looked in on two neighbouring patients we had come to know. One kept calling races at Woodbine, with rising enthusiasm. I once saw a nurse temporarily quiet her by dropping a piece of cookie into her mouth. Then there was a beautiful Japanese woman in a pretty silk coat and slippers, quick-moving and with jackdaw impulses. She liked little objects, especially anything red, and trotted about the halls collecting bits and pieces which relatives and friends and nurses redistributed day after day.

Evenings were peaceful there. After the trays were gone I had my own dinner in the basement cafeteria. Usually visitors ate alone, and hurriedly, before lights out, but one evening I was approached by someone who turned out to be Tim Lilburn. We were both visiting patients, he an old work associate. Without fishing for it, we both soon established the other's occupation: safe conversational ground, not too personal. He had been working in a Jesuit mission in southeast Asia, territory I knew of, as I told him, from Mustard Seed activities and through my sponsorship of a child in Irian Jaya. It turned out that he knew of me through Maggie Helwig, a *Canadian Forum* friend and neighbour of years past. She and Tim were currently working on a poetic version of the Mass, he said, and some other ritual prayers. We ran into each other once or twice more in Riverdale, and the contact spurred me on to read his poems. By following the biographical sketches on the flyleaves of his books, I know that he went on to teach out west.

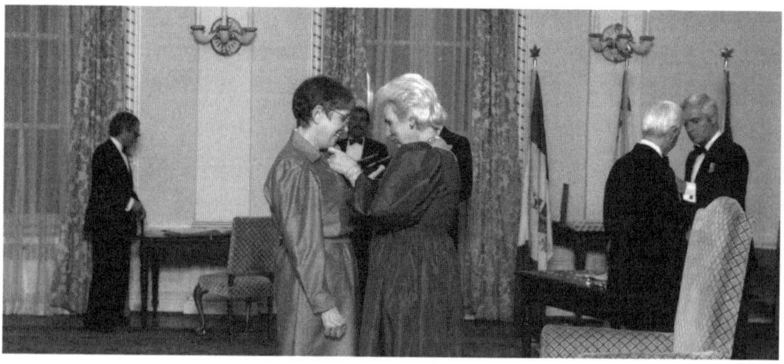

Margaret with Governor-General Jeanne Sauvé, Order of Canada presentation, 1985. (Photo: John Evans. Credit: University of Manitoba Archives and Special Collections, Margaret Avison fonds, Box 1, PC151)

MY MOTHER'S DEATH AND AFTER

I knew nothing of the communal life in Fellowship Towers in my early days there. I left for work by 7:30 a.m. and never returned from Riverdale until after 9:30 lights-out. All this began to change with Mother's death. It occurred on June 7, 1985 over night 'somewhere between 4 and 6 a.m.', but word did not reach me until 8:45, when I was in the office. The hospital asked me to come, sign some papers and take out Mother's belongings. Everything felt odd, so out of sync with my normal day and any of my normal human contacts. My first impulse was to call Ted, but of course he was dead. I wanted more particulars before calling my sister and her family in Ottawa, so, after phoning A.J. and Mrs Stewart to explain the closed office, I made my way to the St Clair West subway station and thence to Riverdale.

An unfamiliar ward nurse on the familiar floor led me behind the bed's curtains and stood there with me. Mother's mouth was a gaping chasm ('By the time we found her, rigor mortis had set in.') They *had* managed to close the eyes. When I kissed her forehead, it was not dry, but cold. I signed something in the nursing office, then a nurse I had not met before appeared with a large grocery bag full of Mother's personal effects and conducted me to the downstairs office where I was asked to sign a form giving permission for an autopsy. In the elevator this woman said briskly: 'That's what it is, eh? It all ends up in a paper bag!' And I heard myself firmly declaring, 'No, that is *not* all there is!'

When I returned once afterwards to thank the 3-to-7 p.m. nurse who had been particularly kind to Mother, it pleased me to hear her tell about their daily speech therapy sessions. Once very recently, speaking with the painful persistence of the therapy sessions, Mother had slowly said to the nurse: 'You seem to understand me. Please tell the nurses "thank you".' (She never made this heroic effort to speak to me. We communicated silently, and by lingering over whatever good food the trays contained. That was enough.)

Was there a notice in the paper? Somehow, Vi Montgomery, a resident at Fellowship Towers, knew the time of the funeral, for family only, with the Rev. George Lowe officiating, and guessed that relatives might come back to my apartment after the service. (There was no second service at the crematorium, and burial arrangements for the ashes, alongside my father's in the Necropolis, had been made in advance.) I was especially thankful for Vi's thoughtfulness because of a rebuke I received on returning from the funeral. The driver who brought one of my nieces on ahead with the flowers had left some, too cumbersome for her to carry all at once, on the lobby tables. 'Get those funeral flowers out of here,' a staff member barked as I came in. I did, and put the lot into my bathtub upstairs, later to be broken up into bouquets.

Up in my apartment, the electric kettle had not been plugged in, and a huge pot of water on the stove was barely warm. Flustered, I was glad that Ruth was bringing some sandwiches, but aghast at my bare shelves (dishes enough for me and an occasional guest, no more). Then there came a rattling sound in the hall: Vi's husband Wes with a tea room cart loaded with cups and saucers, a cream and sugar set, and spoons. 'Vi thought you could use these,' he said. 'I'll come back with the cart when you're finished.'

That was almost the moment to overcome my aching tearlessness. But no proper weeping came for two years more, and then out of a blue sky, untriggered, at the office, the sore sobbing began. I had to close up for the day and occupy the space defined by Marian Anderson's singing of the spiritual, 'Sometimes I feel like a motherless child'. The inadequacy of any 'tribute' we could utter had made us all content to keep the funeral service liturgical, simple. In *No Time* there are several poems explicitly about the Riverdale days, with memories and meditations, out of this time.

During Mother's illness, at our family doctor's suggestion, I had attended an open meeting for caregivers at the Clarke Institute of Psychiatry. The introductory speech, outlining areas of concern as a guide to discussion, was brief and stimulating. As I listened, I developed an awed respect for women with 'difficult' mothers-in-law, or with mothers whose caregiving child was so resented by a competitive sibling that maternal feelings had to be smothered for the other child's sake. If illness complicated the dependency, a caregiver's own children would inevitably suffer neglect to some extent: no parent home after a child's fall, for example, to give comfort and Band-Aids. Hearing one account after another of household managers under these pressures, I saw my own situation in a better perspective. I had longed for children, as some unmarried women do. The domestic work at the Johnsons had helped, and Mother's growing dependence satisfied this longing. My personal needs were met by our adult daughter-mother relationship.

Now that Mother was dead, all her roles over the years bemused me. What I waited for, and was in time rewarded by, were vivid memories of Mother at characteristic lively stages of life: her sharing out of household responsibilities in our school days, so justly and with such openness to revision for any good reason. My father called and chaired these family conferences, but deferred to her agenda at them. We then conceded that the demands of their church responsibilities made some wriggle-room necessary. The fact that allowances adjusted to cover our clothing purchases and incidentals were entrusted to us as well, was certainly Mother's ruling. She knew that in his accounts Daddy painstakingly noted tiny expenses (a bottle of ink, a donation at some meeting), but overlooked, for example, items like candy ('Feel in my pocket,' he would say at the table after dessert, 'there may be something there'), or even major repairs to the car. Mother's firm direction, especially when Nanny or some long-term guest or kitchen help was added to the ménage, kept our core family stable and cohesive.

Now that her care was all behind me, I thought I'd get back into the swim, at work certainly, and at Fellowship Towers where I hoped to become acquainted with my fellow residents. In addition, a nurse I'd known at Knox Church met me for coffee one afternoon and proposed that I volunteer at St Michael's Hospital Palliative Care Unit. Anne Gauntley, in charge of palliative care volunteers, would interview me first, but I would enjoy meeting her, as indeed I did. In the inevitable hierarchy of hospital management, a volunteer appointment at that time also involved gaining the approval of the hospital's overall director of volunteers, who took a confronter's stance during my interview. It was a surprise at the end to be told that I was accepted.

Anne's direction of my further preparation for the job, in six Wednesday evening training sessions, was objective, memorable, enjoyable. There were videos of the pioneer palliative care unit in England, which Anne and Shirley Herron, the palliative care unit manager, had visited. There were also videos about palliative patients themselves. All these years later, I vividly remember one about a woman who was encouraged to focus on the time she had left, with the result that she roused herself out of a considerable slump by asking whether she could try to play the piano from her wheelchair. Happily for her and her fellow patients, she could play, and well: singsongs evolved among the patients who could sit in the lounge. There was another patient, enfeebled and nearing his end, but sustained by the leaves of a shrub outside his window. In another sequence, a woman close to death peacefully announced to the nurse on rounds, 'It will be tomorrow.' Just for a moment, she explained, she had experienced levitation, though still lying flat, seeing herself laid out on the bed below. Her death did occur the following morning.

Once the six-week course was completed, each new volunteer was scheduled for a half-day's work per week. We were counselled to plan a happy movie or social date afterwards, so as to avert heavy-heartedness or reversion to our past mourning times. The volunteers with whom I've talked since agreed with my finding that our time of personal grief had given us perspective, a measure of acceptance, that had helped us to be objective as we met patients in their final weeks. Since Anne had won my respect, however, I followed her advice and often walked home after my stint, discovering a new area east of my usual downtown routes and finding new leafy back ways and quiet streets with small houses and no traffic. Nothing of my volunteer morning lingered then.

I have worked out my own ways of walking a distance. First, venture far enough to feel a steady rhythm with your whole body, so that after the jolt of any necessary stop, as at a curb, you are easily released into the remembered pace. Sometimes, to strike the 6/8 rhythm that is most sustaining, I dream up words to repeat ('chlorophylled shrubbery' one day) so that neither side of my body feels unequally stressed. The established rhythm brings on a slight dissociation of sight and hearing, so that undirected receptors allow the world around to flow uncensored into consciousness. A dry, dusty, chicken-coop smell seems part of seeing small frame houses, fronts blanked to the street. A final stage, synaesthesia – also the state necessary to writing a poem – is hard for the depersonalized experiencer to sustain. The detachment-with-stimulated-emotion is the state in which a fleeting phrase or the glimpse of a remembered scene is a signal: catch this now, or it's gone forever. Groups of student writers have heard me cite a related discipline: Gladys Story's sound counsel to me as a teenager, to eschew for ten years the first person singular in my poetry.

Volunteer training continued, in a sense, during regular monthly meetings, on Wednesdays between 6 and 8 p.m. One of the first seemed designed to emphasize harmony between Protestant and Roman Catholic volunteers. No sectarian stress was evident among the mixed group of volunteers I joined, but perhaps the history of St Michael's Hospital (long managed by the Sisters of St Joseph, but latterly brought wholly under business management) made the sisters sensitive to any threat of incursion on the values their hospital represented. Hence the tactful, almost defensive, way the sister who addressed us began, eager to stress the common cause as she spoke about the positive attitudes conducive to good palliative care.

Once we relaxed from the feeling of being managed by this needlessly diplomatic start, the learning session was excellent, so useful indeed that I stuffed my notes from it into the 'maybe autobiography' file. The theme was hope: our metaphors for hope from seasonal cycles, our signals of hopefulness, the discipline sometimes necessary to staying hopeful; and the bedrock value of Christian hope. Since each person has value, this life is *not* all there is, and spiritual strength is available for enduring and dying.

The sister concluded by playing for us a recorded song about a rose, from seed through growth under the gardener's care, to the last stages of flowering. Each stage had its beauty. This 'accentuate the positive' note fitted the symbol to her theme without denying the end of the cycle. My notes conclude with afterthoughts: 'It *was* inspirational, helpful too – so why does it stir in me a *yes, but?*' I did not want to take a negative stance, but I wanted nothing 'cheering' to deny those almost overwhelming experiences that affect the tenor of difficult days until they are worked through. The better I knew the Bible, the more it helped me understand this process: its stories are often stark in their realism about bad times and prolonged sufferings. The Storyteller rides the storm with us, and here and there throws in challenges more awful than I could ever dream up – and to people already, in their own view, pressed past endurance.

In my younger days I rejected sentimental Sunday school lessons that dwelt on God's care for us in terms of little leaves opening in spring, the fragrances in April and May, and so on. The ice storms of winter, the dark months, or violent storms after warm days – these were never part of that story. It takes insurance law to admit to those 'acts of God'. Butting against easy faith is not a good attitude, but God tolerates and deals with it, slowly teaching the honest, positive side of realism, that power in the Joseph stories, in the Old Testament histories, in *Habakkuk,* in Mark's gospel: blunt narratives all. All these stories informed my thinking on those walks home after each palliative care unit shift.

A few years earlier, my friend Joan had passed on to me her copies of *The Second Mile* magazine, published by William Pope in Nova Scotia. Knowing that I liked the idea of putting my poems 'out there', but not the publicizing part, she suggested that Mr Pope, whose Lancelot Press also published books, might be interested in my poetry. I could not have known then that the Popes' son Robert, a vigorous young artist already making a mark with his work, would soon be diagnosed with cancer. During the ensuing years, he produced a remarkable documentation, in paintings, of the course of a cancer patient's illness from the sufferer's point of view. The impact of his work, some of it reproduced in book form, has been meaningful to physicians and families and hospital staff, and ultimately became the focus of his father's life after Robert's death in 1992.

Of all this I had suspected nothing when we first corresponded. Mr Pope agreed to consider a manuscript, I sent him the poems on hand, and *sunblue* was published in 1978. This was followed after my mother's death by *No Time* (1989). Through that book, Joan and I met William and Isabel Pope in Montreal when it won a Governor General's Award for Poetry. That was the beginning of a good friendship.

It intrigues me to consider the various publishers I've known over the years. *Winter Sun* appeared, in England, though the efforts of Kay Coburn, and the publication of *The Dumbfounding,* with Norton, in New York, was entirely arranged by Denise Levertov. *A Doctor's Memoirs* had to be 'promised in advance' to make the amorphous project seem worth the family's investment (paying me for my time). They wanted 'a good publisher'. I remember John Gray, sitting in his Macmillan office, listening to my proposal that he risk committing himself to an unwritten manuscript! He looked more like a university professor than a businessman; his thoughtful silences during that interview were impressive. But finally, to my amazement and joy, he did agree to 'take' the unwritten book.

When Mr Pope decided to retire from publishing, Richard Teleky, editor of my *Selected Poems* (Oxford), was the one who directed me to Brick Books as a possible distributor of *sunblue, No Time* and *Not Yet But Still.* When I had another collection ready, I sent the manuscript to Brick, and they agreed to consider what became *Concrete and Wild Carrot.* Kitty Lewis, the manager, explained that the care Brick takes about quality meant that no manuscript would be accepted until a thorough process of selection had taken place. Then one of several editors, scattered from coast to coast, would take on the editing.

My editor was Stan Dragland, now in Newfoundland. He took scrupulous care, had me rewrite one scant poem I refused to omit ('Remembering Gordon G. Nanos'), and improved punctuation and many other details of the manuscript. This close attention was very different from that of any other publisher/editor I had known, but it came to be something I appreciated. (It helped that Stan was my *Pom Seed* friend and operator of UWO's old press, many years earlier.) Stan's incitement to prepare a manuscript carefully helped equip me to cope with the Porcupine's Quill's editorial staff's work in preparing, with Stan and Joan, the three volumes of *Always Now: The Collected Poems.*

Throughout the period of these varied dealings with publishers, I kept on writing and earning a living until retirement in 1986, when writing and working on revisions of new poems continued, with Joan's computer typescripts increasingly invaluable, especially before cataract surgery, and even after, since my vision was still partly impaired. I did sometimes find myself in a dry spell, though. At such times, my life's vocation would seem to recede from me. 'In the eyes of others,' says W.H. Auden in *The Dyer's Hand,* 'a man is a poet if he has written a good poem. In his own, he is only a poet at the moment when he is making the last revision to a new poem. The moment before, he was still only a potential poet; the moment after, he is a man who has ceased to write poetry, perhaps forever.'

During the first years at Fellowship Towers after Mother's death, my old contacts overlapped with the new ones. It helped that residents from Knox Church perpetuated that connection as long as the Knox van was running. Joan was the volunteer driver who called for passengers at both Christie Gardens and Fellowship Towers seniors' residences, then drove us home again after morning and evening services. As a passenger, I learned to know some of my fellow Knox members much better.

Mrs Cora Hanna had been a missionary nurse with Hudson Taylor's China Inland Mission. Sunday after Sunday I had observed her peaceful face in church, sometimes as she sat beside her son Grant, also a missionary, when he was home on furlough. His joyful concentration during hymn singing taught me to try harder to make hymn words mine as I sang. Only later did I learn that Mrs Hanna's husband had been killed by bandits in China. She had the presence of mind to drop to the ground too, clutching one of their children, and, when the coast seemed clear, escaping with her child south to Cheefoo where, now a single mother, she served as school nurse.

Ninety years old when she moved into Fellowship Towers, Mrs Hanna said she missed making pies for the family every Saturday. As we waited for the van Sunday mornings, her white sandals became the focus of attention. Her doctor had cut a hole in their tops to ease her buckling toes, and she kept wearing them in winter, with only loose galoshes atop. The sandal straps were soft, and it became my job to buckle them solidly to prepare their wearer for the high narrow steps into the van.

Then there was Mr Stanley Austing, gaunt, a great long-distance walker. In his nineties he had walked from a southern point in Papua New Guinea to the mountainous tribal area in the north where his missionary son worked. On until his one-hundred-and-second birthday, increasingly bony and thin, he still walked daily, his tall frame oddly tilted backward. ('Here's my feet, my head's coming,' someone quipped.)

The Rev. Dr and Mrs Alexander MacLeod were two others in that van with bonds to the Far East. Dr MacLeod had spent the World War II years in a Japanese prisoner of war camp. All he would say about it was that he needed immediate medical care when brought back to San Francisco, before proceeding to the east coast for three years' hospitalization. Mrs MacLeod, repatriated before the Japanese invaded their area of China, had concentrated on music, piano teaching, while waiting for him long and anxiously in New England. Now she and Mrs Harriett Hanes, her good friend at Fellowship Towers, worked together to provide 'Friday Night Music' hours for the other residents. Mrs Hanes carried her own hi-fi player down to the public lounge and drew on an astonishing library of tapes. She introduced each number with biographical notes on the composer and, sometimes, simple comments on the work itself to make it more accessible to untrained ears. Refreshments ended the evening, always with a diabetic choice for Dr MacLeod and some others.

At Christie Gardens the Knox van picked up several other passengers, among them Mrs Vera Mathews and Mrs Mary Fitch, two women of force and intelligence whose frank comments the rest of us deliberately incited. In time, as passengers dwindled, the van was discontinued. Fortunately, Fellowship Towers had a sequence of fine chaplains and we enjoyed the Sunday morning services in the chapel there.

Four chaplains stand out in my memory. The Rev. Dr Bob Irvin was a precise thinker, theologically, both an intellectual and an evangelical. For some years he had been a Dean at the Moody Bible Institute in Chicago, in the very brick building I walked past in my pagan days there. He taught us, a miscellaneous group of retired old people, as carefully as if we still had years to work with the principles he elicited from the texts.

The Rev. Dr Gordon Stephens had also been an academic, and was still engaged in the study of biblical archaeology. He insisted on his identity as the son of a blue-collar father, as one whose life had been changed in his early twenties by conversion at an evangelical meeting. Acceptance was immediate in his new church community, but he confessed to us the fears he felt in his early prayer-circles. When his turn came, he would stand and grip the back of his chair so tightly that its legs rattled against the floor. He did not propose any prayer circles at Fellowship Towers!

The Rev. John Kershaw was a third outstanding chaplain. He and his wife Vivian brought many gifts to his ministry among us. With a philosopher's mind, a concern for individuals and a background in psychology, he could encourage troubled residents confidently, with a reverence for the person consistent with his vocation. Besides the teaching sessions in the chapel, thoughtfully prepared and taught with conviction, he and Vivian hosted various informal get-togethers. Some Saturday afternoons, for instance, they gathered us residents for a 'storytelling' time. The stories were not instructional, simply good plots, well-written. Then followed a great treat: fresh baking Vivian had brought, and hot chocolate.

From Pastor Kershaw's many comments, and from his regular

prayers for Pastor Georgi Vins, we knew how deeply involved he felt with Russian Gospel Ministries, a mission founded by Vins and subsequently merged with another mission to form Frontline Missions International. Vins and his church would meet in the forest to evade hostile Soviet intervention, but, even so, he was eventually captured and sent to a Siberian concentration camp. Christians outside Russia spread the word and agitated so effectively that he was ultimately released in 1979, but stripped of his Soviet citizenship and forcibly exiled from his homeland to the U.S.A. There he founded his mission, working for the church in the Soviet Union until his death in 1998.

In spite of their strong ties to Pastor Vins' work in Ukraine and Russia, the Kershaws seemed securely anchored in Fellowship Towers. We residents reassured one another that they would be staying because of Mr Kershaw's health problems, which he did not conceal from us. Probably to encourage several stroke victims among the residents, he described the stroke he had suffered: tearfulness in the initial period, he told us, was physical in basis, not emotional. Patience through a slow recovery period must have been drawn from his spiritual dependence, for it could not have come naturally to such an intense, goal-oriented man. He also took delight in nature, and therefore in Robert Bateman's art, and in his own hobby, painting.

We were incredulous, then, when he announced one day that he would be leaving us to take over Pastor Vins' job as director of RGM. His headquarters would be in the States, but he would be travelling at least twice a year to Ukraine, secretly carrying funds to the church there. The farewell gathering was memorable: crowds came from all sixteen floors, and the collection was in proportion to the residents' esteem for the Kershaws, who were the focus of a standing-room-only audience when the presentation was made. No chaplaincy couple before or since has had the Kershaws' gift of reaching every kind of Fellowship Towers person on his or her own terms.

At the time of this writing, the present chaplain, the Rev. William (Bill) Hubbard, is another strong personality with another gifted wife, Karen. The contrast with the Kershaws is striking, Pastor Hubbard's background being military. After World War II, his father was stationed in Germany with the Canadian Army Occupation Force. Away from this context, as a young adult at a Baptist missionary's meeting,

Bill first made contact with and was overwhelmed by Scripture and the words of Jesus. Though respectful of his home, he was rueful about his parents' lack of enthusiasm when he gave them the good news of the impact that Christian teaching was having on his own life.

He retained a warm eagerness to offer Christ to everyone, simply expecting that the gift of salvation would be welcomed naturally, in his own generous spirit. He had not grown up in the anaesthetizing familiarity with evangelical teaching that in later years breeds, not contempt, but dreary indifference in those who rebel early, freeing themselves from the strictures of 'should' and 'ought' before finding their own approach via the touch of awe that enables believing to come first and anchor the knowing of truth.

The consequence has been a very different ministry here, shoring up shaky faith, encouraging faith in those open to hearing the word, alerting long-term believers to expect newness, always, from God. Pastor Hubbard is an eager student, yet also, from a stance of intense and genuine caring, practical in his approach to day-to-day life, to our lives, the lives of his own growing-up children, and our whole Toronto community. The variety of pastors at Fellowship Towers has highlighted the wonderful uniqueness of every human being, that created basis for all human woes and wonders in relationships.

From its beginnings in early piano lesson days, then resuming a few years later when our music teacher was old and dying, my relationship with Joan continued to develop through participation in our home Bible study group, membership in the same church, involvement in Evangel Hall's Sunday evening services, as well as during my mother's last years, in the church visitation evangelism programme and all through Fellowship Towers days. And, as mentioned earlier, at a time when I was reluctant to publish, Joan was the one who encouraged me to submit the manuscript of *sunblue* to Mr Pope at Lancelot Press.

In my later years, I discovered how essential for me, so given to impulse (the underside of openness to nature and fleeting insight), was Joan's objective, logical, disciplined mind. She could have had a university career, teaching philosophy, if she had not chosen to accept the responsibilities of family life. The disciplines she had learned exposed my tendency to self-indulgence, to statements so fuzzy in outline as to be virtually evasive, even untrue. Learning is always painful; making a good friend has costs. But the reward, a true friend in old age, continues to be astounding and delightful to me.

Joan became the reader to whom I ran with any new poem. Instead of a reaction of 'wow', what followed – and I came to expect and want this – was a close reading: what do these four lines mean? Does this stanza belong in the poem? In this place? Are you sure this is the word you mean? This title doesn't seem to introduce what you've written. On her computer she would produce typed copy (I write in longhand, as I did even in the days when my fingers would work on the typewriter keys). I had tried a computer of my own, but resisted it every inch of the way. 'A Chip on Her Shoulder', written for *Hi-Lites,* the in-house paper here, records my reaction.* Now that the internet is taken for granted, I comfortably drift farther and farther out of the swim, grateful for a friend who does necessary e-mailing, and types texts in bold print for my easy reading. Thanks to Joan's computer, the pile of manuscripts began to grow. 'Don't you have enough for a book here?' Joan asked again in the late nineties. *Concrete and Wild Carrot* was assembled and sent off to Brick Books as a result.

During these busy days at Fellowship Towers, friendships developed with residents like Margaret Dingle, who was always carrying a book. One day I asked her to show me the title, and we talked easily from then on. She wore a handkerchief dropped from the ears over her lower mouth because cancer of the jaw had left her without control of her saliva. Once a conversational basis was established, however, she focused totally on whatever the subject might be, ignoring the covering's impediment and thus enabling me to ignore it. Her objectivity and her Christian radiance lasted even to final days in Sunnybrook's palliative care unit.

Another dear friend, Canon Dr Ina Caton, managed for a while to keep an apartment in Fellowship Towers and to prepare her own food, although her sight was failing. She maintained ties with Little Trinity Anglican Church, a long distance south and east. The chaplains here sometimes invited her to lead prayers at midweek chapel meetings, or, occasionally, to teach. Whenever she spoke, the chapel was filled with

* The essay is reprinted in the 'Documents' section which follows.

awed silence. We understood why Wycliffe College honoured her with a doctorate towards the end of a life of service. Her work had included Sunday school responsibilities throughout a forbiddingly wide, under-populated area of northern Saskatchewan. She could tell many a tale of treacherous back roads, drifted-over ditches, gatherings sparsely attended or not at all when roads were judged by parents to be impassable.

Finally recalled to Toronto, she looked forward to the scholarly libraries she had been ravenous for but cut off from for many years. It was a spirit-stretching discipline to discover that now, with both leisure and books, she had to contend with diminishing eyesight. By the time she came to Fellowship Towers, a cataract had well-nigh closed her 'good eye'. After her doctor had discussed the pluses and risks of surgery on that eye, she asked us to pray for a wise decision. The operation did widen her rim vision, for a time anyway.

All through her days here, Ina offered a small-group Bible study in her apartment to any of us who wanted it. Because she couldn't see well enough to read her notes, she engaged the aid of magnifiers to help her read onto tape both the passage of the day and her textual comments, to be played back before group discussion ensued. Facing reality, Ina eventually applied for a room in Belmont House, where more extensive care was assured. How we missed her when her long wait ended abruptly, since space could not be held.

After Mother's death I gradually became involved in resident activities. Someone nominated me to the large executive group, headed in those days by Bill Bodden. Perhaps he knew of my Knox connections. He was a Presbyterian too, an elder in his church, and a very confident president of 'Yongestirs', the residents' council. Bill's name evokes that of Edythe Forsyth, another leading light of that time, the person who planned Talent Night programmes, agitated for light-hearted entertainment and worked hard to make these evenings a success. She was a little bit of a thing, with a cane, then two canes, then a walker, but she never mentioned her health limitations. On her urging, I became a member of the programme committee. Meeting in one anothers' rooms, we drew up a fine list of possible programmes, even offering to host them so that no questions could arise about who would take responsibility.

At the next executive meeting, our committee's report was called for, our list of possible programmes was proudly handed to the chairman – and nothing more was ever heard of it! Mrs Forsyth was quickest to rise above this disappointment, just as she rose above her narcolepsy, the strange malady which startled her new friends, for she 'came and went' in responsiveness, even in consciousness. The episodes were unpredictable, but never lasted long; we all learned to wait through those moments, then resume whatever we were discussing without breaking step. When Bill Bodden died, the residents' executive dwindled. His was too hard an act to follow.

Other changes came. Some residents died,* some moved to nursing homes, some to family members' homes. Some returned to out-of-town locations dear to them from earlier years, among familiar landscapes and lifelong friends with whom they were still in contact. But others, like Mary Horne, my late friend-down-the-hall, showed no interest in a residents' outing to the very district where she and her husband had raised their children and later lived in retirement. 'This is where I am now,' she said comfortably of Fellowship Towers.

Organizational skills and lively ideas for projects returned with a new generation of residents. Never before had Yongestirs been so cheerfully *stirred.* The meetings grew until they filled the auditorium. Under presidents Connie Stokes and then Genevieve Carder, new ideas proliferated and new committees were struck. The library, on the far side of the auditorium, began to grow more inviting. Mrs Emma Austin, who had helped shape a good church library before moving to Fellowship Towers, made up a card catalogue and put the shelves in order. Readers welcomed the new system, though for some years none of her successors had the time or the cataloguing skills to carry on such orderly work. For a while, an inexperienced young staff person from the activities department was given responsibility for the library, but long-standing residents objected. The shelving had been put in by residents, Wes Montgomery insisted, so the library should again be the residents' responsibility. A library committee took over, purchasing books with income from the Towers' annual bazaar. For low-vision readers, the public library brought in selections of large

---

* See 'For a Salty and Sainted Friend', *Not Yet But Still,* and 'Audrey: A Posthumous Portrait', *Concrete and Wild Carrot.*

print books on a rotation basis. When Genevieve Carder was president of Yongestirs, she helped readers to find the books they wanted and even placed notices and reviews of new books on every floor of the residence. With the constant flow of older residents out and new residents in, the tradition of volunteer library management is still being handed on.

Throughout this period in Fellowship Towers, I was showing my poems to Joan, my friend and enabler. Together we assembled the contents of *No Time,* and *Not Yet But Still,* and sent the manuscripts to Mr Pope. *Concrete and Wild Carrot* was readied after Mr Pope had retired from publishing, and sent to Brick Books. Nearly a year passed before the book was accepted and the editorial revisions cleared up. The background of my current life is reflected in the book. The Ramsden Park poem, for instance, refers to the lovely park, on the west side of Yonge Street just north of Fellowship Towers, where I still like to walk or sit. 'Dividing Goods' grew out of residents' discussions, heated or reflective, about 'leaving money' to distant family, or 'saving for my estate'. 'Balancing Out' remembers a frequent Sunday morning fellow worshipper at Knox Church, near the Scott Mission, no doubt the source of the coat mentioned in the poem. Gordon Nanos, of 'Remembering Gordon G. Nanos', was a quiet and much-loved resident. Part 2 of 'Other Oceans' comes from early hours at my bay window desk overlooking the Rosedale Valley. Part 7's 'post-modern' lines probably echo things learned from listening to the radio, and, increasingly, the TV. (Before successful cataract surgery I depended on the media.) 'Lament for Byways' and many other poems reflect Toronto walks over the years. Glimpses would register in my rhythm-hypnotized mind, and return long after, unsummoned, with astonishing vividness.

When I was first told that *Concrete and Wild Carrot* was nominated for a Griffin Prize, I was overwhelmed by word of its lavishness. Surely it is the most generous award for poetry anywhere! It is offered by Scott Griffin, a successful businessman with a strong interest in poetry. His wife told me later at the Edinburgh Festival that, bewildered by his success, he once turned to her for counsel. Her response was to remind him that, while he might worry about having too much money, most writers worry about having too little. And because he had always enjoyed poetry so much, why not set up a poetry prize?

The night the awards were to be announced, one for Canadian poetry and one for international poetry, the van driver who was attempting to deliver me and three friends to the address on the printed invitation seemed as much at a loss as we were: that's how new to us all Toronto's Distillery District was in 2003. After arrival and a social hour, my three friends were led off to different places in the dark dining room. My table was within sight but not within hearing of theirs. I was seated, among others, with Michael Ondaatje and Adrienne Clarkson, then Her Excellency the Governor General. All those at the table seemed to know one another well. Because social chit-chat has long been a difficulty and an embarrassment to me, I was happy enough to be somewhat out of the conversation. Food was brought, keeping us all busy in the dark, unsure what our forks had speared until it was in our mouths. We all laboured under a like disadvantage, though, and managed right through the banquet.

The occasion of a dinner before the presentation of an award is difficult for writers whose working life is solitary. Most are confused by a confounding of identities: the day-to-day person is different from the writing person, since the latter has suffered a shift of viewpoint towards a presence speaking from, as well as to, the unknown readers. But that presence lacks legs to receive an honour.

Poetry has a limited public. Publishers need some measure of return from marketing these books. Publicity around a prize-winning book brings them increased profit. Yet prizes, annual 'top ten' lists in the newspapers, and the like, seem to devalue what they mean to celebrate. What if no *really good* book came out for three years running? Would any panel of judges say so? And does there have to be a 'star' in every year's cast of poetic performers? On the other hand, quite apart from market considerations, income from publishing poems is scant. By rewarding excellence in less popular arenas like poetry, generous donors certainly buy time for writers to write.

How the Griffin Prize presentations began that night, I cannot revisualize. I do remember rising and making my way forward when my name was called. There were insecure wooden steps up to a platform. Seeing that my cane would perhaps miss them in the suddenly glaring stage light, Mr Griffin courteously and simply helped to haul me up. On stage his elbow was very welcome as he steered me across to the podium. Other people said things, then my turn came after an envelope was handed to me. It struck me how remote the secluded writer's home base was from this exotic, dark-and-stage-lit, very public place. Without time to collect myself, I said what came to me involuntarily: 'This is ridiculous!' The audience out there in the darkness did not gasp or wait for sensible elaboration. Their instant laughter, surprised but friendly, made my remark seem all right. I did say some other things, and I hope they redeemed the situation by conveying something of my respect and appreciation.*

After the presentation, younger people began to dance somewhere out in another area, but the Griffins were quick with their guidance toward the van which had been prearranged to convey me and my friends safely back to Fellowship Towers. I particularly remember Mrs Griffin managing to heave me up the van steps under cover of fixing over me a shawl-cape I'd brought, which might have dragged and tripped me.

And it was not all over. The prize money was overwhelming, but for me the primary value of the award was that it included travelling to Edinburgh that summer to do a reading at the Festival of Books. Years earlier, on the approach to Le Havre with the Johnson children in my charge, I had glimpsed a far coastline which someone on deck

---

* In her letter about the 1990 Governor General's Awards (see 'Documents', page 294), Margaret records having involuntarily said the same thing ('ridiculous') in a CBC interview with Shelagh Rogers following the ceremony. If she had been up on preparing acceptance speeches, she might have followed the lead of Wallace Stevens' 1955 'On Receiving the National Book Award for Poetry', a photocopy of which was in her possession: 'Awards and honors have nothing to do with this [the incalculable expanse of the imagination as it reflects itself in us and about us]. The role of awards and honors in the life of a poet is simply to bring him back to reality, to remind him, in the midst of all his hopes for poetry, that he lives in the world of Darwin and not in the world of Plato. He does not accept them as true satisfaction because there is no true satisfaction for the poet but poetry itself.' In her Griffin acceptance speech, Margaret went on to explain that 'all this [fuss] seems very remote from the impulse that makes a poem', but 'ridiculous' had already won the hearts of the audience. At Margaret's request in 1991, Shelagh Rogers had kindly omitted the first 'ridiculous' from the aired interview.

Margaret at The Griffin Prize reading, Toronto, 2003. (Photo: Patricia Fry)

said was England. So near and yet so far, I gazed at that magical source of my language and invaluable reading until I became aware that the four children, readied for disembarking, were beginning to squirm. Scotland held that same magic attraction, and now I would set foot there and travel, west to east, across the country.* England remained out of range, but I was glad to be spared the London crowds, yet to be able to talk by telephone from a safe distance to Sigmund, my war refugee friend and German language coach, who lived there.

* For an account of the Scotland trip, see Joan Eichner's 'The Griffin Prize for Excellence in Poetry', in *Hope and Healing: The Robert Pope Foundation Newsletter*, Spring 2004, 9–12.

POETS LEARN FROM POETRY*

Poets learn from poetry. My learning has been haphazard, dependent at first on hearing the poems I liked in a school's curriculum or those we had to memorize. Ever since, I have both read and written with my ear. In my younger days, 'creative writing' courses were unheard of. Poets were famous Englishmen, we thought – and I liked Robert Browning's lively but verbose long poems better than his wife's lyrics. More natural to my ear were the few modern American poems that turned up in our readers.

In my early teens, I wanted to choose for myself what I would read. I hunted for poetry in my father's library (which was largely theological), and took Palgrave's *Golden Treasury* up our cherry tree, with a cushion. My perch proved unromantically awkward, and a thirteen-year-old made no headway with the poems. They were written in an English language I would have to learn from books. Then in the library, far too early, I found Robert Bridges' *Testament of Beauty,* stiffly English to my Canadian perception, though its solemnity moved me. The incantatory music of Francis Thompson's 'The Hound of Heaven', too, stuck with me long after I first read my father's copy.

What I read apart from school was mine in a special sense, my choice. For example, Thomas Hardy's *The Dynasts,* its architectural vaults and spaciousness, suited the frame of mind of a groping reader in those Depression years. And the border ballads read to us by Miss Gladys Story in her after-school poetry club, one brief precious high school term (she died soon after), gave *time past* a new magnetic force, and wakened in me a hunger to learn how poets spoke in faraway places and times.

It is hard, at the end of life, to remember which experience came

---

* First published in *Arc,* Winter 2004, in slightly different form, Margaret intended this essay – 'Poets Learn from Poetry' – to end her autobiography, but she was not given time to reach the last chapter of her own story. Some of the items collected in the 'Documents' section of this book do carry that story a little further, but, as was stated in the Preface, they were not integrated.

before or after another, although certain discoveries in early adulthood stand out. Somehow I had my own copy of D.H. Lawrence's poetry; I felt the electric charge of his diction and imagery. To me, another poet, a Canadian, Archibald Lampman, certainly flashed a new glimpse of what poetry really is:

> Sometimes I hear
> The dreamy white-throat from some far off tree
> Pipe slowly on the listening solitude,
> His five pure notes succeeding pensively.
>
> (from 'Solitude')

The mesmerizing chant of patches of T.S. Eliot put iambic pentameters into my own vatic utterings! And his echoing of street talk, encouraged by Ezra Pound, Ezra says, taught me to listen in my place and time, though I never heard anything to rival 'O the moon shone bright on Mrs. Porter/And on her daughter/They wash their feet in soda water' (*The Wasteland,* Section III).

Then came Elizabeth Bishop's *North and South.* It took my breath away because of the poet's matter-of-fact focus, in everyday words so precise that she seemed to speak of things I, or some double of me, had seen before. (When I read her line 'A great-uncle painted a big picture', I felt she must have visited my uncle's living-room and seen its large framed amateur painting of a lakeshore at night where the path of the moon gleamed across the ripples – to a focus somewhere left of one's shoulder!)

A later American style, imagist verse, I knew through the eyes and voice of W.W.E. (Eustace) Ross – too restrictive for my temperament but disciplined, clear: a new virtue to cherish. Yeats's jewel-set words reinforced these values, in a more lyrical style, inimitably; his 'Sailing to Byzantium' lingers in my ear over the decades. William Carlos Williams showed me the motiveless precision of simplicity in style; he wrote with the careless freedom of poems shed around the edges of a busy medical practice.

At the other extreme from these widely respected poets was Robert Penn Warren. His 'The Ballad of Billie Potts' is a rollicking dark story written for the ear's delight (e.g. 'For Little Billie never was much of a hand with a pen-staff': the Southern accent was automatic, as I read). It takes a rare plot-sense to sustain suspense through a long poem like that.

Another poem in my memory, although I never 'learned' it, is E.B. White's 'I paint what I see' from a 1930s *New Yorker*. In fact I *mis*remembered it. To start with my wording:

> 'What do you paint when you paint a wall?'
> Said John D.'s grandson Nelson.
> 'Do you paint just anything there at all,
> like a hunting-scene or the trees in fall?'
>
> 'I paint what I paint,' said Rivera.*

The actual text reads:

> 'For this, you know, is a public hall
> And people want doves, or a tree in fall,
> And though your art I dislike to hamper,
> I owe a *little* to God and Gramper,
> And after all,
> It's *my* wall ...'
>
> *'We'll see if it is,' said Rivera.*

I am not a scholar. My jackdaw's familiarity with verse comes from leisure reading, although prescribed reading was necessitated by a Government of Ontario grant in return for two years' subsequent university teaching when a student population was cresting, in the 1960s. Two poets, in those years of graduate study, registered indelibly in my awareness, even if not traceably in my writing. First, bp Nichol. He and I exchanged light-hearted verses while he worked on

---

* Margaret doesn't misremember the poem, except that the first stanza's refrain is '*"I paint what I see," said Rivera.*' What she calls the 'actual text' is the final stanza of the poem, and she omitted lines three and four of it in her *Arc* article. Only the last stanza was printed in the *New Yorker*, on 20 May 1933. She must have come upon the whole poem elsewhere.

the same library level where my carrel was. 'In Eporphyrial Harness' (*The Dumbfounding*) is one of my scribbles for him, and he published one of his for me, 'Not What the Siren Sang But What the Frag Meant'. Second, Byron: my thesis work on his *Don Juan* made mischievous and conversational usage clearly apt for poetry, a welcome note, given my tendency to solemnities.

American writers have refreshed me consistently. My spontaneous notes in a college library's edition of early Dickinson poems I ruefully remember; at the time my response, seemingly one-on-one, was irrepressible. Walt Whitman's voice was audible in his work, though I kept listening for more poems as musical as his 'When Lilacs Last in the Dooryard Bloomed'. Vachel Lindsay's Chicago celebrations appealed to me, another city dweller. Because the Lowells were a storied aristocratic family, I resisted Robert Lowell's lyrical authority, but resistance melted away when I read 'For the Union Dead', his evocative, New Englander's memorial poem.

Robert Frost's precision, nobody has touched. Theodore Roethke's 'My Father's Waltz' had such an impact that I went on and on reading him, finding my own highlights in his work. In the sixties the Beat Poets carried all before them; even in Toronto, I rode with the floodtides. It was unexpected and very touching at a UBC poetry conference in 1963, when Allen Ginsberg followed me out to a quiet spot on the night campus to speak kindly about my first public reading of 'The Dumbfounding' earlier that evening. He said it had communicated.

The poetry of Wallace Stevens I hunted up because one or two commentators on my first book (*Winter Sun*) saw his 'influence' in it. (Was it the dense texture of his verse? Not likely the caustic undertone.) When I read his 'Emperor of Ice Cream', it recorded willy-nilly in my memory – though years passed before I tumbled to the fact that it was about a dead girl, laid out.

W.H. Auden I prize above all, not for the poetry primarily, but for the astringent wisdom of his prose work, *The Dyer's Hand.* Every poet needs that book!

Anthologies help me identify poets I want to look further for, as do magazines. In one British journal devoted to other (prose) matters, I tripped over a brief poem that charged all my circuits. It was signed Micheal O'Siadhail. Coincidentally, I mentioned the poet to someone off to visit in Ireland. In triumph she returned with an autographed copy of O'Siadhail's *Hail! Madam Jazz* for me. It was well worth her trouble.

I long to know Homer and Virgil. In graduate school I was game to try for a Ph.D. when a sympathetic professor, who introduced himself as Billy Wallace, said he would sponsor a thesis on my proposed topic, 'Figures of Speech in the translations of Homer by Alexander Pope and Robert Lattimore'. But he suffered a sudden heart attack and died. He had known that my only Greek was gleaned over one summer from an Oxford graduate who had answered my Toronto 'Want Ad' for a tutor! All other potential thesis sponsors in Classics considered my knowledge inadequate for assessing translated figures of speech.

Dorothy Sayers' *translation* of Dante, with the Italian text on facing pages, in paperback too, made that classic accessible to a grateful amateur. Translations of the Bible gave me one ancient, monumental source truly explored. I found it fascinating, in time inexhaustibly nurturing: the poetry and the story-telling astonished me when, after my conversion to Christian faith, I found, increasingly, that daily reading kept pace with everyday living.

All is grist to one's mill, I suspect. But it all informs, inly forms, the place where one's voice arises. Very early I learned to notice pacing in what I read, for example, the languor of 'With how sad steps, O Moon, thou climb'st the skies!' (from a sonnet of Sir Philip Sidney); or the crisp 'Desiring this man's art and that man's scope' (absurd words to come from William Shakespeare in his Sonnet xxix).

For me, a recognizable experience is expressed in another sonnet by Sir Philip Sidney (from his 'Astrophel and Stella'):

> Thus, great with child to speak, and helpless in my throes,
> Biting my truant pen, beating myself for spite:
> 'Fool,' said my Muse to me, 'look in thy heart, and write.'

Looking into his heart was safer for him, using the formal conventions of poesie in an earlier day. For us now it might be taken as inviting therapeutic writing, an abyss against which my grade nine guide, Gladys Story, warned me.

I do not prescribe for other writers my scramble to gather in various poets' musics. Writing with my ear forced it upon me because I could avoid picking up any one voice only by mixing voices this way.

In the seniors' residence where I live, any number of us can go on, from memory, if someone starts Byron's first line 'The Assyrian came down like the wolf on the fold....' All of us once had it as 'memory work' in elementary school. All of us also knew Robert Louis Stevenson's *A Child's Garden of Verses* (the idea of a bed with a 'counterpane' was wonderfully exotic!)

Rhythms create community, just as finding a 'voice' depends on hearing many voices.

DOCUMENTS

Among the following items, letters are printed with Margaret's ampersands, dashes, underlinings and the like so as to catch as much as possible of her epistolary style.

Margaret at the Brighton, Ontario home
of the Rev. Dr A.D. and Mrs Judy MacLeod, 1998.
(Credit: Don MacLeod)

Cars

Advantages of setting out on an autobiography in old age? It strikes me that I was fortunate to grow up before cars. Car trips in my memory began in the childhood years – the deeply moved novel wash of time and other people's lives mile upon mile through the darkening side window in the back, mile after mile of stunned wordlessness. But that is not the same as being bundled about, strapped into carseats, climbing about in public cars, surely a different rhythm of child's motion than I can imagine, shaping them forever in some ways. O I remember these 4 a.m. drives from [the] farm in Union to London market, in the back of the truck beside my cousin Jean, our legs dangling out, the centre-line of the big road, the longest stretch, sucking in the roadsides as we sped along – steady motion but not closed in, dominated by the fragrance of the berries in their boxes and crates behind us in the truck. Still our world, not other people's ... *[Margaret's ellipsis]*

Space

From childhood, over all the years, awareness of space, planets, stars, beyond these again, has murmured within me. The world is a little ball tossed among many of many sizes, so far off that the night sky doesn't shine but only twinkles? Somehow the idea got mixed up in my mind with the law of gravity, so that in my bed I might suddenly panic, clutching the *[This breaks off mid-sentence.]*

Vanity

Does it take vanity to go on in an art? I have gone through swings between phony self-deprecation and equally phony over-confidence, trying to find an unphony balance. The Christian concept of a 'calling' has helped, and of a 'gift' – one of many gifts to every believer. Writing for fun in childhood, was fun – but it gained recognition at home and at school, gratifying but somehow burdensome. One early experience came when a Stratford company performed Shakespeare's *A Winter's Tale* at the Royal Alex Theatre, and Mother (who budgeted for the family in those Depression years) had top gallery seats for herself and me – so high that the statue-that-comes-alive in the play was visible only from the floating-rib area down. It was exciting, stifling, risky (on an awkward tilt over the remote orchestra-and-stage level). Something precipitated out in my mind there in the dark, never uttered before: 'I will write things that lots of unknown people will be reading one day and feel the way I'm feeling here.' In hindsight I see, too, that Mother's ambition, in music, made secondary for the sake of marrying my father, was transferred unwittingly to me. The 'first person singular': now I see the wisdom of Gladys Story's warning against it, that late September afternoon in 1931. It took years to relax into an 'I yam what I yam' – in one of the comic strips [*Popeye*] we used to lie face-down reading on Saturdays as children. Then it became even a shield against praise not for the poems but for the transitory fame.

Coming to Terms with Tolstoy

[Written for a cash prize during Margaret Avison's undergraduate career. As a beginning on the subject of the Doukhobors, it is succeeded by another essay, 'Poetry and the Doukhobors'. We have followed Margaret's format, including her method of ellipsis, which omits a fourth dot for a full stop. Brackets are hers. The typescript essay is followed by a handwritten page headed 'Tolstoy Quotes in Old Script', which locates for Margaret's own sake the page numbers of quotations she has used, and others she has not. The titles of the books from which she quotes are absent, though, and are not bibliographically useful, so we have not reproduced the page here.]

NARRATOR: In the sequence of fables he adapted for children, Leo Tolstoy tells a story of a man blind from birth. The blind man asks 'What colour is milk?' No answer succeeds in communicating anything. For the blind man, writing-paper means dryness, rustling; flour means velvety palpable depth; rabbit-fur means softness and warmth; snow means coldness. The colour of milk cannot be conveyed to him.

Trying to understand Tolstoy, the human being Leo Tolstoy, is as baffling as trying to comprehend the colour of milk if you have never seen milk and have no idea what 'colour' really is.

He was a Russian; he lived 82 years, from 1828 until 1910; he wrote certain novels so widely read that they have become part of the human air we breathe. This much is definite. This much is common knowledge.

But Tolstoy will not stay put in the past, to be studied. Whoever looks further into his writings finds himself being prodded and asked questions and forced to admit contemporary pressures in an unnerving way. It seems impossible to come to terms with him, unless you come to terms with everything else first and know precisely where you stand. His biographers, as a result, can never give a rounded view – only the view from where they stand – and each of them seems to be talking about a different man. Much that he said and did invited distortion. Tolstoy refused to worry.

TOLSTOY: 'Of course I do not think it is worthwhile publishing in the papers a contradiction of the opinions falsely attributed to me. You cannot wish good health to everyone who sneezes.'

NARRATOR: Even the facts are bewildering. From 1854 to 1856 Tolstoy served as a commissioned officer in the Crimean War and his account of the Napoleonic campaign is a masterpiece of military history; yet he is equally well-known as a pacifist spokesman. He rooted his life deep in Russian soil; yet Tolstoyan communities flourished in England and the United States, and the Doukhobors were brought to Canada by funds Tolstoy established, after negotiations between Tolstoy and the Laurier Government in Ottawa. Tolstoy's teachings are the basis of the Freedomites' adamant boycott of public schools in British Columbia: yet Tolstoy founded a public school himself, taught in it, and helped to train other teachers.

How can we approach a man so full of contraries? It is like listening to a complicated fugue. Each voice must come through if the whole is to take shape for us.

His fellow-writers are perhaps the most trustworthy witnesses – Turgenev, who was at the peak of his career when he met the young Tolstoy; or Gorky, who remembered and recorded conversations from the last period of Tolstoy's life. Both men found themselves often at odds with him.

In one conversation Tolstoy had startled Gorky with the comment that he had known very few happy days; as he put it, 'I have never lived – I cannot live – for myself, for my own self; I live for show,

for people.' Gorky reflected afterwards, and drew his own conclusions:
GORKY: 'I believe it ... He was not happy. Though it is not true that he lived for show. Yes, what he himself did not need, he gave to people as though they were beggars; he liked to compel them, to compel them to read, walk, be vegetarians, love the peasants, and believe ... People must be given something which will either satisfy or amuse them, and then: let them be off! Let them leave a man in peace, to his habitual, tormenting, and sometimes cosy loneliness in face of that bottomless pit – the problem of the "essential".'
NARRATOR: These sentences fall strangely on our ears, if we identify Tolstoy as the author of *War and Peace* or *Anna Karenina.* How could anyone say that Tolstoy talked to people in order to get rid of them? In the great stories his insights are uncanny; it is as though he entered into the very identity of the people he described. What can Gorky's words mean – unless this man changed wholely [sic] in his later years. Yet when Tolstoy was still in his twenties he roused a similar response from Turgenev, whom he had visited.
TURGENEV: 'Tolstoy ... calls Paris a Sodom and Gomorrah and compares himself to a stone lying at the bottom of a river and being gradually covered with slime ... He is a queer man. I have never met anyone like him, and I don't understand him at all. He's a mixture of a poet, a calvinist, a fanatic and a fine gentleman ... more honest than Rousseau and, at the same time, an unsympathetic character ... (pause and change of tone)... but ... when this wine has done fermenting it will be a drink worthy of the gods.'
NARRATOR: The violence of Tolstoy's feelings was as marked in Paris in the 1850s as it was when Gorky knew him a half-century later. Yet there had been one radical change. The 'fine gentleman' Turgenev detected had gone through many fires during that same half-century. In his student days Tolstoy confessed himself both vain and aloof. His upbringing had been demi-royal. He was accustomed to the aristocratic life of the landed nobility. But gradually all the appurtenances of such a life took on a strange senseless look for him. He has described a typical morning, as it then struck him.
TOLSTOY: '... Boots, shoes, galoshes, several pairs soiled the previous day, are already being cleaned and made to shine like glass ... Clean linen, washed, starched and ironed, is being made ready with studs, shirt buttons, buttonholes, all carefully inspected ... If the person be

active he rises early – at 7 o'clock, i.e. still two or three hours later than those who are making all these preparations for him. Besides … clothes for the day and covering for the night, there is also a costume and foot-gear for the time of dressing: dressing-gown and slippers. So he undertakes his washing, cleaning, brushing … Then he … takes the things he needs, such as spectacles or eye-glasses, and distributes in different pockets a clean pocket-handkerchief, a watch with a chain (though in almost every room he enters there will be a clock), money of various kinds, small change … But at last all is complete and the day commences, generally with eating … The men for the most part smoke cigars or cigarettes at this time, and read the newly arrived papers. Then they leave the house for their offices or business, … in carriages … Then comes a luncheon of slain beasts, birds, and fish, followed by a dinner consisting, if it be very modest, of three courses, dessert, and coffee. Then playing cards or music – or the theatre, reading and conversation, in soft spring armchairs, by the intensified and then shaded light of gas or electricity. After this tea, again eating supper, and again to bed – a bed shaken up and prepared with clean linen … to be mussed all over again. Thus pass the days of a man of modest life.'

NARRATOR: The smothering superfluity of things oppressed Tolstoy more and more, and in time he fought himself free. He swept away every excess, down to the bare rocks. His food, furniture, and clothes had to be the simplest possible. What services he needed, he insisted upon performing himself. He often walked from Moscow to his country home – a distance of 130 miles. He adopted the simple peasant costume, so that more than once, tramping the roads in bast shoes and seeking wayside shelter, he was turned away from the door, a tribute to the success of his new role that never failed to fill him with glee. This rugged regimen was not imposed on the rest of his family, and some absurd situations arose in consequence. One visitor has described a breakfast in the Tolstoy home: a table crowded with all that is required to serve a large family; everyone eating and chattering; Tolstoy entering with an egg in one hand, a contraption for hot water in the other, boiling his own egg and, when he has fished it out, making his own coffee – because he scorned to use the labours of others for his own simple needs.

Did Tolstoy realize how maddening people found him? Well, in the midst of his young family he once wrote a 'Bulletin of the Patients of Yasnaya Polyana Lunatic Asylum' (Yasnaya Polyana was the name of the family estate). This Bulletin was composed for the family Letter-Box. Imagine it being read aloud that evening with whatever anonymous pieces the other members of the household had contributed. Tolstoy had included everyone, though the case-history of the smallest child read succinctly: 'No. 16: under investigation. Mania: doing up buttons.' As for his own case …

TOLSTOY: 'No. 1: Sanguine complexion. One of the harmless sort. The patient is subject to the mania known to German lunatic doctors as Weltverbesserungswahn [world-reforming delusions]. The patient's hallucination consists in thinking that you can change other people's lives by words. General symptoms: discontent with all the existing order of things; condemnation of every one except himself, and irritable garrulity quite irrespective of his audience; frequent transitions from fury and irritability to an unnatural tearful sentimentality. Special symptoms: busying himself with unsuitable occupations, such as cleaning and making boots, mowing hay, etc. Treatment: complete indifference of all surrounding the patient to what he says; occupations designed to use up all his energies.'

NARRATOR: 'Busying himself with unsuitable occupations' – how Turgenev would have endorsed that charge! He had made it himself, before Tolstoy's self-analysis was written …

TURGENEV: 'You write that you are very glad you did not follow my advice and become a pure man of letters. I don't deny it; perhaps you are right; still, batter my poor brains as I may, I cannot imagine what else you are if you are not a man of letters: a soldier? a squire? a philosopher? the founder of a new religious doctrine? a civil servant? a man of business? … Please help me out of my difficulties and tell me which of these suppositions is correct. I am joking; but I really do wish beyond all things to see you under way at last with all sails set.'

NARRATOR: Twenty years later Turgenev was still hopeful, though by now with an undercurrent of philosophical resignation. From Paris he wrote a Russian friend, in November 1871:

TURGENEV: '… I am very glad that Tolstoy's health is now satisfactory and that he is at work. Whatever he does will be good if only he does not himself mutilate his own handiwork. Philosophy, which he hates, has revenged herself on him in a strange way; she has infected him, and the enemy of rationalizing has plunged head over ears into rationalization! But perhaps all *that* has fallen away from him by now and left only the pure and powerful artist ...'

NARRATOR: The relationship between these two writers was not an easy one. Their natures were too dissimilar. Count Ilya Tolstoy tells a typical story of a visit Turgenev paid his father.

COUNT ILYA TOLSTOY: '... At last, when it was beginning to get dark, a woodcock flew over Turgenev, and he shot it. "Killed it?" called out my father from his place. "Fell like a stone; send your dog to pick him up," answered Ivan Sergeyevitch. My father sent us with the dog ... at last Turgenev came to help us, my father joined in the search ... "It may have got away along the ground," said my father, puzzled. "It is impossible that the dog shouldn't find it..." "It fell like a stone, I tell you," Turgenev insisted. There was no finding the woodcock, and the incident left an uncomfortable atmosphere behind it, as if one or the other of them must be very much in the wrong ... And this had to happen, just when they were both so anxious to avoid every sort of misunderstanding! That was the very reason why they had carefully fought shy of all serious conversation and spent all their time in sport. When Papa said good-night that evening, he whispered to us that we were to get up early and go back to the place to have a good hunt for the bird. And what was the result? The woodcock, in falling, had caught in the fork of a branch, right at the top of an aspen tree, and it was all we could do to knock it out from there. When we brought it home in triumph it was quite an occasion, and my father and Turgenev were even more relieved than we were.'

NARRATOR: This was Turgenev's last visit to Russia. He died in France, in the autumn of 1883. A few weeks before the end he wrote to Tolstoy:

TURGENEV: 'Dear Leo Nikolayevitch: I have not written to you for a long time ... I cannot get better, and it is useless to think of it. I am writing to tell you how glad I am to have been a contemporary of yours and to make my last and sincere appeal to you. My friend, resume your literary work! ... O, I would be happy if I could believe that my appeal would have an effect on you! I am done for ... I can't walk, I can't eat, I can't sleep, but it is boring to repeat all this. My friend, great writer of the land of Russia, listen to my prayer ...'

NARRATOR: Again and again Tolstoy recorded the conflicting drives that he could never explain to Turgenev's satisfaction He was only 29 when he wrote in his Diary:

TOLSTOY: 'Laziness, boredom, and sadness. Everything seems useless. The ideal is unobtainable. I have already ruined myself. Work, a small reputation, money. What for? Means of enjoyment – again, what for? Soon an eternal night ... It is only now that I have understood that it is not the life around one that must be arranged symmetrically as one wants it, but that one must break oneself up, make oneself pliable, so as to adapt oneself to any life ...'

NARRATOR: Tolstoy speaks of his systematic work, his long arduous mornings at the desk year in and year out, with something akin to self-contempt. The dissatisfaction came in waves.

TOLSTOY: '... Here, as in the country, I am still not working with my pen, and, do you know, this abstinence satisfies and makes me happy. From habit and from self-love, and from the wish to befog oneself, one wants to write and to get away from the life around one, but no irresistible force impels me to write, and I have got rid of that indulgent judge within me who formerly approved of anything I scribbled. I abstain from writing and feel a kind of purity, such as one feels from not smoking ...'

NARRATOR: Of course Tolstoy was not consistent in this attitude, as witness another rueful letter to a fellow-author not long afterward:

TOLSTOY: 'You are hard at work and may God help you at it! It was high time. I say this to myself more than to you, though I also know that when one is accustomed to work at a certain depth of creation and cannot reach that depth, one cannot force oneself to it ... I have begun a mass of things, all of them things I love – only I cannot dive down to the proper depth, but keep floating to the surface.'

NARRATOR: Gorky tells us that Tolstoy was often evasive and abrupt when talk turned to books and writing.

GORKY: 'It always seemed to me – and I do not think I was mistaken – that Leo Nicolayevitch was not very fond of talking about literature, but was vitally interested in the personality of the author. The questions: "Do you know him? what is he like? where was he born?" I often heard in his mouth. And nearly all his opinions would throw some curious light upon a man ... Of Anton Tchekov, whom he loved dearly: "His medicine gets in his way; if he were not a doctor, he would be a still better writer." To me he once said "You are an inventor ..." When I answered that Kuvalda had been drawn from life, he said: "Tell me, where did you see him?" He laughed heartily at the scene in the [official] court ... where I had first seen the man I described under the name of Kuvalda. "Blue blood," he said, wiping the tears from his eyes, "that's it – blue blood" ...'

NARRATOR: Tolstoy returned to the charge of 'invention', still in conversation with Gorky but thinking now of his own work too.

TOLSTOY: 'We are all of us terrible inventors. I myself, when I write, suddenly feel pity for some character, and then I give him some good quality or take a good quality away from someone else, so that in comparison with the others he may not appear too black ... That's why I say that art is a lie, an arbitrary sham, harmful for people. One writes not what real life is, but simply what one thinks of life oneself. What good is that to anyone, how I see that tower or sea or Tartar – what interest or use is there in it?'

NARRATOR: In this frame of mind, Tolstoy could justify his lambasting journalism but not his early fiction. There can be no doubt about his gusto in controversies. For example, listen to his artful glee in protesting what we would call today a high-level PR campaign.

TOLSTOY: 'The Russian and French peoples have been living for many centuries with a knowledge of each other ... [but] all these millions of French and Russians imagined suddenly that in some especial fashion they were enamoured of each other ... The moment one of the Russian commanders had drunk to the health of France, it became known to the whole world; and the instant the Russian admiral had said: "I drink to beautiful France", his effusion was transmitted round the globe ... such was the solicitude of the papers that they commemorated not merely the toasts, but the dishes ... "Consommé de volailles; petits patés ... Faisans à la Perigueux ... Casseroles de truffes au champagne ... Parfaits à l'ananas ..." The speeches made were also published, but the menus were more varied than the speeches. The meaning of the words was always the same – We love each other tenderly, and are enraptured to be so tenderly in love ...

Those that expressed their sentiments of love especially well on these occasions received orders and rewards. Others, either for the same reason or from the exuberance of the feelings of the givers, were presented with articles of the strangest and most unexpected kind. The French fleet presented the Tsar with a sort of golden book in which, it seems, nothing was written...; and the Russian admiral received an aluminium plow covered with flowers, and many other trifles equally astonishing...

At the same time tens of thousands of telegrams flew from Russia to France and from France to Russia. French women greeted Russian women, and Russian women tendered their thanks to the French. A troupe of Russian actors greeted the French actors; the French actors replied that they had laid deep in their hearts the greetings of their Russian colleagues. The Russian law students of some Russian town or other expressed their rapture to the French nation ... Russian children wrote greetings in verse to French children; and French children replied in verse and prose. The Russian Minister of Education assured the French Minister of Education of the sudden amity toward France of all the children, clerks, and scientists in his department. The members of the Society for the Prevention of Cruelty to Animals expressed their warm attachment toward the French ... Every one sent congratulations to every one else, and thanked some one for something. The excitement was so great that some extraordinary things were done ... For instance ... one woman, having put on a dress composed of the colours of the Franco-Russian flags, awaited on a bridge the arrival of the Russian sailors, and shouting "Vive la Russie", threw herself into the river, and was drowned ... a Russian sailor who appeared to be in perfect health, after having witnessed these exciting scenes for a fortnight, jumped overboard in the middle of the day and swam about, crying "Long live France" ... Thus ... finally ... not alone those on the spot, or merely nervously predisposed persons, but strong, healthy men were affected by the general strain and were betrayed into an abnormal condition of mind. I remember even that whilst reading distractedly a description of these festivities, I was suddenly overcome by strong emotion, and was almost on the verge of tears ... In many of the articles ... a naive satisfaction is clearly expressed that no one during them alluded to what it was determined, by silent consent, to hide from everybody, and that only one incautious fellow, who was immediately removed by the police, voiced what all had in their minds by shouting "À bas l'Allemagne!" ... "Down with Germany" ... No one is thinking of war; only milliards are being spent upon preparations for it ... in France and Russia. But all this is done to ensure peace!...'

NARRATOR: No wonder Turgenev was agitated about Tolstoy's

polemics. How seldom a great satirist ever returns to simple directness! How often anger has dominated and subverted a style! It is remarkable, in Tolstoy, that though he wrote many such pieces, they never became typical. On first impressions a reader calls this the style of Tolstoy's 'late period'. But was there any break in his life, any essential change of focus? In externals, in the way he lived, in the struggle to make his principles operative, the changes were progressive and radical. But the basic impulse was constant. His anger at society's recourse to violence, for example, was first recorded on that youthful trip to Paris, before any of the novels of the so-called 'first period'. He watched a criminal being guillotined, and his diary rings with the absolute conviction that was to be a lifelong goad:

TOLSTOY: 'When I saw the head part from the body and how they thumped separately into the box, I understood, not with my mind but with my whole being, that no theory of the reasonableness of our present progress could justify this deed, and that though everybody from the creation of the world, on whatever theory, had held it to be necessary, I knew it to be unnecessary and bad.'

NARRATOR: A few years later a political execution attracted widespread notice in Russia. Legal or social arguments meant nothing to Tolstoy. No theory interposed distance, or comforting perspective, on the human reality.

TOLSTOY: 'I could not drive from my eyes those hanging attenuated figures. The image of the woman ... especially oppressed me. I clearly pictured to myself how she placed her head in the noose, and how she involuntarily adjusted it, moving her head till the noose lay under her windpipe; and then, when the stool had been pushed from beneath her feet, and the cord pressed the soft gristle of her throat tight to the hard vertebrae of her nape ... I suffocated and repeatedly swallowed saliva to assure myself that my throat was not yet squeezed up ... I saw those protruding eyes fixed in amaze on the inexorable nearness of something terrible, and the blue face under the black cap ... The horror of it all! The horror!'

NARRATOR: Was Tolstoy using this awful occasion as a whetstone for his conscience? It is a bitter charge. A lesser man shrivels at the thought, and recoils from ever treating such a subject again. For Tolstoy the revulsion was not from such topics but from the hysteria in his own attitude. It is instructive to compare that feverish passage on capital punishment with the detached power of Tolstoy's style years later, in his tract on vegetarianism, for example.

TOLSTOY: 'The next time I visited the slaughter-house … it was the Friday before Trinity … a warm June day. The smell of glue and blood was even stronger and more penetrating than on my first visit. The work was at its height. The dusty yard was full of cattle, and animals had been driven into all the enclosures beside the chambers. In the street, before the entrance, stood carts to which oxen, calves, and cows were tied … By the fence stood the cattle dealers' horses. The dealers themselves, in their long coats, with their whips and knouts in their hands, were walking about the yard, either marking with tar the cattle belonging to the same owner, or bargaining or else directing the passage of the oxen and bulls from the chambers … I went into the compartment where small animals are slaughtered – a spacious chamber with asphalt floor, and tables with backs … Here the work was already finished; there were only two butchers in the chamber. One was blowing into the leg of a dead lamb and patting the swollen stomach with his hand; the other, a young fellow in a frock besmeared with blood, was smoking a cigarette. There was no one else in the long, dark chamber, pervaded with the smell of blood. After me there entered a man, apparently an ex-soldier, bringing in a young yearling ram, black with a white mark on its neck, with its legs tied. This animal he placed upon one of the tables, as if upon a bed. The old soldier greeted the butchers, with whom he was evidently acquainted, and began to ask about when their master let them have time off. The fellow with the cigarette approached with a knife, sharpened it on the edge of the table, and answered that they had a free day on public holidays. The live ram was lying as quietly as the dead inflated one, except that it was briskly wagging its short little tail, and its sides were heaving more quickly than usual. The soldier pressed down its uplifted head gently, without effort; the butcher still continuing the conversation, grasped with his left hand the head of the ram, and cut its throat. The ram quivered, and the little tail stiffened and ceased to wave. The fellow, while waiting for the blood to flow, began to relight his cigarette, which had gone out. The blood flowed, and the ram began to writhe. The conversation continued without the slightest interruption.'

NARRATOR: Tolstoy stubbornly defied anything that threatened to dwarf or limit him. The cost could be great, but he saw what the alternative was too – it is obliquely stated in one of the fables he adapted.

TOLSTOY: '*The Duck and the Moon.* A duck was floating down the river; she had been hunting for a fish, and all day long she had not found one. When night came, she saw the Moon in the water, and thought that it was a fish, and she dived down to catch the Moon. The other ducks saw this, and began to make sport of her. From that time forth the Duck began to be ashamed and lose courage, so that whenever she saw a fish under the water she would not seize it, and so she died of starvation.'

NARRATOR: His failures, other people's exasperation, distaste – he allowed none of these things to restrict his range. And the result was, finally, a great story like 'The Death of Ivan Ilyitch'. When he was an old man, Tolstoy found himself telling Gorky, very unwillingly, about a sordid incident in the autumn streets of Moscow many years past. To Gorky it was not an unusual story. But Tolstoy hated the thought of anyone writing on such a subject. 'Why?' asked Gorky.

GORKY: 'He looked straight into my eyes and smiling repeated: "Why?" Then thoughtfully and slowly he said: "I don't know. It just slipped out ... Yes, it's necessary to write all about everything, everything." Tears came into his eyes. He wiped them away, and smiling, he looked at his handkerchief, while the tears again ran down his wrinkles. "I am crying," he said. "I am an old man ..." And very gently touching me with his elbow, he said: "You, too – you will have lived your life, and everything will remain exactly as it was, and then you, too, will cry ..."'

NARRATOR: Tolstoy spoke, then, as though his reformist zeal had been directed toward changing the world. Yet that idea could be reversed: the zeal was equally, and perhaps more cogently, a digging in of his heels whenever the world threatened to change his human stature, to water him down, to rob him of his vivid perceptions and his keenest sensibilities. He himself says as much, in a statement intended to be simply political:

TOLSTOY: 'Only people who have something which they will on no account and under no circumstances yield can resist a government and curb it. To have power to resist you must stand on firm ground. And the government knows this very well, and is concerned, above all else, to worm out of men that which will not yield, in other words, the dignity of man. When that is wormed out of them, government calmly proceeds to do what it likes, knowing that it will no longer meet any real resistance ...'

NARRATOR: Governmental pressures were not the only threats Tolstoy recognized. Their occupations, he saw, insulated many men against human awareness, against fundamental human concern. And his view of the dignity of a man spurred him to attack this institutionalizing pressure, too.

TOLSTOY: 'You say to these people: "Your work is useless, perhaps even pernicious, for the following reasons; pause and consider them for a moment ..." They will not listen to you, but scornfully reply: "You men have leisure to reason about such matters, but what time have I for discussions? I have worked all my life and work does not wait. I have to edit a daily paper with a circulation of half a million; I have the army to organize, the Eiffel Tower to build, the Chicago Exhibition to arrange, to cut through the Isthmus of Panama, to make investigations on the subject of heredity, telepathy, or to find out the number of times such and such a word occurs in the works of such and such a classic author."

... In my opinion, not only is work not a virtue, but in our defectively organized society it is more often a means of moral anaesthesia ...'

NARRATOR: In Tolstoy's eyes, research and scholarship were clearly suspect too, reader and scholar though he was himself. Before he was 30, for example, he sulked to his diary about his 'idleness' during one five-day period when he had devoured two of the longer novels of Thackeray. Later in life he mastered Hebrew in remarkably short order, but felt guilty about losing himself in the pleasure of such study. Basically he feared bookishness as just another evasive tactic.

TOLSTOY: 'That is the worst of educated men: they cannot speak about any great question till they have read everything that has been written about it, for fear some one should say: "But have you read Schwarzenburg?" – and then, if they have not read Schwarzenburg, they are done; whereas a good, ignorant merchant like T., who has read nothing, but is keen on his own subject, will stick to his guns and do something with it.'

NARRATOR: The intellectual enthusiasm of the 19th century put Tolstoy on his guard too. Scientific advances made an exciting climate, and he was aware of the temptation to be swept away by 'microbes in the shape of a comma' (his own delighted phrase). But he constantly reminded himself of the need for ballast; the sense of wonder was as important as man's mastery of the physical world, and neither could take the place of direct human feeling.

During the years at Yasnaya Polyana Tolstoy plunged into experimental teaching among peasant children. To his chagrin, he found that he did not really *know* much of the science he had taken for granted since his own schooldays. Why do winter and summer alternate, for example? He went about checking up and found not one educated adult who could give a clear explanation, though they all tackled the question with immense confidence. No wonder the peasant children in his school felt a lack of authority in such teaching then …

TOLSTOY: 'I in my childhood believed that the world was round, and the like, but I did not understand it, and so it is with them now. It was always far easier for me to comprehend what my nurse told me: that at the end of the world the earth and the sky met, and there at the end of the world the women wash their linen in the sea and mangle it on the sky.'

NARRATOR: It was not a question of deciding to tell children the stories rather than teaching them science; what Tolstoy was learning was the depth of conviction necessary to good teaching.

TOLSTOY: 'Sometimes the teacher and the pupils get carried away, and instead of one hour the class lasts three hours. There have been cases when the pupils themselves cried, "More! More!" And they exclaim against those things which bore them. "That is stupid! Go to the little ones" they cry contemptuously.'

NARRATOR: Clearly this school of Tolstoy's had the quality of an exciting experiment.

TOLSTOY: 'They sit where they like: on the benches, tables, window-sills, floor, or in the arm-chair … As soon as one of them decides that he will sit in a certain corner, all his friends, pushing and diving under the forms, get there too, and sit together looking about them with faces that express as much satisfaction as though, having settled in that place, they would certainly be happy for the rest of their lives. A large arm-chair (which has somehow found its way into the room) is an object coveted by the more independent personalities … One dislodges the other and, curling up, sprawls with his head far below the back, but reads, like the rest, quite absorbed in his work ... In my opinion this external disorder is useful and necessary, however strange and inconvenient it may seem to the teacher ...'

NARRATOR: One day Tolstoy proposed that the children should write a story of peasant life ... One of them bade Tolstoy to write it himself in competition with them, and he set to work too until Fedka climbed on the back of his chair and interrupted him by reading over his shoulder. Tolstoy gave in, and began reading aloud what he had written so far. Several of the children gathered and had ideas for going on with his story. Semka and Fedka particularly had eager suggestions and new details and Tolstoy began to write as hard as he could to their dictation, having constantly to ask them to wait.

TOLSTOY: 'We worked from seven in the evening till eleven. They felt neither hunger nor weariness, and were even angry with me when I stopped writing; and they set to work to do it themselves turn and turn about, but did not get on well and soon gave it up ... Next day we set to work to continue the story. When I asked Fedka if he had thought of a continuation, he only waved his hand and remarked "I know, I know! – Who will do the writing?" ... We resumed ... and ... the boys showed the same enthusiasm and the same sense of artistic truth and proportion ... All this had evidently occurred because the actual writing was a difficulty to them ... We had obviously succeeded in finding a more natural and inspiring method than any we had previously tried.'

NARRATOR: Informal though it was in his school, Tolstoy noted an easing of relationships when he was with his pupils in the open air. One winter evening, when senior classes broke up around 9 o'clock, he was persuaded to walk back towards the village.

TOLSTOY: 'We walked without speaking, occasionally slumping through the soft, ill-trodden path; the white darkness was so dense as to seem to waver before the eyes; the clouds hung low as if something dragged them down upon us; there was no end to that peculiar whiteness in which we alone crunched over the snow; the wind soughed in the bare tops of the poplars, and silence reigned in the woods ...

Fedka suddenly stopped. "But how did you say that your aunt was killed?" he asked ... "Tell us! Tell us!" And I told them again that terrible story of the murder of the Countess Tolstoy; and they silently stood around me looking into my face. "It must have been terrible to go by night when she lay there murdered," exclaimed Fedka; "I should have run away!" ... Semka picked up a dry branch from out of the snow, and began to strike the frost-covered bole of a linden. The hoar-frost fell from the branches, on his cap, and the echo rang through the forest. "Ilyof Nikolayevitch," said Fedka (I supposed that he was going to speak of the Countess again), "what is the good of learning to sing. I often wonder, I really do, why we sing!..."'

NARRATOR: The children, like the horsemen he met on hunting trips or the peasants who taught him how to make shoes or mend roofs, were refreshing company for Tolstoy. Their direct forceful speech appealed to him strongly, and their closeness to nature. His own physical vitality was immense. Like his character Levin in Anna Karenina, he was a landed proprietor with a genuine love of the land. The chapter where Levin joins his peasants at haying, and learns the rhythmic endurance, the practised control of swinging the scythe – this chapter speaks unmistakably in Tolstoy's own voice. And it was written many years before he chose to live the simple life. Outdoor work all his life filled a deep need with Tolstoy.

TOLSTOY: 'It is good to have a friend, but he may die or go away or one may not be able to keep pace with him; but Nature to which one is wedded by a Notarial Deed or to which one has been born by inheritance, is still better. It is one's own bit of Nature. She is cold, obdurate, disdainful and exacting, but then she is a friend one does not lose till death, and even then one will be absorbed into her ...'

NARRATOR: Like all extraordinary men, Tolstoy looked to find peers everywhere. Of course all too often, instead of the candour he expected, the human exchange between human beings, he would find himself listening to a kind of empty gabble. The disappointment could chill his response to the peasants:

GORKY: 'He would come out looking rather small ... in simple clothes ... Russians who judge people by their clothes ... began to pour out a stream of ... familiarity: "Ah, you are one of us! ... Hail for ever. I bow low to you." Or ... "Leo Nicolayevitch, though I disagree with your ... views, I deeply respect in your person the greatest of artists." And suddenly, under ... his ... crumpled blouse, there would rise the old Russian *barin*, the grand aristocrat; then the noses of the simple-hearted visitors, educated and all the rest, instantly became blue with intolerable cold ...

One day I was returning from Yasnaya Polyana to Moscow with one of these "simple-hearted" Russians, and for a long time he could not recover his breath, but kept on smiling woefully and repeating in astonishment: "Well, well, that was a cold bath ... He's severe – pooh!"'

NARRATOR: With people of his own circle, Tolstoy's exasperation was even less held in check. For example, in the administrative corridors of Petersburg one morning ...

TOLSTOY: 'I met a pair of Orlov Generals who made me shudder. It was just as though one were standing between two sets of rails with goods trains passing. To enter into the minds of these Generals I had to recall the rare days of drunkenness I have experienced, or the days of my very early childhood.'

NARRATOR: Balancing his gloom when he felt cut off from human communication like this, there were times when Tolstoy felt an exhilarating kinship with his fellowmen.

TOLSTOY: 'Yes, the means to gain true happiness in life is, without any law, to throw out from oneself in all directions like a spider an adhesive web of love, and catch in it all that comes – an old woman, a child, a girl, or a policeman.'

NARRATOR: What would Tolstoy feel, as an old man, if he read through the diary he kept in his early years and came upon this entry:

TOLSTOY: 'Went to a funeral in the evening. The prayers touched me. Love is suffocating me – both physical and ideal love ... I am extremely interested in myself. I even love myself because there is much love of others in me.'

NARRATOR: Instantaneous sympathy with everyone in the world – that had been, surely, a fair illusion of youth. So much had happened since those days. There was the terrible time when he became aware of Russia's innumerable poor.

TOLSTOY: 'I began to devise a plan of philanthropic activity in which I could exhibit my goodness, [but] ... I felt all the time in the depth of my soul that it was not the right thing.'

NARRATOR: There were years in his school and years of struggle against his inherited way of life. Then famine struck certain provinces of Russia, in 1891–2. Tolstoy poured out money, collected more, set up free eating-houses, and supervised the distribution of food and seed. In the midst of all this activity he wrote a friend in a tone of utter discouragement:

TOLSTOY: 'You will say: "Why then do you go on?" – Because I cannot escape, and because … I … think I am not doing this work for my personal satisfaction … The oppression comes not from the practical work, which on the contrary is cheering and attractive, and not from dislike of the occupation, but from a constant inner feeling of being ashamed of myself … There can be none but living help for living men … To wish to do good without sacrifice, is like wishing to move a body without expenditure of force …'

NARRATOR: Through all these dark days, Tolstoy's perspective seemed to be shifting, as though the very ground under his feet were shifting. He records a glimpse of human life in that period, in a strangely conceived, highly powerful series of images:

TOLSTOY: 'There are worldly people, heavy and wingless. Their sphere is down below. There are strong ones among them: Napoleon. They leave terrible traces among men and cause an uproar, but it is all on the earth. There are those whose wings grow equably and who slowly rise and fly: monks. There are light people, winged, who rise easily from among the crowd and again descend: good idealists. There are strong-winged ones who, drawn by carnal desires, descend among the crowd and break their wings. Such am I. Then they struggle with broken wings, flutter strongly, and fall. If my wings heal I will fly high. God grant it …'

NARRATOR: Trying to live according to his convictions brought new problems. When he forswore his own right to his property, in his fifties, he left his substantial royalty income in his wife's hands – uneasy at this cavilling with the forthright course he advocated, but unable to involve his family in the consequences of any other course. One evening he discussed the question with a friend, and tortured himself with the thought that you could measure men's readiness to serve the truth by watching how they reacted to their family's opposition. The men themselves were at fault, if the families' disapproval prevailed.

TOLSTOY: 'It means that there is in us something that renders it possible for others to suspect us of being insincere and playing at simplification. Only because they see this something do they raise their voices against the undertaking which threatens to undermine their accustomed ways of life. If but for a moment they saw that we really could not endure this life of landlordizing, that it stifles us, sickens us, and that we should die if we did not change our life – believe me they would not find a word to say ...'

NARRATOR: Critics of Tolstoy's radical disorientation sometimes forget that he himself was often wracked by doubts.

Part of Tolstoy's contemporaneity for us is the way he seemed to sense the issue of our time: man against technical efficiency and society's mass pressures. Part of his appeal is his sterling assertion of human values. Part of his vulnerability is his complete failure to comprehend or accept the fact that man is a social creature too. All his social concepts were essentially negative.

Tolstoy's role in the Doukhobor migrations to Canada can only be seen in the context of these ideas.

He found his own life inextricably involved with a deplorable society. His ideal for economic life was primitive self-sufficiency, which seemed to him a human good in itself, and a real alternative to the growing complexity of the world. But every time he opened his eyes, the nightmare of the social reality was still there. Often in those days he was like a man fighting off tormentors, ridden with a directionless sense of urgency, craving release.

Into this scene stepped the first Doukhobors he had ever known: visitors on their way to Siberia where their leader Peter Verigen had been exiled. And behold, as they told him about their community, he felt he was meeting his own theories of Christian anarchy clothed in flesh and blood. The persecutions of the sect because they refused to bear arms for Russia he had heard of already. And the Russian Government was newly embarked on ruthless measures of repression.

Thus it was that Tolstoy made the Doukhobors' cause his own. Not only was he instrumental in publicizing their need, establishing funds, and arranging for their emigration to a new homeland. He also had much to do with the formulation of the Doukhobors' beliefs, though such a statement would have astonished him at the time. Scarcely any of these people could read, and the persecutions had cut them off from the rest of the world. But in Siberia Peter Verigen, their leader, became acquainted with some of Tolstoy's ideas, and passed them on as instructions to the Doukhobors. His messages followed them to Canada: Tolstoyan principles at second-hand, out of context, often garbled. Some of the tenets of the Sons of Freedom today can be traced to this source.

Right from the first there were divisions in the Canadian Doukhobor community. They showed baffling unwillingness to sign any legal documents, even the claims to their own property. Canadian officials were at a loss, and Tolstoy, when he wrote the Doukhobors, seemed to lend support to the most extreme faction:

TOLSTOY: '... Dear brothers and sisters, I know and understand the difficulty of your position in a foreign country, among strangers who give no one anything freely ... I know how difficult it is ... but I know also that ... you must not live as the world lives, each accumulating property separately for himself and his own family, and withholding it from others ... The Christian teaching cannot be taken piecemeal: one bit taken and another left ... If people, accepting Christ's teaching, have repudiated violence, law-courts, and wars, they must also repudiate property. For violence and law-courts are only wanted to retain property ...'

NARRATOR: Tolstoy could not have foreseen such fruits of his teaching as the 1902 Pilgrimage. He had protested against inhuman conditions in the mines. The Saskatchewan Pilgrims cut the metal fasteners off their clothes. His arguments against the exploiting of animal labour – an extension of vegetarian teachings – led them to loose their stock into the autumn prairies, strip off their leather boots, and set out to find an orchard Eden. As they walked the cold came on. Their nights were spent in the open on the outskirts of uneasy villages. Some had to be carried; November snows deepened; in the end they were bundled into freight sheds hundreds of miles from home, and shipped back to the frontier farms they had abandoned in exaltation a few weeks earlier.

TOLSTOY: 'My view of this movement among the Canadian Doukhobors is that materially they have injured themselves. But this movement has shown that there lives in them what is most precious and important – a religious feeling not passive and contemplative, but active, drawing them to the renunciation of material advantages ... and that this feeling is more precious than anything else ...'

NARRATOR: Tolstoy's tone is odd here – the actual experience was not clearly in focus for him. Certainly, too, he was not helping ease the strain for either the Doukhobors or the worried Canadians. And yet ... it is easy to see his failure and overlook our own. Policies towards the Doukhobor extremists have shifted with parties and outside pressures over the years. But how conscious have we been of the fact that, in Tolstoy's words, 'there can be none but living help for living men'? And how well has the 'dignity of man' been remembered in these policies, the dignity that Tolstoy feared governments wanted to 'worm out of men'?

His respect for a man's human stature was an art of listening well, and with relish, even though he sometimes expressed a dark foreknowledge of how heavy a price would be paid for the chasms he saw separating people. In his last days, two peasants visited the old man ...

TOLSTOY: 'They came both so strong and fleshy; says one: "Well, we've come uninvited", and the other says: "With God's help we shall leave unbeaten" (and he broke out into childlike laughter, shaking all over). We shall soon cease completely to understand the language of the people. Now we say: "The theory of progress", "the role of the individual in history", "the evolution of science"; and a peasant says: "You can't hide an awl in a sack", and all theories, histories, evolutions, become pitiable and ridiculous, because they are incomprehensible and unnecessary to the people. But the peasant is stronger than we are; he is more tenacious of life, and there may happen to us what happened to the tribe of Atzurs, of whom it was reported to a scholar; "All the Atzurs have died out, but there is a parrot here who knows a few words of their language."'

NARRATOR: Gorky gives us a picture of Tolstoy at that time:

GORKY: '... what a vast amount of life was embodied in the man ... I once saw him as, perhaps, no one has ever seen him. I was walking over to him at Caspra along the coast, and ... on the shore among the stones I saw him ... sitting with his head on his hands, the wind blowing the silvery hairs of his beard through his fingers: he was looking into the distance out to sea, and the little greenish waves rolled up obediently to his feet and fondled them as though they were telling something about themselves to the old magician. It was a day of sun and cloud, and the shadows of the clouds glided over the stones, and with the stones the old man grew now bright and now dark. The boulders were large, riven by cracks ... He, too, seemed to me like an old stone come to life, who knows all the beginnings and the ends of things ... I cannot express in words what I felt rather than thought at that moment ... everything blended in one joyful awareness: "I am not an orphan on the earth so long as this man lives on it."'

NARRATOR: Gorky's dwindling vista is not the Tolstoyan ending, though. The actual story of Tolstoy's death is dreadful, and desolate: squabbles among literary executors, discord, loss and illness at home, increasing tension and estrangement – and finally the dying man rambling off to the solitude that eluded him still, and getting no farther than a country stationmaster's. It is a sequence of negations.

A man of contraries, Tolstoy himself reminds us that negation is only one half of the strange business of dying.

TOLSTOY: 'I remember once when a bear attacked me and pressed me down under him, driving the claws of his enormous paw into my shoulder. I felt no pain. I lay under him and looked into his warm, large mouth, with its wet, white teeth. He breathed above me and I saw how he turned his head to get into position to bite into both my temples at once, and in his hurry or from excited appetite, he made a trial snap in the air just above my head and again opened his mouth – that red, wet, hungry mouth, dripping with saliva. I felt I was about to die, and looked into the depths of that mouth as one condemned to execution looks into the grave dug for him. I looked, and I remember that I felt no fear or dread. I saw with one eye, beyond the outline of that mouth, a patch of blue sky gleaming between purple clouds roughly piled on one another and I thought how lovely it was up there ... and now whenever I think of death I picture that situation to myself, because I have never been nearer to death than then. I recall it, reflect on it, make comparisons, and see that death – real, serious, all-absorbing death – is, thank God, not dreadful ... one's soul is serene and at peace.'

Miriam Waddington

[A scrap giving some context to a post-university relationship.]

We were fellow-writers, and she had invited me when she was hostess to some of the 'Montreal Poets' whose early fame had come before them. On that evening, too, we met Esther and Earle Birney. In 1942 his *David and Other Poems* came out and bowled us all over.

Irving Layton and Patrick Anderson appeared among us too, with their new poems as well as issues of *First Statement* and *Preview*, eager for manuscripts. The stimulus of the Montreal Group helped some writers in Toronto to emerge, and terrified others, although we all eagerly read their periodicals.

To Miriam Waddington

[71 Spadina Road, Toronto, June 9, 1945. Avison had reviewed Irving Layton's Here and Now *for* The Canadian Forum, *May 1945. He wrote a scathing response, which was printed with Avison's reply in the June* Forum.*]*

Your letter has so much packed in it that I have great pleasure contemplating a reply, but great difficulty in 'couching' it. One odd thing – you are more you, – the solitary human being, not the poet but the person through whom their own poetry can find its channel – in that letter than I have known you to be. You speak of the constraint of our friendship. I know of course what the strangeness is, although I am not sure why it is. But here is a theory – reject it if it seems wrong to you.

An artist is highly self-conscious and inalienably solitary. But with human beings, his relationship shares other people's definitions, & therefore with his friends he is even less self-conscious & solitary than the non-artist, because a new kind of innocence has been introduced by the very fact that his artistic conscience makes it clear to him that he need never feed on other people for his real, interior and impersonal, success. Therefore his friendship can afford to be clearer, and in many ways closer, than that between people who cherish, albeit unconsciously, mutual suspicions. But between two artists the case is different. They understand each other best in their art. Being conscious of you as a poet, I am both anxious to read what you write, and wary of intruding on your inviolate person in a way that nobody except another poet would be capable of doing. Also, when other people ask me about my affairs I can take their question conscientiously, and answer it in the same way I used to answer requests for information at the Institute. I used to think it was phony to be so serious about subjects which deserved seriousness only on a basic level where articulation would be the same difficult and exact thing that it is in the form of poetry. But it's not phony, not when the questioner invites you to meet him on a casual plane. But from you such questions had to be parried. If I answered you in a gemütlich flow of easy confidences it would be a rather unworthy travesty. Therefore our conversations were always more decorous, more formal, than either of us talking to other of our friends. And therefore our meetings were infrequent. Our basis of real communication remains sure, though. And in measure as I respect you as a poet, I am utterly confident that whatever you do & feel as a private person will be part of your individual integration, & that the details of your affairs can best be recognized by me in the degree of serenity from which you write. So that when I read your last Forum poem, my pleasure (aesthetic) was heightened by the pleasure of a friend who sees a developing resonance & self-realization contributing to the power of creative imagination in someone they like personally.

There. That is probably pretty muddled, and perhaps pompous too. But it was worth a try eh?

Re Layton's book – I am really contrite to have affronted him. Honestly, you know, I never anticipated such a reaction. I was obsessed those weeks with the conviction that poetic values are constantly being debased, by admixture with the amour propres of poets who owed themselves both more respect and more humility, and by the acceptance of both critics and readers generally of the alloy as an inevitable part of the true metal. Layton is certainly making a lot of mistakes in his writing. Hell though, so am I. He knows if he is a poet. I certainly would not be so impertinent as to decide that question, since I have no interior evidence. He might be fooling himself that his writing at the moment has a purity which it simply hasn't. Well, I thought, I'll clear that out of his way bang right off. Compromise on crucial points is in the long run more painful, & 'kindness' in this context is condescension. If only I had worded my review more scrupulously it might have been okay to say all the things I said. Since it appeared, I read for the first time that little book of Rilke's published as Letters to a Young Poet. It made me wish Rilke, & not I, had been Layton's reviewer. Read the book & tell me what you think of it.

What you say about the 'native tradition' is good – But the maple leaf in capital letters standing all by itself is associated for me with …

a market brand of bacon. What I mean is, that your roots, your genuine patriotism, is not a national thing if you are Canadian. It is our peculiar good fortune to be in one of the few nations in the world where the concept of nationalism is somehow absurd. Our feeling is for a distinctive climate & locale, made up of the tangible & the intangible, the natural & the civilized, of our apprehended environment. And as long as we are not tricked by Lorne Pierce [publisher of the Ryerson Press] & his ilk (which I suspect [A.M.] Klein has been, in his own way) into confusing this feeling with the invoked nationalism of the credos, it is certainly a vigorous, generative element in us.

You ask what I am doing now. I have just finished a temporary job at Simcoe Hall (8 hrs daily of typing envelopes), have banked up a few editing and proof-reading jobs to do in my room, & have campaigned like crazy because of our elections, particularly this week after the desperate outcome of the Ontario vote Monday night.* Whether my awkward campaigning really is any contribution I don't know. But there again, it's worth trying. Although at bottom I keep feeling that if I could persuade the electorate to a man to read all of ee cummings, nobody would have to worry his head again about Drew et al. They would disperse like the foul mists in the sunshine. Shall I try my kind of campaigning, & drop the political kind? That wd be equally distorting. But don't you get terribly tired of having to insist that politics, economics, art, mores, are all one piece, and that isolation of any aspect is impoverishing and emasculating the whole communal life? If people wd only be reasonable about economics and intuitive & emotional about aesthetics – but no, they go in reverse. And demd if I know how to shift their gears!

Write me again if you feel like it.

Margaret

---

* In the Ontario provincial election of 1943, George Drew, leader of the Progressive Conservatives, had formed a minority government with Ted Jolliffe, leader of the Co-operative Commonwealth Federation (CCF), forerunner of the present-day New Democratic Party. In 1945, seeking a majority, Drew called an election and won it by exploiting Cold War tensions, including fear of Communism. Jolliffe's party was reduced from 34 seats to 8.

To Miriam Waddington

[71 Spadina Road, December 13, 1945. The first paragraph, welcoming the publication of Waddington's Green World, *has been omitted, as has a later paragraph of 'news'.]*

As you probably guessed, I sympathize with your uncertainty re the literary groups in Montreal. I'm not giving in and conceding that Spengler was right in denying the possibility of poetry in our epoch – not by any means. But I keep feeling both astonished and bewildered by the fake unities of our cultural world: as if the only reliable cohesive force in our society is sheer animal apathy – the conversion of an ideological war into a national one being one symptom of that apathy – an insistence that the real fight lapse into shadow-boxing again – sinister and mutilating as the shadows may be, the end of the bout is only weariness. Sooner or later the genuinely cohesive forces, which will split our society even as they unite the segments, will begin to operate. Of course the multiple signs that the segments are already, as it were, perforated ready to be torn, are very evident – Ford, Property Owners Assn. fights etc. But the forces for division are offset by that stronger cohesion of apathy. The rebel still pays his carticket into the slot 5 minutes after professing a thorough-going anarchism and so on. And you can't merely resolve to pursue a violent course, you can't legislate the releasing of genuine forces; even as a political minority in your plans for your minority policy you can't predetermine that effect. It is no accident that a Serbian assassination touches off an imperialist war. You can't elect the social catalyst. In the meantime, the poet, whose reservoir is the whole of the continuing human tradition, is forced to speak either in broken generalizations, or in a painfully personal specific reference. His problem is to join his voice with the continuing human tradition. But at this moment in history, a recognition of that tradition would show up the inadequacy, the absurdity, of the common hope that if we rub along a little longer with our eyes shut we will be in an approximation of Victorian (or Russian) security soon. So the poet finds it difficult to express what few wish to recognize, and is rejected at the bottom if he succeeds.

There. That is all really too general in terminology to be exact, but it is an effort to articulate The Fear. In concrete terms, perhaps all I should be saying is that I find writing increasingly difficult in proportion as I feel anxious to express things. Maybe the jaundiced analysis above is merely an extension of a personal sense of inadequacy and incompetence.

Anyway, there are many good hours in my weeks. The variety of part-time jobs I am doing gives me a chequered, insecure, delightful sequence of weeks. Some hours I do clerical work in the Registar's office, others proof-reading at home, others editing for the Institute, others typing for Dr Brady, and one hour a week lecturing to a Pass English 1st year group at Vic. The income, though irregular in flow, is surprisingly copious. The psychological effect is all, I think, to the good. If my social conscience begins to bother me, I am free to adapt my schedule so that its demands may be to some extent satisfied. If I need a quiet morning on the streets or in a library, I can let each of my employers think that one of the others is employing me. Best of all, if I ever had any illusions about having a tangible identity, they are dispersed. Happily my respect for the rest of the world, vegetable, animal, and human, has increased enormously as my self-respect has shrivelled. It is an absurd, terrible, beautiful, rigidly defined life, and heigh-ho to it.

I hope you don't mind this kind of introversion Miriam. It is easy to write these things to you, and yet the result is so inexact that I almost prefer a 'newsy' letter, as a gesture of friendship. But that isn't the kind of letter I want to receive, so I can only ask you to draw my arguments out onto solid ground....

Gradually people see less of each other. Gradually our generation is discovering the *locked* door, the drawn blind, the wind-scoured boardwalk. And gradually a new generation is discovering Murray's coffee, Left Book Club evening study groups, Chinatown dinners, and Sunnybrook Farm wiener-roasts. It is funny that I find it easy now to realize that I will be 48 – 50 – 65. Maybe that is part of the chastening aftermath of my spring and summer petticoat panic. I don't know whether I ever told you, but via Bobby Adamson of the Institute I drifted into a habit of frequent drinking and serious (o serious) discussing with a crowd of Winnipeg boys all at least a decade younger than myself, & from there shot straight into a state of foolish infatuation which was simultaneously so phony and so poignant that I spun like a top for weeks and weeks. I have finally extricated myself, and by now the only scar is a niggling awareness of my foolishness. But it is a sober morning-after, and, like so many incidents in the long sequence, a new iron door slammed shut behind me closing off a former retreat. So again heigh-ho.

Well – confidences are boring aren't they. I can't tell you how little any of that [here an arrow to the previous paragraph] matters by now. Except insofar as every particular sharpens the outline of all particulars, it was a hell of a waste of precious hours. And o my, Miriam, I want to write something decent before I die. I hate everything I've done up to this minute. And time goes too fast.

Write me, as you promised to do –

Margaret

To F.R. Scott

[November 29, 1946. In a note clipped to her photocopy of the letter, Margaret has written to Joan Eichner, 'Could the parts circled here in red [and black] fit into the "Short Term Jobs" section?' We have included all of the letter but a brief first paragraph, since the excerpts would have had to be properly integrated to be completely intelligible. However, we have italicized the parts Margaret picked out.]

Dear Mr Scott

Your note disturbs me, as have the inferences of conversations. I'm afraid that by shelving a difficult topic I have succeeded only in generating some esoteric atmosphere; and now, to prove that an illusion, I'd like to try to cope with the topic straight.

Please be patient while I state the obvious. As a student I put poems in the College magazine without thinking twice, & simultaneously becoming aware of *The Forum*, in that. But then earning a living began to sop up the idle time conducive to preparing Mss. And then all in a year – *because of [A.J.M.] Smith's researching for his first Anthology – demands began to become onerous. There was a 'Writer's Group' that cost a whole precious evening every time I went. And a 'First Statement Group' that not only took an evening but bespoke more time, because it wanted canvassers for subscriptions.* And [Ronald] Hambleton had his proposition &, no sooner had I collected for him more pieces than I felt half-way justified in submitting, than Dr Robins made another anthological proposition. *I felt confused & went down to Lorne Pierce to retrieve Mss, & he talked about Canadian Poetry as if he were a missionary but at the same time revealed that he was publishing Hambleton without having even glanced at the Ms. So I pulled mine out* almost as a gesture of trying to fight my way out of cobwebs. Free time is so scarce. And publishers in Canada have such a wry knack of turning into persons. Hambleton asked me to give him some things for *Reading* and slammed up the receiver in dudgeon when I said I hadn't anything. You asked me for something at McNaught's, and Birney wrote asking, & then Crawley. Each time the request was more like a personal letter than a publisher's, & each time I felt more concerned to behave courteously in a social dilemma than even roused to consider the question of poems & public. *Most of the people who approached me didn't even know what I write, & had no way of assessing whether it was any good. All they knew was that I'm a Canadian.*

This seems to me a ridiculous situation. I feel that the immediate point of contact with these people is always of secondary importance to both them & myself, & so have evaded rather than offering up living hours to fight my way through into the clear. *Surely my central responsibility is to accept the responsibilities that society makes compulsory for an adult, and then to write the best things I can, as much as I can. Of course I write for a listener. And of course I think of publishing as the anxious despatching of the message corked in a bottle on the big world-ocean. But I feel no urgency towards that. If the message is worth corking, it must be clear. It never will be fully clear either, I know that. But when it should go out, it will. And if water will get in & dissolve away the paper, why it will.*

So if I acted evasive about showing you pieces, what then? I think I know what that wd be. I'd be afraid you'd read them as magazine material, or even that you'd tell me I'm good, rather than recognizing the image of the bottle-sender on the desert island, & acknowledging the hopeless loneliness & the absurd fool-out-on-a-limb terror & excitement of picking a bottle out of the wrack on your stretch of desolate beach. All poetry, even the poetry that fails, has to be that.

[Written in the margin, with an arrow pointing towards the second line of the foregoing paragraph] i.e. when poets get together they are hard put to it to be persons. The dilemma is mutual, natch, though this paragraph doesn't show how.

If you said I was good, it would be destructive, not as the destroying of some rare delicate thing at all, but the same way goodness of the left hand can be tainted if the right hand catches on. In fact I'd go one stage further, & say that the labels, both artistic & moral, are misleading & irrelevant. If a thing is, it is. If it partly is, amen. If it only tries to be, or only has an illusion of is-ing, well, amen.

Sometimes I think the longing to establish the listener is one that has to be fought down. If you have that false sense that the listener is there listening, you are too eager to brake your utterance. Emily Carr called her first bk *Klee Wyck* or something. But then 'The House of All Sorts' – it's enough to make me wretched to write that. Her inner ear was overwhelmed by a sense of community. The world was closer & warmer, BUT NO LONGER NEW. Think of the first man who said 'God be with you.'

Sometimes for long weeks the world is close & warm to me. The office full of living people, & the papers full of real problems, & the library full of wise bks & sociological symptoms (the two categories?) And for long weeks I am busy & efficient & purposive & cheerful like a sparrow. And then I realize that the sky is mussed with rift, and the air in my room is cacophonous with echoes of the day's voices, & the ideas in my head are all gummed up with other people's labels. And gradually I remember again about the desert island.

I wouldn't have tried to tell it to you if I didn't know you knew about it. Whether your attitude to it is anything like mine doesn't matter. That's private. May heaven & hell continue self-appointed.

Sincerely yrs,
Margaret A.

To Miriam Waddington

[71 Spadina Road, Toronto, December 6, 1947. Much of this letter is about Miriam Waddington's thesis, sent to Margaret Avison for response. We reproduce only one paragraph here.]

Capetanakis is a fine poet eh? His criticism I liked less. Some of the essays seemed to me to overbalance because of the very reckless concentration of focus that makes the poems so good. Also I've good [sic] a sensitive spot about any indulgent conciliatory quips about the spinster-genius. However I must concede that his Dickinson poem is technically uncanny, & that I haven't looked at Charlotte Brontë for years. One thing certainly, it's a delight to read criticism by someone who, primarily, feels the excitement of literature. Sometimes I feel that all the critics & Eng. Profs feel about art the way a garment mfgrer feels about bolts of cloth. We're all getting so damned articulate & self-deprecatory about the subjective whim of cultural 'taste' that it's glorious to be confronted with the old indefensible human enthusiasm & hectic cheek again....

Yrs, Margaret

To Cid Corman

[10 Washington Avenue, Toronto 5, Canada, 26 June 1953. We include the middle of this letter, dropping the first three and the final paragraphs.]

Trying to arbitrate a <u>sine qua non</u> for poetry is silly, but one seems to have to. I'd make it mastery. To be on top of the so powerful unarticulated, on top of one's limited self as if escaped from it, on top of ..., [Margaret's ellipsis] attitudes or feelings towards the many other limited selves too, out of whom the unarticulated is partly forcing itself. And in technique, on top of tradition or experiment, not ducking past or present or future, simply listening & giving to listen. Which, coming back to perfectness [the third paragraph of the letter, past the throat-clearing, began very obliquely to discuss 'perfectness' in the context of 'your long poem'] is too high a demand to ever be fully met, poetry in mortal ears giving only clues to what it is always.

These observations must not constitute a claim on your time which sounds too full. All in the course of things I'll turn up there one year or you here again, & we may pursue such.

With Mr Shapiro I am, I feel, at an end. The last postcard praised a most ignoble, joke-rhymed piece of unhealthy occasional verse which

I had deliberately enclosed as bait. Makes me shiver to realize how dangerously close he was to even accepting this morbid morsel for pubn. I must learn to keep my private jokes private....

Sincerely yours,
Margaret Avison

To Cid Corman

[10 Washington Avenue, August 18, 1953.]

First, the article on [Charles Olson's] *Projective Verse.*

However often I read it, let it have its way, it remains (good) autobiography.

Serious meaning finds right form. Every close, hence exclusive, definition of kind of meaning/form risks excluding a poetry that may be tomorrow, unpredictably. E.g. p. 14 'one perception must immediately & directly lead to a further perception, must must must MOVE, Instanter, on another'* = lateral motion is the only (or only good?) kind. What about one perception so steadied, so held, that more more more umbrella upsided out of it (Yeats's whorl/gyre)?

The man-and-nature relationship (pp. 20–21) makes me want to say to this particular man, Bless you, go to it, don't mind us. By 'us' I guess I would mean to fence off where it wouldn't intrude on him the thing social workers call inter-personal & inter-group relations. Besides me (and other like human creatures), and tree, stone, sun, maggots, trapdoorspiders – besides these are money, history, languages, night edition help wanted columns. Pound's usury maybe? – Anyway, something that chokes the breathing, but is part of every breath.

I guess I believe every manifesto is solo (Latin for one). Especially

---

* Margaret has lower cased some of this and leaps from the middle of Olson's paragraph to the end. 'ONE PERCEPTION MUST IMMEDIATELY AND DIRECTLY LEAD TO A FURTHER PERCEPTION ... must must must MOVE, INSTANTER, ON ANOTHER!' (Robert Creeley, ed., *Selected Writings of Charles Olson.* New York: New Directions, 1950, 17.)

with poets. God send this one courage of his convictions & send the rest of us our own c. & cs

PS. I delight in [Olson's poem] In cold hell in thicket almost daily.

Margaret Avison

To Miriam Waddington

[10 Washington Avenue, Toronto 5, Ont, March 23, 1954. The first and last paragraphs of chat have been omitted.]

It's interesting what you say about writing prose. Something I can completely sympathize with too. Except that poetry also grows increasingly difficult for me, although in proportion the attempting of it grows more exciting. You know how impatient I used to get when people exhorted me to travel & 'have experiences' as if that were the way of establishing the handy reservoirs from which a writer draws? I still believe these exhortations derive from a myth, but I begin to see how the myth arose. It's simply that a writer, always in some part of his being preoccupied with a writer's problems, needs to husband the moments when he turns his full awareness on them. In the days of the literary life – socially – a poet would keep the hours of reading, feeling, working at poetry, up to their necessary intensity & spontaneity by plunging inbetween into whatever currents offered, viz., travel & 'experiences'. A job, humanly experienced, however, can perform the same function. To be able to *know* the least sympathetic human being in the miscellany of contacts a job imposes, is not only a reviving distraction, but also proves the poet's working hours. I couldn't try to write so that Mr X, for example, would respond if he read it, but I can try to write a statement as valid for Mr X, in his full differentness from me, as it is for the surest poetic censor. And a few lines that bear up under that challenge will likely bear up.

Does this seem sensible? One always suspects anything consoling of being rationalization, but that can spoil some absolutely natural breathing-spaces, so I'm more on guard against suspicion perhaps than against the suspect –

Sincerely, Margaret

To Eleanor (Godfrey) Graham

[June 2, 1954, Hotel Graham, Bloomington, Indiana. The lower part of the sheet on which this letter was written contains a few words – 'Hardy 30 Poems' and 'Barnes' poetry – analogy with Hardy' – and a quantity of doodling. Avison turned the sheet upside down and began her letter.]

The foot of this page are my notes on the first John Crowe Ransom class. Submitted in evidence. His two assignments were more fun than anything he said: 1) Take the Collected poems of Hardy & choose 30 which would be a 'Selected poems' volume – a task he apparently has from Knopf, & be prepared to justify your choice should any particular poem be challenged; 2) compare Wm. Barnes [English Dorset dialect poet] & [Thomas] Hardy (not on paper, just for talk tomorrow). I spent the afternoon with the Library copy of Barnes, & have a new enthusiasm – partly because it was a selection I had, & the bigger older books of him were all I'd looked at before. We'll read some later? Mr Ransom is a slow starter, I think. Impeccably dressed – the only man I've seen in a jacket since I arrived in Indianapolis Sunday; almost timid – he panicked after each question he asked far more than the students, & not able to bear the anguished pause, let each opening close him back into more speech; also the room where the seminar had been called was locked at the hour appointed, & through the glass of the door could be seen a solitary boy doing homework of some kind, but the rest of us didn't like to act with Mr Ransom, plainly identifiable, gently trying the handle of the locked door from time to time, looking perplexed, & moving away to lean hot & tired against a wall. A young man from some other nearby office finally intervened or we might never have had a class. What surprised me, he seemed to anticipate hostility & to approach his course by defending himself for not adhering to this that & the other school. Two students walking behind me afterwards said he had obviously mellowed too much, & was resting on his laurels, & they thought they'd try to switch to Fiedler's course. However I think the first meeting too inconclusive to be discouraging, & as I say I really relished the assignments, so I shall withhold judgement & go again tomorrow. My other course is Whitehall, on Language & Literature. He is definite, confident, compelling, & invites to all sorts of games I'm game to try. But to him the 'schools' are meat & drink. He is 'formalist in linguistics, Gestaltist as opposed to the Behaviourists in criticism'. Maybe I'll be able to use those terms meaningfully by the time I return, but much of his first 2-hour stretch bewildered me. Assuming you'd be interested, this is the content of his lecture: the study of language has had three phases 1) orthodox, its concepts derived largely from philosophy, its rules based on Greek &, later, Latin, & assumed to be universal (Plato & Aristotle through the 'golden 12th century' to the 18th century which elaborated the static system by adding rules based on analogies, & codified rules to give the middle classes an index of correctness). 2) historical. The 19th century began to appreciate how far orthodoxy derived from Latin, a comparatively static language, & therefore was not furthering the study of changing languages (living ls); in exploring the changes, comparative language study & principles of relationship were developed. 3) Structural Began with imagism, 1917, insists on pattern everywhere, has already defined itself in 3 schools: European or formalistic, very exciting he says, but all done in either Czech or Russian about Slavic literature, pretty inaccessible; Copenhagen School, a 'glossematic linguistics' which starts with genres & works painfully towards syntax & diction; Americanist School, the anthropologists' approach, emphasizing techniques & productive of various lexicons & grammars rather than critical principles (because they concentrated on Indian languages & later other primitive people's languages). We are going to apply all this to English. And it will be a game, because I recognize from what he said that I am still firmly pre-19th century in my use of syntax etc. O, he says the mind is a binary computator, has to think in terms of opposed pairs of things always. Is this right?

Poor Eleanor, I hope you have time to read so many words. And that you are being kept well supplied with books – Isabel [Fraser] or Joan [Lampel] would either one delight to serve you there, I know. Hugh will surely be recovered by the time this reaches you, & they will be in a pitch of conference work. I wish everybody were here too, it's such a beautiful campus, about the size of High Park, wild but cared-for, pine groves & catalpas & beeches & some huge trees that grow what look like blackberries which are ripe now & sticky underfoot, brooks & bridges, red-earth paths, cat-birds & jays & cardinals & warblers of all kinds, much heat. The buildings are just all right, but mostly concealed in foliage anyway. Rich, but more like banking-houses inside than school. Throngs of students from 9 to 90 are hard at it all day – breakfast is at 6:30 in the student cafeterias, & all offices go thrivingly before 8 a.m. The Library is hot, so I choose to read on a bench within sound of the Music School, a lovely meld of all instruments, but piano predominating.

Eat as well as you can, & tell me if there is anything particular I should report on.

Love,
Margaret

To Eleanor (Godfrey) Graham

[An excerpt, undated and unaddressed, though Margaret has indicated the addressee on a sheet of paper attached, and the subject matter clearly follows that of the previous letter. The underlining – wavy on the paper – may have been Eleanor Graham's.]

We assembled at 8:15 as bidden in a large theatre-lecture hall in the Business & Economics Bldg. On the blackboard were still some notes on marketing & insurance rates. On either side of the podium are huge dismally abysmally horrendous murals of machines & men of business & feet rocking the cradle (approx.) Mr Ransom & Mr Empson sat demurely on 2 straight chairs at the left of the podium while the last stragglers found seats. The capacity of the hall would be about 4 times Room 8 (U.C. [University College, University of Toronto]) & it was pretty well filled, since the delegates to a conference on East-West relations had been invited as well by the School of Letters. A few Chinese & Japanese & one or two Indians & the rest like us; maybe an older group though. 30–40 ages mostly.

Mr Ransom finally walked over to the lectern – powder-blue cotton cordurory suit, white shirt, navy bow-tie, pink of face, pale-blue of eye, white of hair, & welcomed the East-West people, & introduced Mr Empson. His notes shook in his hand so badly he kept trying various devices to steady them while he told us that, next to himself, Mr Empson was the most senior Fellow of the School of Letters, had twice come to it when it was at Kenyon College from China, had graduated in Mathematics from Cambridge, published so & so, & this year had been good enough again to make an extended trip to be with us, this time from England, where he had been living since 1952. And that the East-West Conference delegates would know him perhaps primarily for his BBC Voice of Asia wartime broadcasts. And he walked down to the first row, & left the platform to Mr Empson. He stood up & pulled his notes out his pockets, producing with them a pocket watch on a tremendously long black ribbon, which fell (the watch) & had to be picked up & then some notes had to be picked up – a studied piece of deadpan pantomime. All being in order, he took stance, raised his arms, & said 'These are not pyjamas I am wearing, but my Chinese Communist uniform.' Told us how the British foreign office advised him to buy it while he was teaching in China & went into a long, half-aloud half-soliloquy highly impressionistic account of an all-day Communist parade somewhere undesignated in urban China. Throughout earnest people kept slipping up the aisles to the few empty seats at the front – though even in the front row I am sure most of the words were quite inaudible. There was a pitcher & glass on the lectern, & he kept pouring water indiscriminately into the glass & over his notes. Finally he crouched low over his notes, looked up from that stance, & said owlishly that he saw that his topic was supposed to be Language & Criticism. But it didn't interest him much, now that he had written his book. Unless someone wanted to attack it. The book we knew – he'd come to that in a minute. Meanwhile he wanted to tell us (stretch of inaudible muttering –) from perhaps 4 minutes of which I heard that he had gone to the Civil War area in China because that was a nice quiet place to write his book on Pastoral. Anybody who was interested would have read this, like the one on language. What interested him at the moment (he kept rambling & coasting back & forth & around the whole podium, perilously close to losing his balance at each turn) was the indignity he had suffered in being put on oath before entering the U.S.A. Then he went into a long disjointed rave about American puritan smugness & why every non-American was quite right to hate them. People kept laughing, out of sheer nerves I think, though the clowning was deliberate, until I felt wrought up almost to the point of tears. Particularly as Empson kept stopping & saying half to himself 'I feel I'm not getting this across to you.'

Suddenly at the end he read a new translation from a piece of Chinese opera, & it was real poetry. By that time, though I had found his tirade politically meaningless, I felt as if I were in the crucible where poems are made. (A whole lot of soliloquy-reminiscences of Hong-Kong for example, which had been full of American war correspondents when he was last there & was consequently 'horrible', & how the only companion he found was a British policeman who had worked with Chinese communists all through the war & was now paid to work Malaya, shooting any Ch. C. he could see.) The routine for these Forums is a one-hour speech, a ten-minute intermission, then a discussion period. The speech last night went on until 9:40. I left then, because I felt the question-period would just be a show, & it had been an artist in the pillory, misbehaving but not betraying the artist for one moment, & I was afraid if the discussion got ugly I might make a foolish speech.

The school was troubled in atmosphere this morning – journalists sped out to telephones to copy early at key points (political). I gathered most people were solely concerned lest newspapers make something of it, but otherwise undisturbed. I had a lovely 2-hour class in linguistics, which grows better each time. Mr Whitehall said reading a poem required the same kind of practice & rehearsing as playing a sonata & made us do metric analysis so hard it vindicated this statement. One of the analyses was of Sailing to Byzantium. You would have enjoyed it.

It's still very hot. I'm going to read Hakluyt now, & Pope, one in each hand as it were. (Neither have anything to do with the course, just the holiday-part.)

Love –
Margaret

To Miriam Waddington

[552 Spadina Crescent, Toronto, June 9th, 1956. The first, throat-clearing, paragraph has been omitted. Here, Margaret says that her Guggenheim Fellowship was to be for ten months; in the autobiography proper, she says eight.]

Maybe you saw – or maybe not – that I got a Guggenheim ($280 a month for 10 months, starting Sept 15). Due entirely to the good public relations work done by my 'references' – FR Scott, AJM Smith, A. Brady, N. Frye, & K. Coburn – for I had no published work to submit. I'm still dazed, for I had no real hope at all after the application went in. They insist on a minimum of six months in the States, & I'll probably go to live somewhere around Chicago, that being accessible to libraries & also on the CPR direct route to Galt. My parents are reasonably O.K., but it would be distracting to be much further away than that. My reactions have been funny, after the initial startled incredulity. It was fun giving cause for rejoicing to various friends who have had to moan with me over so many things in the past 10 years. That I continue to like. The notoriety I do not like: for so long I've been building up a lovely philosophy of defeat that now, instead of welcoming a success, underneath I just fear that I've turned out to be the wrong sort – or I'd continue failing! Last, & probably most worth pondering, is a conviction that the ten months really just constitutes a tremendous headstart on what I ought to have the sense to make a more sensible life. I know that it's unrealistic to expect to be able to earn a living as a poet. But I refuse to accept that that means the only alternative is a 9 to 5 job. The year as a domestic was good in all respects except physical – it was too hard, and therefore for lack of energy & strength the privacy it permitted in free time was lost as far as any good steady writing was concerned. When I finally had to give up, I stumbled into a small public relations firm. Thank heaven the Guggenheim rescues me from a long-term commitment there, for it is a corrupting, distracting, attractive kind of work, & for lack of other ideas I'd probably have hung on at it too long. One of the limiting factors is always a degree of responsibility in Galt. Apart from that, I'd try living further afield for a while, I think. But anyway, this free year should set my feet on a path of steadier loyalty to the one purpose I find meaningful for me, & maybe when it's over I'll be able to figure out some less compromising way to live – and with all my heart I hope I'll resist any temptation to 'use' the notoriety to get me a job!

Too much autobiography, but it's out of the way now. You'll want far more to know how I plan to use the time next year. Ever since your first letter, and more concentratedly since the second, I have been trying to pin down the notions in my head, and the closest I can come is this: to try to realize the difference between poetic present time & historical present time. The social revolution since 1918 is hard to understand from inside it where our generation is: Maybe for your children there will be a degree of perspective. Wouldn't you give your eye teeth to know what they'll make of it when they are our age? The [sociologist David] Riesman kind of problem is out of my field – though reading what sociologists make of it all is helpful. But what strikes me is that art means freedom from chronological time. A living past is as much present as past. Nowadays a small proportion of people get much sense of the past, & a much smaller one any living sense of it. Without it, their poetic understanding is crippled. And it may be irrepressible optimism speaking, but I think poetic understanding could be, and one day will be again, a widespread thing. I think people need it, & are at present suffering from lack of it – that lack is one dimension of current unhappiness and restlessness. From the writer's point of view it is very hard now too. You & I know we can draw nourishment from Chaucer, Turgenev, Pope, Aymé, Cowper, Campion, Joyce. But the moment of poetic reality, that makes us write, is usually more limited. Your mirror, in Queen's Quarterly, is a beautiful poem. A sense of a ghostly 'other' most real being, hidden in a generally accepted historical kind of being, given only in fleeting reflection. That's it. [Nelson] Algren, say, writes poignantly of the present, but the living past won't consort with his 'present' time. Chr. Fry [Christopher Fry, English playwright] writes a pastiche of past excellence, makes it lively, but fails to touch present reality with it. Eliot uses a device for escaping chronological time that is religion's, not properly poetry's, so fails to speak for us, even though he can speak of us.

Where this leads I don't know. But it's fun, eh?...

As ever – Margaret

Poetry and the Doukhobors

[The mention of Mrs Polanyi (Ilona Duczynska) late in this essay means that it must post-date 1956, after the Hungarian Revolution which drove the Polanyis out of their country to Canada. Between 1953 and 1959, Sons of Freedom children, taken from their parents, were domiciled in a sanatarium in New Denver, B.C. They were there at the time of Margaret's writing, which must therefore have been sometime between 1956 and 1959. In The Canadian Forum *Vol. 44 (March 1965), 280–81, Margaret reviewed Simma Holt's* Terror in the Name of God: The Story of the Sons of Freedom Doukhobors *(Toronto: McClelland & Stewart, 1964.)]*

There may be poems by Canadian Doukhobors, but if so, the material is not to hand – the one art mentioned in most accounts of the Community is group singing – in Russian. This is not a consideration of the Doukhobors' poetry, then.

The connection between poetry and the Doukhobors is not a logical one. But to stick to logical connections involves compartmentalizing the world, and diminishing ourselves: from microcosms to specialists. It is usually specialists in political economy or education or folkways or law who make statements about the Doukhobors. Therefore it might fill in some of the waste places in the account to ponder the Doukhobor story from poetry's point of view.

There is an implied distinction there, between 'the specialist's' point of view and poetry's point of view. At one stage of cultural development the makers of poems and those who enjoyed poems were simply Everyman. To speak of poetry's point of view is an awkward personification now that we have lost poetry as a common language. The sense of the phrase comes out more clearly by indirection, e.g., some such proposition as this.

The specialists are concerned with facts – and the disciplines of their 'fields' help them to maintain disinterestedness. But the problem they assess may withhold some of its aspects from the disinterested.

The Doukhobors have experienced acute tension with the rest of the Canadian community. Their immediate neighbors have felt the tension too, and though they are therefore far from disinterested, they are participators in the problem, not observers of it. For us, at a remove, it should be possible to consider the story without disinterestedness, but yet with objectivity. The facts, the hints, the legend, what we have in common and where our understanding falters – admitting all these for no predetermined purpose may give us a better living sense of a social problem, and may show us our own situation in new perspective too.

To call this approach 'poetry's point of view' is simply to give it a convenient name. The phrase is vague; it suggests some sort of brooding over the whole of a subject. Does it presuppose learning from all the specialists, and adding further perception – a kind of post-specialist compendium of fact and impression, thought and feeling? Think of the variety of subjects where a 'poetic approach' might be attempted. It sounds hopeless. Everyone who attempted a poetic approach would have to become a man of one subject – so diverse and explicit are the specialists' contributions. Even then, he might never get through to the post-specialist perspective, might bog down in scholarship, or lose some faculties of perception or feeling on the way.

And yet ... it is a suitable role for poetry, to be a fool and rush in. The learnedness of our time so often cheats us of learning. There are many subjects that have yielded too little human meaning for all our careful study. The subjects escape us as they hide out in the various accepted pigeon-holes. This process has been our bulwark against bias. The generalizations have seemed the only trustworthy means of transport into areas beyond direct experience. And so article after article, book after book, deals with its subject under the three key headings: social, political, economic. Can a subject like the Tunisian border war or Indonesia or the Doukhobors really be conveyed or understood, without some fourth dimension in the approach?

If life is too short for a post-specialist approach, perhaps Everyman can breathe again, or, to turn it about, perhaps each specialist can rediscover his poetic understanding, and suffer the modifications of his disinterestedness that this implies. For example, a modified political scientist would be able to apply his learning to the Doukhobor community, derive his conclusions about political institutions, but tell more about the Doukhobors than he does now. Is this a foolish hope? Either way? Let that question remain in the air, for the time being.

For people primarily interested in poetry, the Doukhobor story has many fascinations, besides the straight story itself. It leads to reflections on the difference between a small, defined rural community and the shapeless community of big cities and world intercommunication. It raises questions about corporate beliefs, and fanaticism. And it forces us to examine the relation between poetic understanding and action, i.e., a poet's responsibility.

• • •

In 1895 the Doukhobors were undergoing persecution in Russia because of their pacifism and resistance to authority, and Tolstoy was at that time strenuously advocating pacifism and Christian anarchy. It is familiar history: how Tolstoy espoused the Doukhobor cause, publicized it abroad, acted as intermediary when asylum was offered them, sponsored their immigration into Canada at the turn of the century, and made financial contributions as well as commitments on their behalf.

The Doukhobors seem to have differed from other Russian sects chiefly in their rejection of any regulation from any state or ecclesiastical institution, and their development of the doctrine of living revelation. Each man was exhorted to listen to 'the Christ within'. It was natural that as experience and persecution called for coherence in the community, the leader would become preeminently the voice of 'the Christ within', the channel of divine revelation, and he seems to have been regarded as a more-than-human authority. Since the tradition was passed on by word of mouth, and guarded jealously from outsiders, only accident led to any written statement of beliefs. Such an accident was the exile in Siberia of the leader Peter Verigen. The instructions he relayed back to the sect show Tolstoy's influence strongly. His epistle of 1896, for example, is chiefly made up of passages borrowed verbatim from Tolstoy's *The Kingdom of God Is Within You.* (If Doukhobor practices seemed foreordained to appeal to Tolstoy, Tolstoy's title seems uncanny in its pertinence to the Doukhobor doctrine.)

Tolstoy's letters to the Doukhobors and his tracts about them are didactic, often the prosiest of prose statement.

But the experience from which Tolstoy wrote, with such startling projective force as to create a new kind of Doukhobor community, was poetic experience. In *War and Peace* he became the world he portrayed. His individual identity was the identity of his characters and, more than that, of social groups, of a people. And having become the world he knew, for all the initial exuberance of the transmutation, led to an awakening horror for Tolstoy as time went by. He sought the good not as an individual seeks, not as a prophet pointing the way, but as society embodied and become conscious of itself and its evils.

To a Russian perhaps the process looks less eerie than to us. Nicholas Ignatieff used to describe a key word in Russian that defied translation – the word *sobornost*. As far as I can recall, his approximate translation was, not 'I think', but 'the communal feeling thinks itself through me'. In English we do hint at the idea by calling someone 'the voice of his time'. This note sounds in many discussions of 'The Wasteland' and 'Gerontion', for example, as though Eliot had written for a voiceless generation and need not be seen as personally responsible for the state of mind he projected.

To leap from Peter Verigen's versions of Tolstoy's vision to T.S. Eliot's poetry is a real leap. The Doukhobor tradition was an oral one, an accretion of individual revelations, hymns, Scriptural images, crystallized and elevated by the isolation and hardships the sect suffered. In written form the tradition does not exist, and it is only a guess that hymns and chants made the body of doctrine into communal poetic statement of a kind. With Eliot, the communal borrowings are 'tags', the words of the poems are his, the experiences are our common experience only through the device of the 'objective correlative'.

One episode, the long pilgrimage in Saskatchewan and Manitoba, clearly illustrates the Doukhobors' very different understanding of the world. But our awareness of the contrast may be heightened by the preliminary attempt to define our own position.

In attempting to compass an understanding of the world, we are all to some degree relativists. We are not happy with a doctrine that unifies the world by relegating some areas to outer darkness. But relativism so far is commonly felt as a woolliness, a dubiousness about any conviction – although our feelings are still deeply involved with convictions. The best we can do, in the meantime, is realize the parts within our grasp as fully and precisely as possible.

The process of making our realizations specific has been, of course, very salutary in literature. The nineteenth century's reaching out for understanding led to some overweening claims for poetry and some loose wishful thinking about society. The need to affirm our common humanity we still feel, strongly. But the fragmenting pressures we know make the nineteenth century's awareness of evil seem facile indeed. In order to rescue poetry from the vapours, we have distilled it into essence, separated off from our longings and our drives as religious or political creatures. If there is to be a connection, we want it to be one we control. The step is clearly taken in Sartre's *What Is Literature?*, a re-appraisal that reflects the intense stresses of the 1940s in France.

'The poet sees the reverse side of words ... Instead of first knowing things by their name, it seems that first he has a silent contact with them, since, turning towards that other species of thing which for him is the word, touching words, testing them, fingering them, he discovers in them a slight luminosity of their own and particular affinities with the earth, the sky, the water, and all created things ... Doubtless, emotion, even passion – and why not anger, social indignation and political hatred? – are at the origin of the poem. But they are not *expressed* there, as in a pamphlet or in a confession ... Emotion has become thing ... The word – the *phrase-thing*, inexhaustible as things – everywhere overflow the feeling which has produced them.

'How can one hope to provoke the indignation or the political enthusiasm of the reader when the very thing one does is to withdraw him from the human condition and invite him to consider with the eyes of God a language that has been turned inside out?'*

Such statements incite an attitude they do not justify, or even condone. Exaggeration for emphasis can be further stepped up by readers longing for a key principle. Formalism in poetry seems to me as meaningless as 'contentism'. Nothing exists prior to its taking form.

---

* *'What Is Literature' and Other Essays.* Introduction by Steven Ungar. Cambridge: Harvard University Press, 1988, 30, 34. Margaret's typescript differs from the above in two ways. *'The poet ... sees words inside out,'* she begins. Later, it's 'The words – the *phrase-thing*, with the inexhaustible quality of a *thing* – everywhere overflow....' Perhaps she wished to improve subject-verb agreement.

Its forming – as thought, pamphlet, confession, or poem – is its coming into being. Sartre focuses on the words of poetry, as anyone who deals with poetry must do. But the poet is not the only one who approaches words inside out. A child called Penelope will grow up with strong Penelope characteristics, evoked by the name, for example. And the *thinginess* of words varies with the poet. The faintly luminescent things Sartre describes as the poet's words make one think, from pure contrariness, of some of Hardy's words that are more like builder's stones. He has his moments of verbal felicity of course. But it is through a jumble of a line sometimes that Hardy's poetic utterance comes through most powerfully.

Turning words inside out, or turning things inside out, freshens and extends awareness – and so serves poetry's turn. When Auden sees the gasworks in play, he renews its meaning for the man who works there. But Auden's definition of poetry as play, like the formalist's definition in terms of technique, are just ways of fighting off fraudulent demands. If our view of the cosmos is chaotic, a clear view of one detail perfectly realized is better than a faked or over-simplified or delusional view of the whole. And we no longer make the explicit claim of seeing eternity in the grain of sand. Our closest approximation is so heightening our awareness of the grain of sand that the dark questions start forth as foil to such clarity.

The Doukhobors' view of the cosmos was firmly defined. Belief, emotion, practical experience, were all unified, and extra pieces that won't fit into any unifying schema for us relativists, the Doukhobors saw as flaws of vision that would melt away in the blaze of true comprehension.

The pilgrimage of October 1902 was their natural response to new insights derived from Tolstoy's new teachings. To one group of Doukhobors, vegetarian reasoning implied that subjecting animals to man's uses was everywhere wrong. That meant no leather. Subjecting men to vile conditions of work in places like mines had been condemned by Tolstoy. That meant no metals. So this group of Doukhobors let their cattle and horses go free, cut the metal hooks and fasteners off their clothes, threw away their leather boots, and set off into the world, carrying some bread and apples. It was well into autumn when they left their lands north of Yorkton, Saskatchewan, 'to reach a warm country where there would be no government, and where they would eat fruit from the Trees.' Aylmer Maude's* description continues: 'Accustomed to a life of industry, some of them had to pray hard to be saved from the temptation which assailed them, to work ... Some among them were convinced that as they were obeying God's will, he would send a second summer instead of a winter; and for a while they really enjoyed fine weather. On November 3, when the pilgrims had reached Foxwarren, the weather changed; a sharp north-east wind arose, and snow soon began to fall. Sleeping in the open, as they had to do, was a severe penance.'

The helter-skelter misery that ended this pilgrimage is familiar: police intervention, resistance and nudist demonstrations in protest, finally a herding of the pilgrims into sheds in Winnipeg. By dogged insistence the authorities finally forced them to return by rail to their homes. The officials were bewildered to find these hungry, exhausted, half-frozen, barefoot people resisting shelter and warmth. One of the pilgrims later gave his account, and made it clear that physical frailty and winter were only apparent obstacles to them, on their way to that harmonious life in nature to which their vision had committed them. These are his words:

'We went through sixteen villages in all. When we were stopped naked, we were much beaten with twigs, all in blood, so that it was terrible to see us.

'Then we were surrounded by some twenty men, and were not allowed to enter the village. And night came on, the weather was bad, rain and snow and wind. Then we clustered into one heap, and lay on the ground one on another. And those who guarded us stopped for the night near us; they put on their sheepskin coats and cloaks. We remained naked; and really it was wonderful to ourselves that in such a wind we were not frozen. Those who stood guard over us publicly announced that the cold that came on was a very great cold, but not one of the naked was frozen ...'

It is as though the 14th century impinged on the 20th ... We may be moved by the history of the children's crusade, but we would have

---

* Aylmer Maude was a biographer and, with his wife Louise, translator of Tolstoy. Maude accompanied the Doukhobors to Canada and wrote a book about them entitled *Peculiar People* (1904).

to 'handle' any such incident swiftly and firmly today.

True, some of our assumptions are searchingly challenged by such carelessness of life and blithe unconcern for scientific fact.

The valuing of every individual human life is counted a primary, hard-won, highly prized basis of our civilization. Yet the Doukhobors see war as the betrayal of this value – or, less dramatically, our acceptance of social institutions they dread as forces contrived to grind down the individual's sacred potentialities. The urgings of a man's spirit, they say, cannot be denied simply for the sake of his survival on earth, for if it is so denied, the survival is after all merely perfunctory.

This intensity of conviction we cannot but honour. For us, though, it can be seen from outside. The moment you admit the existence of comparable intensities in other societies or ages, you classify your own romanticism, as it were. Even more for that, perhaps, the unswerving firmness of these true believers makes an appeal to us. Compromise is no longer a virtue as it was during 18th century England's equipoise of complexities. [Handwritten in the margin: 'expand'.] Nothing dovetails that way in our society, except contrived or ill-realized pieces we feel are only two-dimensional. Poetry longs to crash through into depth, at least.

But the crashing through is empty gesture if it denies part of what we know. The Doukhobors believed a second summer might occur for their holy pilgrimage. We know too much about the earth's relation to the sun for that. The solar system was just part of subjective reality for the pilgrims, and so available to divine disposition. For us, it is not so much, nowadays, that we believe it a rigid impossibility for divine intervention to operate on such a scale – for magnitudes do not disprove magnificence. Partly perhaps in our bones we remember the rabbis of old who thought poorly of themselves if they were the occasion for a miracle – since the *ordered* miracle was momentarily marred by the occasional, specific one. More literally, we are too conscious of the ramifications if the solar schedule were to be adjusted to our needs. A double summer here would make us anxious about Australia's crops, and even if the antipodes could be fitted in, we owe a reverence to some possible, unthinkable fragment as important as ourselves somewhere about the planets or the Milky Way. No, it is not mechanistic theory that blocks us from emulating the Doukhobor pilgrims' faith. It is just that we cannot re-limit our horizons. Science has not cheated us, only stepped up the terms. Oppenheimer, after all, is a poet too.*

So we would have to deal firmly today with a children's crusade or with another pilgrimage. And this resolution does not, surely, reflect any smugness. We may be able to recognize the glory of vision that stirs simple people at such moments, and yet we cannot but act according to whatever perspectives reason and considered historical experience have yielded us. There is no point in crying 'fanatic' and staying inside with a book of Wallace Stevens – or Traherne; for that is the very refusal to take account of an alien world that we condemn in the radical Doukhobors. But neither is there anything to be gained in picking at the careful, limited affirmations of those who are attempting the poetic approach today and looking about us instead for an exalted psalmist or even a sombre glebey [an Avison coinage] Langland to emerge.

Perhaps this sounds like an endorsing of Phyllis McGinley's poem 'In praise of diversity'. One of the reasons that poem is in an anthology of light verse, though, is that it leaves out of account the feelings of the Canadian farmer next-door to the Doukhobor land whose hay goes up in smoke, or the feelings of the constables who have to act for the majority and control the Doukhobors' excesses.

The response of the Canadian authorities has often been patient. But some incidents have called for resolution, and there have been, naturally enough perhaps, instances of exasperation and rough treatment.

Zubek† has incorporated the following conversation in his description of the Sons of Freedom:

> 'I haven't the nerve to burn my house yet,' said one matron looking around her bare but neat two-roomed house. 'The barn shall go, but I can't bear to part with my house.'
>
> 'Never mind now,' comforted her guest, a burnt-out refugee. 'Tomorrow you may think differently. No one knows how the inner voice will speak tomorrow. It is another day – let it take care of itself.'

---

* J. Robert Oppenheimer, theoretical physicist, 'father of the atomic bomb', was certainly interested in poetry, whether or not he wrote it.

† John Peter Zubek, *Doukhobors at War.* Toronto: Ryerson, 1952.

Although it is not the women's voices but Zubek's derisive voice we hear there, the burnings he did not invent. They recall the Russian sect that taught literal baptism by fire for the faithful, among whom, in the last thirty years of the 17th century, there were said to have been a total of 8,834 victims of suicide by burning, usually collective suicides, in barns and so on.

The confusion of this savage tradition with Christian anarchy was an irony Tolstoy did not foresee. He would surely claim, though, that persecution here is what keeps alive the traditions of the era of persecution in long-ago Russia. The parents who committed arson in the 'twenties were in jail long enough for resentment to register indelibly on their children. These children, now grown up, are the fanatical group who defy the British Columbia school laws. About a hundred of *their* children are shut away from them in New Denver, an adapted sanatarium, and permitted no holidays, and only visits every other Sunday from their families – and that through a wire fence – until they are fifteen years old. The *Maclean's* article on this truancy punishment quotes one Freedomite's stubborn assertion that the government will succeed only in strengthening the next generation's 'firmness in the faith'.* He is very likely right.

What the Canadian authorities are doing in New Denver is indefensible. But the principle that guides us is clear enough: a basic minimum of conformity is required of minorities in any society. A common reaction to Doukhobor disturbances among people here is 'let-them-go-back-to-Russia' – or let them go to Uruguay or the States or wherever their migratory longings may direct them at the moment. From poetry's point of view – to go back to that useful and indefinable phrase – it is clear, though, that there is no society, no country, no asylum on the face of the earth, where the promptings these people see as divine revelation would not lead to tensions and suppression.

---

* If, as seems likely, the article referred to is Sidney Katz's 'The Lost Children of British Columbia' (*Maclean's*, May 11, 1957), the passage in quotation marks is Margaret's. The passage she is drawing from may be one in which Katz quotes 'Doukhobor John Perepelkin' as follows: 'New Denver is making good Sons of Freedom out of our children.... Wait and see what happens when they get out' (101).

In adolescence most human beings know that that is true. There is an early perspective when the whole adult world appears as a massive conspiracy of compromises. Sometimes we are uneasily aware that a truth is lost when this perspective is lost – or rather when it is shuttered off by foregrounds. Something akin to the drives the Doukhobors experience persists in our society, and not only in what we call the 'lunatic fringe'. Liquor, stock-car racing, even the hypnotic flirting with fear that has become cosmic fear, show that the Doukhobor extremists are not really five centuries removed from us. Freud's diagnoses, which made people uncomfortable enough, were still a welcome consolation for a while – but soon explanations turned into questions again. Locating roots only leads to awareness of the soil that nourishes them, the sun that draws out change; the vast unknowables impinge more than ever when one new detail is brought into focus.

There are violences compacted in all of us. Whatever other ages and other cultures offered as explanation or as outlet, for us there is no common agreement on how these violences can be accepted and suffered.

We do not envy the Doukhobor extremists their communal release. We see too clearly its destructive aspects. And we want the voice of reason, not drowned, but included in any ultimate orchestration with our other powers and latencies.

We do envy the Doukhobors a certain whole-heartedness, at least impulsively. For us, the nibbling and gnawing of contingencies so frets conviction that we are half-disposed to condemn as pretentious any preference we still feel for grandeur, encompassing belief, and as excess any gravitas that is at the same time high-spirited. (High spirits are, for us, a comic exercise, with a pointedness not to be taken seriously.)

Contingencies, like the season's inevitable darkening during the pilgrimage, may have left the rapt Doukhobors untouched – though even here it may be argued that their conviction did not founder only because the unbelievers (the RCMP) intervened in time. Perhaps martyrdom would have crowned the pilgrimage for them, though, if no one had intervened. It is in the meaner dimension of day-to-day living that contingencies can be seen undermining the Doukhobors' uncompromising principles. For example, the University of British

Columbia's report* tells of the government commission's attempt to relocate a community of the Sons of Freedom sect. The Freedomites' spokesmen insisted that they were all farmers, 'a claim inspired largely by the mystic virtue which they attribute to the simple life.' Members of the sect refused to consider relocation in a semi-urban area. Yet the fact was that all of them had been earning part of their livelihood in non-agricultural jobs; their farming was primitive in method and ill-adapted to the climate and to market requirements, their properties were without exception run-down. The commissioners had to hunt for some relocation where other jobs would be possible, while maintaining the polite fiction that all the Sons of Freedom were as purely and simply farmers as their doctrine of the good life demanded.

The Doukhobor community is not the only one where actual practices fail to chime with the community's favourite version of itself. We still teach the virtue of thrift, but our economists know, and our budgeting reveals, how little thrift is valued in our consumer economy. The theories that exalt work as an individual's contribution to society, necessary to both his functioning as a social being and to the world: how well does this fit with our actual experience, where automation is a creeping paralysis in labour circles, and thousands of people in city offices are kept distracted, and remunerated, at what they know in their hearts are made-up jobs that contribute nothing needful to the world, and far from fulfilling them as individuals, school them in the poisonous practices of killing time?

We do not covet the Doukhobors' emotional release, then, nor, upon reflection, the unshakeableness of their conviction. But what about their wholeness, their communal experience? True, many Doukhobors have abandoned the old ways for partial or total adaptation to the rest of Canada. But the group that remains manifests a degree and range of shared understanding beyond anything we know.

For us, comedy is still a common language perhaps. Tragedy is not. It is a wonderful pleasure to hear the same funny story, that has travelled as if by magic, in different cities and in different kinds of

---

* *Report of the Doukhobor Research Committee.* Vancouver: University of British Columbia, 1952.

company – even when you discover that a TV programme or a *Reader's Digest* is what has given it currency. For the delight is in the common response. When poetry was an oral tradition, we wonder, did it complement and exalt the experience we know only in terms of a joke now? It is easy to be nostalgic, and to lose the past in the mists of sentimentality. A recent book that celebrates the folk-tradition – W. Kenneth Richmond's *Poetry and the People* – is more rough-shod than sentimental. It is full of self-contradictions of great persuasiveness, and lovely passages and quotations; but his theory involves a desperately clean sweep. For example this:

'The decline is demonstrable. Shakespeare ... Milton ... Dryden ... Pope ... and then the lesser "Dunciad" fry – Eagle, buzzard, magpie, sparrow ... insects.'*

According to this thesis, the Normans, then the court, finally the universities, diverted the fair stream of English poetry, so that the last clue we have of what the common touch might have meant is Shakespeare. But we cannot un-think what has riven the structures of common articulations for mystery, however poignant we may find the old carol of Mary and Joseph from which Richmond quotes:

> Then up speaks the little child
> In His own Mother's womb
> 'Bow down, you sweet cherry-tree
> And give my mother some.'

There is another folk-poem cited by Richmond as a sample of what we have lost:

> March yeans the lammie
> And buds the thorn
> And blows through the flint
> Of an ox's horn.

And this time we are truculent at his regrets. For surely some lines of that quality have been written since folk-poetry vanished into the

* W. Kenneth Richmond, *Poetry and the People*. London: Routledge, 1947, 130.

ground and may be being written today. To my ear, for example, James Reaney's 'The Horn' creates out of this word something wholly comparable. The difference is not in what exists as poetry, but in who hears it. And if poetry becomes increasingly 'difficult' – to use a cover-all word – the folk-thesis could be inverted: instead of people resentful of an exclusive caste of literati, an abandoned remnant of poetry's court refusing to give up the residual delight of talking among themselves. In fact, with actual poems in our hands, we would be hard put to it to accept the notion that poetry is becoming increasingly 'difficult'. Most of it now, most of it over the three centuries Richmond condemns, is accessible. And anyone who dislikes the court or college flavours has only to make poems with others of his choosing. For Jack Clemo – poor, handicapped, without wide social acquaintance or formal education – the poetic image is the Cornish clay-pits. Has he, by the magic of this non-elite background, any wider audience than a scholar like Beddoes?* And is the texture of his verse very distant from that of the college caste? Here is the concluding section of Clemo's poem, 'The Excavator':

> Yes, this is Christian art
> To me men could not school
> With delicate aesthetes. Their symbols oft
> Tempt simple souls like me
> Whom Nature meant to seal
> With doom of poetry,
> And dowered with eye and brain
> Sensitive to the stain
> Of Beauty and the grace of man's Ideal.
> But I have pressed my way
> Past all their barren play
> Of intellect, adulthood, the refined
> Progressive sickness of the mind
> Which throws up hues and shapes alien to God's
> Way with a man in a stripped clay desert. Now
> I am a child again,

---

* The poet Thomas Lovell Beddoes (1803–1849). Margaret's poem, 'The Earth That Falls Away' in *The Dumbfounding*, takes title and epigraph from Beddoes.

With a child's derision of the mentor's rods
And a child's quick pain,
Loving to stand as now in outlawed glee
Amid the squelching mud and make a vow
Which joy no priest or poet takes from me.

I cannot speak their language; I am one
Who feels the doggerel of Heaven
Purge earth of poetry; God's foolishness
Laugh through the web man's ripening wisdom spun;
The world's whole culture riven
By moody excavations Love shall bless.
All staining rhythms of Art and Nature break
Within my mind, turn grey, grow truth
Rigid and ominous as this engine's tooth.
And so I am awake:
No more a man who sees
Colour in flowers or hears from birds a song,
Or dares to worship where the throng
Seek Beauty and its old idolatries.
No altar soils my vision with a lax
Adult appeal to sense,
Or festering harmonies' magniloquence.
My faith and symbol shall be stark.
My hand upon these caterpillar-tracks
Bogged in the mud and clay,
I find it easier to pray:
'Keep far from me all loveliness, O God,
And let me laud
Thy meaner moods, so long unprized;
The motions of that twisted, dark,
Deliberate crucial Will
I feel deep-grinding still
Under the dripping clay with which I am baptized.'*

---

* *The Map of Clay.* With an Introduction by Charles Causley. London: Methuen, 1961. We have followed the format of this version: Margaret's typescript has a complex set of indentations.

Clemo's defiance of aesthetes and sophisticates is his individual assertion, but he knows that the people who receive and require his poetry, if any, will be – the little minority who read poems still.

In other words, it is social distrust that separates poetry and audience, and nothing necessarily in the poetry itself. The Hungarians wrote in the peasant language, not as poets apart, but as poets among, the people. Yet the few poems I know – thanks to a translation project Mrs Polanyi has undertaken here – speak the same poetic language as that marooned minority, the English-speaking poets, with a difference only in a higher ratio of very fluent, highly productive writers.

It would rob the world of its reality to pretend that poetry could ever have universal appeal. In the days of folk-poetry, as now, a responsiveness to words, to sounds, to relationships and sense impressions, were essential to full enjoyment of poetry. It does not need Colette's discrimination to detect, as she baldly puts it, that Shakespeare is sometimes very hard to take because he accepted terms from the vulgar who clamoured for his clowns and fairies and forced him, an entertainer, into what she called his Noel Cowardesses. There would be no poetic gain today if bebop rhyming were incorporated in verses, to meet the demands of the mythical TV audience.

It is a boring, frittering occupation, to predicate the kind of society where poetry would be both good and popular. Poetic principles cannot be carried over wholesale into the political arena, either. In the case of policies towards B.C.'s Doukhobors, it is hardly advisable for us to assert our common humanity by trying to melt ourselves down and reshape ourselves on the basis of a certain shared substratum of violent feeling.

But just as, in poetry, social mistrust can mark a good poem with irrelevant caste-inflections and, if we are not on guard, these can be allowed to condition poetic judgment until caste-inflections limit the poetry – so our sense of the differentness of Doukhobor fanatics can bring out in us such a passion to eradicate the differences, that we merely breed further fanaticism. Rigidities of judgment, formulated principles held against all comers and past all reason, are alien to the poetic approach. There must be flexibility, the expectation of the unpredictable, however uncomfortable that is for regulators. An administrator's utopia would be a world of robots.

For example, one group of Doukhobors staged a strange demonstration in Vancouver in 1944, to publicize their post-war plan. They proposed putting Hitler and his corps on a Pacific island, with plenty of fruit, tomatoes and spinach, but no meat, liquor, or tobacco. The leader of the group paraded nude, except for a headdress of oranges in a net with white streamers. It is not surprising that the programme found few supporters. But it is sad somehow that our response was only the Black Maria.

Doukhobor rigidities are not without charm. For example, dancing is condemned among them because they think of dancing as inevitably linked with Salome and the fate of John the Baptist.

And their deviations from the rigid standard they set themselves lack the candour that, in art, breaks out joyfully as irrelevancy or paradox. This candour appears amply in Tolstoy's writings, as in this 1851 entry in his journal:

'How strong I seem to myself to be against all that can happen; how firm in the conviction that one must expect nothing here but death; yet a moment later I am thinking with pleasure of a saddle I have ordered ... and I fall into despair because my left moustache is higher than my right, and for two hours I straighten it out before the looking-glass.'

If we react with martinet stiffness to outbursts of Doukhobor enthusiasm, of course the rigidities are not all on our side. Some of the sympathy Canadians feel for Doukhobor truancy is perhaps misplaced. It is doubtful whether they would accept any school system, even one reformed beyond the best educationists' wildest dreams. Their objection is in principle, a principle hard for the authorities to pin down. Alexander M. Evalenko* has reported, in translation, the only explanation the Doukhobors gave him, viz., 'Who has not heard of the words of Tolstoy that all universities are just so many insane asylums?' If they studied a living Tolstoy text, they would come upon the folk-schools he taught himself. They would find the wonderful

---

* Alexander M. Evalenko, ed. *The Message of the Doukhobors, a Statement of True Faith by 'Christians of the Universal Brotherhood' and by Prominent Champions of Their Cause.* New York: New York International Library Publishing Company, 1913.

stories of Tolstoy's tireless search for methods that would waken the peasant children's interest and relate the vast world beyond them with what they themselves knew directly, and, best of all, his devices for encouraging their creative powers. Remember his discovery that the boys failed to write good stories because the physical difficulty of shaping words on the paper inhibited them? And how it turned out, with Tolstoy writing to their excited dictation, long after school hours, after the dinner-hour; how he flagged at last and was suffered to rest; and how the boys battled the ABC's in an effort to carry on without him, fell asleep at last at their labours, and woke at daybreak only to resume their dictation, their story consuming them till it was all written down? Tolstoy had no objection when one of these boys went on to more advanced schools, and became a writer in turn. What he condemned was the school system's emphasis on nationalism, and war, and negation. But the condemnation is all that remains of this tradition to the Doukhobors in Canada. And so the pacifism, and the individualism, which they cherish so fiercely, has been increasingly nourished only on dreams and negation.

Of all the reflections that arise from pondering the subject of the Doukhobors, this may be the most pointed. It is intriguing to consider what changes – in viewpoint and emotional release – there are, between a primitive community with one firm belief, and our one-world relativism. The exaltation that reveals itself at high points in the Doukhobors' history is kin to something we still know, some source we have not learned to tap, that is nonetheless forceful in us. The persistence of a peasant culture, in Canadian society, refreshes our interest in the folk-sources of literature, and the changes that social complexity has brought about. But above all, the Doukhobors, for whom Tolstoy has finally meant only sterile dogma, remind us to beware of too-easy assumptions about the fruits of universal literacy.

The poetic approach is various, adapted to living human experience. The insights of art are lost when they are hardened down into formula. Is it better, perhaps, to restrict poetry to the few who will prepare their understanding for the shock of contact? Or is the poetic vision valid only in a visionary world – a 'divine discontent' that has no relevance in the context of popular experience? Was it a false dream, to suggest that the expert – the political scientist and so on – might one day recover and apply in his work the receptiveness, the flexibility, the burning clarity, poetry can develop in the human imagination? If, in some guise, poetry again became universally accessible, would eccentricities and morbid cultism be its fruits?

It seems unlikely that our society need add to its worries a fear of the poet's effect on the people. We smile a little to overhear Yeats's troubled reflections on his social responsibility (in 'The Man and the Echo'):

> ... And all that I have said and done,
> Now that I am old and ill,
> Turns into a question till
> I lie awake night after night
> And never get the answers right.
> Did that play of mine send out
> Certain men the English shot?
> Did words of mine put too great strain
> On that woman's reeling brain?
> Could my spoken words have checked
> That whereby a house lay wrecked?
> And all seems evil until I
> Sleepless would lie down and die.
> (Echo): Lie down and die....

And yet ... Karl Shapiro's tone has an ambiguous wryness, where he gives his chorus of poets these lines (in 'Trial of a Poet'):

> ... We took on ourselves the calls of conscience.
> It came to us when the priests stumbled
> And kings and presidents mumbled and failed.
> If not us, who? If not missionaries and cranks,
> If not the eccentric, the insulted, the poor,
> Who would accuse and alter
> The fatalism of inferior habits?...

The poets, mark ... 'If not missionaries and cranks'.

Dependent/Dependant

In an interim sometime, perhaps before full-time work at the [Evangel] Hall, I depended on assignments, as typist or shorthand stenographer, through an agency called Office Overload. What I remember from the initial interview is disagreeing with the interviewer, who objected when I said there were two correct spellings for 'dependent/ant'. Her dictionary agreed. She was very surprised, and gave me exacting placements on that basis.

There are several writers in residence, named or not....

*[*Rintrah, *vol 1, no. 1, Winter 1972, first and last number of a student publication at the University of Western Ontario.]*

By ten in the morning many people have been disposed of – public school children, high school personnel, and all responsible adults are tucked away with their varied busy work. Most college people are either caught up in a mirror image of these, or in hiding, or strung out along main traffic routes providing or accepting something misnamed a hitched hike. The quieter streets are left to occasional dogs, squirrels, the birds who walk a lot, cats, pre-school children, and stray others. The coherence of their outdoor comings and goings is not readily apparent; cross-relationships, however, when they spring up at random, are sensed to be permanent.

You cannot follow the stray individual, for his route by definition is unpredictable, and your following presence would have a predictive and therefore invalidating effect. You might meet him later, but the meeting (the in-come, in fact) will be in a recognized place already known. But the stray knows, in spite of your best appearances, that you too have known or could know what it is to be out of range, of necessity unrecognized – that is the writer's confidence in readers and he too is a reader.

Most writing in and around the university is public or purposive or required, and therefore tends to vanish into the busy work world or its mirror image: essays, letters and signals, persuasion, social gesture, therapeutic run-off. But verbal events of absurd independence keep occurring too, so that the side-streets become an end accomplished. Blank maps are thus unscrolled for other explorers from newly fixed frontiers. It is good that a few publishers on the campus are now appointing themselves to open the unmarked ways.

1990 Governor General's Awards

[Pages 3 to 9 of a letter to her sister Mary that Margaret meant to include in, or incorporate into, her autobiography. The date is unavailable, since Margaret did not photocopy the first two pages: most likely late January 23, 1991, since her trip to Montreal was from January 21 to January 23. Ellipsis is Margaret's.]

Now for the Montreal part. Joan called it 'queen for a day'. The 1st class VIA trip, taxi & chit, $150 room at 'Le Méridien', prepaid, messenger with 'an important envelope for Madam' soon after we arrived, etc. For breakfast ($12.50, buffet in the hotel, me paying). That day, the 22nd, I had pancakes & real syrup, bacon, real grapefruit juice <u>and</u> 3 prunes with whipped cream plopped on by mistake (I thought it was yogourt), bran muffin, coffee. There is a concourse under the hotel, & the batteries had run out on my flashlight – for going to the bathroom at night without turning on the huge lights & waking Joan. So we went down, bought a) batteries b) a longer 1/2 slip for the dinnertime dress – & browsed a long time in the bookstore, which had <u>NOT ONE</u> of the French short-listed books in the huge section of 'Littérature Québecoise'! But the children's books were fun, & I found some beautiful postcards of Montreal. Back upstairs to see whether the creases from the suitcase had come out of the suit (afternoon) & dress (dinner) – they had enough to not need paying a presser who <u>could</u> have fixed things but cost a lot & might have been nerve-wrackingly unpredictable in timing. I, solo, had been bidden to another floor (at 1:15) to meet the other 'winners' & the Canada Council ladies who did the logistics, dressed & ready for the 3 o'clock ceremony. On VIA the waiter had given us biscuits & cheese & peanuts, Joan had brought some dried fruit, & the bar in the room offered orange juices & pops etc, – so these we ate for lunch & off I went (skirt & red blouse & jacket & respectable black shoes, tho flat heeled), leaving Joan to cope until 3 minutes before the ceremony began.

The start was: being greeted in a sort of Reception Suite by Josiane Polidori of the Canada Council & three other hostesses from there; introduced in rapid succession to all the authors & illustrators there so far (I knew one only, of them all); continuing cycles of introductions as others arrived.... At last all were assembled & we were led through hotel & underground passages and dark bare echoey backstage spaces to the Place des Arts where the ceremony would be. (I learned only then that James Campbell & a symphony had given a gorgeous concert there the night before, Monday.) (Could not have come by a ticket at the last minute I later learned.) There was a 'set' on stage, poster-style & some sculpture-dimensioned posters, a bare floor, a long table (right), 2 chairs right of the table, a huge space & a lectern & microphone (left) & 3 chairs right of the lectern. We were given a printed sheet showing the award categories (no people's names – the actual programmes were hidden until AFTER the ceremony and the distribution of awards), & we were summoned in the right sequence – my place 12th of 14 – to go up steps (right) onto stage, pause at the first 2 chairs where GG & Lady wd shake hands, clump across to the mike, say something (!!) (the first we'd heard of this) – just like the Grammies, find steps (left) off the stage, & sit in a new special row from whence we'd be led elsewhere ... That rehearsed, but NOT our speeches – we were led to a place backstage where room dividers created a barely adequate space for us standing rather bunched & told to wait: someone would distribute our cheques discreetly, there – because no money must change hands in front of the GG! While we waited some made speech notes. I had no pen, no paper, no peace there to do anything because we were all nervous and tended to chatter, the French to one another or, courteously, in English to us, etc. The one person I knew by sight was Nino Ricci (novel in English). I remember good conversation with Daoust, the French poet, & the one I liked best, Melançon who with his wife had translated A.M. Klein's *The Second Scroll* into French; he described the meticulous way they worked, separately, editing each other's parts, switching; 23 dictionaries & nine years' work in all; and she was home, ill, & he hated accepting kudos that were so jointly earned. Time palled, feet hurt, faces paled, & we'd only each other, till a CC lady came in & slipped us each a $10,000.00 cheque (mine is in a separate account in the bank till I gain a little perspective & sense of reality – Thurs. I did that).

She left & we each stowed our envelopes. I found it a great icebreaker to ask others what they planned to do with their money. Nino thinks he will live off the interest! Paul Morin, illustrator, has wanted a recording studio for ages & means to start that business with his, & hopes it becomes a source of income to support his painting. Melançon has debts, but one son has longed to go with a highschool friend for a year's exchange in Spain, & they hope to enable him to go. Etc....

Suddenly, in came the GG & Mrs H. Hands shaken all around, intros, congrats, thank yous. Many had drunk things at all these receptiony intervals, & we left the 2 royals to have some & were led off into the darkened theatre to a reserved section at the front where our guest had been taken & told to save a seat, so we were sprinkled about – the Chairman & 2 came to chairs (left stage), told us to stand (all the crowd), in came the Hnatyshyns, in dead silence, no anthem or fanfare, they sat, we sat. Speech by Lefebvre, Eng & Fr by turns; speech by Joyce Zemans of CC, ditto. The parade of awardees began, I tried to attend while composing myself & my speech as best I could there in the dark. Some seemed too long, so I kept cutting ... when # 12 came I got on stage, on very sore feet by then after 2 hours standing, got hand shaken & a bound copy of my book given me, clumped to mike, & here's exactly what I sd. (Never before written down till now!): 'Thank you (facing CC people etc.) I also feel grateful to a publisher who has been very generous and longsuffering over several years: Mr William Pope of Lancelot Press, Hantsport, N.S. May I commend the Can. Council for taking such a solitary trade as writing, and such a remote thing as a stack of books, and translating these, astonishingly into a social and public event like this.' Stumble off down the other set of stairs. Someone in a fuzzy sweater in the dark whisks me off to a waiting CBC microphone & telephone & girl, Shelagh Rogers asks 'What do you think of your GG award, Margaret?' and I say – totally taken by surprise – in a high falsetto 'It's ridiculous!' She promised soothingly to edit that out, & I must have said something else though I know not what. Fuzzy sweater led me back the opposite aisle to a special row in the dark, where I could hear the last bit. (Nino Ricci ended his remarks with 'Merci, Thank you, Grazie.')

Some friends & observers moved in on the people who'd won awards, but the CC ladies separated them & corralled us up onto the stage again for a series of group photographs – 'like an athletic team', said the GG. I was wedged next to Mrs Hnatyshyn and asked her about her children, and she told me while flashbulbs flashed away – she seemed a lovely person.

Then we all went to the lobby, and Joan & I both hunted for Mr and Mrs Pope, unsuccessfully, until a CC lady located them for us. It was good to meet them. They had just arrived around mid-day, but seemed serene and game, although only one (the 'publisher') was invited to the dinner the Bank of Montreal was giving. More standing amid swooping trays of shrimp etc., more sipping Perrier Water amid many cheery unknowns, everybody very friendly ... Finally Joan & I wriggled free of the crowd and limped away via under-cover-route to the hotel & finally the room. Poor Joan had to wear her sore shoes some more, but I'd brought sandal-like comfortable low shoes and they were passable with the Laura Ashley cotton dress. By the time we were changed, it was time to meet Mr Pope & get a taxi downstairs for the Bank of Montreal, & the dinner.

By then the day had gone on a little too long – as this letter has. It was excellent salad, chicken, etc. but hard to chew, took too much energy (the chicken was not tough, it was delicately boneless & perfectly done, just my jaw felt like a machine with 2/3rds of the power cut off). Fortunately my table-mate was a brilliant talker – a banker, Czech, with experiences of living in Japan, coming to love Outremont, corporate contacts all over that gave him a liking for the people he dealt with – & he compared 'insularities': those of England, Japan, Quebec – very alike, wellnigh impermeable to outsiders. By now he is aware that he & his wife (Hungarian in origin, a painter), despite fluency in French & long years of citizenship in Canada, will never be accepted as part of this community – & he doesn't care to contemplate living in any other part of Canada. My own wits, & words, were working about on a par with my jaws, but my ears got me through, thanks to this man.

We got a taxi back to the hotel, & Joan invited Mrs Pope to join us in the Foyer, where we settled in the bar for fruit punch all round – friendly time despite the din of a piano-player too close to us. Wed. breakfast? Potato latkes & bacon & pineapple and prunes, and a muffin, and REAL coffee. Checked out. And spent the precious remaining 2 1/2 hours exploring Old Montreal on foot – free & anonymous & off the hook and happy – VIA home, through a fine-blowing snowstorm, to the 10 o'clock news (where you came in, in this letter.) –

I won't do such a long screed again, I promise.

Love, Margaret

Interview with Cristina Cassanmagnago: Margaret Avison's Voice

[Interview with Cristina Cassanmagnago in Rivista Di Studi Canadesi/Canadian Studies Review *12, 1999, 81–87. This is a slightly edited version of an interview conducted in Toronto on August 5, 1994. The language barrier caused some errors and produced less well articulated versions of material that appears elsewhere, so we have omitted instances of both. Punctuation has been adjusted. Readers will note that wording here is occasionally doubtful. Margaret must have had no opportunity to reconsider. All but centred ellipsis is original.]*

• • •

CC: You converted to Christian faith in 1963. Could you please tell me how you reached this point?

MA: Gradually I see that it started when I was eight years old. My grandfather, whose wife had just died, came to live with us. We lived in view of the mountains in Alberta. I sat on his knee and he told me about Abraham, the sacrifice of Isaac, the story. He never pointed morals. He told story after story and it mattered as much to him as to me. He was talking to me as to another adult from his loneliness, his sense of death and being abandoned by his wife, and for an eight-year-old, that stayed with me permanently. And there had been other people over the years. I didn't know at the time that they were the golden stepping stones to faith. I can remember I was very depressed once, and my father came. I was working here and he came to a meeting here. We had lunch and he met an old friend of his who had been a minister, a man of about five foot one with a bald head, and he said, 'What are you going to do in life?' and I said, 'If I knew I'd tell you' and he said: 'There is a Lord. Ask Him.' I didn't think of it again. But over the years these things accumulated and after I believed, I could see things right back to the beginning, preparing for the stage when I began to search seriously. Then I was driven to read Scripture for at least two years. That is a dangerous occupation for an unbeliever!

• • •

CC: So your life changed after your conversion.

MA: I could smell the flowers in the grass, the first morning as I walked. I hadn't had my senses so vivid for years.

CC: You prefer to be considered a poetess of human experience rather than a writer of religious poetry.

MA: Those terms are invented in a secular century. 'Religious' writing, devotional writing, hymn writing and general writing from someone with religious feeling are quite distinct. Devotional writing is all written in prayers and I think intended to be heard. Religious writing is deliberate teaching. 'Paradise Lost' qualifies there. It takes a theme that is like a sermon, only it is poetry. For me Hopkins, though he writes religiously, is in the general category. He is writing from human experience, which in his case includes his vocation.

CC: You are frequently compared with Hopkins.

MA: I know. People speak of me and Hopkins because they are comfortable with anything Christian, as they are not comfortable (because they feel betrayed into the secular) if they get to somebody else. As you know, I chose Byron for my thesis on purpose. If God is anywhere, if He is present, you can study anything. This narrowing down to things you are safe with almost suggests that you are losing your faith, it seems to me. Once Jacques Maritain, a French philosopher of the Catholic Church, was here at St. Michael's lecturing back in the thirties, and it was a marvellous lecture in aesthetics. I just hung on because I am not good at philosophy. Then there was a discussion and it was all very upper levels of religious thinking, and somebody in the audience said, 'How do you approach Baudelaire?' There was a long silence and then a little smile. He could have fitted that into his aesthetic theories in a minute, but he didn't ... What he said was: 'My friend, you won't take Baudelaire away from a Frenchman!' That taught me something at the age of 22 that has been with me all my life. Hopkins and I may be alike in faith, but faith is not a subject, it is a reality. Life, and any human beings – all of us – potentially or actually have to do with God, whether we know it or not.

CC: Could you please explain the relationship between poetry and your faith. Do you want to link them, or...?

MA: I don't want to link them any more than I want to link anything. It sounds as though there is an equal level. It is more to be suffused with what God wants, and if he wants me to drop literature that is okay. C.S. Lewis once said he had discovered there was a great temptation to write from an insight rather than live from it, act from it. I have learned what that is. If I get excited by something I am reading –

devotions in the morning, or something that comes to me – then the temptation is to turn it into a poem, but lose the point of it for that day. Let it live a bit, see if it is really direction for something up ahead and often it is. I've just been readied for something and it isn't really a poem. That's the kind of thing I mean.

CC: I have often read that you converted to Christian faith, but there is no mention of a specific church. Do you think it doesn't matter what church a believer follows?

MA: Each of us in any church cherishes the traditions of that church, but the key thing we have in common, and we mustn't forget, is that Jesus Christ is Saviour and Lord. I heard the message in a Presbyterian church so I just followed on, in due time joined it. I might have heard it in a Catholic church and then I would have joined there. You can meet other people on a common ground, because I know somebody who says: 'The heart and soul of Judaism is the heart and soul of Christianity, that God is one.' If you start with that attitude to a Jewish friend it is quite different from starting: I do believe in the Messiah and he doesn't. If it were not for the Jews we wouldn't have the roots of our faith; if it were not for the monks through the dark ages, copying Scriptures by hand, we wouldn't have our Bible. The Reformation should have been within the church, because it was just restoring what had been so cherished over the centuries. I don't mean that differences don't matter in a positive way, that each of us cherishes his own tradition, but we should keep our eyes on a common ground.

CC: *No Time,* the title of your last collection, makes me think about waiting ... about the future ...

MA: There is another pun sense in that too; because the common complaint of mine is: 'there is no time for this ... there is no time for that'; and also I have been very preoccupied with God's timeless awareness and how we live along this little string of yesterday, today and tomorrow, and there is a disjunction in understanding, and so that is hidden in the title too, I think. A preoccupation. I just had fun with the title. 'No time like the present' is another idiom in English. It is how you seize a moment, a common saying in English ... I have a feeling about language that when you choose a word or an expression with two or three meanings they are all valid or you shouldn't use it and if a reader finds four or five others they have to be valid. You have to control where the word can go for anybody, just by the rightness of the word, or someone will be misreading …

• • •

CC: Reading your poems I have noticed that you mostly use free verse. Could you explain the reason for that choice?

MA: You write sonnets, you are writing right back to Shakespeare; you write quatrains as a Canadian, you are writing back to Bliss Carman. It is the revolution I spoke of in the late '30s and '40s. We were trying not to be like traditional English poets, not to be like Bliss Carman. That meant hiding the rhymes, complicating the rhythms. Free verse is a little freer definition than I would give it, and sometimes if you look for it you'll see that the pulse still is iambic pentameter, God help me, because that is what I have read so much. That rhythm dominates except in poems that are written in anger which tend to be tight in rhyme and rhythm; or poems of wit, joke poems.

CC: I have noticed that sometimes you change your poems, you think them over and then write them again … [Cristina is thinking of 'The Butterfly' and 'Design'; we skip to Margaret's general answer]

• • •

MA: Yes. Revision, as I grow older, gets more and more agonized … I find I have to sharpen the sense of final sections. My energy ran out before I got to those sections in the first writing. The energy is always best at the beginning and I tend to peter out and when I reread, I see … ah, here you have to fill it out.

CC: *Sketch* is also the title of some of your poems.

MA: Well … as an artist can make a quick sketch in order not to forget, there is a certain kind of writing that is like that. I see, so I'd better record it. And you have poems like that; you can group some of them to become the core of another kind of poem, but some of them just stand as they are.

CC: When I read your poems I am always impressed by your images. They're real, very strong …

MA: Now that I'm old, there is a sense sensitivity that fades a bit … yes, more skeletal structure stands out now, less surface beauty.

CC: You translated Hungarian poetry because your friend asked you to help her and because of the political and social situation of Hungary at

that period. Was this an important experience for you?
MA: I think that the big thing I came away with, after an introduction to literature I hadn't known, was the sound. She made tapes, she read beautifully in Hungarian and the 'Bartók' particularly … I have had Hungarians say when I read it aloud, it is exact, it is the music … That was important with 'Bartók', because Illyès knew what he was doing and the words had to evoke the music. It's a little rhetorical, particularly for Illyès who is usually plain: compare that with 'Of Tyranny in One Breath', so spare, so tense. The voice, if you translate, you have got to pick it up. But this language is syllabically very different from English. So to work with the sounds and try to convey the music was very exciting … and music and meaning and voice are important together. Writing from the ear is always precious to me. What looks like unrhythmic, unrhymed verse is precisely adjusted especially at line endings where English uses a strong syllable, naturally, not the grammatical light word-endings normal in Hungarian.

• • •

CC: Is there something else you would like to say?
MA: I think one or two things. One thing is I don't like the process of rapid reading, the habits we form of … because many books are for information we skim. I do like a lot of space around a statement, that you can sink into. Writing complicatedly is trying to focus meaning. If somebody will go slowly then they'll discover there is another kind of reading and that will make it possible for them to read Beowulf and Dante and many rich things that now are out of reach except through people who are privileged and have taken courses. I think a lot of people get cut off from this habit of good reading. But I have come to see that if you can be simple as well as making people go slow … 'You can't take Baudelaire away from a Frenchman'; Maritain's whole lecture is in the simple statement. So that is what I would like to be able to do. What about my future … It is trying to get simple.
CC: But in your last poems you are simpler. For instance in 'Detroit … Chicago … 8 a.m. … platform 5'?
MA: Yes it is clear. I like the one 'Discovery on reading a poem' for that reason. I wish I could get the light of a born Irish kind of laughter in the saddest places. That is the other thing I would love to come to if I am allowed to. But it is important that you don't take me too

seriously, and I don't take me too seriously either. The closer you get to death, the less it seems to matter about the poems, you know.

CC: You speak of death quite often. For instance in *No Time* there are two groups of poems dedicated to two dead people, your friend and your mother.

MA: It is something you don't think about as easily when you are young, because it has a terrible impact for a young person, but when you are my age, people are slipping outside [probably slipping away] all around you all the time. I had a couple of severe illnesses that could have finished me. I got better. 'It's neither here nor there', as they say. It does put the poetry in proportion.

Ray Souster and the Contact Days

[Written for a Greg Gatenby-organized Harbourfront 'Tribute to Raymond Souster', June 17, 1998, but most relevant to the 1950s. Margaret did not attend the evening – her piece was read on her behalf – but perhaps Souster went her one better by ducking his own tribute.]

Raymond Souster is 'self-effacing', everyone agrees – so let's begin with a look at his face: sober, responsible, gentle and patient, eyes active, missing nothing, and always lurking around his mouth the hint of an amused smile. The setting? He is making a group of writers known to one another.

And Ray is still at it. E.g., would I have come upon Richard Woollatt's first book (*Eastbound from Alberta,* 1981) if Souster had not found him first and worked with him as a co-editor of collections of poetry (1975 and 1980)? Indeed would R. Woollatt have bothered making his poems available at all but for Souster's prodding? I would love to know how many others there are like this.

Some of them go back (like me) to the '50s. It is as yesterday to us, though it may seem something you hear about in a classroom to later generations. But *we* were young then. During the Depression and the War and its aftermath, who had time for poetry or cared about it? Except a poet like Ray. He 'brought us out', on smudgy pages from a mimeograph machine, in early collections and little magazines, and brought us together through his Contact readings. A small following developed, and heard, and began to share his excitement about fresh winds blowing and widening horizons.

When Greg Gatenby first told me about his plan for this evening, I had an instant recall of Ray playing host to Cid Corman. After the Corman reading he brought Cid and a bottle of something or other to my room – as I remember some other plan had fallen through. It's not clear to me now which are things we talked about then and which arise from Corman's later writings – things about poor villages in southern Italy, or the New England spastic poet [Larry Eigner]; nobody knew he could read – he could not speak – until he heard Cid Corman reading poetry over the local radio and, with astounding enterprise, managed to announce himself through a typed message! (A book of his was later published in Boston.) Cid Corman was doing in the American northeast what Ray Souster was doing in Toronto.

Reviewers speak of Souster as 'the poet of Toronto'. Indeed local streets and faces and buildings and small happenings, through his poems are lit up over and over again, in all our weathers: slush-deep sidewalks when wet flakes continue falling, through bone-hard windy days in the canyons of downtown, to springtime and the softening of every outline then. There is Babe Ruth's home run against the Toronto Maple Leafs at the old ballpark on Hanlan's Point. The Island lagoons. The roller-coaster that one night just took off from the (now vanished) amusement park at Sunnyside, sailed off out over the lake, and just kept going.

But Souster's true scope was wider, as his editing and Contact planning show. This is the man exasperated by any arbitrary barriers between poets in various parts of the world. Ezra Pound's *Make It New* spurred him on. He learned from William Carlos Williams, and many of the readers he brought to the readings were young Americans. Ray fought against regional rivalries and barriers too. He was quick to acknowledge in the B.C. magazine *Tish* a lively new movement and welcomed its influence as it spread eastward. From all areas of Canada came the young unknowns whom Souster introduced to readers in the early anthologies he edited, *New Wave Canada,* and *Unit of Five.* (The former was dedicated to W.W.E. Ross whose poems, part of the imagist movement, were well-known in the U.S, but not in Canada.) Incidentally one of his magazines included, for the convenience of beginning poets, a list of 22 little magazines coast to coast with addresses and names of editors hospitable to poetry!

Who was Ray Souster – an editor? a custodian of new talent? the organizer of readings? the encourager of interested readers and audiences? Did he dodge behind such identities because he was shy about being spotted as primarily a poet? I think so. One of the poets he admired was e.e. cummings, and I think of him when I read cummings (in a high school *Spectator* in Ottawa Hills, Michigan, 1955): 'As for expressing nobody-but-yourself in words, that means working just a little harder.... Why? Because nothing is quite as easy as using words like somebody else.'

Doesn't that suggest Souster? And he certainly worked harder than anybody else! For one thing, he lived the common lot that he liked to write about, working the 44-hour week of that period, before and after his wartime years in the RCAF. Was he earning for the sake of a fringe of time to read and write? Not so! Think of the letter-writing, telephone-calls, posters, consultings, that lay behind his Contact readings. And the livelier hours of preparing those collections of other young writers. How and when did he do his own writing?

There are 62 items listed under Souster's name in the Reference Library's holdings! Yet I say to you, Ray: you knew perfectly well that publishing many fugitive little books of poetry, and finally letting seven hefty volumes of *Collected Poems* follow – each volume unmanageably heavy to haul down from its shelf – this tactic of publishing but eluding attention somehow worked pretty well. Has anyone been able to gather a satisfying sampling of Souster on their own poetry shelf?

Perhaps Souster relished the language of the Sports page and the pub conversations after hours more than the language of lyrical tradition. Yet he wrote his lyrics too: 'Queen Anne's Lace' ('that shyest filigree of wonder/found among grasses') which has the wistful final stanza:

> You will imagine poems
> as brief, as spare,
> so natural with themselves
> as to take the breath away.

Tradition, however, was dangerously close to an institution, Souster's *bête noire*. He would agree with W.H. Auden: 'A poet and an illiterate peasant, if they enter a government building ... both sniff in any official world the smell of unreality in which persons are treated as statistics' (from 'The Poet and the City', in *The Dyer's Hand*). And so alongside Souster's delicate vignettes there are political fulminations, bursts of wrath over insidious social pressures, aggrieved narratives about the oppressed. And then again there is his gnomic verse:

'Merry-go-round' (the poem in full)

Still grabbing
at that golden ring?

The ride's the thing.

OR

'Now in November' (in full)

At the end of the eavestrough
winter's first icycle

now pierced by the sun
and dying
one stubborn drop at a time.

OR

'Prayer' (in full, with its verbalized noun)

Daylight my darknesses.

'Lit Crit' is baffled by Ray's accurate self-knowledge about his own work. He did write long poems; one of them, 'All the Long Way Home' (in *Riding the Long Black Horse*, 1993), is one of my favourites. But elsewhere he says:

I'm not sure I'm ready for epics;
there are far too many little songs
the others have left unsung.

Equally unpretentious were those Contact readings, held in the Isaacs

Gallery, on the west side of Yonge north of Bloor, or in the YMHA at Bloor and Spadina. The first one I remember electrified us and made us all look forward to the rest of the series. Because that night the visiting poet was a boy with glowing eyes and thick dark hair and a child's rosy cheeks, from Montreal, reading his embossed, hieratic, sure-footed gold-threaded poems – his name was Leonard Cohen. He was probably reading from his *Let Us Compare Mythologies* (McGill Poetry Series, 1956). 'I have the tools, I know how to use them,' Cohen is reported as saying much later (in *Strong Voices,* 1988) 'but the content becomes more and more difficult.' We heard his lyric voice that night, before many pressures honed his utterances and made them both more and less accessible.

Greg Gatenby tells me that I had a role at some of the meetings, and not just as that one-time impromptu hostess, but I have no memory of hosting the open conversation that the visiting poets wanted after their readings. Probably developments in form and diction predominated. I recall Zukovsky's spidery outlines, how he netted a true reading; and Creeley's appalling bed-rock homing-in, not one syllable wasted. Another of the American readers, Denise Levertov, took my address at the end of her evening, and we have exchanged occasional books and postcards over the years since. I met another reader later, by chance, at a gathering in somebody's room in New York, Leroi Jones (that was still his name then).

The reader who stands out for all who attended, I would guess, is Charles Olson – partly because he is a presence, physically and dynamically. His essay, 'Projective Verse', was already widely known. It begins: '... "closed verse", that verse which print bred and which is what we pretty much have had, in English and American ... It led Keats, already a hundred years ago, to see it (Wordsworth's, Milton's) in the light of "the Egotistical Sublime"; and it persists, at this latter day, as what you might call the private-soul-at-any-public-wall....' The contrasting 'open' verse that Olson proposed, he demonstrated. The 'breathing', the physical ex-pressing/ex-haling from a particular person's being and energy and intention, was shared forth that night, first in three translated versions, each making its own full poetic impact – 'Variations Done for Gerald Van de Wiele'. To this day I hear Olson's voice whenever I read them. The exacting art of public reading he made evident when he began his 'A Newly Discovered "Homeric"

Hymn' – you can find the text in *The Norton Anthology of Modern Poetry*, ed. Richard Ellman & Robert O'Clair (1973). He gathered his forces visibly for this poem, standing there. And began … and stopped dead, perspiration shining on his head. 'I started too high on the scale,' he explained. Prepared himself again. The carefully mounting intensity worked: the reading communicated that poem, permanently.

When I decided I couldn't be here to read this in person tonight, I looked up Ray's phone number (it's in the book) and called him to make sure he'd understand. He chuckled. 'I'm not able to go myself,' he said; his reasons sounded valid. But he ended by saying: 'It wouldn't matter if what they said about me that night was good or bad – having it about me – I'd feel uncomfortable.' He would wince at how well this fits the words of the English, polished, well-known writer, Robert Graves (in 'The Poet and his Public'): 'The only demands that a poet can make from his public are that they treat him with consideration, and expect nothing from him; and do not make a public figure of him – but rather, if they please, a secret friend.'*

Putting Computers in Perspective, or A Chip on Our Shoulders

[This appeared in Hi-lites, *the newsletter of Fellowship Towers retirement home, June 1999.]*

Communication is amazingly extended and eased by the new technology. That is, communication with others in the know, who have the right equipment and the skills. But is communication cut off too – between users and non-users? Some may learn, some have learning thrust upon them, but many do not learn – for lack of opportunity or energy or capacity.

It's a fact that the world changes and over generations we adapt. Trains created local communities. Cars gave us a life of flow instead of roots. Airplanes opened up horizons worldwide. When TV was new, some people were resistant at first (and now we may wonder why we didn't listen to ourselves back then!).

---

* *The Crowning Privilege: The Clark Lectures, 1954–1955.* Also *Various Essays on Poetry and Sixteen New Poems.* London: Caswell, 1955, 191.

For people our age, it would be useful to stop feeling isolated from the new generations, and start assessing the prospects ahead. We have the time to think, and we have some perspective on our ever-changing times, to help us size up our grandchildren's technological revolution.

Before we go any farther, let me confess that my learning is at the outsider-beginner stages. From where I stand, I have some questions. Somebody told me that computers work on a principle of yes-no options. Does that eliminate maybes? Is a computer, then, an inappropriate instrument for any questions in the grey area?

People talk about E-mail, and doing research in a Harvard Library from a cottage in Muskoka. *Where* are the messages in the interval between sending and receiving? I never really understood the telephone, but at least I could see the wires. Radio waves unnerve me if I think about them. TV impulses being converted into sound and line and colour mystify me even more. Now is our beautiful sky full of data? Do we breathe them all? Or are they zipping straight up into the stratosphere in tiny vertical stripes?

Why did computers proliferate so suddenly and haphazardly? I can remember when a whole wing of the U of T Physics building was needed to house the first computer on campus. And now 'laptops'! Did the supply create the demand, or vice versa? It seems as though new models become obsolete before their owners have had a chance to master them. If this goes on, will enough people be able to keep pace? Does pressure to be the first explain why the designers didn't agree in advance on standardized codes? Or why they don't provide a master manual at this stage, translating one set of symbols into the other?

Of course a new branch of learning will coin new words – that has always been a convenience for the specialists, who in turn use roundabout explanations to tell laymen about their work. But computerese crops up everywhere. A local gift shop sells a 'mouse pad' – and it's not for a rodent. Journalists use 'interface' in a way that suggests some eyes-nose-mouth encounter. And so on.

Is it an accident of history that the onset of 'the post-Christian era' coincided with 'the computer age'? And is it today's defiant shrugging off of history that dictates the plastic quality of its new words? Plastic, not organic. There are roots and matted interweavings, across continents and down the centuries, underneath the words we have inherited, the language that shapes our responses, our understanding, our wit, e.g. (*rad*ical, *rad*ish, e*rad*icate)!

Quick connections, and gradually resonant overtones: we need them both. Maybe we can reaffirm the essential words that will never pass away, too, to this high-flying worldwide-reaching new generation. Especially if we appreciate how, through them and their internet, there is in fact no longer any west or east.

Clothes

[A scrap with '"Retirement Home" section' written on it.]

Buying clothes I dislike. What I enjoy is costuming for my mood when I dress in the morning, although this involves cluttered stowage places, hanging or folded away, and reliance on a friend's choices of proper wear for an occasion, the buying of which she is good enough to supervise, selecting wisely the fabrics and styles. The easiest laundering is by machine: from Washington Avenue, in London, etc., this involved a laundromat; at the Lascelles apartment and in this Seniors' Residence, the use of quarters in slots for smaller but similar machines. As a consequence, the elastic of waistbands tends to weaken, a lesson I learned on a subway platform one day when I felt my ankles softly hobbled, and had to step gracefully out of a black half-slip and nonchalantly tuck it into my bag as the train came in. It is safer to carry a safety pin always, this incident suggested. To replace slips with weakened waists is not simple. Younger women wear varying hem lengths year by year, and the dowdy length best for me is not always easily found.

Interview with Sally Ito: The Quiet Centre Inside

[From Tim Bowling, ed, Where the Words Come From: Canadian Poets in Conversation. *Roberts Creek: Nightwood Editions, 2002. Original note to interview: Sally Ito is the author of two poetry collections,* Frogs in the Rain Barrel, *Nightwood 1995, and* Season of Mercy, *Nightwood 1999, and a collection of short stories entitled* Floating Shore, *1998. She lives in Winnipeg.]*

SI: In his poem 'The Dead Poet,' Al Purdy, speculating on the origins of his poetry, asks 'how else explain myself to myself/where does the song come from?' Do you have any explanation of where your voice came from, of why you became a poet?

MA: My mother valued, yes, overvalued, my earliest verse, even sent one piece to the local paper's children's page when I was seven. Nobody I played with knew or cared, so her pleasure pleased me. My mother's early encouragement did prompt me to go on writing, and to read whatever came my way later. Prose. Poetry was inaccessible at first. I started with *Palgrave's Golden Treasury,* and it palled! But I still can see the brown-linen boards of D.H. Lawrence's *Poems* – accessible and explosively exciting. Soon I was writing echoes of T.S. Eliot too, and then of Elizabeth Bishop. Widening acquaintance with poetry, and life experience, gradually freed me to write as I liked. There was nobody to stop me.

SI: How have your feelings about poetry, the reading and writing of it, changed since you were in your twenties?

MA: Youth: lyric flow. Late teens: English courses and more verse-music in my ear – too much Melville and T.S. Eliot for a while. In 1938 (at twenty) the poems in English from colonial Canada, though beautiful, seemed more relevant to field and forest than to the Depression and its looming solution, war. After 1945, American poetry came in from many contacts here and in the U.S. Experimenting energy peaked when our daily rounds brought bp Nichol and me together. By then new surges of vitality came with new Christian faith, and poetry lost its status as my first priority. Finally, life experience and aging led to delight in words' derivations and histories, a more deliberate style, and some awareness of the need for exacting revision.

SI: Have you felt your vocation as a poet to be a solitary affair? How important do you think 'community' is for the poet? (By 'community' I mean a community of other poets and writers.) Do you find talking and consulting with other poets to be helpful? For example, you mention 'experimenting energy' coming from your contact with bp Nichol.

MA: It has been solitary for me. In 1940 I graduated with a debt and needed a job. Depressed at first, I began to let the everyman-quality of workdays whet me. The stress between nine-to-five and evening (books and notebook) proved stimulating – a pattern that was to persist. Family and family health concerns increased. Every experience feeds the reservoir that poetry taps. Of course, each of us makes choices. Only after twenty years' writing did I venture much. For example, Professor Warren Tallman organized an event at UBC which I attended. The stimulus of conversation with many writers was welcome, especially after meeting George and Angela Bowering over coffee. Moreover, down the years in Toronto I attended the readings organized by Raymond Souster, Toronto's eminent poet. A young, rosy-cheeked Leonard Cohen, with abundant black hair, came with work that evoked the huge dimensions A.M. Klein had opened to us all. There were fine American poets in the series, too. I enjoyed other writers as other opportunity offered, like that wonderful chance encounter with bp Nichol. However the fight for private time continued to be a primary concern.

SI: How did you meet bp? And what effect did he have on your work?

MA: We met in the University of Toronto Library stacks in the early 1960s. He was then employed putting away books on a lower level where I had a carrel, a desk where my work materials could be left, during M.A. studies. As I walked towards that desk one morning, bp, an unknown stack boy, was waving a fist with a rolled up manuscript in it, saying softly but intensely to a co-worker 'It's good. It's really good. They send it back after a half-glance, if that. Won't anybody READ my poetry?' Without breaking pace as I approached, I said 'I will', and without a beat missed, bp slammed it into my hand. Instead of doing dutiful work at my desk, I read it with growing delight, and, when time came to go, I left a small note, promising the precious manuscript back the next morning – although I made it clear that my enjoyment did not mean I could move bp any closer to publishers (no doubt he knew the same addresses). Of course I enthusiastically offered any words he wanted to use as a blurb. Over the months our correspondence flourished, on scraps of paper, just fun to light the lower level where we were immured. I can't remember whether I attended some of bp's readings that year or later, or when I heard his group [The Four Horsemen] perform, or over what years received his delightful periodicals and mailings. (My set of such materials is now in York University Archives where a friend placed them when I had to clear my shelves in a sudden move.)

One morning, during library days, I vividly remember. Spring, a frantic season on campus, and bp elatedly cried 'Come out! A friend from Vancouver is outside! You've got to meet!' He and I and bill bissett sat in the sunny triangle of grass (northeast of the old building, now the medical library) and, again, all the essentials were in place. bill's *th influenza uv logik* (Vancouver, Talonbooks, 1995) later showed the mutuality in that buoyant friendship-language. bill had a capacity for suffering, and bp for compassionate wholeness. Together they were discovering their own freedom of word and gesture. Influence? Little, in writing. Concrete poetry, though, and the comic book (e.g. *Captain Poetry*) were now within my ken as a reader. I would play in now and then for the fun of those exchanged notes. One of my notes appeared in one of his papers once ('In Eporphyrial Harness'). Dear bp! The *person* he was nourished me over the years, humanly speaking.

SI: I know of some poets who have had their work used in liturgy and worship. Do you see your poetry as primarily something to be read in books? Or to be read aloud to an audience? Who do you see as your reader?

MA: I write to be read – I answer for myself only. I have enjoyed formal readings by other poets; oral rhetoric lifts the poetry off the page, sometimes. Tim Lilburn's is such, whether read or heard. My readers are the completers of what the text began. I address them as co-creators, unknown but for sure out there, and exacting.

SI: What *is* a poem, in your definition?

MA: We discussed this topic in a university English class I taught in the 1960s. My small senior 'A' class set the topic they wanted to discuss from September to May as: 'What is a poem?' That was their topic, up to me to devise a method. In each class someone was named to lead the next class's discussion, illustrating and explaining his definition based on one poem of *his* choosing, photocopied the week ahead so that everybody had a copy. When he presented his 'A poem is … (such and such),' the others were to challenge his definition from that poem and from any others they were planning to choose in turn or simply others that we all could look up in a common anthology. One by one, definitions were knocked down, or edited down, until in May we were all satisfied. Their conclusion: *A poem is that form of art in words that requires from the reader the same creative energy as from the writer.* To me, this was an exercise done in fun but at some level I concur with the conclusion they came to.

SI: I grew up as a writer in an environment of creative writing

programmes, of federal and provincial arts grants for writers, and of early publication opportunities in literary magazines across the country. I know this is a much different environment than the one you experienced as a young writer in Canada in the forties and fifties.
MA: Yes. Before there were any grants, some younger poets fostered a politely anti-establishment stance. For example, F.R. Scott published a satirical poem on the Canadian Authors' Association's tea-parties. In Montreal, Irving Layton and Louis Dudek led a more rambunctious break with the past, circulating mimeographed magazines, some in Toronto too. While they were in Toronto, Miriam Waddington and Earle and Esther Birney encouraged writerly company. Time limits curtailed my participation. The Canada Council was born. I had a vision that it would set up kiosks everywhere, opening our books to everybody, to the publishers' delight. Repeatedly I urged this upon the Council. Government grants to individuals still evoked unhappy associations: McCarthyism in the U.S., propagandist art in the Soviet Union, and censorship of writers in Nazi Germany. I had stated the alternative (to grants) so forcefully that, to be consistent, I never applied to the Canada Council for a grant. Yet I have gratefully accepted the Governor General's Award, twice. And I did apply for the Guggenheim Award when the opportunity was opened to me.
SI: How important have reviews, awards, other honours been to your feelings about your work? Is competition healthy or unhealthy for a poet?
MA: Any 'recognition' – even a bad review – does help me. I write to (from and for) readers, and am therefore heartened to know somebody out there has read what I wrote. Awards? Cash helps, temporarily. Awards help publishers sell books, we hope. 'Honours' can be an encouragement but can end up distracting from a writer's privacy and working time. 'Competition?' The word's metallic taste is already there in 'awards'. Open competitions can launch new writers, true. Surely, though, no writer wants to 'win' when that means another writer 'loses' – and may for a time even believe the judges' assessment, not his own convictions.
SI: In your early years, did you have anything in the way of classes or an inspiring teacher that might have influenced you as a poet?
MA: I had contact for one term in the fall of grade nine, with one teacher, Gladys Story, who influenced many, me among them. She

was never my classroom teacher, but she asked to see my notebook from home, and made a few marginal comments, in fine red ink. One of them counselled me not to 'use the first person singular in any of your poems for ten years.' After her death I learned more of writing just as reading and life enabled.

SI: Sage advice! Was there anything else in the early years of your career that encouraged you to become a poet?

MA: 'Career?' I was a wage-earner. Any job I did well meant dangerous promotion towards a 'career,' i.e. a time-eating job. So I had to move on whenever 'career' threatened. Daytime with everyman did make free time light up. I never thought of myself as 'a poet', never wanted 'to be a poet', and I wince if someone introduces me with reference to my poetry. The choice life made for me is one with which I heartily concur: to 'be' a human being, no more, no less. I *did* take the writing of poetry seriously as far back as I can remember – but never, God help me, did I or do I want to take myself as a poet seriously.

Now back to Gladys Story. In the fall of my grade nine year, she announced a 'club' after school, 4 p.m., and people up to grade thirteen came. She read poems – ballads, English poets from several centuries and some recent writing too. World War I permeated her thinking, and added poignancy to her reading of Sassoon. We were spellbound. That first meeting, to help her assess who was interested in such a club, perhaps, she asked each person to bring some of their writing. Former pupils came back from university to sit in and absorb the selections of poetry – all from England – that enriched our understanding. She died after Christmas. I was in on only one term with the club, but the reading and her notes on my poems were a profound influence. In high school years my plan was to study math and physics in university. A burst appendix in the middle of grade thirteen meant I could not make up the labs in time. To avoid repeating a whole year, I switched to arts.

SI: How did your poetry writing develop in your university years?

MA: My undergraduate years were 1936–1940. All periods of English literature, especially the freshman course on Renaissance poetry, enriched my response to words and delighted my ears with new cadences, rhyme patterns, rhythms. In those days English began at the beginning, Old English and Chaucer, and ended with Thomas Hardy. Any contemporary poetry we read on our own, off campus, like we did our own poem-writing.

SI: And what of your years of post-graduate study? I know from reading your biography that you took an M.A. in English and that you also went to Chicago on a Guggenheim scholarship.

MA: There was a gap of twenty-three years between my B.A. and graduate school, which I entered in the mistaken hope of becoming a teacher. Teaching I enjoyed, but after two years of it other things came. Graduate school was made feasible by Ontario's subsidies, in order to staff colleges for a bulge of incoming students. A good year of classes and writing the Byron thesis, and then two drearier years towards the doctoral written and oral exams gave me qualifications, 'all but thesis'. There has been no thesis. All cut into time to muse or write. The stack-time exchanges in verse with bp Nichol kept fresh air blowing in, as did the quiet centre inside from a brand-new faith (conversion in January '63 of the year I enrolled). Some of *The Dumbfounding*'s poems came even then.

SI: What was your Chicago experience like?

MA: I received the Guggenheim in 1956. On the application I asked for 'eight months in Chicago to live as a poet' – such I designated then for that purpose. Chicago was the place I chose because my ailing parents were accessible from there. My request was in general terms because I did not want to commit myself in advance to producing something at the end. In fact, most of my work was organizing, revising, and typing old manuscripts. The outcome was a clean copy of the *Winter Sun* poems, a long accumulation with new poems of the Chicago days interspersed. The experience was glorious. Wonderful libraries. The Art Institute near the Chicago Public Library. *Poetry* magazine on the same campus as the Chicago University Library. I visited *Poetry*: they had published a group of my poems earlier. There I met Frederick Bock, then the assistant editor, a fine poet who became a good friend until his untimely death from cancer. Everywhere the friendly Americans included me, if I could find time to socialize. I took time from working mainly to go where good jazz was playing, evenings.

SI: What was the critical climate like during your period of study in Chicago?

MA: The Chicago period blurs with other times. Dominant in the late fifties were critics who made the poem's text the primary object. They approved a closely-textured style, significant in all its parts. I read and relished Blackmur, I.A. Richards ... the 'new critics'. They had influence on us, but no poet writes from prescription. Frederick had been part of a creative writing class, at Iowa University – the first time I had ever heard of such a class.

SI: Did you ever have a sense of yourself as a Canadian poet, in particular?

MA: Never 'as a Canadian poet'. My schooling had included British and ancient history, but little Canadian history. Knowing at least the southern part of Canada, B.C. to P.E.I. first hand, intrigued by Quebec, blank about U.S. history, I did have a sense of belonging. The lack of patriotism here I judged a Canadian virtue. Books in English, poetry included, were without boundaries for a reader.

SI: What was your view of Canadian poetry?

MA: 'Canadian poetry' struck my generation as echoing English verse *as* rural, remote from our experience of ardent pacifism, the Great Depression, then World War II with its sudden industrialization. Leo Kennedy's *The Shrouding* first woke me up to somebody in Canada who reacted as I did, and wrote poems.

SI: By 'Canadian poetry', do you mean the work of earlier Canadian poets such as Bliss Carman, Archibald Lampman and Charles G.D. Roberts, for example?

MA: Yes. Carman, Lampman, Campbell, F.G. Scott (F.R.'s father) etc.

SI: I've not heard of Leo Kennedy – who was he? How and where did you encounter his work?

MA: My generation read the first experimental periodicals and found him in the *The McGill Fortnightly Review* (we also found F.R. Scott, A.J.M. Smith, and A.M. Klein there). Although he was born in England, Kennedy was educated in Quebec in Catholic schools and McGill. Here was someone with elegant form and a modern voice: we took notice when his book came out – *The Shrouding.* I do not know what happened to him later.

SI: Did your experience of pacifism, the Depression and the war create any conflict for you between poetry and politics? It sounds like you wanted poetry to be about something different than what you were currently reading at the time.

MA: Looking back, I think it was the 'poetic language' that we all wanted to change. We learned music from the Georgians but we craved common spoken words in poems – *and* reference to contemporary experiences. It was natural for political identity to grow alongside wage-earner identity, around the edges, perhaps. Certainly I was involved with a political party and canvassed in pre-election weeks. I saw no conflict with poetry in this communal concern.

SI: I want to ask you now a question about writing in forms. You have written sonnets, especially in your earlier books, but did your desire to use 'common spoken words in poems' eventually steer you more towards free verse?

MA: What felt passé were poetic subjects as much as elegant language, which demonstrated unawareness of a whole new social context to be spoken from, and to. Diction can declare the inclusiveness of communal concerns. Perhaps good writing is *always* non-elitist? As to your question, no. Everyday diction appears in various kinds of verse from the sixteenth century on. And the term 'free' verse is purely negative – free from requirements. *All* verse must observe some constraints, rhythms, consonant patterns, echoes, stresses that fall as the meaning dictates, etc. These are unobtrusive requirements, but still not 'free verse'.

SI: Did you and your peers think of moving more towards narrative-style poems to bring that 'story and novel' readership experience to contemporary poetry readers?

MA: Pondering what others in my time might have purposed reminded me of someone's quip that in those days *status quo* had become *fluxus quo.* Poetry readers will always be fewer than novel-readers in our day, since journals and newspapers and work reports condition our reading habits. To be jerked about by shorter lines that yield meaning only after rereading and quiet consideration, calls for unfamiliar habits. It was not so in Victorian England, when poetry had a wide and demanding audience. Poets tended to run to excess then. In our day we all found Earle Birney's 'David' inimitably beautiful, of course. It was a narrative poem that every reader in Canada knew!

SI: I asked the previous question because a number of poets today are also prose writers. I myself write short stories and am currently working on a novel. I see working in the different genres as quite different experiences. Did you always only write poetry? Or did you ever want to write fiction?

MA: By my own choice, poetry was what I did. My prose writing has come through assignments: for example, a ghost-written biography paid for by the subject's children; a grade seven history text, paid by an educational publisher; pieces I was hired to do during my years of free-lance work; occasional articles, invited usually, or book reviews, long ago. Novels require a capacity for plot structuring which has been left out of my make-up. Even narratives amongst my poems are, in the main, among the discards – they usually don't work.

SI: I think there is a distinct difference between the 'kind of mind' required for writing the different genres. Tim Bowling has spoken of the art of writing poetry as a 'discipline of consciousness'. When you write poetry, do you have to be in a certain 'state of mind' to do it? Is it a consciously cultivated state of mind or one that arises from the unconscious depths spontaneously?

MA: A 'certain state of mind' concurs with the writing, yes. I think it comes of intensity of focus, i.e. not from 'cultivating it', although I can remember doing so at thirteen or fourteen. When I wanted to write, I would play the melody of Schubert's 'Am Meer', dreamily, at our piano – nobody else at home. Then I would go upstairs as carefully as if I were carrying a brimming cup, to the desk and the special pen and notebook for poems. I smile at the memory.

SI: Your playing of the piano reminds me of what other poets I know do – they get in the mood, so to speak, by reading poetry or listening to music. I do find reading other poets to be inspiring although I don't necessarily read them specifically to write poems. You speak of 'intensity of focus' – do you find that to be a spontaneous thing or deliberate (in that you will concentrate on something specific in order to produce a poem)?

MA: The question you have here is not clear to me. Fact, now: I resist having to write. Do so only when something nags me, preoccupies me, has to be cleared away. Analyzing my procedures is beyond *me* – though others write poems *and* write about process. We're each unique as human beings! E.g. Rilke, John Clare … Pope … Coleridge, my own family members!

SI: I understand your resistance to analysis of procedure. However, when I was taking creative writing in my undergraduate years, we were asked to 'analyze' a poem we had written ourselves. For me, it turned out to be a rather illuminating exercise in terms of making something 'unconscious' more conscious. P.K. Page wrote of 'hearing a phrase' that came to one like a boomerang; one had to catch the thing before it curved away into the nether parts of the mind. From that phrase, she would then 'build' the rest of the poem. I found that metaphor of the boomerang quite apt.

As the spiritual is often the topic of your poems, I wonder how you craft the metaphor for those 'moments least accessible to lisping human terms' that you have described in your essay 'Muse of Danger'. Certainly you caution writers not to derive all their inspiration from such moments, but on those occasions when they do, how should they go about it? Or to be more specific, how do you go about it?

MA: The 'how-to' will likely be unique for everyone in Christ writing poems. I was early struck by C.S. Lewis's warning not to use scriptural insight for poetry if it was meant for action. If it is an insight for poetry, my 'method' is like trying to identify a hopping little bird before it flies – to discover something barely glimpsed, for my own sake.

SI: Yes, I do identify with that 'method'. I've often used poetry to 'tease' out meaning from scripture – in particular, meaning from narrative passages where it is not always clear what motivates certain biblical characters. As for other passages in scripture that are more 'theological', I tend to want to work with them more in prose than in poetry although certain 'notions' do occasionally hop about like the bird you speak of.

MA: Thanks to a friend, I'm learning not to use other people's words (the *jargon,* as the outsider hears it). She also warned me against moral-tag endings. Our faith is not fable.

SI: I agree; avoiding the 'jargon' is of paramount concern. And moralizing is also a distinct temptation. It often parades itself as 'closure' but may not be at all aesthetically pleasing or satisfying. The main problem I have discovered is finding a more deliberate and meditative sensibility that comes from a refining of spiritual consciousness. I was mildly surprised to see how precisely 'mysticism' can be defined in the Catholic encyclopedia, for example. It kind of takes the lyrical 'wind out of one's sails', if you know what I mean.

MA: 'Mysticism' is a word I'm nervous about. Fruitful meditation is all I know. By that I mean a balance *I* need, to avoid inwardness.

SI: You spoke of 'lyric flow' as part of your poetry in youth. And then in your later years, you thought of poetry in terms of a 'delight in words' derivations and histories, a more deliberate style, and some awareness of the need for exacting revision.' I sense a shift here between the lyric to the more meditative – a shift that I am currently negotiating myself. I wonder how you made such a transition or shift.

MA: In my own experience lyric flow was a gift to youth, an overflowing ease like an athlete's ease, confident, full of energy and drive. One rides with it as far as possible. But to push on when it isn't a given is to risk writing parodies of one's own earlier poems. At that point, word, music, word-sounds, images no longer simply cluster and come almost of themselves. Contriving them is useless. Head-knowledge, life-experience etc., gradually change the process. Impulses of feeling become less important than quickened interest in some visual object, or a vividly imagined situation. This reads like a law for all poets! I speak only of what seemed true for me.

SI: In *Not Yet But Still,* how did you come to write about Job, in poetry? Since yours is such a long poem, I imagine that it wasn't spontaneous but a very deliberate and contemplative act.

MA: 'Job'? At issue were two questions that had nagged at me over years, and had to be explored and cleared. 1) I had to face God's 'permissive will', in suffering, and hang on to that and yet Satan as instigator; and 2) in the light of Job's emotional struggle (through trying to figure it out), I needed to ponder the emotional component of the Godhead in the whole drama. That called for a solid, step-by-step restraint in form and language – hence, the style that put off any readers bringing in their own expectations of 'a poem'. One's natural reaction to the scriptural text would be overwhelming awe – hence wordlessness: this was the struggle behind putting down the words. Nobody has yet accepted my 'Job' as a poem, so maybe it isn't. It can be discarded or forgotten: that's not my business.

SI: Did you see your writing of 'Job' as a 'practical application' of scripture in that the Book of Job is one that demands meditation/contemplation rather than 'service' in the form of action? I see your poem as a form of 'hearing the Word and doing it'.

MA: No – no 'oughtiness' pushed me into it. Every believer reads the Book of Job over the years, finding shifting emphases, different questions etc. every time. I worried at one time about the validity of the teaching by Job's friends: should I heed it? Was it sound theology? If it was, then why did they need Job's prayers so sorely at the end? None of my earlier readings led to a poem. For this poem, my search was for God, as THE Friend. Underlying it was a recurring incredulity about the Father's love for me, I think. Certainly I wanted to know Him better as Person. And a person has emotions. What were His feelings – veiled by the Scriptural text? That incentive made the poem a preoccupation until I took it on.

SI: Earlier you spoke of poetry 'losing its status as [your] first priority'. Was this a result of your 'new Christian faith'? If so, how did poetry recover its place in your life afterwards?

MA: I was forty-five when I encountered the living Jesus. Up to then I had been 'good', obeying Exodus 20:3–17 but unaware of a fallen nature. I was familiar with the stories of the Bible. The idea of the Fall had conveyed dark Miltonic imaginings. But suddenly, that day in 1963, the first two Commandments bowled me over – 'Thou shalt have no other gods before Me' and 'Thou shalt not make unto thee any graven image' – but I was steadied by Exodus 20:10 ('But the seventh day is the sabbath of the Lord thy God ...'). We are to share the Creator's rest and joy – every week! What looked like a sacrifice (that 'priority') turns out to be a good investment. On the brink of yielding, and accepting the Lord, I cried: 'But don't touch the poetry!' As 'Person', in my *The Dumbfounding* says, at that point solid walls closed in. There was no deal till I threw in the poetry along with myself.

SI: I can certainly identify with that! I know you eschew the identity of the 'poet' in order to avoid the vanity of the title, and yet as poetry writing is one of the things that humans do, it's not easy to depart from the identity it gives one if one does it well. In other words, it can still be seen as a kind of gift ... certainly we can write our poetry for the eyes of God only, but is it not still meant for the eyes of humans as well? To nourish them in faith and worship? Otherwise we would all be satisfied in writing our poetry in the sand. What we do with the responses of humans, however, has more to do with ego than perhaps the actual writing of the poetry does. I don't know ... I think the topic of selfhood in Christ and selfhood through writing is a constant source of conflict for some believers. It is for me.

Going back to your earlier work, I was struck by your mastery of the sonnet. I'm curious as to how you developed such deftness at that form. I find that writing in forms requires a kind of diligence and concentration that that 'lyric flow of youth' isn't always amenable to (I think here of Frost's old line about writing free verse like playing tennis with the net down ...) I've sometimes experimented with biblical poetic forms – trying to write a psalm, for example, but I find it very, very difficult.

MA: I write with my ear. Some poetic forms originated in music. There is no parallel in prose creative writing. Sounds in poetry are musical, words are primarily tactile: to paraphrase Sartre, a writer's words are primarily not the ones in the dictionary, but the ones he knows from the reverse side where he can feel their surfaces, texture, knobbiness, curves ... Playing with sound and texture becomes instinctive. No proper poet ever *planned* alliteration (that one was accidental!). Reading oceans of English poetry schools the ear to rhythm and rhyme. Doing it seldom just comes. There are patterns to learn. Rhythm is no problem if English verse is inside the ear. (Fighting off iambic pentameter where it is inappropriate, or dull, is the bigger problem.) Rhyme schemes have to be learned. This whole area is the place for analysis – not how a poem originates or how to make it come.

Tricks –

1) write the rhyme scheme on the right margin of your page, every draft, so you don't have to keep checking line endings. As your lines establish the a-sound, the b-sound, etc., add the sound opposite *a* and *b* on the margin, etc.

2) If you are stuck with a weak word just for the sake of rhyme, and *cannot* do better, switch it to be the earlier line, so that the good rhyme will please the ear and (we hope) all will be forgiven.

3) If it's not getting in your ear fluently, quit the poem and do a da dá da dá da dá a while to yourself. Too much sweating will show. It ought to begin to flow. I wrote one triolet (a poem of eight-syllabled line where line one recurs as fourth and seventh, and line two as the eighth). It never had much life – too much carpentering and it never did become easy in the ear as I wrote. *Deftness?* Practice, and reading with your ear.

SI: Do you still write poems in forms? (I noticed a few rhyming poems in *Not Yet but Still.*)

MA: Sometimes. The themes and the way I feel about them guide the tone of voice, diction, level of style, formal or open lines.

SI: Another particular aspect of your poetry I find compelling and that I see throughout all your books is your use of weather and landscape imagery. I'm struck at how skillful you are in your descriptions of the seasons and the landscape at different times of the year. Your work seems to explore 'terrains' – a word whose deeper meaning I've found in your work. I notice that many of your poems begin with a natural image – a gaze that leads into a deeper seeing. Is that often how your poems start – with that intensity of focus on some natural phenomenon? Does that first line (so many of which are stunning in their poetic impact) just come to you? And is it from there, that you develop the rest of the poem?

MA: It is true that skies, weather, surroundings, do move me – but not *to* anything, not purposively. Just a form of rejoicing in natural being in general.

But first line 'coming?' An image from gazing at something? No. Not in my experience. I'm sorry, I can't analyze how I work, though I know some poets can.

SI: With your poems, how much do you revise?

MA: Second day after writing, often extensively. Fussing with details, ongoingly. I wish I had done more of this early on!

SI: This brings me to ask how your books were put together. The typical thing today for a poet starting out is to 'study' creative writing in a workshop or class, then publish a few poems in literary magazines, and then eventually assemble the poems in some cohesive sequence and send out the manuscript to small presses. Somewhere along this process – and I would think this would vary from person to person – the 'poet' identity is formed in the mind of the individual enough to provide him/her with the impetus to submit and/or often resubmit their work to publishers. Did your attitude about writing poetry change with the publication of a book? I don't intend this question to be about poetic identity per se but also about artistry in terms of getting a book 'out there to be read' and how deliberately shaping a book for readers is different than, say, 'writing for oneself'.

MA: You ask about four things here: (1) Preparing manuscripts – selecting and discarding, reassessing and revising. (2) Submitting poems to periodicals: for me this began with high school and college student papers. Because I knew two people from other contexts on the *Canadian Forum* board, I submitted poems to that paper. And so on. (3) Arranging poems for a book: for me it is usually scattering individual poems so that the reader will find an easy transition from page to page. I once tried a topical arrangement *(Not Yet But Still)* – a mistake, I now think. It forced a reader from too much entrée to too much pudding, all at once. (4) Finding a book publisher: it is indeed a matter of 'submit and resubmit', as I found with *Winter Sun*, which was many times rejected, like most first books. My second book, *The Dumbfounding*, Denise Levertov *requested* when Norton New York requested *her* to assemble six poetry books pronto, to open out their catalogue which they considered too heavily academic. Then through his periodical I learned about William Pope and his Lancelot Press in Nova Scotia. He was friendly towards my manuscripts and published them until he retired from publishing.

SI: I know you have a new book coming out. What is it called?

MA: The new book, *Concrete and Wild Carrot*, should appear later this year. It will be published by Brick Books.

SI: As you look back on the many poems you've written, is there one in particular, or one book perhaps (excluding the most recent one), where you feel you came closest to an accurate rendering of your impression of life?

MA: No one poem, no. Over a lifetime of writing, 'impression of life' undergoes many changes. I do notice recurrent responses to events and climates of opinion, punctuated by impulses of playfulness, and periods of withdrawal – time to digest all I've read and to refuse to keep up with all I haven't read. The one piece that says it all may lie up ahead somewhere, and seems to move on as I move on. This is not a negative statement!

To Burton Hatlen

[November 30, 2004. Burton Hatlen was organizer of the conference named below. This letter is not written in Margaret Avison's free and independent style, but is rather a letter of recommendation, a response to Hatlen's request for one. Still, it fills a gap in her own record. Robert Creeley also attended the conference and was glad to see Avison there, as was Ted Enslin.]

Please use any or all of the following sincerely appreciative comments about the National Poetry Foundation's 'Poetries of the 1940s,

American and International' Conference which took place at the University of Maine, Orono, this past June.

The programme of the Conference tempted me to the very edges of my stamina (my mid-80s), offering such a range of high quality topics and lecturers/readers that it was difficult to choose among them.

Initially and throughout I was struck by the eager receptivity of the delegates, students and faculty alike. It was this quality of attentive listening that lifted my confidence and encouraged me, when it was my turn to do a reading. I came to realize how helpful creative writing courses are in awakening students' ears.

Many poets read from their works. Among the readings I heard, Bob Perelman's strict diction and metropolitan references were impressive, as was Jennifer Gosetti-Ferencei's quiet rendition of her powerful poetry.

As a member of the panel on 'International Perspectives II', the same Jennifer Gosetti-Ferencei reflected elegantly on the poetry of Miklos Radnoti in the context of Hungary's mid-century stresses, making her subject pulse with ongoing relevance. Another excellent panel's subject which also painfully echoes on into our own day was 'Poetry in the Japanese-American Internment Camps'.

Supporting such events, there was an enticing selection of books available in the Conference's book room, with participants well represented.

For me, the outstanding and deepest delight lay in store at the very end of the Conference: Theodore Enslin's careful communication of his current, beautiful, structured, aural poetry. It was unforgettable.

I owe you, and the National Poetry Foundation, a debt of gratitude for memorable exposure to poetry of the 1940s, in your country and beyond – and for your thoughtful provision of drives and meals throughout my stay.

Sincerely,
Margaret Avison

P.S. This is an official communication; an unofficial one will follow.

M.A.

Interview with D.S. Martin: A Conversation with Margaret Avison

[Margaret Avison was interviewed by the poet D.S. Martin at the Write! Toronto *conference, November 13, 2004, presented by the Word Guild. The interview appeared in* Image 45, *Spring 2005.]*

IMAGE: In your foreword to the first volume of *Always Now,* your collected poems, you say of your response to the natural world, 'In time the mood tilted towards a conviction that an ultimate purpose prevailed, and is good.' When do you feel it is best to let this good exist in a poem without drawing the connection to God, or even to leave this good hiding in the underbrush?

MA: Writing a poem I start with whatever the theme is, and I never pointedly bring in or leave out any reference to faith. Some poems immediately arise out of reading scripture or thinking about it. Oftener it just permeates, I hope, and reflections might come through, but I don't think there's a place in poetry for any kind of propaganda. If you're very worked up and angry, the poem may sound propagandist. I've done pieces like that, but there it's the anger you're to notice and not the propaganda.

IMAGE: A friend of mine once asked you a question before an audience and was very reassured when you told her you saw no difference between writing poetry in secular and Christian circles. Please explain why you believe this to be true.

MA: I think, simply put, it's myself that does the writing, and I am myself when I write. It's myself when I'm with Christians, and it's myself when I'm with people who don't know anything about the faith. I would hope to be myself everywhere. The poetry is just another dimension of that. As I've said before, propaganda is alien – unless you're doing something like hymn writing. You have to have strict rhythm, rhyme and content in a hymn, and in any case it's not really a poem, it's a hymn. Aside from that, I can't think of another exception where you want to teach in a poem.

IMAGE: Sarah Klassen has written in the journal *Prairie Fire,* 'It is Avison's unique accomplishment to write, in and for a secular world, about faith and God, with intelligence and without becoming either sentimental or preachy.' What has contributed to this accomplishment? Do you write primarily for a secular audience, a Christian audience, or perhaps for yourself?

MA: Writing for yourself is where it begins. When you are very young you begin writing out your feelings. But when you are older, you write for somebody, always. The somebody is not faceless, but it's never anybody in your immediate circle. You develop a sense of a readership from whom you pick somebody to address – an unknown somebody, that is, the reader who receives the poem. It isn't a poem until it is received. It's important to find the person to receive it and get beyond being your own private poet.

IMAGE: How has being a writer and reader of poetry affected the way you read scripture?

MA: Poetry has helped me to know that in reading the Word, scripture, it's important to read every word. I don't know Greek and Hebrew, but I've got lots of translations to help me. Similarly I think in poetry it's always true that every word matters. You revise by cutting out and boiling down. Words are a good training for realizing the unchangeableness of the Word.

IMAGE: Your poem 'What John Saw (Revelation 4)' includes the lines:

> Least moments given, though,
> can open onto
> John's comprehender: here,
> there, then, always
> now, because unchanging, who
> made light and ponderous rhythms, time, and all
> pulsing particulars.
> John saw him rainbowed in glory –

In your 1993 Pascal lectures at the University of Waterloo, you quote the sixth-century philosopher Boethius as saying: 'Eternity then, is clearly a property of the mind of God. God ought not to be considered as older than the created world in extent of time, but rather in the immediacy of his nature.' Were you thinking of this when you wrote 'What John Saw'?

MA: I don't relate the two myself, although perhaps there was an unconscious connection. With no training in philosophy, I remember working through Boethius in preparing the Pascal lectures. I hoped that wide reading would help me put the experience and prevalent doctrine of our times into historical and ideological perspective.

'What John Saw' refers to and was initiated by reading chapter 4 of Revelation, and by a startling assertion in Isaiah 45:7 that has gone on working in me ever since I first read it: 'I form the light and create darkness' (NIV). Luther's translation introduces the concept of evil in this verse. As I read it, the passage implies that God *comprehends* evil; my interpretation is based on the etymology of 'com-prehend'. God is good: he encompasses evil. This biblical elaboration freed me, a former inquirer, from uneasiness at a heaven too good to be real or endurable. Faith left me with some of that uneasiness until I read Isaiah's answer.

IMAGE: Prior to your conversion to Christianity, you were already a successful poet, having won the Governor General's Award. Did being a public figure make it more difficult for you to turn to faith, or at least to begin talking about it?

MA: No. Publicity got in the way of reading and writing. I wish it could be deferred until people are dead. I haven't ever really been a public figure. I have been a private person always. Neither honours nor conversion changed anything in that regard. And I have never found it difficult to talk to anyone about my faith, in public occasionally or in private. Being known as a poet did not make it more difficult for me to turn to faith either. Coming to faith enriched my subject matter.

IMAGE: I remember reading about the time you threw your Bible across the room. It would be delightful to hear you tell us about that.

MA: Well, I was brought up in a Christian family. Then I had an experience of the world, and decided my parents' faith was a lovely story. It just didn't fit, so I became an agnostic for many years.

When I was about forty, I was working on proofs and smoking in the basement of the library where I had a job upstairs at Victoria College at the University of Toronto. A girl came in and said, 'Do you know the joy of knowing the Lord Jesus?'

I said, 'I know the theory, and as you can see I'm busy.' And then I thought, well, no. That's not kind. I can be nicer than that. And I looked up at her and her face was just shining.

'I never have been beset by doubt,' she said. 'Would you do something for me? Would you attend this church some Sunday evening?' And she wrote down the name.

'I won't make any commitment, but thank you,' I said, and I politely took her note. Two years later I found her note and complied, and began to hear the gospel preached there at a nearby church in Toronto. Two years after that, I said to somebody coming out, 'I'm sick and tired of this. You all talk of faith, and you've got it. I don't doubt that. I haven't got it. What am I supposed to do?'

And she said nervously, 'Go and see the minister.' So I went to see the Rev. Dr William Fitch. 'Well,' he said, 'you won't like the answer, but I'm going to tell you to go home and read from the Gospel of John before you go to work every day.' I said, 'Okay, it's a deal,' and I did.

Every morning I got up extra early. With a cup of coffee I would sit and read. The book seemed to me like one little plaque followed by another little plaque, with no sort of design, and with a lot of nonsense in between. I was bewildered, but I pressed on. And one morning I came to John 14:1. Seven o'clock in the morning, and there I was: 'You believe in God; believe also in me.' 'In you?' I said. I had such a strong sense of the presence of Jesus in the room that I said it aloud. 'Well, okay. I'll believe in you, but don't touch the poetry, because it's all I've got left.' Suddenly, it was as though I was enclosed in marble; everything just absolutely froze. So I picked up my Bible and threw it across the room, and said, 'Okay, take everything, then!' And I put my coat on and went off to work. Gradually during the day I knew something was a little different. And that was the beginning.

Before faith, I thought I knew what a Christian professed, thanks to believing parents, access to a theological library, and years of hearing good preaching. But in my young adult life, doctrine had come to feel like a burdensome harness, hindering free learning and exploring. Therefore when faith was given, after I had returned to taste sermons once again and agreed to read through the Gospel of John, it was simply faith in Jesus. 'The Dumbfounding' is an attempt to state in plain terms how the mystery of the gospel now newly enveloped me.

The Dumbfounding

When you walked here,
took skin, muscle, hair,
eyes, larynx, we

withheld all honour: 'His house is clay,
how can he tell us of his far country?'

Your not familiar pace
in flesh, across the waves,
woke only our distrust.
Twice-torn we cried 'A ghost'
and only on our planks counted you fast.

Dust wet with your spittle
cleared mortal trouble.
We called you a blasphemer,
a devil-tamer.

The evening you spoke of going away
we could not stay.
All legions massed. You had to wash, and rise,
alone, and face
out of the light, for us.

You died.
We said,
'The worst is true, our bliss
has come to this.'

When you were seen by men
in holy flesh again
we hoped so despairingly for such a report
we closed their windpipes for it.

Now you have sought
and seek, in all our ways, all thoughts,
streets, musics – and we make of these a din
trying to lock you out, or in,
to be intent. And dying.

Yet you are
constant and sure,

the all-lovely, all-men's-way
to that far country.

Lead through the garden to
trash, rubble, hill,
where, the outcast's outcast, you
sound dark's uttermost, strangely light-brimming, until
time be full.

IMAGE: John North, of the University of Waterloo, has quoted you as saying that although your father was a minister, you went on 'a long willful journey into darkness.' How has this impacted your subsequent faith walk, and your poetry?
MA: The darkness was simple: agnostic head-work. And I think I have every sympathy with people who resist someone's insistent evangelizing, because I was there so long. I've done courses in witnessing. I've done the routine things one does, just as in the early days I tried to do what all the Christians around me seemed to be doing. I didn't succeed in imitating anybody. By now I'm comfortable to be me and a Christian, to go wherever I go and wait for a chance to communicate, whether by being, or through some conversation that opens the way.
IMAGE: You often slip a question mark onto a statement, or a single word, changing it into a question. For example in 'Meditation on the Opening of the Fourth Gospel', from your collection *No Time,* you say:

Come? In flesh and blood?
Seen? as another part
of the 'natural world' his word
flung open, for the maybe imperiller,
in what to us was the
Beginning?

What has led you to this technique?
MA: One reason I do it is in order to get under the text. I particularly like to ask these questions of something familiar in scripture, to try to read it in a new way. Something familiar can become unfamiliar as you approach it. Sometimes my questions are a way of feeling my way into a subject, and sometimes they're straight questions.

IMAGE: Do you write many poems that don't rise to the level of publication, and how do you sift through them?
MA: Sometimes they just need revising. In those cases I have a sense there's something there, but I haven't quite got it in focus. I have a drawer called 'To Revise'. But sometimes they are awful – too personal, too particular. I just know they haven't got really put together, and there's no use keeping them. The very bad ones I very humbly send to the archive at the University of Manitoba where my stuff is being held, so people can see how very bad my writing sometimes is.

Sometimes a bad poem comes from priming the pump. After a long period where fortunately I can read for a change, and I don't have to write, I'll begin to pull back into wanting to write, and sometimes I have to write a bad poem to get it going.
IMAGE: In *No Time* you had revised your earlier poem 'The Butterfly', but in the first volume of *Always Now* the earlier version reappears. Why didn't you decide to include the revised version?
MA: I had revised it because it's entomologically incorrect. A butterfly is not a moth, and the last line has to have *moth*. But when the time came for it to appear in *Always Now*, I decided, I don't pretend to know insect life, and I left it the way it was written originally, so that the moth – the meaning of the moth – can come in on the last line the way I want it. I went back to my mistake.
IMAGE: You have translated poetry from the Hungarian. Would you describe what that experience has taught you?
MA: I've read translations where I wished the translator had a native speaker as an informant. I got into translating Hungarian because of Ilona Duczynska, who wanted to publish English versions of certain poems. Our procedure was one of the most exhausting I've ever been through. She would read the Hungarian version onto a tape, and we'd have long sessions at a desk, going word by word. A poem might use the word for *stone*, and I'd say, 'Well, is that a crag, or a pebble, or is it in a building? What does that mean?' And she'd tell me. Bit by bit we'd get the literal meaning right. Hungarian is like Finnish, I think: the lines tend to end with three or four light syllables. English does very badly in serious writing with lines ending in light stresses. They tend to produce rather rollicking poems, which the poems of Ferenc Juhász, for example – a peasant for whom communism meant a university education and an enormously expanded universe and a divorce from

his peasant family as he grew – were not.

It was necessary to listen again and again to the sound of the Hungarian, staring at the meaning, until I could imitate the sound in the English; and Ilona was very exacting there. But it was a process that paid off. There's an 'Ode to Bartók' by Gyula Illyés in that group, and a Hungarian listened to it and asked, 'How did you get the sound of the poem?' Well, I didn't. Ilona did. I see why translations often read like nothing written with the ear, as a true poem is; it happens when there is no Ilona to say no.

IMAGE: Denise Levertov referred to you as 'that profound Canadian poet'. Would you describe your relationship with her, and how she was helpful to you in your early years?

MA: I met Denise when I was visiting New York once. Somebody introduced us, and we went to her apartment in a loft building on the East River. She liked talking about poetry, and so did I, so we exchanged a little talk about poetry, but mostly it was about New York and what I should see when I was there.

Later, at a conference organized at the University of British Columbia to introduce Canadians to American writers, Denise was one of the featured poets. I had a very minor role, but I got to know Denise a bit there.

Later she was approached by Norton publishers in New York, who had been accused of doing nothing but technical books and wanted to do some publishing in the humanities. They asked Denise to find them six poetry manuscripts to publish, to right the balance.

Denise telephoned me and told me to send a manuscript for Norton. I said, 'Oh Denise, you won't like it,' but she told me to send it anyway. The manuscript was *The Dumbfounding* – all devotional writing in that period.

Her history? She was Jewish, but her Jewish father escaped to England before the actual fighting forced him out of Germany. He became a clergyman in the Church of England in Denise's childhood. When the war broke out, she became a nurse and went to France and became Jewish again for the cause. There she met a Jewish-American soldier and they married. For years and years her interests were all literary. But when her son was ten, his father began insisting that he have a bar mitzvah and attend rabbinical school, and that alienated her. Gradually she returned to the Christian faith, and she died a Roman

Catholic in Seattle. We kept in touch all through the years.

IMAGE: Did it surprise you when she also became a Christian?

MA: No. Because I had had to fight my way out of childhood too, and I understood – though I couldn't adequately grasp the impact on her of the war, of course, and of her Jewish family history.

IMAGE: Tell us about your friend Joan Eichner, your friendship through the years, and the ways she has been a help to you.

MA: We were friends from the early fifties, when we both had the same music teacher. Joan went on to become a musician and I didn't, partly because my parents moved out of Toronto and the piano went with them. Years intervened. She was in Japan and Austria and all over the place, and I didn't even hear from her, but when our music teacher was hospitalized, we met at her bedside and just picked up where we'd left off – beautifully.

I've got a poem called 'To Joan'. She was driving a big, old van for the church, picking up all the lame and infirm and elderly, here and there, me included.

To Joan

The pulpit led a prayer:
'Thank God who brought us here.'

I prayed, 'We couldn't come unless
Joan came by car for us:
help me tell truth in this
while praying thus.'

'The power of kindness, providence, skill,
derive from Me whose power is over all.'

The act of God is found
lovely for being through my friend,
nonetheless His because
blessings, in her (through whom), also make final pause.

Joan edits marvellously. She's the person I run to with every new poem. Sometimes she looks at it and says, 'I don't know what you mean here,' and that's the part I revise. I can't type any more, my hands having deteriorated, and she does it all for me. I accept this as from a friend. It's a gift in late life to have your first real friend like that.

IMAGE: I've heard you mention your admiration for George Whipple. Are there some other poets – perhaps less established poets – whose work you also value?

MA: Oh, yes, I read more poetry than prose for enjoyment – such poets as Robyn Sarah, David Solway, David O'Meara. Richard Osler has a lovely poem quietly remarking on a lady in an airplane across the aisle reading *How to Know God.* There's an empty aisle seat between him and the lady, and he keeps thinking, *The God she wants to know is perhaps in the empty seat.* It's that kind of poetry.

IMAGE: In your poem 'A Kept Secret' you make a deeply provocative statement: 'Darkness is changed/once it is comprehended; it becomes/knowledge, beyond our reach.' Would you elaborate on this for us?

MA: I vividly remember the superb moment which occasioned that poem: a large bird flew up into a tree, and the combined play of tree-shadow and sun, darkness and light, were part of the exhilaration of the event. Poetry can use concepts without taking them too seriously, as in this poem. I was writing poetically, not philosophically, even though 'comprehended' might seem to refer to Isaiah's statement. The poem merely tries to express the wonder of creation as seen in a flash.

IMAGE: It seems to me you are deeply concerned with the origins of words. Is the etymology of a word more significant to you than what the word has come to mean in our time and our culture?

MA: It's not just a comparison of usage and etymology in present practice. Words are tools. Sartre said he always approaches a text from the underside to *feel.* He fingers the words underneath before he gets the meaning. Etymology enriches that very much, and gives you echoes. Also it keeps you from going wild with a word, because you have to keep your associations within its various meanings over years, but not stray beyond that. So yes, it matters.

IMAGE: When I reviewed your book *Concrete and Wild Carrot* I described your work as 'urban nature poetry' – which seems a bit of an oxymoron. A number of poems in that book, such as 'Pacing the Turn of the Year', 'Towards the Next Change', and 'Ramsden' seem to be about watching people or nature in Toronto parks. I wonder if you'd prefer to be writing about nature in a wilder setting, or is there something particular about nature within the city that is attractive to you as a subject in itself?

MA: I love being out of the city, but I don't drive a car, and the nature I know is here. 'Concrete and wild carrot' says it: it's the concrete of the city, and the wild carrot you can find by walking along mews and laneways or looking through the subway window along the open cuts.

IMAGE: Do you see being a poet as a calling?

MA: Yes. *Calling* and *work* are treated as synonyms by Webster. My work as a poet is a calling in that sense. It is based on natural drive and natural ability, as opposed to being a spiritual gift, which is something given only *after* one believes – I had been writing for years before my conversion – and given by the Holy Spirit, as opposed to a natural gift which develops from one's physical and genetic inheritance.

IMAGE: What advice would you give to younger poets, particularly to those who want to write of faith and reach out to a secular audience?

MA: They have to find their way. I can't tell a young poet what to do, nor can I look at young poets' manuscripts or first books anymore. My time is shorter every day, because it takes me longer to dress and undress the older I get, and there just isn't time to do what I used to love doing. So, to each his own way.

IMAGE: Do you see poetry as something much more than self-expression? Do you have any comment about the trend in our culture to think of poetry – and indeed all art – as only expressing oneself?

MA: I could quote one of my ninth-grade teachers, Gladys Story, at Humberside Collegiate in Toronto. She was a very unusual teacher, a wonderful teacher. She introduced me to 'Border Ballads'. She was only there the first term – she became ill and died shortly after, but that first term she had a four o'clock poetry group. She accepted people's manuscripts, and she read aloud from some. Former students came back from university to attend the group. One night she asked the person who wrote the ode 'To an Apple-Core' to stay afterwards, and I did. She asked to read my notebook, and in my notebook she wrote, 'For ten years I would like you to write nothing using the first person.' I think in a way it's gone a little too far with me. I think 'I' could come back into my poetry more now. But still on the whole it was very sound advice. If you feel, you should feel for the people out there to whom you're writing, as well as for yourself. It's hard to

discover that unless you're forced to it by somebody like that teacher.
IMAGE: Just over thirty years ago you said, 'How poetry matters in the context of human distress and God's recreating power I am unable to define.' Have the intervening years shed any light on this for you?
MA: No. It's far too trite to say that people who have a tough time with something in their life are improved by poetry. I don't think they always are. It can go either way. There's some learning that brings you closer to all the people out there you're writing with and for, but I don't know if that's under one's command. It's a mystery, isn't it? I've got a poem about people who've lost a first child. There's just no way of saying anything about it.
IMAGE: How has your faith changed your approach to the writing of poetry?
MA: I think not at all. That first morning I was quite willing to give it all up, and before work the next day I wrote of the parable of the sower and the seed compulsively ('A Story' in *The Dumbfounding*). I had promised, but I wasn't held to my promise. I was enormously grateful not to have to give up poetry when I came to faith. It had held first place in my life, and I was willing to give it up, but the Lord did not require me to.

However, my approach to the writing of poetry has evolved somewhat since. My beliefs were obtrusive at first: moralizing tags in the last line or two of a poem, for example, and some of these were edited out before publication. Poems kept developing out of the new excitement of Bible reading, some with text references, some narrative, some exploring this rich new territory. (Many of these thematically weigh down *No Time,* but nevertheless are reprinted in the third volume of *Always Now.*) Gradually there developed a peaceful confidence that my Lord knew who I was, knew my joy in writing with my ear in our good language, and had freed me from any obligation except a thankfulness for his companionship.
IMAGE: As you've mentioned, the Porcupine's Quill is in the process of releasing your collected poems. The second of the three volumes was just out in the fall of 2004. Are you planning to publish another new collection, or will you simply be adding new poems for the third volume which appears next year?
MA: There will be some new poems in that third volume. I haven't come to a crashing stop. But I surely cannot live very much longer.

They take care of old people too well in this society.

IMAGE: You obviously have a lasting legacy. How would you like future generations to see you and your work?

MA: I hope there will be future generations, and I wonder if they will be reading. I don't know how to answer that. I think if people read there will be poets among them, and poets find poets. I think that a lot of things in our society are moving away from communicating in words toward a way that I don't understand, toward the visual – and some of it I think is very good – but it's a world I don't know.

On Xmas

In 'Midwinter Wassailing' (*New Yorker* Dec 22 & 29/97, p.15) Bill Buford says that 4th Century Christians appropriated this ancient holiday to become the church's celebration of the birth of Christ, and for centuries afterward all Christendom rejoiced and made merry at Gallic Noel, Norse Yule or British Christmas. But, he records, Cromwell banned Christmas because he saw it as an excuse for 'carnall and sensual delights'. In New England and Massachusetts similar views led to a twenty-two-year outlawing of Christmas celebrations, with a stiff fine for any lawbreaker who forbore labour or feasted or otherwise made a difference on December 25th.

Although all these facts were new to me, I was not astonished because of my mother's attitude to Christmas. Her background was strict Methodist. But my father was a Father Christmas, Jolly old Elf, and jubilant head of our family celebrations. His huge delight in the traditions drew us all in. He wore a red 'smoking jacket' and kept a grate fire ablaze. He made sure that we children started on Christmas early. Long before daylight, he would fill up the chinks in our Christmas stockings with a big beautiful orange right in the toe. (Oranges were a Christmas treat in Alberta back in the late twenties.)

Mother, we early guessed, was a reluctant follower in his wake. She would have disabused our minds about Santa Claus if it hadn't made her feel disloyal. She enjoyed preparing the special cookies and snow pudding for dinner, and her roast turkey always deserved the high praise it received at and after the table. But she told us stories about cold Melton Mowbray pie, sliced at midnight Christmas Eve, for her childhood family celebration, after the evening together at church. Father had missed any kind of family Christmas during his early years, having been a foster child in an Ontario farm community, initially with a loving but elderly couple and after their death moved hither and yon. All the family life he had missed, all the celebrations he had watched from afar as a boy, were crammed into the short years of our growing-up – and we loved it.

My sister perpetuated the warm rosy everybody-gather-round feast we'd known long ago. My brother had new traditions for his own family – carols for family and friends around his piano every Christmas Eve. He and his wife Ruth seemed to love hosting a Christmas dinner, with their house all decorated and fragrant with cedar boughs.

On my own, I reverted to Mother's and Grandpa Kirkland's quieter celebration. I even tried to avoid joining the family at my sister's and Frank's in Ottawa one year when I was working till 1 p.m. Christmas Eve and again at 9 a.m. on Boxing Day. It was peaceful and enjoyable on my own, curled up reading, or listening to radio music while preparing breakfast. But a Christmas Day deliveryman rang the bell down in the landlady's front hall, and tramped up to my second floor door bearing a roasted turkey. The family had all felt blue about my solitude until Ruth remembered the delivery business's special seasonal offering. That cheered them all up. I telephoned to thank them, enthusiastically, but I cannot remember eating any turkey. I had no carving knife, for instance. The adventure of disposing of it where it would not be 'wasted' must have been fun, but I can't remember one wisp of that.

When we were all young, I was one of several guests invited to a recently-married couple's apartment, for dinner. The husband was hosting us in the living-room while his wife was putting the dinner she had prepared into a serving-dish to bring it in. But oh, there was an odd, soft crash, if you can imagine such a sound. The host went fast to the kitchen door and saw that the flour bin (out for thickening the gravy?) had upended, dusting many surfaces as well as the floor in the kitchen. He was a good husband. He and his wife looked at the mess in silence for a moment. Then he stepped back, said quietly 'Oh, I beg your pardon,' and closed the kitchen door. How did the dinner party go, in the end? That was evidently not memorable.

• • •

Christmas is like that, to me. I am both the bride and the young husband, eager to enter into the spirit of a happy occasion and prepared to offer my best all round, with a few gifts chosen and hidden until the paper-and-ribbon stage arrives. Then cards begin to come into my mail-box. I decide I'll answer them 'afterwards', so it won't be 'all over for another year on Dec. 26th'. But it is. January and February deadlines begin to impinge. 'They' won't mind, I think, if I haven't written my cards, ar answered theirs, as long as they don't think I'm ill or senile or dead. It's all very well to say 'I don't do Christmas any more.' Nobody much wants to do it, but they don't let 'want to' eclipse 'ought to' as I've done. O, O, O …

In my case it's not an accident – crash – but Christmas makes me remember that flour-bin before dinner, every year. As I try to step clear, I hear again that man's 'Oh, I beg your pardon,' and I close the door on it, despite my raddled conscience.

Last photo of Margaret, July 2007, with Joan Eichner.
(Credit: Greg Scharf)

Slow Breathing

[A poem on the subject just addressed. Like 'A Novel in Miniature' it appears in Listening: Last Poems. *Toronto: McClelland & Stewart, 2009. It seems fitting to frame with poems an autobiography by a woman who lived and breathed poetry.]*

What a quiet rainy interlude with
Christmas over, nothing
doing till New Year's – most
people still
recovering, or dutifully
dealing with the
fall-out! (Even my
'list' isn't started yet. I mean
of presents, let alone cards.)
Guilt I have self-indulged me with too
long to learn that
guilt is an
ineffectual, transparent
veil
exposing rather than
excusing further
ducking of due
demands. Oh dear, like the
new year's, they're all
ahead up there!

Relax! The quiet light
falls on the undemanding pages of
a perhaps new
book, or an old
paper – not on
a proper yearly-presents' record
(though such for yesteryears existed), no
nor any small-size
stationery. N.
B: allow no pen in hand

unless a pushy
poem blocks all al-
ternatives even on
December twenty-nine. The dishes
are in the sink. It's past
time for peeling carrots, pulling
leftovers out of the fridge, putting the
kettle on.

Old age too is an
unfestive interlude,
lamp-lit, yes,
but out of touch with all but
a few, if any,
kinfolk or old friends. Take
heart! The seasonal
sidewalks are lively still; once
again ice-rinks resonate
with bright dazzle, cornering blades, and thuds.
                    Remember that
the longest stretches were the busy
but beset ones, still remembered: offices,
schedules. Losses.
                    These shatter
the heart, ripen a
person's experience before
the last-of-light is, once-
for-all, the new
threshold.

SIGNIFICANT DATES

Compiled by Joan Eichner

Portrait of Margaret, 1991. (Credit: John Reeves)

1918 Born in Galt (now Cambridge), Ontario.

1920 Family moved to Regina, Saskatchewan.

1924 Family moved to Calgary, Alberta. Margaret attended Central Public School, completing grade six.

1929 Family moved to Toronto (age eleven). Grades seven and eight, Annette Street Public School. Grades nine, ten and eleven at Humberside Collegiate. Grade twelve completed at Alma College after autumn hospitalization (for anorexia nervosa) in Toronto General Hospital. Grade thirteen at Humberside Collegiate.

1936 Entered Victoria College, University of Toronto.

1937 Parents moved to Ottawa (Dominion United Church).

1940 B.A. in English, University of Toronto.

1940–42? File clerk in North American Life, then a few months at Gage Publishing (proofreading, editing).

1943–45? Canadian Institute of International Affairs – Library, then Information Service.

1945 Clerical work in Office of the Registrar, University of Toronto.

1948 University of Toronto Library, Order Department. Freelance editing in spare time, including rewrite of a grade seven history of Ontario for Gage.

1951 *History of Ontario*, Toronto: W.J. Gage & Co.

1954 Summer school at the University of Indiana.

1955–56 Nursemaid and home help to family with four children, Toronto and France.

1956–57 Guggenheim Memorial Foundation Grant: spent eight months in Chicago preparing manuscript of *Winter Sun*.

1957–1963? Six years of freelance work including translating Hungarian poetry with Ilona Duczynska, assisting professors Alexander Brady and Kathleen Coburn with research and editing, ghost-writing Dr A.I. Wolinsky's autobiography, summarizing theses for the School of Social Work.

1960 *Winter Sun,* London: Routledge and Kegan Paul and *A Doctor's Memoirs* (with Dr A.I. Wolinsky), Toronto: MacMillan.

Governor-General's Award for Poetry (for *Winter Sun*).

1963 January 4: Conversion to Christian faith.

August: Vancouver Poetry Conference; father's death, mother's move to Toronto to live with Margaret (this family responsibility to 1985).

The Plough and the Pen, comp. I. Duczynska, Toronto: McClelland & Stewart.

Entered University of Toronto Graduate School (M.A. thesis on 'Byron and the Newspapers', how the style of *Don Juan* reflected the new journalism of Byron's day).

1964 *The Research Compendium,* Toronto: School of Social Work.

M.A. degree.

1964–66 Doctoral studies including final examinations. Did not proceed to thesis.

1966 *The Dumbfounding,* New York: Norton.

1966–68 Taught two years at Scarborough College, University of Toronto, and volunteered at Evangel Hall (Presbyterian storefront mission).

1968–72 On staff of Evangel Hall.

1970 *Acta Sanctorum,* Ilona Duczynska, comp, London: Peter Owen.

1972–73 Eight months as Writer-in-Residence, University of Western Ontario.

1973–78 Worked in CBC Radio Archives, Toronto.

1978 *sunblue,* Hantsport: Lancelot Press.

Involved in Visitation Evangelism at Knox Church.

Began work as Secretary, Mustard Seed Mission.

1982 *Winter Sun/The Dumbfounding: Poems 1940–66,* Toronto: McClelland & Stewart.

1983 Doctor of Letters, Acadia University, citation by Alex Colville.

1984 Moved to Fellowship Towers Seniors' Residence.

1985 Officer, Order of Canada.

Doctor of Letters, York University, citation by bp Nichol.

Mother died June 7.

1986 Retired from Mustard Seed Mission.

1988 Doctor of Sacred Letters, Emmanuel College, Victoria University, citation by Prof. Jay Macpherson.

1989 *No Time,* Hantsport: Lancelot Press.

1990 Governor-General's Award for Poetry *(No Time).*

1991 *Selected Poems,* Toronto: Oxford.

1993 Gave the Pascal Lectures at the University of Waterloo: *A Kind of Perseverance.*

1994 *A Kind of Perseverance,* the 1993 Pascal Lectures, Hantsport: Lancelot Press.

1997 *Not Yet But Still,* Hantsport: Lancelot Press.

2002 *Concrete & Wild Carrot,* London: Brick Books.

2003 Canadian winner of the Griffin Poetry Prize.

Jack Chalmers Award for Poetry, Canadian Authors Association.

Read from *Concrete and Wild Carrot* at the Edinburgh Festival of Books, Scotland.

Always Now: The Collected Poems, Volume One, Erin: The Porcupine's Quill.

Participated in a 'Write! Toronto' Seminar (Christian writers' The Word Guild).

2004 Read at the National Poetry Foundation's 'Poetries of the 1940s, American and International' Conference, University of Maine at Orono.

Always Now: The Collected Poems Volume Two, Erin: The Porcupine's Quill.

Interviewed at *Write! Toronto* (The Word Guild).

2005 *Always Now: The Collected Poems* Volume Three, Erin: The Porcupine's Quill.

Leslie K. Tarr Career Achievement Award for outstanding contribution to Christian writing in Canada.

2006 *Momentary Dark,* Toronto: McClelland & Stewart.

2007 Margaret died as the consequence of a broken hip on July 31.

ACKNOWLEDGEMENTS

Archives and Special Collections, Harriet Irving Library, University of New Brunswick (Cid Corman Fonds MG L 21) and Library and Archives Canada (F.R. Scott fonds MG 30 D211).

Matthew Holmes and *Arc*, for permission to reprint 'Poets Learn from Poetry' (*Arc 53*, Winter 2004).

The Director of *Revista de Studi Canadesi* and Cristina Cassanmagnago for permission to reprint parts of 'Margaret Avison's Voice' from *Revista 12* (1999).

Mary Kenaghy, D.S. Martin and *Image* magazine for permission to reprint 'A Conversation with Margaret Avison', from *Image 45* (Spring 2005).

Silas White and Sally Ito, for permission to reprint 'The Quiet Centre Inside', from Tim Bowling, ed. *Where the Words Come From: Canadian Poets in Conversation.* Roberts Creek: Nightwood Editions, 2002.

McClelland & Stewart, for permission to reprint 'A Novel in Miniature' and 'Slow Breathing' from *Listening: Last Poems,* Toronto: McClelland & Stewart, 2009.

Thanks also to *The Hermes* (Humberside Collegiate Institute), *Hi-Lites* (Newsletter of Fellowship Towers), the University of Manitoba Archives and Special Collections, CBC Archives, the University of Toronto Archives, Marion D. Cameron, Prof. Dean Irvine and the Rev. Dr Victor Shepherd. Special thanks to David Kent for bringing his expertise to bear on the manuscript.

Thanks to Patricia Fry, Don MacLeod, Karen McKim, John Reeves, Newsome Photography and Greg Scharf for permission to reprint their photographs.

The cover image is by Will Gill. Thanks to Susan Sherk who holds this work in her collection and also to photographer John Haney for the reproduction.